BECOMING RIGHT

PRINCETON STUDIES IN CULTURAL SOCIOLOGY

Paul J. DiMaggio, Michèle Lamont, Robert J. Wuthnow, Viviana A. Zelizer, Series Editors

BECOMING RIGHT

How Campuses Shape Young Conservatives

Amy J. Binder and Kate Wood

Princeton University Press

Princeton and Oxford

Published by Princeton University Press, 41 William Street, Princeton, New Jersey 08540
In the United Kingdom:
Princeton University Press, 6 Oxford Street, Woodstock, Oxfordshire OX20 1TW

press.princeton.edu

Binder, Amy J., 1964–
  Becoming right : how campuses shape young conservatives / Amy J. Binder and
Kate Wood.
    p. cm. — (Princeton studies in cultural sociology)
  Includes bibliographical references and index.
  ISBN 978-0-691-14537-2 (hbk. : alk. paper)   1. Conservatism—United States.
2. College students—Political activity—United States.   3. Education, Higher—
Political aspects—United States.   I. Wood, Kate, 1980–   II. Title.
  JC573.2.U6B53 2013
  320.52084'20973—dc23
                                        2012029765

British Library Cataloging-in-Publication Data is available

This book has been composed in Sabon and Trade Gothic

Printed on acid-free paper. ∞

Printed in the United States of America

10 9 8 7 6 5 4 3 2 1

To Edward, my love
A.J.B.

To Geoffrey, for everything
K.S.W.

Contents

Preface

For more than half a century, critics located in right-leaning think tanks, foundations, and the media have championed the cause of conservative undergraduates, who, they say, suffer on college campuses. In books with such titles as *Freefall of the American University* and *The Professors: The 101 Most Dangerous Academics in America*, conservative critics charge that American higher education has become the playpen of radical faculty who seek to spread their antireligious, big-government, liberal ideas to their young undergraduate charges.[1] In this portrait of the politicized university, middle-of-the road students complacently absorb their professors' calculated misinformation, liberal students smugly revel in feeling they are on the righteous side of the political divide, and conservative students must decide whether to endure their professors' tirades quietly or give voice to their outrage, running the risk of a poor grade. Administrators, according to the critics, do little to stop the madness.

Universities' abdication of responsibility toward their undergraduates is said to have both academic and social consequences. Academically, faculty are accused of turning their backs on Western-centered liberal arts training in favor of highly tendentious, politically correct curricula housed in the "studies" departments—ethnic studies, queer studies, Latin American studies, women's studies. Sociology, political science, and most of the humanities also come under attack, and even the crazy lone math professor who walks barefoot to class (for some reason a popular image) and rages against Republicans and foreign wars becomes a symbol of a widespread problem on American campuses. Socially, conservative critics say, things are no better, and they condemn undergraduate peer culture for being fast, loose, and fueled by drugs and alcohol, behaviors that go largely unchecked by the adults who are supposed to be in charge. In the area of administrative policy, the conservative critique extends to affirmative action in hiring and admissions, which detractors deride as anti-meritocratic and unjust and which, they contend, led in the first place to the vocal populations on today's college campuses claiming victimhood and demanding a left-oriented curriculum. Critics point to administrators' decisions to bar ROTC from campus (a practice some elite universities began after the military implemented Don't Ask, Don't Tell), to institute policies that coddle Muslim student groups, and to turn a blind eye to faculty who clearly and regularly cross the line between "teaching and preaching."[2] But at the most general level, the critics argue that a hostile political atmosphere exists on campuses that militates against intellectual diversity of opinion and actively promotes only one of the nation's two major political parties.[3]

To mitigate the effects of what they perceive to be an overwhelmingly liberal environment, conservative organizations have sprung up to help right-leaning students. One such organization, led by David Horowitz, has produced the Academic Bill of Rights to protect students "from the imposition of any orthodoxy of a political, religious or ideological nature," and has established chapters on campuses nationwide "collecting documentation of political abuses in the classroom."[4] National cosponsored events such as the National Conservative Student Conference introduce thousands of students each year to the celebrities of the Right.[5] Meantime, organizations such as the Leadership Institute train students in how to "take back your campus" from radical professors, and the Clare Boothe Luce Policy Institute encourages "brave young women [to] share their experiences of what it's like to be conservatives on liberal campuses."[6] More intellectually styled organizations such as the Intercollegiate Studies Institute and the Institute for Humane Studies seek to sponsor young conservative journalists and Ivory Tower–bound graduate students through internship programs at such venerable institutions as the *Wall Street Journal*, or through summer seminars at which they can discuss the work of the free market economist Friedrich Hayek or the philosopher of personal liberty Russell Kirk.[7] Added to this is a proliferation of conservative-funded think tanks on university campuses—the Hoover Institution at Stanford University and the Mercatus Institute at George Mason University are but two of the best known—that serve as centers for conservative thought. According to conservative critics, all of these organizational strategies, from promoting animatedly partisan conferences to sponsoring intellectually invigorating seminars and internships, play a crucial role in minimizing the marginalization that conservative students feel on campus and improve the chances that right-leaning students will remain active in conservative circles.

Yet over the period of time in which these organizations emerged and have flourished, they have attracted little systematic notice. The movement to build a corps of young, ideologically dependable lawyers, journalists, congressional staff, voters, and academics has been a central priority of the political Right, but few have investigated the effort to mobilize right-leaning students on college campuses, or how those students experience their undergraduate lives. While social scientists have given considerable thought to progressive politics at the university level (with examples like Doug McAdam's *Freedom Summer* and Fabio Rojas's *From Black Power to Black Studies*), far too few have looked at the identities and political activities of self-described conservative undergraduates and their sponsors.[8] Every once in a while journalists—in the place of social scientists—take up the issue and ponder college-age conservatism as a kind of exotica that occurs on university campuses or at national conferences.[9] And certainly a cottage industry of conservative websites and publishers has directed attention to the phenomenon of conservative student activism.[10] But these anecdotal forays into the conservative student phenomenon are hardly disinterested social scientific studies. Moreover, while recent academic studies have looked at faculty's political beliefs and behaviors, or have investigated the growing sector of conservative organizations aimed at other strategic goals, the mobilization of conservative *students* has been all but left out of the analysis.[11] As a consequence, neither scholars nor university administrators nor parents nor concerned outsiders know whether the accusations leveled against universities—or the organizational tactics designed to counter the problem—resonate with the conservative students on whose behalf critiques are made and solutions created.

As the first book-length study to be conducted on the contemporary campus Right, our research sets out to fill a gap in the public's understanding of the most recent wave of conservative cadre building. In this comparative case study of students at two universities, we look at how conservative undergraduates think and behave politically in different college settings, and how these actions connect to a variety of other political phenomena in the broader U.S. culture. By deciding to study two universities closely—one an elite private university on the East Coast, the other a large public university system in the West—we are able to explore similarities and differences in conservative activism across different campuses. Not content simply to survey undergraduates about their political commitments, we went directly to students and alumni/ae to talk with them personally about their lives before, during, and in some cases after college. We wanted to know whether they felt they were in a political minority at their universities, as the critics contend; whether they were upset about their peers, faculty, and administrators; and what they did about it if they were. We wanted to learn what the turning points had been in their ideological orientations and what forms of conservative activism they engaged in while in college. We were interested in conservative students' career aspirations and their positions on particular political issues. In addition, we asked our interviewees about whom they knew in the larger world of conservative thought and politics, and the degree to which they connected with larger networks that advocated conservative positions. Most intriguingly, we were eager to find out whether there might be something one could call a national way of "acting like a conservative" on college campuses or whether local circumstances instead created meaningful variation across the universities we studied.

The following pages provide answers to these questions. Although we are careful not to contend that we have described all of the possibilities for conservative action in colleges and universities across America, among our most important discoveries at Eastern Elite University and the campuses in the Western Public system is that while conservative undergraduates across the country may share many of the same political beliefs—they support small government, low taxes, and individual responsibility—the political *styles* students use to express these commitments are highly distinctive on different college and university campuses. Organizational settings matter significantly for how undergraduates come to see themselves as political actors, how they envision responding to their peers and professors on campus, and how they picture the rest of the world and their own futures within it. Because "college" does not denote a single experience or phenomenon (even within the relatively privileged portion of the higher education sector of four-year residential campuses that we investigate here), students on different campuses end up having strikingly divergent approaches to being conservative. These variations are not so much a matter of doctrine as they are one of disposition and tactics, and they reflect both the organizational differences between universities that shape students' everyday lives and the imagined trajectories that these students project about their lives after college. Although one could not be faulted for imagining that a college-educated conservative student graduating from Eastern Elite University would be more or less like a college-educated conservative graduating from the Western Public system, we have strong evidence that indicates otherwise. Indeed, our findings show that the particular university a student attends has a significant impact on how that student decides to go about being a conservative—if not so much in what he or she believes, then in how he or she expresses those beliefs. These different styles, we contend, are in no small part connected to the styles present in the larger political culture in which we all participate.

ACKNOWLEDGMENTS

This book is the result not of two people but of many. Yet before we go on to thank others, we would first like to acknowledge each other in this effort. Amy would like to express genuine gratitude to Kate for bringing her passion and extraordinary talents for research to this study, even while she has been writing a fascinating dissertation of her own about university culture. This has been a true collaboration in every sense of the word—in spirit, shared vision, and just plain hard work. Kate can only begin to thank Amy in just these few words. Working on this project as a graduate student has been both challenging and rewarding, and she has been extremely fortunate over these past several years not only to have had Amy as her co-author but also as a mentor. Every grad student should be so lucky.

It may not be customary to thank our series editor before others on our list, but when that series editor is Paul DiMaggio, the sociologists among our readers will understand why he gets top billing. The man is a marvel in giving constructively critical comments, which pushed our project to the next level. We have learned so much from working with him that it's hard to know what to say besides a simple "thank you." Of course, if we didn't have to worry about house style, that last bit would actually be italicized, underscored, decorated with emoticons, written in ALL CAPS, and followed by a large number of exclamation points.

Several organizations have supported this work. The Spencer Foundation's Small Grants program may have "small" in its name, but its funding in the area of the New Civics initiative sponsored travel, interview transcription, undergraduate research assistance, a bit of graduate student stipend, and even a sliver of sabbatical. Thank you to Susan Dauber and Lauren Jones Young for their interest in and support of the project. The generosity of those at the Center for Advanced Study in the Behavioral Sciences at Stanford University has also been a great gift. A good part of the first draft of this book was written in Study 43, but there were other wonderful joys to be had at the center, too, not least the friendships forged or strengthened with Tori McGeer, Enrique Rodriguez-Alegria, Nancy Whittier, Gary Alan Fine, Joan Barbour, Cynthia Pilch, Iris Litt, Iris Wilson, Tricia Sota, Liz Lambert, Stephen Kosslyn, and Linda Jack. Thanks go as well to the Academic Senate of the University of California–San Diego, which has always provided needed funding at crucial moments, and to UCLA's Higher Education Research Institute for providing access to survey data.

We have great colleagues and dear friends at UC San Diego who have been helpful in so many ways. We see them frequently and learn from them always in enjoyable social settings, but also through the institutionalized auspices of the Sociology Department's Culture + Society Workshop, the Workshop for the Study of Conservatism and Conservative Movements, and the Inequalities Workshop. Although this list is not exhaustive, we would like to officially thank the faculty members who came to know the work best—Mary Blair-Loy, John Evans, John Skrentny, Jeff Haydu, Robert Horwitz, Tom Medvetz, Isaac Martin, Kwai Ng, and Bud Mehan—as well as previous and current graduate students Michael Haedicke, Stephen Meyers, Michael Evans, Lisa Nunn, Ian Mullins, and Erin Cech. We would also like to thank our research team. Our quantitative analyses benefited tremendously from the work of graduate student Geoffrey Fojtasek. We also received considerable assistance from undergraduates Lindsay McKee DePalma, Lauren Bernadett, Teresa Chu, Adam Kenworthy, Joanne Chen, Adina Bodenstein, and Alice Chao, many of whom are now pursuing or have completed graduate studies of their own. The very smart and savvy administrative staff members in the Department of Sociology have been a great help in budgeting, organizing, and finessing the logistical parts of this project, particularly Stephanie Navrides, Tanya Pohlson, Manny dela Paz, and Susan Taniguchi.

There really isn't a sufficient way to thank Mitchell Stevens for everything he has added to this research project (and to Amy's overall life project since graduate school). His is a very special sociological imagination that combines deep knowledge of culture, organizations, higher education, and all manner of other disciplinary concerns. Mitchell is also part of a higher education/education mafia from which we have gained a great deal and to whose ongoing projects we hope to contribute: Elizabeth Armstrong, Richard Arum, Josipa Roksa, Jal Mehta, Steven Brint, Neil Gross, Scott Davies, Michèle Lamont, Pam Walters, among others. Others around the country who have commented on particular aspects of the project deserve thanks as well: Ed Walker, Marc Ventresca, Ann Colby, Bill Damon, Laura Stark, Gary Alan Fine, Chiqui Ramirez, Rory McVeigh, David Meyer, Ronnee Schreiber, and Sarah Willie (although this list is hopelessly incomplete). Nicki Beisel, as always, is in a class by herself.

We have presented portions of the manuscript in progress in many venues, including the departments of sociology at the University of California–Berkeley, the University of California–Irvine, Rice University, the University of British Columbia, and the University of California–San Diego, as well as at Stanford's Center for Advanced Study in the Behavioral Sciences, the Center for Adolescence, and SCANCOR, and at the annual meetings of the American Sociological Association. We thank many interlocutors in each of these forums; their questions and comments have been extremely helpful to us in thinking about our cases and our arguments. We also thank the editors of two volumes in which some of the research described in this book was previously published: Lisa Stulberg and Sharon Weinberg, editors of *Diversity in Education: Toward a More Comprehensive Approach* (Routledge), and Neil Gross and Solon Simmons, editors of *Professors and Their Politics* (Johns Hopkins University Press).

We have benefited greatly from the work of a team of transcribers headed by Loretta Sowers. Our sincere thanks go to Dorothy Tuzzi, a goddess among transcribers, who made opening up every new transcription document an unexpected pleasure. Not satisfied to simply do a marvelous job of transcribing our interviews, she sent commentary, ancillary information (thank you, Internet search engines!), and nuggets of her terrific wisdom. If we couldn't find any other reason to get back into the field collecting interview data, the anticipation of working with Dorothy again would provide enough incentive.

In addition to Paul DiMaggio and the other Culture Series editors at Princeton University Press (Michèle Lamont, Bob Wuthnow, and Viviana Zelizer), we would like to thank the acquisitions and production staff of the press for their interest in our work, especially Eric Schwartz and Nathan Carr. Thanks, too, to Marjorie Pannell, for her excellent copy editing. Any mistakes or oversights in content are, of course, our own.

Many friends and family members made the process of writing pleasurable. Amy especially thanks Mary Blair-Loy, Marnie and Lew Klein, Rowan Schoales, Elyana Sutin, John Skrentny, Mitchell Stevens, Charles St. Hill, Daniel Blaess, Laxmi deLeo, and the entire Binder clan for their love and support. Lois Binder, the clan's matriarch, is the person who bred the love of politics in her daughter. What a gift! Profound gratitude goes to Edward Hunter, who provides love, comfort, gloriously wide-ranging conversation, yoga buddyism, Manhattans straight up, and gourmet Mexican meals at the Sweet 'n' Drowsy. Kate thanks Richard Buxton, Andrew Hall, Jennifer Moorman, Ariel Dekovic, Allison Roselle, Erin Cech, L.Z. and Y.E., and, of course, all her fellow graduate students at UC San Diego. Bill Hoynes deserves a special note of thanks for his encouragement, mentorship, and steadfast support, without which she would not have pursued an academic career (and so certainly would not be writing this!). Kate also thanks her parents, brother, and in-laws, for bearing with her; Hannah, Josh, and Emmeline Close, for providing support when she needed it most; and Puff, for her cold nose and unconditional love. But her deepest thanks go to Geoff, for being who he is.

Finally, to our interviewees: We thank you so very much for sharing your time and thoughts with us. We hope we have rendered your experiences faithfully.

BECOMING RIGHT

Chapter 1

Introduction

In 2004 and again in 2007, members of the College Republicans on a campus we call Western Flagship, the main campus of the Western Public university system, staged an eye-popping event known as the Affirmative Action Bake Sale.[1] The Bake Sale is a widely recognized piece of political theater that conservative students put on at many universities across the country, at which members of right-leaning campus organizations sell baked goods at a higher price to white passers-by than they do to, say, African Americans or Latinos/as. The event is said to highlight while also parodying the deleterious effects on all students of affirmative action policies. Student sponsors contend that the event opens up important campuswide discussions of a pressing issue that all too frequently remains unacknowledged on university campuses. But when students talk about what it is like to actually stage the event, and to get others' reactions to it, it is clear that they revel in the sheer fun and provocation their activity stirs up. According to one interviewee, the Flagship campus chapter of College Republicans elicited a strong response from liberals in 2004:

> So we're out there and it's like five College Republicans, wearing our little College Republican stickers. . . . And for about half-an-

hour, community members would come by and say, "Oh, I'm a white guy and I've got to pay a dollar" and "Oh, I'm a Hispanic guy, damn I feel so oppressed by the white man. I've got to pay 75 cents." I mean, people really were getting into it. But of course, meanwhile, there's a noontime rally organized by the diversity thugs with the tacit approval of the [university] administration and stuff. They've got their bullhorns out, they're angry, they've got their signs. They're out there for half an hour getting themselves all ginned up. And of course, [a Flagship administrator] is there, the [Flagship] police commander is there, all this stuff, and so we're sitting there. And I have no problem with protesters; I *want* the protesters there! There's cameras everywhere! (Chuck Kelley, Western Flagship)

This event, which drew crowds of campus administrators, police, and protesting students, is one of a number of confrontational actions that conservative students stage on college campuses across the country, alongside Catch an Illegal Alien Day (when students marked as illegal immigrants are chased down and mock-imprisoned), the Global Warming Beach Party (during which environmental concerns are ridiculed with suntan oil and beer), and the Conservative Coming Out Day (a twist on LGBT coming-out celebrations, when conservatives proudly announce their presence to the campus). Even in university systems like the University of California, where affirmative action in admissions has been banned since 1996, conservative students stage these kinds of events, such as Berkeley's highly publicized Affirmative Action Bake Sales in 2003 and again in 2011.[2] Conservative students who put on events that we have labeled "provocative" are tickled to rile liberals at their universities and are supported in their theatricality by national organizations established to foster such conservative activism on campus.

On a different college campus 2,000 miles away from Western Flagship, which we call Eastern Elite University, such an event is considered verboten—not by college administrators and faculty so much as by conservative Eastern Elite students themselves. At this private university, most right-leaning undergraduates denounce the act of pushing liberals' buttons as sophomoric, as well as ineffective at recruiting potential fellow travelers or encouraging debate on an issue. The head of Eastern's College Republicans said:

> Look, I don't think something like that is helpful. Yes, maybe it gets a point across to some students. But overall it just makes people mad. . . . If you're making someone mad in the course of trying to make a broader point or in the course of trying to influence someone, then great, go for it. . . . [But] what person walks up to a table to buy a cupcake and realizes that "[this] is an Affirmative Action Bake sale," and then walks away thinking, "Wow, that was a great illustration of the problems with affirmative action. Maybe I *will* rethink my views on that." . . . The only thing that I have ever seen come from putting on events like that is divisiveness and anger and lack of communication. (Derek Yeager, Eastern Elite)

Others at Eastern make it a point to say that such an event would be unsuitable for the sensibility of their campus, where "[students] tend to be a little bit more intellectual" (Calvin Coffey, Eastern Elite). At Eastern Elite, most conservative students argue that it is beneficial to conduct respectful arguments and to try to reach out to the other side, to learn from their political adversaries, and to create a well-tempered conservative presence on campus. While their conservative beliefs are no less ardent than those of their counterparts on the Western Public campuses, Eastern Elite University students disdain the national conservative organizations that encourage such theatrical events, accusing those groups of having a reputation for being "not as thinking" (Nicole Harris, Eastern Elite). Instead of engaging in provocative public actions, most students at Eastern Elite extol the virtues of a style that is more deliberative—we call it "civilized discourse"—to be used among themselves, as well as with faculty, administrators, and their liberal peers.

There is, however, more to this story. These dominant styles of conservative expression on the Western Public and Eastern Elite campuses exist within a broader spectrum of activity that includes some additional options. While the two styles described above are the most highly valued forms of conservative expression on their respective campuses, other approaches can be found as subordinate, or what we call "submerged," styles, appearing sometimes with greater and sometimes with lesser intensity, depending on student leadership in any given year.[3] At Western Flagship, for example, members of the College Republicans in some years may lean toward wanting less confrontational actions and engage in relatively institutionalized forms of party participation to create a style we call "campaigning." Going against the prevailing wisdom requires a stiff spine, however. When student leaders on the Western Public campuses use this submerged style and try to get others to support campaigning over provocation, they often draw criticism from their peers for not being "super-conservative" enough (Kody Aronson, Western Flagship), for being "an abomination" insofar as campaigning encourages students to "[kiss] the ass of the National GOP" (Chuck Kelly, Western Flagship), or for simply being "lame" (Karl Hayes, Western Satellite). (We should note quickly that Western Flagship is part of the larger Western Public university system, which also includes the Western State and Western Satellite campuses. When we refer only to this main campus, we will say Western Flagship; when we refer to these schools as a group, we will call them Western Public.)

At Eastern Elite University, meanwhile, the submerged style of campaigning gets a decent amount of support from a subset of students—particularly those in the College Republicans, and especially in election years—because it is seen to be reasonably aligned with civilized discourse. Campaigning is simply an added layer of practical activity on top of what most Eastern Elite conservative students are already trying to do: convince folks to think about conservative ideas, consider GOP platform positions, and have good debates. But more notably, an expressive submerged style of conservative insurgency, which we label "highbrow provocation," thrives in the pages of the campus's conservative newspaper and is a kind of pedigreed *National Review* style. Though often producing extreme discomfort among those conservative students who practice civilized discourse, a handful of conservatives at Eastern Elite participate actively in penning intense, philosophical, and at times vitriolic editorials and essays within the paper's pages. Targeting the "ironies of campus life" (Henry Quick, Eastern Elite)—by which this interviewee meant multiculturalism, political correctness, the overprotection of campus minority groups and women—newspaper staff *are* provocative, just not in the same way that student activists staging Catch an Illegal Alien Day or the Bake Sales are. Highbrow provocation is not "activist" in the sense that activism means going out on the quad and publicly riling people up; instead, it mainly takes place in the world of words and ideas. And it is also more thoroughly submerged at Eastern Elite, meaning that however much negative attention highbrow provocation gets, there are only a few people on campus who actually use it, whereas on the Western Flagship campus, provocation is mainstream. It should also be pointed out that the highbrow provocation style fails utterly on the Western Public campuses: Although one of our Western State students tried to engage this style on his campus, he conceded there was no audience for it.

What all of this means is that the patterns in conservative styles across the two universities we studied are strong, stark, and deserve sustained analysis: Something is happening on college campuses such that provocation prevails in the Western Public system (with campaigning as a submerged style), whereas civilized discourse dominates at Eastern Elite University (with both campaigning and highbrow provocation in submerged positions). These patterns suggest that while conservative students may have a steady presence at universities across the country, and that they are also to a large extent *ideologically* united under a conservative banner across these campuses, students' political *styles*, their ways of expressing their conservative ideas, are systematically varied. This holds true not only for students' styles and tactics as articulated through political events but also for their everyday perceptions of the classroom experience, their thoughts about the activities of faculty and peers, and the ways they conduct their social lives. While this does not mean that every last conservative student on these campuses comports with the dominant or submerged styles prevalent there, when we look at the overall patterns among groups of students, the patterns are striking.

Should we be surprised to discover that there is such considerable variation in conservative styles across different university campuses? In some important ways, yes: this is an unanticipated finding. In the few years leading up to the 2008 presidential election, when we were collecting the bulk of our data, and since, there has been a visible trend toward a narrowing conservative style promoted within the core of the Republican Party, with highly partisan confrontational tactics emerging as the regular means of doing business.[4] Examples include members of the Republican Party shutting down the government in 1994 under the leadership of then Speaker of the House Newt Gingrich and Sarah Palin's mocking tone at the 2008 Republican National Convention when referring to the Democratic presidential candidate Barack Obama's history of community organizing.[5] While the Republican Party is not synonymous with conservatism, most people who identify as conservative vote that party's ticket. Given the party's trend toward confrontation, it is therefore not unreasonable to imagine that during the time of our data collection, 18- to 22-year-olds with conservative leanings would have participated in a more or less shared repertoire of national-level, right-of-center beliefs and values, and that all students would have used at least some elements of the provocative style on their home campuses. In addition, this age group is wired in to multiple forms of widely disseminated media, from Facebook pages devoted to conservative causes, to 24/7 streaming cable news channels featuring such celebrity pundits as Sean Hannity, to constantly updated blogs written by those on the political right. Had they been interested in investigating conservative views on "what is wrong with the liberal campus," our interviewees would have encountered mostly the thoughts and ideas of "movement conservatives" who are located in conservative-funded think tanks, foundations, and media outlets and who often champion the cause of right-of-center undergraduates.[6] Students could even have laid their hands on the *Campus Conservative Battleplan*, distributed by the Young America's Foundation, an organization that provides ready-made posters and flyers depicting Nancy Pelosi, Michael Moore, Hillary Clinton, and Noam Chomsky as the bugaboos of the Left and sends out prepackaged plans for staging protests against liberal policies.[7]

On the other hand, we also know that despite American conservatism's shift toward a narrower stylistic range since the 1990s, the political Right, like any other ideological grouping, is a varied camp.[8] Conservatism has always been heterogeneous—if not racially and ethnically, then at least in terms of the issues that fall under its umbrella, the organizations that are in place to advance its goals, the intellectual concerns of its most scholarly advocates, and the styles to which its different proponents adhere.[9] As the conservative author and columnist David Brooks writes, there is a long-standing division between mainstream Republicans and "self-described conservative revolutionaries," a typology that was updated in 2011 by the Pew Research Center for the People & the Press, which divides self-identified conservatives into "staunch conservatives," "mainstream Republicans," and more independent-minded "libertarians."[10] National conservative political figures such as the 2012 GOP primary candidates Rick Santorum and Mitt Romney differ on both issues and style of address, and pundits such as Bill O'Reilly, George Will, and Charles Krauthammer offer different modes of political analysis.

The same is true of conservative organizations targeting college students. While the national organizations sponsoring battle plans are the largest, most vocal purveyors of conservative ideology to undergraduates, a handful of other organizations, such as the Intercollegiate Studies Institute, educate, sponsor, and mobilize a more self-styled intellectual student. Some of these organizations espouse a type of conservatism more in the manner of Edmund Burke, in which "corrections" to the established order are tolerated and the tempered disposition is valued. Or they may hark back to William F. Buckley's "full-throated passion of the agitator" in his book *God and Man at Yale*, whose style today can be found in such media outlets as the *Weekly Standard* and *National Review* and which is redolent of the highbrow provocation style we see at Eastern Elite University.[11]

But the larger political culture of conservatism in the United States is not the only context influencing right-leaning college students. At the level of the college campus, students' academic and social experiences also shape their conservative styles. As both Burton Clark and Mitchell Stevens have pointed out in separate studies, universities cultivate unique institutional characters.[12] Selectivity in admissions, the quality and frequency of faculty-student interactions, differences in historical institutional sagas, the promotion of particular types of student career aspirations, the physical landscape of campus life—all of these affect the in-college experiences of students on any given campus, and may be supposed to influence the styles of political discourse and action that are seen to be reasonable there.[13] What is utterable or even celebrated political discussion or classroom interaction on one campus might be viewed by students at another school as questionable or even completely outside the realm of possibility. While such known campus features as a school's reputation for academic excellence or for being a party school clearly lead to selection effects—eager college applicants choose campuses that fit who they think they are now and who they would eventually like to become; likewise, selective colleges choose those applicants who they believe will enhance their school environment—we should also expect that elements of the campus culture will influence students once they are enrolled in college. Further, though undergraduates certainly enter colleges and universities with differing personal histories, including varying experiences of social class, race and ethnicity, and religion, an extensive and long-established body of literature indicates that the campus itself is an institutional environment that influences students in significant ways.[14]

So, to be sure, students' background characteristics and experiences with the wider political culture are salient for their political development, but at the same time, the influence of the school context in which students find themselves immersed cannot be ignored.[15] In this book we demonstrate that conservative students on any given campus share unique, local repertoires of conservative ideas and styles that differ from those available on other campuses, and that these local repertoires for action influence students' understandings of what is appropriate to say and do politically at their university.[16] The kinds of interactions that conservative students have with one another, with members of their broader campus settings, and with the traditions and everyday practices of their schools provide the crucible in which conservative politics are forged out of individuals' pasts and the broader political culture in which they participate. Political actors, we argue, are *made*, not born, as colleges nurture and enhance particular forms of student conservatism.

Making sense of the styles and discourses of conservative students on the campuses of Eastern Elite University and the Western Public system, then, is both complex and important. It is important to understand the range of conservative styles that exist and to track the extent to which college-age conservatives across university settings are similar, and thus have sufficient unity to form and maintain a national constituency for right-leaning action—perhaps particularly these days, as members of the Tea Party express disdain for more deliberative-style "Establishment" conservatives and moderates.[17] One might say that conservative style—as much as, if not more so, than political ideology—is what primarily differentiates right-leaning candidates, pundits, and intellectuals in our current political culture. We therefore need to know how these styles develop in the first place and what role universities play in this process. It is equally important to know where divergences among conservative students lie, since such knowledge can help explain the factionalization that has occurred among current conservative leaders.

But the project is also complex, since understanding these styles requires looking at several components of college students' lives in combination with one another. At the broadest scale, understanding these styles involves tracking the many different national organizations with which conservative students come in contact, with an eye to each organization's rhetoric and preferred targets of attack. The styles promoted by national organizations such as the Young America's Foundation often reflect the repertoires of still larger political entities, such as the conservative base of the Republican Party or various right-leaning media outlets such as Fox News. At a level closer to students' everyday experiences, it also involves analyzing conservative undergraduates' extensive dealings with the different structures and cultural practices on their home campuses, from the campuswide organizational arrangements that all students encounter (classrooms, dorms, course registration policies) to the smaller groups that are specifically political, such as right-leaning campus clubs. If campuses influence political styles, as we believe they do, it is in large part through students' concrete interactions with their campus's shared cultural ideas and organizational structures that such an impact occurs. We think of these as opportunity spaces for political styles.

These campus-level opportunity spaces come in many different forms. Universities that house students all four years, for example, create a different sense of community than do institutions where most students live off campus in apartments or in the fraternity or sorority system. Students who live in on-campus housing during their college years sometimes describe themselves as existing in a bubble or a hothouse, where they get to know a large number of their peers. This sense of community affects how "in your face" conservative students might be willing to be with their politics, since being overly confrontational risks losing precious social capital built up through close spatial proximity. At universities where most undergraduates live off campus, on the other hand, it is easier to take the gloves off when expressing political views, since any given student knows fewer people on the whole campus, and those who remain anonymous—well, their feelings don't matter as much. Another example: universities that have deep pockets and can provide ample funding to all student clubs may breed a greater sense of trust among conservative undergraduates than do institutions that are suspected of funneling limited resources toward favored groups. Such largesse makes it more likely that conservative students will tend to be solicitous, not snarky, toward administrators. Conversely, conservative students who go to schools where resources are tight (a common situation at large public universities) and who regard the distribution of those resources as far from transparent are more likely to feel alienated from administrative decision makers and to think they have a right to be combative. This sets a different tone for political discourse and style on their campus. Still another form of contingency: universities that have smaller student-to-faculty ratios and generally teach students in seminar settings rather than large lecture halls allow students to see faculty as generally approachable fellow human beings. On the other hand, on campuses with larger student-to-faculty ratios and bigger classes, faculty may seem more like inaccessible aliens than concerned supervisors and, therefore, subject to more confrontational attitudes. The list of examples goes on, but all of these opportunity spaces, in one form or another, influence the types of political behavior that students will think are appropriate for engagement on their campus. The particularities of campus settings, from this perspective, play a critical role in creating distinctive types of political actors.

At present, social scientists know very little about the organizational structures and cultures that affect conservative students' thinking and action. A small number of scholars have studied the original conservative student movement of the 1960s and 1970s (led by the Young Americans for Freedom), and there is a growing literature on the conservative movement at large, which has changed American society enormously in the past several decades, written by historians, political scientists, sociologists, and journalists.[18] But very few authors have written specifically about today's conservative college students' thoughts about their education and their lives beyond college, let alone how conservative styles might manifest distinctively on different university campuses. The few exceptions among scholars who have studied contemporary college students—such as April Kelly Woessner and Matthew Woessner, who have used national survey data to research conservative students' perceptions of their professors and experiences in college, and Ethan Fosse, Jeremy Freese, and Neil Gross, who have looked at the question of why conservative students do not pursue doctoral degrees—have not been able to capture the greater context of conservative students' college experiences or their varying modes of expression.[19] We should know much more about who conservative college students are and which parts of conservatism they identify with, how they become conservative in the first place and how they develop their political identities on campus, and whether and how they intend to be active in politics in the future.[20] Since college-age activism is often an important step to leadership in the larger political arena, knowing about students' activities in college across different campuses—and across the conservative spectrum—is a crucial area of study.

In presenting the argument that universities have a large influence on conservative political development, we must introduce two caveats. First, to argue that political style is an organizational accomplishment that occurs on campuses is not to claim that students arrive at college with no ideological commitments derived from family, community, media exposure, or prior political and schooling experiences, or that students are blank slates to be written on by educational institutions. Students' prior identities are important and must be accounted for, even while we observe that once students enter a university, that institution's existing structures and culture channel them into distinctive types of conservative style. Second, and related, students are not automatons molded seamlessly into these styles. There is plenty of agency to go around, as students take stock of their identities on campus and think strategically about how their actions will ultimately connect with their future careers and social lives. There is evidence in our cases that students assess their options, and then sometimes actively defy dominant styles by taking up submerged styles, or create new hybrid forms of expression out of multiple different styles. They also sometimes decide to opt out of political life on campus if the conservative organizations they are interested in don't seem like the right fit. Or they plot to put together a new slate of club officers when the time is right.

Nonetheless, it is also clear that the informal group settings and formal organizational arrangements that students participate in on campus present considerable supports for leaning heavily into the dominant style of their university and considerable constraints against easily branching off into different styles.[21] Foregrounding these local settings of interaction and negotiation, and particularly the cultural meanings that are shared in them, allows us to complicate the picture of how people become politically involved. Americans seem alternately predisposed to holding, on the one hand, an individualist account of action, in which independent actors are seen to be the crux of rational decision making about how to conduct their lives, politically or otherwise, and on the other, a culturally deterministic account of action—a sort of "their culture made them do it" stance.[22] But looking at how conservative students are embedded in campus-level organizational structures reveals how neither individual identities nor broader cultural repertoires, in isolation, fully capture variation in political styles.

Another way to say this is that we understand higher education to be a politically formative institution that hones preexisting ideological commitments into particular political actions. The importance of universities to students' politics goes far beyond affecting their attitudes or educating them in vague lessons of service learning or civic participation. Rather, we see universities playing a fundamental role (at least for some students) in providing the cultural tools for constructing political *selves*: individuals who not only hold certain values or beliefs about the world but who have learned how to express and practice those ideas in real time and in real situations. The importance of this cannot be overstated: college is not just about academics and human capital formation and the social network ties forged with friends and future colleagues. It is also about the production of certain forms of citizenship in vital and frankly partisan ways.

STUDYING CONSERVATISM AT EASTERN ELITE AND WESTERN PUBLIC UNIVERSITIES

To this point we have said a lot about how we will analyze the experiences of conservative students but little about the two cases we studied, or the details of how we conducted our research. In this project we focus on Eastern Elite University, a single campus, and the Western Public university system, which is home to a flagship campus, a land-grant university, and smaller satellite campuses. As stated earlier, our main focus in the Western Public system is on the Western Flagship campus, though we draw on data from two other campuses in the system, Western State and Western Satellite, which are more conservative than the main campus.

Obviously, the generic names of our comparative campuses are pseudonyms, as are the names of most of the campus organizations and individual student and alumni/ae interviewees we use throughout the book. Although it was not our first choice to keep the institutions anonymous, we did so as a necessary concession to the Institutional Review Board at Eastern Elite, whose administrators granted us approval to interview undergraduates on their campus only on the condition that the campus not be identified in our work. We have taken great pains to obscure the identifying characteristics of our two universities, which we accomplished by commingling the actual attributes of the two universities we studied with the attributes of two peer institutions of each. For example, to come up with specific descriptions of Eastern Elite's social organization—its physical landscape, residential arrangements, student-to-faculty ratio, general education curriculum, and conservative clubs (all of which we think in some significant ways influence conservative styles)—we combined information from Eastern Elite itself with that of two other private, elite universities on the East Coast. We did the same for Western Flagship, blending its specific characteristics with those of two other public flagship campuses in the western United States. In creating these composite school profiles we veiled the specific identifying features of the universities while keeping the general institutional flavor of each. This should not be interpreted to mean that we think all eastern private universities are just like Eastern Elite, or that Western Flagship is perfectly representative of its peer institutions.[23] They are not. We simply use these profiles to be able to discuss our main campuses with a good deal of specificity while keeping their identities anonymous.

During the summer, fall, and winter of 2008 and into early 2009, the first author conducted 58 in-depth interviews with members of the Eastern Elite and Western Public communities.[24] Four out of five of the interviews we conducted on our case-study campuses were with students and recent alumni/ae who self-identified as conservative (for a total of 46), and 12 other interviews were with faculty, administrators, donors, and other students on those campuses who had unique perspectives on campus conservatism. Of the 22 total conservative student or alumni interviewees on the Western Public campuses, 15 respondents were current students and 7 were alumni/ae.[25] Of the 24 total conservative student/alumni interviewees on the Eastern Elite campus, 10 respondents were current students and 14 were alumni/ae.[26]

In addition to the 58 campus interviews, the first author also conducted 15 interviews with leaders of national and regional conservative organizations that lend support to conservative students and alumni/ae from across the country (and often specifically to those who have interned at those organizations), as well as with 19 students and alumni/ae at UC San Diego, some as pilot interviews and some later to check what we had been finding at Eastern and Western.[27] The total number of interviews conducted for the project is 92. As we stated above, in keeping with our guarantee to mask the identities of our universities, all campus interviewees were assigned pseudonyms, but with their consent, we use the real names of the national organizational leaders whom we interviewed. All interviews lasted from one to two hours. After the interviews were completed and transcribed, the second author systematically coded the interviews so that both authors could identify trends and generate concrete empirical claims about our findings.

Initial student and alumni/ae interviewees were selected on each campus after we read about conservative activities on the Internet, and then located students who were active members in such clubs as College Republicans, antiabortion groups, pro-abstinence groups, student government, anti-gun control clubs, religious clubs, and campus newspapers (both mainstream campus newspapers for which our interviewees served as conservative columnists and conservative newspapers). We did not seek out, nor did we hear about, groups at either of these two universities that supported overt racist extremism, as has been evidenced at Michigan State University, where an infamous British neo-fascist, Nick Griffin, was invited to speak to a Young Americans for Freedom chapter.[28] Nor did we seek to interview students whose *predominant* form of conservative identity was religious, first, since other scholars have already studied such students quite thoroughly, and second, since there were no organizations that we became aware of on campus that were both foundationally religious *and* explicitly politically conservative.[29] That said, we talked with several students of faith who were involved in the conservative-oriented campus organizations that we did study, and several of our interviewees identified with the Christian Right's primary social issues, such as opposing abortion and gay rights. Some of our interviewees also were actively involved in nonpartisan religious organizations, such as Catholic student clubs or evangelical campus ministries.

After we came up with an initial pool of interview subjects, we then asked early respondents for the names of other conservative students and alumni/ae they knew, and interviews were conducted with all students on these lists who were willing to be interviewed. This chain-referral sample methodology mostly ruled out students who were not visibly active in conservative politics on campus since it was more difficult to find out about them, although a few such respondents were located on each of the campuses and were important sources of information. But in general, our student and alumni/ae interviewees were known at their universities for the conservative politics they wrote about, ran political campaigns on, staged events for, or otherwise expressed in their campus political activities. They were generally enthusiastic members in their organizations, even if they didn't always think of themselves as activists or as the key leaders of those groups. We sought students who represented the dominant style on campus as well as those who seemed skeptical about the ways things were usually done. We do not claim that the students we interviewed are representative of all conservatives on these campuses, and certainly not conservative students at all other types of universities and colleges in the nation, from Christian liberal arts institutions to community colleges. But what we *do* have in our sample are conservative students who have been educated in state-system public universities and a national elite university—in other words, the types of young people who are likely to be the conservative leaders of tomorrow. Although we have missed some forms of conservativism as a result of our case-study design and our decision to study the most active students on campus, our methodology does allow us to understand—with a depth and detail that are unique to our project—the kind of conservative college students who will make a difference to conservative intellectual thought and conservative politics in the future.[30]

Although all of our interviewees identified one way or another as conservative in ideology, they varied on many demographic characteristics. The majority of students interviewed from both Western Public and Eastern Elite were white men; however, people of color and women also are represented within the sample. Students from both schools came from a range of class backgrounds. The interviewees' social class standing—nearly always a difficult variable to deal with in this type of study—was determined using qualitative data. Rather than inquiring as to individuals' families' net worth or specific cultural competencies, we asked our respondents about the occupations of any coresiding parents or guardians during their pre-college years. We also inquired as to the highest level of education completed, and the institution(s) their parents or guardians attended. With as complete information as possible (some of our interviewees were quite masterful at evading questions about their family backgrounds), we found that while Eastern Elite respondents on average tended to come from families with higher educational and occupational status, students at both Eastern Elite and Western Public displayed extensive variance.[31] Both groups included parents whose highest level of education was a high school diploma or GED, as well as parents who had received graduate degrees. Correspondingly, parents' jobs ranged from unskilled labor to the professions. Interviewees also varied considerably in their religious beliefs, with Catholicism the most common faith among religious students at Eastern Elite and various forms of Protestant Christianity among those at Western Public. Perhaps surprisingly, given the state's reputation for being a stronghold of the Christian Right, more conservative students in our sample at Western Public identified with mainline Protestantism than with evangelicalism, and more Western Public students than Eastern Elite students declared themselves non-religious, perhaps because of greater libertarian leanings in that western state. Finally, though students on all three Western Public campuses were more likely to come from within the state, the Western Flagship campus in particular attracts a significant population of out-of-state students, and interviewees from both Eastern Elite and Western Public represented all regions of the United States.

In addition to conducting interviews, we also collected and analyzed newspaper articles from both campuses and garnered troves of data ranging from a box of nostalgia given to us by one of our Western Flagship conservative club leaders to publicly available online data on conservative organizations. Finally, we analyzed a national dataset made up of surveys of first-time matriculating undergraduates at four-year universities that had been collected in 2001 by the UCLA Higher Education Research Institute (HERI). We use these national surveys to map the political composition and demographics of student bodies across four-year American universities, which serves as the context in chapter 2 for the information we collected at our two case-study universities.

The logic of the comparison of Eastern Elite University to Western Flagship University rests on several dimensions of institutional similarity and difference. First, we selected these two campuses as our primary locations because both are prominent examples of campuses that conservative critics often point to as paradigmatically liberal strongholds, though for somewhat different reasons. (Western Flagship University employs particular faculty members who have come under heavy attack in the conservative media; Eastern Elite University is just generally known as spawning liberal elites.) These two universities are also similar insofar as they are both religiously unaffiliated and they are Research I institutions, meaning that they train both undergraduates and graduate students through the PhD level and give high priority to research in addition to teaching. Notable differences distinguishing Eastern Elite from Western Flagship include geographic region, the public/private divide, admissions selectivity, visibility to East Coast centers of power, and having or not having sister institutions in a larger state system. In its selectivity and prestige, Eastern Elite represents somewhat of an outlier or an extreme case for university campuses. Likewise, in its reputation for being located in a very liberal community, the Western Flagship campus also represents something of an extreme case for a public state university. But using these extreme cases provides considerable analytical leverage, revealing institutional attributes that would be difficult to tease out among more similar institutions.[32] Although it is not possible to generalize from these two case studies—two universities cannot capture the full array of higher education in this country—our findings are suggestive for understanding many of the experiences that conservatives have had in university environments in the first decade of the twenty-first century, and for how different political styles are crafted in the early years of peoples' lives.

In the next section we briefly describe our primary campuses and then proceed to an outline of the rest of the book.

DESCRIPTIONS OF THE TWO CAMPUSES

Eastern Elite University is one of the leading institutions of higher education in the world, boasting faculty members at the top of their fields in virtually every department. Yet Eastern Elite is not just a research institution. It is a university that showers its undergraduate students with individualized attention and nurtures in them the sense that they are a special population and entitled to the very best that higher education has to offer. The university crafts this impression of student worthiness via many avenues, from the online testimonials prospective applicants can read years before ever setting foot on campus, to a freshman orientation program brimming with activities that underscore students' belonging to a close-knit community, to daily occurrences of centuries-old traditions, like bell-ringing, that become the pleasant background noise to life as an Eastern student, to the academic environment on campus, which creates occasions for students to regularly interact one-on-one with faculty.

Unlike state schools (and indeed, unlike many other private institutions), which cannot afford a seven-to-one student-to-faculty ratio and a huge number of small seminar classes, Eastern Elite's impressive endowment allows it to place enormous emphasis on faculty accessibility and professors' clear demonstrations of concern for the welfare of their undergraduate students. Ladder rank faculty, not graduate students or adjuncts, teach undergraduate classes, which makes Eastern a fortunate institutional holdout in the changing structure of American higher education. But of course, this is one of the main reasons (besides bragging rights) that students work like crazy to get into Eastern; why they apply to this school, which has just a 9 percent acceptance rate; and why parents who can afford it invest roughly $50,000 a year for their sons and daughters to go there. In classes, office hours, and many other settings, the high-octane, ambitious Eastern Elite student is reminded why she has chosen this campus and what the payoffs of graduating from this school will be. This university is one of the institutions on the American landscape that truly has what Burton Clark would call an "organizational saga"—an account of its place in the educational pantheon that is widely circulated and revered not only by anybody who is directly involved in the university's day-to-day operations but also by everybody else across the globe who pays attention to postsecondary education.[33]

Western Flagship University has a different sort of aura. While it is also a Research I university with distinguished faculty and several top-ranked departments, many undergraduate students come to the Western Flagship campus with the idea that it will provide an all-American college experience.[34] Western Flagship is the jewel in the Western Public university system, with beautifully landscaped grounds, handsome Ivy-League-meets-the-West-styled buildings, a lively college town surrounding it, and a stunning natural backdrop that sets off the campus. Western Flagship has also consistently been ranked as one of the top party schools in the nation. As one student commented in a national ranking of party schools, "It's true, we're just that excellent at partying. It's our way of life."[35] Accompanying this affinity for partying, though, Western Flagship is easygoing and casual, welcoming and friendly, and home to many students who have come from within the state because Western Flagship offers the best education available for reasonable in-state tuition prices. Students earning top grades in high school and receiving SAT scores around the 1200 mark thus want to come to Western Flagship for the educational value as well as the recreational opportunities.[36] That said, admissions are not especially selective; 80 percent of those who apply for admission get in—suggesting that high-GPA students and relatively strong standardized test-takers self-selectively apply to this campus.[37] In addition to in-state students, Western Flagship has a sizable number of out-of-state students (30 percent), who come to enjoy the Western Flagship experience and whose parents are willing to pay a substantially higher price for that privilege in the form of out-of-state tuition and fees.

Although the town in which the Western Flagship campus is located is highly equated with the experience of being a Western Flagship student (students, like other community members, have access to great boutique shops and restaurants, performing arts venues, bike lanes, and bars), neither the town nor the campus itself creates that same sense of belonging to a special, bounded community that students at Eastern Elite enjoy. While school spirit is carefully crafted at Western Flagship through high-profile NCAA sports programs, some factors militate against the "we"-ness that is apparent at Eastern Elite. For one, while more than 90 percent of freshmen at Western Flagship live on campus, that number drops precipitously in subsequent years as students move off campus into apartments or Greek houses. In addition, because of a much more constrained budget and larger class sizes, students do not have nearly the same access to faculty or to university-sponsored events as do undergraduates at Eastern Elite. And although there are freshmen orientation programs and traditions that are designed to pull in all members of the campus community and to create a sense of "who we are," it is notable that the most visible and student-lauded annual event is an informal, if enormous, yearly illicit drug celebration. The "organiza-

Table 1.1. Comparison of Eastern Elite University and Western Flagship University on Attributes of Interest

Attribute	Eastern Elite	Western Flagship
Full-time undergraduate enrollment	7,000	22,000
Percent male	51	50
Percent female	49	50
Percent minority undergraduate	30	15
Percent in-state	15	70
Percent out-of-state	85	30
Percent from public high school	60	90
Tuition and fees (not including room and board)	$40,000	$21,300 out-of-state, $5,500 in-state
Cost of room and board	$10,000	$8,176
Percent receiving financial aid, Year 1	70	40
On-campus housing guaranteed?	Yes, all four years	No
Percent of freshmen in on-campus housing	100	90
Percent of all students in on-campus housing	98	25
Number of applicants	22,800	18,000
Percent accepted	9	80
Percent accepted who enroll	70	45
Mean SAT scores	2100–2210 (based on 3 tests: qual., quant., analyt.)	1150 (based on 2 tests: qual., quant.)
Percent graduating in 5 years	97	70
Student-to-faculty ratio	7:1	18:1
Is there a Greek system?	No	Yes
Percent affiliated with Greek life	NA	16

Note: This information is the product of compiling data on three elite private universities for Eastern Elite University and three public flagship universities for Western Flagship University. Sources of this information were multiple. Data came from the universities themselves (e.g., from their websites), *US News & World Report*, College Confidential, collegeprowler.com, and other such sources. Although these data are accurate for no single institution in either category, they are indicative of the general features of our two case-study universities.

tional saga" at Western Flagship, then, is quite different from Eastern Elite's, a point to which we return often in this study. Table 1.1 shows some of the key similarities and differences between Eastern Elite University and Western Flagship University.

THE REST OF THE BOOK

Having provided a description of how we intend to study and analyze conservative students' experiences on our two campuses and discussed our methods and data, at this point we give a roadmap of what is to come in the rest of the book.

In chapter 2 we scale our questions down to the individual student level to flesh out the question of who right-leaning 18-year-olds are when they enter college. We do this in two ways. One important data source is the surveys administered by UCLA's HERI to thousands of incoming college freshmen and graduating seniors during the 2000s. This national dataset gives information on students' ideological orientations, demographics, and family religious and socioeconomic characteristics. Our second information source is the data we collected on the different campuses we studied, which we use to shed light on our students' and alumni's/ae's formative years in their families and their schools, their early experiences with conservatism, and how they got the politics bug.

In chapter 3 we look at three prominent national conservative organizations that sponsor campus conservatism, since we believe it is impossible to understand the different styles we witnessed at Eastern Elite and on the Western Public campuses without first getting a sense for the cultural repertoires that exist in American society at large. These national organizations—which themselves reflect the same range of positions we would find in national politics and the media—vary in size and types of support offered to students, but more important, they vary in the types of students they attempt to mobilize. In describing the field of these organizations, we also offer a typology of them. On one end are the "populist" organizations, which might profitably be compared in discourse and audience to the Fox News network. At the other end of the spectrum are what we call "refined," more intellectual organizations, which are quite a different animal but not altogether unrelated. Espousing a style of conservatism that appeals to those who identify as more contemplative, these organizations offer distinction to their members. But whatever place on the continuum these organizations sit, they share two things in common: they are unabashedly conservative, and they relay to students the message that "you need us because your campus neglects conservatism." The chapter is devoted to understanding the ins and outs of this conservative landscape.

In chapter 4 we turn to the campus level and begin our in-depth analysis of the institutional dynamics—that is, the organizational arrangements, cultural ideas, and practices in place at our two primary comparison universities—to see how these affect student conservatism at Eastern Elite University and Western Flagship University. We first consider each university's reputation in the higher education sector and explore how a school's standing in the larger field of universities might affect students' perceptions of their experiences as conservatives in college. We then look at the institutional environment, investigating how each university manages such mundane features as course registration, core curricula, and residential living arrangements, to see how these bear on conservative students' experiences in college. We proceed to an examination of conservatives' self-described academic experiences, comparing students' impressions of their campuses with the ideas and styles promoted by the different national conservative critics and organizations. Other sections of chapter 4 look at conservative students' social experiences and the degree to which students on each campus feel connected to a campus community. As several recent studies have pointed out, college is more than just academics; it is a breeding ground for sociability and social reproduction, learned in community with others.[38] This matters, we find, for how right-leaning students "perform" conservatism, insofar as their feelings of connection with or disjuncture from others on campus color their willingness to be confrontational in their politics. We end chapter 4 with conservative students' own accountings of both the benefits and the disadvantages of being on the conservative end of the political spectrum on their campuses, where they say they are ideologically outnumbered.

Chapters 5 and 6 build naturally from chapter 4. In these chapters we look at conservative students' activities in the specifically conservative clubs at each university and examine what students have to say about the ways they conduct themselves as conservatives in those settings. Chapter 5 is mostly about the Western Public university system, with a particular focus on the Western Flagship campus; chapter 6 is mostly about Eastern Elite University. Student-run conservative organizations fit into several categories, with a significant blurring of the boundaries. There are issue-oriented organizations such as chastity groups, pro-life groups, and pro-gun groups; there is the omnipresent College Republicans, which despite being a national organization has chapters that differ considerably in expressive styles across our two cases; there are conservative newspapers, and so on. We describe the range of organizations on each campus and illustrate both their most mundane and most vibrant activities. We also sketch out the internecine battles that exist among conservative individuals and clubs. As we have witnessed in recent national conservative politics, there are many moving parts to conservative ideology (traditional social issues, fiscal conservatism, national security; RNC-supported candidates vs. Tea Party candidates, "birthers" vs. moderates). Holding these parts together is a major accomplishment—an accomplishment that sometimes falls apart on college campuses. Looking at these conservative cleavages on campus is a bit like looking at national conservative politics refracted through the psyches of twenty-somethings.

But the main emphasis in chapters 5 and 6 is to look closely at the conservative styles of undergraduates at Eastern Elite and Western Flagship, and to try to understand what makes these styles so different. There is variation across these campuses in what are considered to be appropriate and legitimate conservative ideas and action, informed by students' understandings of themselves as college students, their involvement in campus clubs and other school settings, and, equally important, their participation in national organizations and their sense of what they are likely to be doing in their future careers. Our analysis of the styles proceeds in three parts in each chapter. We first simply describe the components of each campus's dominant style—what it looks like and sounds like when students engage in provocation in the Western Public system or civilized discourse at Eastern Elite, and how the submerged styles of campaigning and highbrow provocation depart from the dominant styles. We then move to explain the presence of these styles, initially employing what is known as the "emic" mode of analysis, allowing our students and alumni/ae to give us their own accounts of their conservative behavior and actions. And finally, we provide a structural and cultural analysis of our findings—known as the "etic" mode of analysis—in which we as researchers step outside the worldview of our subjects and think carefully about how the institutional features of the two different campus environments (dorm life, off-campus housing, course selection, student body size) create such variability in conservative thought and action. We think all three of these stances toward understanding conservative styles are essential: The first provides a nice lay of the land; the second allows students to tell in their own words how they select from a wider range of options; the last relies on the tools of our discipline to go deeper than "native" informants can usually see on their own.

Though in the foregoing chapters we will have used our entire sample of students to make empirical observations, in chapter 7 we hive off one category of our data and look specifically at the women among our interviewees to examine a phenomenon we call conservative femininity. We are interested in whether and how gender may intersect with other demands of being a conservative member of campus, such as whether the experience of being a woman leads women students to advocate for different political issues, or whether it might make them more or less likely to adopt wholeheartedly, modify, or reject their campus's dominant style. Looking closely at the example of women demonstrates that while the institutional dynamics found on the campus at large and in conservative clubs are highly influential in determining conservative students' political styles, personal and group characteristics such as gender also play an important role. Rather than assuming that campus cultures and organizational structures entirely determine individual and small-group practice, using the example of conservative women we find again that individuals' differing experiences can encourage or discourage their embrace of local political styles.

Focusing on just the women in our sample also gives us empirical perspective on the recent enhanced visibility of conservative women in GOP politics. Women have long played prominent and varying roles in the conservative arena, of course: from the 1940s through the 1960s Clare Booth Luce was a member of Congress, an ambassador, and a high-society supporter of Barry Goldwater; in the 1970s Phyllis Schlafly led a grassroots movement to stop the ERA, while Louise Day Hicks and Pixie Palladino fought busing in Boston; in the 1990s Ann Coulter blasted onto the punditry circuit; and in 2006 both Michele Bachmann and Sarah Palin were voted into office as, respectively, a member of the U.S. Congress and governor of Alaska. But it was not until the 2008 election and Sarah Palin's nomination to the national Republican ticket that media attention to women in the conservative movement exploded. In this chapter we explore what women's increased political visibility has meant for conservative college women on our case-study campuses, as well as how gendered expectations combine with conservative ideologies to create a uniquely feminine conservatism.

Having looked long and hard at evidence from multiple sources of information in the first seven chapters, in chapter 8 we present a more abstract model for thinking about how universities, in tandem with the broader political culture, cultivate distinctive styles of conservatism. Here we explore research in the fields of higher education studies, cultural sociology, political theory, and organization studies to capture some of the more general processes we have observed. We also argue in this concluding chapter that the model we have developed for studying conservatism in this project can be applied more widely to the role that universities play in the development of many different types of student identities. Focusing on colleges as organizational and cultural contexts for personal development is highly portable to other substantive inquiries about student's lives, whether in the political, academic, or social realms.

Before launching into these chapters we think it is wise to say something about our stance as the authors of this project since the subject of this book is about politics—and not only politics generally but politics and the university, the latter being a world we both inhabit. We want to make it clear that when we write about our conservative interviewees' views of the world we are neither condoning nor condemning their perspectives on how society should work—even as our respondents often made statements that could be viewed as indictments of the kind of work we do. Where we were able, we fact-checked the details of the events our interviewees discussed and the people they referred to, and on some occasions we inserted facts where rumors or incomplete or even incorrect accounts had been relayed to us by our respondents, such as when a student indicated to us that an Ivy League university had not allowed a controversial conservative event to take place on its campus but in fact the university had allowed the event to go forward. In this sense we believe we have an obligation to bring reality into discussions when the perspectives we are describing are either clearly or possibly inconsistent with the facts. It can be a tricky business to analyze interviewees' worldviews when those worldviews are highly contested, such as the idea that because the large majority of university faculty identify as politically liberal (an empirical *fact*, established most recently by Neil Gross and his colleagues), liberal views inexorably taint the classroom (an asserted *claim* that some conservatives hold steadfastly while others dispute it).[39] We think our job is to provide basic facts to the best of our abilities, but then to understand how conservative students make sense of them and experience their lives. In this we use an interpretivist approach in which we seek not to provide "objective truth so much as to unravel patterns of subjective understanding," on the assumption that what conservative students believe to be true is shaped by their perceptions and understanding of their world.[40] Readers may not always agree with the ways we have decided to describe our subjects' worldviews, or they may think we have pulled our punches when we might otherwise have "corrected" them, but we hope they will respect our scholarly goals.

Chapter 2

Who Are Conservative Students?

Conservative college students are made, not born. While this may seem like an obvious statement, we often overlook the many inputs that go into people's political development and assume that their political views are more or less static over time. But right-leaning undergraduates, like anyone else, are informed by multiple experiences at different points in their lives, from the political conversations they have with their families while eating their Wheaties in the morning, to the events that student organizations stage in high school and college, to the blogs and Twitter feeds they follow online, to the conferences they attend with hundreds and sometimes thousands of other students. And so we begin with what we might call the smallest unit of analysis in our investigation—individual students. In this chapter we ask a seemingly simple question: Who are conservative students, both in our sample and in the nation at large? Are they richer and "whiter" than their fellow classmates, as we might guess from the images of their elders at events like the national GOP convention? Are they more religious, as polls indicate for the general American population of conservative voters? And what about their families' political backgrounds? Are college-age conservatives likely to grow up in right-leaning homes, as Rebecca Klatch found for the "Yaffers" who were mobilized in the 1960s by the Young Americans for Freedom; or do many of them, much like the Alex Keaton character from the 1980s sitcom *Family Ties*, react against their liberal or moderate parents' politics to become avid supporters of small government, low taxes, and conservative social issues?[1] And just what is the proportion of conservative students in our nation's colleges, anyway?

While we might expect to come by answers to these questions easily, there turns out to be little in the way of a central information trove that can be tapped to enlighten us. We have therefore put together a compendium of such material by relying on a mix of sources that seems most useful for this range of questions. To provide a "thick" account of how young people come to be conservative—what their turning points have been, and who their most influential role models are—we rely on our own data, collected on the Eastern Elite and Western Public campuses, to give us the flavor of how such political development processes work. In our interviews and in the ethnographic settings where we did our research, we talked with college-age conservatives about their early years as children and teenagers, and asked them about their initial and most salient political experiences. We heard stories about students' "Aha!" moments that led them to seek solidarity with other conservative people in their communities, who then encouraged them to dive into the books of Ayn Rand, or become better acquainted with the Bible, or join antiabortion protests, or pitch in on local political campaigns. This analysis provides a vivid account of who our interviewees are politically, and how they first came to identify with conservative causes.

Our qualitative accounts, though rich in detail, are far from representative, and so we also analyze quantitative data from a large-scale study of college students that, while it delivers a rather "thinner" account of undergraduates' experiences, can offer a more representative source of information. This not only provides a way of somewhat checking our respondents against nationally representative data, it also fleshes out a portrait of contemporary conservative college students that previously has not been available. Here we rely on information collected by scholars at UCLA's Higher Education Research Institute (HERI), who since 1966 have surveyed more than eight million incoming first-time/full-time college freshmen in the full panoply of higher education campus types in the United States, from small liberal arts colleges to the largest of state-funded "multiversities," and every kind of four-year institution in between.[2] Collected and published each year as the American Freshman National Norms, the HERI surveys provide valuable information on students just as they enter college, including their basic demographic characteristics, future educational goals, and career aspirations, as well the ways in which they identify their own positions on the political spectrum.[3]

In this part of our analysis we make use of several years' separate reports, as well as a publication called *The American Freshman: Forty Year Trends*, which was issued by HERI in 2007 and shows data on freshmen for the years 1966–2006. After laying out a few of the key trends in students' political identifications over these four decades, we proceed to analyze HERI's national survey data on freshmen for one specific year, 2001.[4] Although the 2001 survey is not as up-to-date or as comprehensive as we would have liked (for example, it is limited to freshmen of more than a decade ago, and cannot show changes over time), we take comfort in the facts that 2001 was a time when many of our interviewees were coming of age (most of them somewhere between their freshmen and senior years in high school), and that 2001 marks the beginning of the eight-year Bush administration, which was in place during most of our data collection.[5]

The key advantage of having full access to this one year's worth of survey data is that it allows us to explore a number of dimensions of what it means to be a college-age conservative. For example, by selecting self-identified conservative students as our primary population of interest, we can compare their demographic characteristics—such as their race, religion, gender, and class status—with those of moderate and liberal students in universities across the country.[6] We can also choose to analyze the data in other ways, such as by looking at different campus types separately from one another, to compare conservative students at private elite institutions most like Eastern Elite University, for instance, with those at selective state universities most like Western Flagship University.[7] The payoff to such an analysis—even as we are providing just the simplest descriptive statistics—is that it more specifically speaks to the particular students in the types of institutions we studied qualitatively. This then not only builds up an information source about conservative students generally but also helps us make better sense of the conservative students at Western Public and Eastern Elite who are at the heart of our research.

WHO ARE CONSERVATIVE STUDENTS, AND HOW MANY ARE THERE ON TODAY'S COLLEGE AND UNIVERSITY CAMPUSES?

THE HERI *FORTY YEAR TRENDS* REPORT

Conservative critics often charge that right-leaning students constitute an embattled minority on college and university campuses, then offer mostly anecdotal examples to make their case. The HERI surveys give us hard numbers to explore the critics' assertions, at least as pertains to the proportion of the incoming student body that self-identifies as conservative.[8] Since 1970, HERI has asked incoming first-year freshmen to state whether they consider themselves to be far left, liberal, middle of the road, conservative, or far right, a five-point scale that scholars often condense to "liberal," "middle of the road," and "conservative"—a convention we follow here.[9] So, just how many conservative students *are* there on college campuses, and how do their numbers compare to liberal and moderate classmates? Figure 2.1 shows us these trends.

Perhaps not surprisingly—because 18-year-old survey respondents may still be forming their political opinions, or are reluctant to take on bold political identities, or are simply following in their elders' footsteps—one of the most enduring patterns in the four decades of HERI surveys is the tendency for incoming students to de-

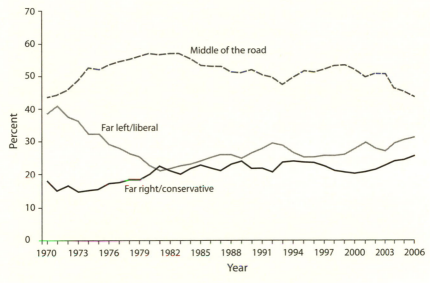

Figure 2.1. Political views of incoming freshmen, 1970–2006.
Source: HERI, *The American Freshman: Forty Year Trends* (2007, 28).

scribe themselves as middle of the road rather than at either end of the political spectrum.[10] As indicated in figure 2.1, middle of the road has always been the political identity that the highest number of new college students report, beating out both liberals and conservatives by wide margins through much of the 40-year period.[11] One interesting take-away observation from this trend is that although conservative critics argue that right-leaning students are in the minority on college campuses across the country, in the aggregate they are in much the same company as their liberal peers, who also find their numbers small compared to the number of moderates.

But this doesn't mean the situation has been static, and the HERI statistics are useful for helping us track the probable roots of the conservative discourse. When we go back to the earliest waves of survey administration, we find one period in which liberal freshmen were considerably more numerous than conservatives in the student population. In 1971, 40.9 percent of freshmen identified as liberal, while 44.1 percent reported they were middle of the road.[12] During this time it would not be difficult to imagine that conservatives (at 15.1 percent of the total freshman population) might have felt more like outliers on their campuses than at nearly any other time since they were outnumbered not only by moderates but also by liberals, by a margin of nearly three to one. The early 1970s, of course, were a peak period for liberal college student activism: The Vietnam War was wildly unpopular, and the late 1960s—replete with countercultural, antiwar, and civil rights demonstrations—exerted a strong pull on the worldviews of young people.[13] While conservative organizations like the Young Americans for Freedom were busy mobilizing college students on the right during this time, they did not have the same reach as their liberal counterparts.

Within just a few years, however, the number of students identifying as liberal dropped precipitously while the number of moderate students grew in kind, and those identifying as conservative also increased. For the only time during the 40-year history of the HERI surveys, freshmen in the early 1980s identifying as conservative surpassed those identifying as liberal. In 1981—the year that Ronald Reagan entered the White House—the number of freshmen calling themselves middle of the road rose to 56.6 percent, and conservative freshmen outpaced liberal freshmen across the country by a percentage point, 22.4 percent to 21 percent.

Since that conservative peak in the early 1980s, the trends have been cyclical. Conservative affiliation gained strength during the first four years that Bill Clinton was president, coinciding with the steep rise in on-air conservative radio and television commentary that was highly critical of the Clinton era, but then declined in the latter days of Clinton's presidency. The latest cycle, beginning with the aftermath of 9/11, shows that those identifying as middle of the road have been losing ground to the two ends of the political spectrum.[14] In other words, at the beginning of the twenty-first century there is a movement away from freshmen reporting a moderate political stance and a movement toward more boldly identifying as liberal or conservative—even while, it must be remembered, there are still more moderates than students on either the left or the right.

UNDERSTANDING POLITICAL IDENTIFICATION

National Survey

The *Forty Year Trends* report is useful for seeing change over time in political affiliation as students enter college, but this overview of data does not allow us to do more fine-grained analysis of students at different types of universities. The first inquiry for which we use the 2001 national survey, therefore, examines the ratios of liberal, moderate, and conservative freshmen entering college at two types of universities most like Western Flagship University and Eastern Elite University, which in the following pages we refer to as "public flagship" universities and "private elite" universities.

As we can see in table 2.1, the proportion of incoming freshmen who identified as conservative in 2001 was smaller at both private elite institutions and public flagship institutions (18.5 and 20.1 percent, respectively) than in the national sample of college freshmen (21 percent)—though admittedly by small margins.[15] Nonetheless, we see that conservative students are slightly underrepresented at the more prestigious levels of educational institutions compared to the higher education sector as a whole.[16]

But much more interesting than simply comparing the percentages of conservatives to other conservatives across different types of campuses is to compare the proportion of conservatives relative to moderates and liberals within each of the campus types. For exam-

Table 2.1. Freshmen's Political Identification as Liberal, Moderate, and Conservative, by Campus Type, 2001

	Private Elite Institutions	Public Flagship Institutions	All Institutions in HERI
Liberal	48.8	35.6	31.1
Middle of the road	32.7	44.3	48.0
Conservative	18.5	20.1	21.0

ple, table 2.1 also shows that liberals and middle-of-the-roaders made up quite different proportions of the student body at private elite institutions than at public flagship institutions, and different again when compared with freshmen at all HERI survey schools. Starting backwards, the data are the following: on campuses of all types in 2001, 31.1 percent of freshmen identified as liberal, while nearly half (48 percent) called themselves moderate; the same pattern held at public flagships, where there were 35.6 percent liberal and 44.3 percent moderate. This is quite a different story from freshmen at private elite institutions, 48.8 percent of whom said they were liberal, with only 32.7 percent reporting to be middle of the road.

What does this mean? Taking just the two campus types of most interest to us, it means that conservative freshmen at public flagship institutions are in the company of proportionally more moderates than liberals on their campuses, while at private elite institutions the opposite is true: Conservative freshmen at schools like Stanford University, Carleton College, or the Ivy League schools attend college with a good number more liberals than moderates. Whether conservative students are precisely aware of such percentages on their campuses is unlikely, but these patterns give us reason to believe that conservatives at private elite schools might complain more vigorously about an overwhelmingly liberal environment on their campuses than their counterparts at large, state flagship universities would. Paradoxically, this is not the case, at least on the campuses we studied. As we explain later in the book, conservative students at Eastern Elite complain much *less* about their liberal peers than do students at Western Flagship—a finding that has much to do with the culture and organizational environment of their campus.

Interviews

Precollege and College Political Identifications

Studying the HERI *Forty Year Trends* report and analyzing survey data on the political affiliations for freshmen in 2001 yields important information on the ratios of conservatives to other students on campuses across the United States. But such data sources cannot tell us what these labels mean to students or how they come to hold these political identities in the first place. For information of this sort we turn to our interview data from Eastern Elite and Western Public.

How do conservative students describe their political positions when given more time and space to answer than a closed-ended survey prompt? We found a good deal of nuance and variation in these responses. First, students at both Western Public and Eastern Elite most commonly characterized their precollege political identity as "conservative" (with one Western Flagship interviewee qualifying himself as a "moderate conservative"), but "Republican" came in second place (including two Eastern Elite interviewees who described themselves as "conservative Republicans"). Perhaps more strikingly, though, each university system boasted four interviewees who identified as *liberal* or *Democrat* prior to their college experience. Table 2.2 gives a simplified version of how our interviewees described their political identifications before coming to college, and compares these with their stated identifications at the time of their interviews.

Given that we were interviewing self-identified right-of-center college students and alumni/ae, it is no surprise that not a single one of our respondents identified his or her current political affiliation as on the left side of the political spectrum. At the same time however, while "conservative" is still the most common response, we see a multiplication of the modifiers students used to characterize their conservatism—something that, of course, surveys cannot capture. For example, one Eastern Elite interviewee explained that while prior to college she had identified herself as a "conservative Republican," at the time of the interview she now "would identify as being either a social conservative or a crunchy conservative" owing to growing commitments around social justice and the environment (though she remained adamantly anti-abortion) (Melissa Preston, Eastern Elite). A Western Satellite student who identified himself as simply a "Republican" prior to college explained that now

Table 2.2 Precollege and Current Political Identifications of
Interviewees

	Western	*Eastern*
Precollege Political Identification		
Democrat	3	2
Liberal	1	2
Republican	6	4
Conservative	(0)	(2)
Conservative	7	11
Moderate	(1)	(0)
Libertarian	0	1
Uncategorizable	0	1
Data missing	5	3
Current Political Identification		
Republican	3	3
Conservative	(2)	(3)
Moderate	(1)	(0)
Conservative	11	18
Catholic	(0)	(3)
Fiscal	(1)	(2)
Libertarian	(3)	(0)
Moderate	(1)	(2)
Progressive	(0)	(1)
Social	(2)	(2)
Libertarian	7	0
Rightwing	1	1
Other	1	0
Uncategorizable	0	1
Data missing	1	1

Note: All data are taken from interviewee self-reports. For both Republican and Conservative, totals identifying as each have been noted on each line. However, for both of these categories, interviewees often reported a modifier, such as "moderate Republican" or "fiscal conservative." As such, totals for these modifiers have been noted in parentheses below the identification each modifies. These modifiers do not sum to the total for each identity; for example, a good number of interviewees identified simply as conservative. Last, "Current Political Identification" in this case means current at the time of our interview.

I'm conservative and situated well within the mainstream of the conservative movement. The label I like to use, for lack of anything better, is a movement conservative with a slight libertarian tinge. That's basically I'm socially, fiscally, and national security conservative. But I'm very oriented towards personal liberty and protection of liberty as opposed to necessarily enforcement of any doctrines, which is where I might break a little bit with the social conservatives. (Bryan Carhart, Western Satellite)

Among our interviewees, then, while we do see a rightward movement overall while in college, the larger trend that we see (at least from students' retrospective depictions) is of an increased fine-tuning of political identification. This appears to come from our respondents having taken in added years of life experience, from interactions with others, from changes in the external world (for example, events that occurred on an international scale, like the wars in Iraq and Afghanistan), and from using all these inputs to more fully articulate their worldviews. This fine-tuning could be one reason why so many incoming freshmen choose the less invested "middle of the road" on the HERI surveys—it is over the course of their college careers that some students refine their political orientations.

The other change in political identification that should be noted in examining table 2.2 is the sharp uptick in the number of Western Public students identifying as libertarian once they got to college. "Libertarian" comes in second place, after "conservative," with "Republican" now a distant third. It is also notable that prior to college, no Western Public interviewees had identified themselves as libertarian, though one Eastern Elite interviewee had. He explained, "I came to Eastern kind of as a libertarian. I mean, I was one of these people who had this kind of juvenile obsession with Ayn Rand [*laughs*]. I quickly grew out of that one" (Vincent Long, Eastern Elite). This interviewee now claims a Catholic conservative identity—which marks quite a distance from his precollege form of identification. In contrast, several Western Public interviewees described their moves *toward* libertarianism. For example, one Western Satellite alumna told us,

The Republican Party is not the same as it used to be. . . . I've just switched from Republican to Libertarian because Republicans can be kind of hypocritical in that they want less government, but then they'll say that they don't want gays to get married, for example, or they don't want marijuana to be legalized. Whereas I think the government should just, hands off everything. (Brittany Urban, Western Satellite)

Western Public interviewees' moves toward libertarianism are significant for all happening *during college*: None of the current libertarians described themselves as having had libertarian leanings prior to matriculating on the Western Public campuses. It would appear, then, that certain features of the Western Public system—in particular, its geographic location in the western region of the country and its emphasis on typical college behavior (which requires something of a laissez-faire attitude toward social life)—create opportunities for legitimately adopting a libertarian political bent, whereas at Eastern Elite, such a possibility is shrugged off, as in the case of Vincent Long, as a "juvenile obsession."[17]

Why Conservatism?

Depending on when they felt they "became" conservative, our interviewees stated many different reasons for having developed their political views. Most commonly, right-leaning students at both Eastern Elite and Western Public initially adopted the opinions of their conservative or Republican families. Some described this as simply reflexive. For example, one Eastern Elite man told us, "It was more that I was conservative by inheritance and I hadn't really decided how I should . . . I knew what the talking points were, or at least what the standard answer was for each issue, but I didn't really understand how it all fit together" (Calvin Coffey, Eastern Elite). Others remembered more contentious relationships with their family members over politics. One Western Flagship interviewee—later a president of the College Republicans—characterized his precollege political identification as being motivated by a bit of adolescent rebellion:

> I do think my parents influenced me, originally in a negative way, because my mom is a libertarian and I always joked that my dad's an anarchist. And so originally I think maybe even my liberalness in high school was probably even to get away from my parents. (Hunter Devine, Western Flagship)

And not everyone came from a right-leaning family: several interviewees on both campuses had one or more liberal parents or close family members. Interviewees also often described parents who, while conservative, were much less politically active than they themselves had become at Eastern Elite or Western Public. In fact, some of these respondents reported that their parents were frankly bewildered by their high level of political commitment during their college years.

For those students at both schools who identified as conservative before arriving at college, a single issue often initially galvanized their conservatism. Issues that concerned conservative students were often related to their own biographies or family histories. Both of these students described being drawn to conservatism by examining the impact of economic policies on their parents' business:

> And my dad always says that . . . he became Republican when he started to make money. And I get that, and really see how those policies, especially tax policies, they're more friendly to small business. My dad owns his own business, so . . . I see how that party benefits my family. And you kind of vote your pocketbook sort of thing. (Stephanie Cohen, Western Flagship)

> [My father] is heavily involved in the auto industry. He . . . talked to me a lot about industry in America and about what it takes to have a successful business. I have taken those lessons to heart and developed sort of a fiscal or economic conservatism from that side of things, by seeing how he has been able to succeed,

and specifically how his company is able to succeed. . . . That is where the economic conservatism stems from. (Darren Norton, Eastern Elite)

Other students mentioned being motivated by issues that were less directly related to their personal experiences but about which they felt no less strongly. Abortion and national elections were the most commonly mentioned among Eastern Elite students, while the Iraq War and the events of 9/11 were the most frequently cited by those from Western Public. Other students who did not tell of a "lightning rod" issue recalled developing their political views through reading influential books (examples ranged from *Atlas Shrugged* to *The Purpose-Driven Life*), or simply having "always been interested" in politics (Conor Denning, Western State).

Burgeoning Political Styles

Among respondents who described themselves as right-leaning before matriculation, we found considerable variation in how they had acted on their conservatism in high school—what we might call their precollege political styles—as well as in their ideological orientations. Across Eastern Elite and Western Public, for example, students described various forms of political engagement that ranged from being relatively apathetic, on one end (most often, identifying as conservative but remaining otherwise politically uninvolved), to actively participating in student clubs, campaigning for candidates, or attending rallies on the other. In addition, among those who were politically active before college, we found that some students from *each* university system described their early political behavior in ways that fit the "provocative" style (which we have identified as typical of Western Public students) or the "civilized discourse" style (which we saw commonly at Eastern Elite).

Those who stated they had been politically inactive in high school frequently attributed their lack of engagement to the political tenor of their home communities, which they reported to be uniformly conservative. This caused them to be unreflectively conservative and apathetic about politics, since everybody around them was pretty much the same. For example, a Western Flagship student said, "I feel like when I went to college I was conservative because I came from a small town and everybody was conservative" (Christina Young, Western Flagship). Others felt that a climate of disengagement in their schools had kept them from really thinking about or investing in their own ideological positions or political manners. As one Eastern Elite interviewee who grew up in a western mountain state explained, "I just grew up with that set of beliefs. It really didn't ever come up in high school. My school was very apolitical" (Elizabeth Tennyson, Eastern Elite).

On the other hand, even before heading off to college, some of the more politically active respondents—at Eastern Elite as well as on the Western Public campuses—pointed to early stylistic proclivities closely related to the provocative style of conservatism. On one occasion for an Eastern Elite student, the development of a Fox News–style mode of political expression happened quite literally, when he worked on a class project that earned him an A:

> The real thing that got me involved in news and politics and journalism, that sort of thing, was in eighth grade we had to do a book report, nonfiction. At that moment, Bill O'Reilly was kind of taking off on Fox News and we had just gotten Fox News on our cable TV. He came out with a book version of his show, *The O'Reilly Factor* . . . and I read it and I thought, "I really like this a lot." . . . My friend and I did a mock *O'Reilly Factor* show [for our project]. . . . We did a split screen and I played the liberal and he played the conservative. (Calvin Coffey, Eastern Elite)

Other students described these inclinations as largely picked up from their families' habits of consuming right-wing media, as this Western Satellite student described:

> Growing up, my parents were always conservative and they would listen to Rush Limbaugh and watch the news a lot, my mom basically. And she would have the radio on AM all day or have it on Fox News. Like, whenever we're together there was

always at least one TV on Fox News. . . . And so I'd be in the car with them and mostly Rush Limbaugh and I'd hear him talking and everything. And I was, "Okay, good." (Victor Irwin, Western Satellite)

In a few cases, family influence was even more direct, with family members actively recruiting the respondents into political activism. As one Eastern Elite interviewee recalled, his mother had him and his siblings out on the front lines of conservatism from a young age: "As soon as we could walk we were holding campaign signs for pro-life candidates and that sort of thing" (Kingsley Griffith, Eastern Elite). Thus at least some interviewees from both Eastern Elite and Western Public were well schooled in the style of populist media and conservative grassroots activism before setting foot on either campus.

We also heard descriptions of precollege political styles from interviewees at both Eastern Elite and Western Public that fit more easily with the civilized discourse style of conservatism. Again, in some cases families were influential, as this Western Satellite interviewee explained:

My dad and I definitely have that political bond in common. I talked with him a lot about it. . . . Some of his heroes are people like Ronald Reagan, people like Milton Friedman. And those people are [the] books I grew up reading, philosophies I grew up understanding. (Lindsey Nicholson, Western Satellite)

For many interviewees, then, their earliest form of political expression came in the form of discussing conservative principles with family members. In other cases, this style was institutionally sanctified via local organizations for teenage conservatives or high school debate clubs. One Eastern Elite interviewee described attending Young Republicans meetings in high school as the time when he "started to critically evaluate my own views. I think that is when I sort of began to make my views my own" (Derek Yeager, Eastern Elite). For others, this manner of conservative contemplation came as a result of self-directed reading or researching the "Austrian economists" (a Western Satellite student) on their own, and then debating their newfound knowledge with family and friends. In all, civilized debate and discussion marked the early political lives of at least some of our interviewees at both Western Public and Eastern Elite, although slightly more Eastern Elite students exhibited this style.

In sum, we find that our student and alumni/ae interviewees from both Eastern Elite and the Western Public system varied politically in some markedly similar ways prior to attending either school. Respondents at both schools described a variety of political identifications, not always coming to college already on the right. Among those from both universities who *did* identify as conservative prior to matriculation, we saw considerable variation in precollegiate political engagement and styles. A good number of our interviewees from both campuses were quite familiar with the provocative style: their families consumed conservative media or were active in protest politics. Others from both campuses had experience with the civilized discourse style, reading seriously about political ideology, debating informally with family and friends or in organized high school clubs, and finding their own distinctive conservative voices. Still other respondents, in contrast, reported they had had virtually no need at all to exercise their conservative muscles during their high school years since their still-forming political ideas were not being challenged in their families, communities, or schools. What this means is that the high school students who ended up in conservative clubs at Western Public and Eastern Elite were nowhere near as remarkably different from one another politically when they entered college as when they exited, a finding that deflates the hypothesis that conservative students are simply self-selecting toward different kinds of campuses.

DEMOGRAPHIC CHARACTERISTICS

Besides simply mapping the proportion of conservative freshmen relative to liberals and moderates (as we did using the HERI surveys) or providing a thicker description of what students mean when they call themselves conservative (as we did using our interviews), we also used our data sources to examine the demographic characteristics—such as race, class, gender, and religion—of those who identify as right of center. Table 2.3 summarizes the gender, racial and ethnic, and religious makeup of our interviewees. On the first two variables noted in table 2.3, gender and race/ethnicity, we do not see substantial differences between the campuses or from the national survey data collected by HERI. No matter how we break down the data, we are looking predominantly at whites and men. However, we see considerably more variation, both between our cases and also in comparing our main campuses to the national survey, when we delve into religion—again, using both national survey data and our qualitative evidence. Last, we examine conservative students' social class backgrounds using parents' levels of education

Table 2.3. Gender, Race, and Religious Preferences of Interviewees

	Western	*Eastern*
Gender		
Men	14	17
Women	8	7
Race/ethnicity		
White/Caucasian	22	22
African American/black	0	0
Asian/Asian American	0	2
Latino	0	0
Other	0	0
Religion		
Protestant	5	4
Catholic	4	11
Jewish	1	0
Evangelical	1	3
Not religious	3	1
"Spiritual"	4	0
Other	2	0
Data missing	2	5
Total no. of interviewees	22	24

and occupational prestige as measures in the national survey, and supplementing these two measures with students' regional origins and their broader discussions of family social class position in the interviews.

Race

National Survey

As indicated by national surveys of voting-age adults, the Republican Party attracts a more racially homogeneous constituency than does the Democratic Party: most of the GOP's supporters are non-Hispanic whites.[18] Is this also true for college freshmen who identify as conservative?

The first thing that we notice in table 2.4 is that at universities of all types in the HERI sample, whites make up a consistently higher percentage of freshmen who self-identify as conservative than they

Table 2.4. Comparisons of Conservative Freshmen to Other Freshmen, by Race and Campus Type, 2001

	White	Black	Asian	Latino	Other
Private elite					
Liberal	72.4	4.6	11.3	7.2	4.6
Middle of the road	66.4	4.6	17.1	8.2	3.7
Conservative	80.9	1.5	9.4	5.4	2.8
Public flagship					
Liberal	72.4	5.8	11.1	7.1	3.6
Middle of the road	72.6	4.9	13.2	6.4	2.8
Conservative	83.9	2.2	7.6	4.1	2.2
All other types					
Liberal	71.5	9.6	5.7	9.1	4.1
Middle of the road	75.2	7.7	6.1	7.7	3.3
Conservative	83.9	4.8	3.4	5.2	2.7
Total	74.9	7.3	6.7	7.6	3.4

do of non-conservatives. At private elite institutions, an average of
70 percent of liberal and moderate incoming freshmen in 2001 were
white, but 80.9 percent of conservatives fell into this racial category; at public flagship institutions, meantime, an average of 72.5
percent of non-conservative freshmen were white, but an even relatively larger percentage—83.9 percent—of conservative freshmen
were white. The clear story that emerges from an analysis of race is
that across all institutional types, whites are overrepresented among
conservative students. Table 2.4 is also useful for indicating that
while African Americans may be the least likely group of incoming
freshmen to identify as conservative, all other minority groups in
the country are also underrepresented among conservatives.

Interviews

As table 2.3 shows, the national data square with what we found in
the Western Public system and at Eastern Elite University: Nearly
all of our interviewees were white, save for two Eastern Elite men
who were Asian American. It would be fallacious to say, however,
that we have no information on race and ethnicity from our interviews simply because we have few students of color among our respondents. To take such a stance would imply that whiteness is
somehow not a racial identity, as when, for example, "diversity"
is taken to mean the presence of people from nonwhite backgrounds.[19] Though we do not examine this at length, it is worth
looking at our students' limited articulations of racialized understandings to better understand the continuing relevance of race in
American conservatism.[20]

In our Eastern Elite interviews, respondents generally shied away
from explicit discussions of race. Only one student expressed some
sense of a white racial identity in relationship to her political views,
noting that she worried it was easy for her to advocate fiscal conservatism as an "upper-middle-class white girl who's had generations
and generations of her family go to Eastern" (Molly Nash Downing, Eastern Elite). The only other Eastern Elite interviewee to discuss his own racial identity was one of the two students of color in

our sample. Kyle Lee described how during his term in office as leader of the Eastern Elite College Republicans, he explicitly worked to add racial and ethnic diversity to the group:

> R: I think when I was president [of the Eastern Elite College Republicans], I was elected to an all-white male board. I was the only non-white member of the board. That was a problem, right? Why weren't there . . . you go into a meeting and it's all white faces. Nothing wrong with that. But when a [school newspaper] *Manifest* reporter comes in to take a picture of the Club, people see that. Oh, a bunch of white boys.
>
> I: So there's nothing wrong with that from your point of view?
>
> R: People are people. Human beings are equal. But the fact that black people can see that picture in the *Manifest* and don't feel welcome to come. Or a Hispanic female comes, looks at the picture and doesn't feel welcome to come. So definitely, by broadening our coalitions on campus, people that *are* Asian or Hispanic that happen to be Republican will see that we are reaching out, they feel welcome to come in. (Kyle Lee, Eastern Elite)

Race and ethnicity thus became an instrumental part of Kyle's approach to leading the Eastern Elite College Republicans, attempting to put a new face—beginning with his own—on the organization. But overall, direct discussion of race only rarely entered into our interviews with Eastern Elite conservatives.

Western Public interviewees were more likely to talk openly about race with us. Many students took the position that American society should be colorblind, and that race is not something that should be taken into consideration when hiring workers or admitting students (relatively unsurprising perspectives, given the Western Flagship College Republicans' multiple Affirmative Action Bake Sales). Several white students mentioned distaste for what they saw as the "victim stance" taken by people of color (Brittany Urban, Western Satellite), claiming that it is not racial identity so much as individual character that matters. As one Western Flagship alumnus stated, "Maybe I've benefited somewhat from the fact that I'm white, but really, I think I've benefited from the fact that I had great parents and [a] great upbringing, and I was very lucky in that respect. And had I been black with the same parents, I think I would have benefited just as much" (Scott Dickey, Western Flagship).

Western Public interviewees overall articulated a stronger sense of having a white identity, and having their race be a salient feature of their campus experiences, than did Eastern Elite students. One woman, sent by a local think tank on what she described as a "suicide mission" to a diversity and tolerance workshop held on campus, recalled:

> And it was just like you can't go to that without feeling like a racist. And I feel like I'm a very accepting person, and I have like gay friends and black friends and, you know, poor friends. . . . I don't understand why I have to be so aware of their situation or their race or their gender in order to be accepting of it. I think *not* being aware of it is actually what is preferable in a situation, and they're just teaching you that you have to walk around recognizing your white privilege. And I think that that makes the situation worse. (Stephanie Cohen, Western Flagship)

In contrast, despite some Eastern Elite students' interests in "making fun of the political correctness that has sort of pervaded this [campus]" (Drew Metcalfe, Eastern Elite), race appears to be one area where even the bold dare not tread. We found that Western Public conservatives were more willing to take, and to be open about taking, more publicly controversial stances in their discussions of race and ethnicity.

Gender

National Survey

A second important dimension to investigate is the mix of genders among conservative freshmen—in particular, to see whether men

Table 2.5. Gender Breakdown by Politics and Campus Type, 2001

	Male	*Female*
Private elite		
Liberal	42.8	57.2
Middle of the road	48.4	51.6
Conservative	58.5	41.5
Public flagship		
Liberal	44.4	55.6
Middle of the road	45.1	54.9
Conservative	56.5	43.5
All other types		
Liberal	41.0	59.0
Middle of the road	40.9	59.1
Conservative	49.3	50.7
Total	43.6	56.4

and women subscribe to conservative political ideology in different proportions in universities across the country, and whether these numbers vary by institutional type. We will go into a great amount of detail on questions of gender when we look at conservative femininity in chapter 7 (so much so that we do not examine our interviewees' views on gender here), but for the moment, we use the HERI survey to open up this discussion.

The first striking statistic in table 2.5 is the comparison between men and women at a variety of institutional types who identify as conservative their freshman year. The HERI numbers show that incoming freshmen who identify as conservative at all other types of institutions are basically split evenly (49.3 percent to 50.7 percent) between men and women. In contrast, there is a significant gender division among conservatives at both private elite and public flagship universities, where conservative freshmen are considerably more likely to be men than women. At public flagship schools, conservative men outnumber conservative women by 13 percentage points (56.5 percent men to 43.5 percent women), and they do so by an even larger 17 percentage points at private elite schools (58.5 percent men to 41.5 percent women). We can see that liberals show pretty much the opposite pattern as conservatives.[21] One clear conclusion to be drawn from these data is that being a conservative on both private elite and public flagship campuses is more of a "guy thing" than a "girl thing," as compared to the wider set of colleges and universities surveyed by HERI—though we will hold off on this point in our interview data until chapter 7.

Religion

National Survey

Religion plays a central role for many people who identify as conservative, as national surveys of the general population of American voters show.[22] Table 2.6 lists the religious affiliations of freshmen in the HERI surveys and shows the proportion of incoming conservative freshman who identify with a particular religious tradition or with no religion at all.

Several interesting findings appear in table 2.6. The first is that university freshmen overall (not just conservatives) are a fairly religious group, with only a distinct minority proclaiming to profess no faith.[23] That said, conservatives are less than half as likely as other students to say they have no religious preference. Indeed, not only are they more religious overall, but they are considerably more likely than their liberal and moderate classmates to identify as born-again Christian.[24] A third item of note in this table is that while conservative students at all institutions are somewhat more likely than other students to identify as Protestant, at private elite institutions Catholics are overrepresented among conservatives compared to the general student population (32.4 percent of conservative freshmen at private elite institutions say they are Catholic compared to 27.7 percent of freshmen at public flagships and 25.9 percent at all other colleges and universities in the general sample)—whereas con-

Table 2.6. Religious Preferences of Conservative Freshmen Compared to Other Freshmen, at Two Campus Types, 2001

	Protestant	Born-Again	Catholic	Jewish	Other	None
Private elite						
Liberal	13.1	3.6	15.9	13.8	16.2	37.4
Middle of the road	17.7	9.0	29.8	7.1	15.6	20.8
Conservative	22.1	20.4	32.4	3.8	11.5	9.9
Public flagship						
Liberal	18.1	6.1	22.7	9.0	15.0	29.2
Middle of the road	22.9	11.5	30.8	4.5	13.9	16.5
Conservative	26.9	23.2	27.7	2.2	11.4	8.7
All other types						
Liberal	19.3	10.8	27.1	3.7	15.1	24.1
Middle of the road	21.9	16.2	33.5	1.5	14.1	12.9
Conservative	23.3	29.2	25.9	0.9	14.5	6.1
Total	21.1	15.9	29.2	3.1	14.5	16.2

Note: "Protestant" includes Baptist, Episcopal, Lutheran, Methodist, Presbyterian, and UCC. "Evangelical" includes all students who identified as born-again; thus, some students may have been counted twice in this table (e.g., an individual who identified as both Baptist *and* born-again). "Other" includes Buddhist, Eastern Orthodox, Muslim, Mormon, Quaker, Seventh Day Adventist, "other Christian," and "other religious."

servatives at public flagships are about equally likely to be Catholic as are students of any other political orientation.[25] Since we had found a strong pattern among Eastern Elite students in talking about their Catholicism, we were quite struck by the same trend in the national survey data.

Interviews

Table 2.3 lists the religious affiliations of our interviewees and shows that nearly half of the students we interviewed at Eastern Elite identified themselves as Catholic. These students often were members of Catholic student organizations on campus and/or regularly attended mass off campus. This raises the question: Why does conservatism—at least among the most active right-leaning students on campus—have such an affinity with Catholicism at Eastern Elite?

Many of the Eastern Elite Catholics described Catholicism as fitting in well with their political beliefs. In some cases, religion appeared to be an outgrowth of political beliefs; for others, this relationship worked in the opposite direction, in which conservative political belief intensified from renewed Catholic commitments. The interview comments from Catholic students below provide examples of each:

> I think my political affiliation grew with my religious belief, . . . or it just happened to coincide at that same time, because I think Republicans at heart think differently than Democrats—that we kind of think that there is some sort of absolute truth out there, there is some sort of moral order to this world. . . . So I think religious life is a part of the Republican Party, even though I do not consider myself a part of the religious right. (Kyle Lee, Eastern Elite)

> I think that part of [my] readjustment of priorities, a big part of the impetus for that was that I experienced a revival of faith when I was a freshman. It was kind of an ongoing process. And that wasn't an instantaneous thing, in reevaluating priorities and then reevaluating my position on abstinence and things like that, but it started the process going, simply because it shook me out of my complacency. (Kris Nagle, Eastern Elite)

Even those Catholic students who were not involved with the Catholic organizations on campus—for example, one student who characterized the Catholic student clubs as embracing "evangelical spirituality, sort of silly music, sort of childish ways of looking at things" (Drew Metcalfe, Eastern Elite)—found their faith to fit well with the "classically" conservative temperament valued at Eastern Elite.[26]

Another student attempted to explain the large number of Catholic conservatives at Eastern Elite in this vein:

> If I were to try to explain why it is that Catholics, why if you're studying conservative students [here] you tend to find a lot of Catholics, I think it's probably more something like any Catholic who is sort of orthodox and serious about knowing the faith and trying to practice it, is going to be steeped in a tradition that goes back 2,000 years. . . . They start off with that general stance and then it develops as they sort of adopt it further and carry it out to its conclusions and start to see things from that point of view. (Nate Quinn, Eastern Elite)

As we'll argue more fully later in the book, the type of traditional emphasis described here is well-suited to the Eastern Elite campus environment and its style of a more contemplative conservatism.

Among non-Catholic Eastern Elite conservatives, we do not find an overwhelming pattern (in part because we lack information on religious identification for several interviewees). But for those we do know about, we see a split between mainline Protestant and evangelical Christian students. Notably also, we find only one interviewee who did not identify as religious, and none who identified as "spiritual but not religious."[27] Thus at Eastern Elite we see quite a different picture of the relationship between conservatism and religiosity than we do on the Western Public campuses.

Given the Western Public system's location in a state known for having a strong evangelical Christian community, and particularly Western Flagship's position as a large public institution, we had expected to find a large number of born-again Christians among our interviewees there. After all, in the national survey, 23.2 percent of conservatives at institutions comparable to Western Flagship identify themselves as born-again. While we did talk to a few individuals who were raised in evangelical households, in the end we wound up with only one Western Public interviewee (a Western Flagship student) who currently self-identified as an evangelical Christian. One reason for this may be that evangelical students on the Western Public campuses have many more outlets for finding like-minded individuals, such as through campus ministries and fellowships, as well as local churches, than would their peers at Eastern Elite; as a result, evangelical students could be less likely to turn to conservative political organizations unless they possessed a particular issue commitment.[28] In contrast, on the Eastern Elite campus, religious students—including evangelical Christian students—reported needing whatever support they could get. As one Eastern Elite alumnus explained, "Well there is a certain, almost anti-religious feeling, like, 'oh religious, how quaint,' or something" among secular Eastern Elite students (Kingsley Griffith, Eastern Elite). Though some Western Public students argued their campuses are "very anti-Christian" (Devin Daleo, Western Flagship), even in just looking at the lists of faith-oriented organizations available to students on these campuses, Western Public students simply have more options.

Though overall we find quite a spread of religious identifications among our Western Public interviewees, perhaps the most striking finding in our qualitative data is the number of students who identified either as not religious or as "spiritual"—in marked contrast to respondents at Eastern Elite. Two interviewees from different Western Public campuses provided explanations for their distance from organized religion:

> But I kind of recoil from organized religion. I believe it's something that . . . I think the writers of the Bible were very intelligent and they had a lot of good things to say but it was written by man. So I recoil from organized religion, but I do have a spiritual side. (Conor Denning, Western State)

> As far as I'm concerned, I'm not particularly religious. I'm I guess more spiritual, as New Age hippy as that sounds! (Eric Leonard, Western Flagship)

Though we can only speculate here, looking at Western Public conservatives' religious identifications in light of what else we know about them, the prominence of libertarian political leanings would seem a likely explanation for many right-leaning students' distance from organized religion.[29] It would also fit strongly with the ideology of being "spiritual but not religious," as students described to us, trying to find the right fit in terms of their faiths.[30] A woman who had been raised in an evangelical Christian household explained:

> You know, at this point I don't belong to a church. And I guess I would describe myself as a committed theist. Not necessarily—I don't have my theology nailed down—I lean towards Christianity but I'm not comfortable saying that I completely embrace orthodox Christianity at this point. So I'm in kind of a weird place, I guess. (Isabel Stricker, Western Flagship)

In short, while we find some points of similarity between what we know about our interviewees' religious identifications, and the national survey data on students' faiths, perhaps the most interesting story here is the extent to which our interviewees' faiths meshed not only with their political ideologies but also with the cultures of their campuses. While on the Western Public campuses we see a broad range of faiths, and somewhat relativistic picking and choosing in creating an individualistic spirituality, among Eastern Elite conservatives, Catholicism prevailed, along with a stronger interest in moral order.

Social Class

National Survey

With race/ethnicity, gender, and religion now accounted for, it is important to use the HERI survey to explore conservative freshmen's social class backgrounds. One of the central claims in this book is that the particular university campus plays a highly influential role in shaping the political styles of conservatives on that campus, so much so, we argue, that students do not just neatly reenact in college the political styles they have been exposed to in their families but rather come to embrace the dominant or submerged conservative styles of their university. Yet at the same time that we make this argument about the role of campuses in the process of political development, we also know from more than a century of sociological research that individuals' tastes and dispositions, as well as their political opinions, are given shape by their social class and status origins.[31] One might imagine, therefore, that students whose families are better educated and occupy higher-prestige occupations will already display something of a more "refined" style—even in their politics—as learned in the family before college, and will be more likely to attend private elite institutions. Perhaps the civilized discourse style that we see so prevalently at Eastern Elite, for example, is merely a reflection of what conservative Eastern Elite students have learned earlier in their upper-middle-class family homes, while the greater tendency of Western Public students to use the provocative style is simply an echo of their humbler social class origins. This is an empirical question that our survey and interview data can help answer. While our interviews are of greater use in addressing these questions head-on, we begin with the HERI national survey data to understand the patterns we find at our primary case-study schools. We use two indicators available in the HERI dataset to discuss the social class backgrounds of conservative undergraduates: freshmen respondents' reports of their parents' educational attainments and of their parents' occupations.[32]

Parents' Education

We begin with parents' educational attainments, which are reported in table 2.7. Here we compare the educational attainments of conservative freshmen's parents with the attainments of parents of other first-time freshmen entering college in 2001.[33]

As table 2.7 makes clear, the general population of freshmen attending private elite universities has parents with higher levels of educational achievement than do freshmen attending public flagship universities. For example, the table shows that freshmen at private elite institutions are less likely to have fathers who ended their

Table 2.7. Parents' Highest Educational Attainments: Comparison of Conservative Freshmen to Other Freshmen, by Campus Type, 2001

	Father			Mother		
	HS	College	Postgrad	HS	College	Postgrad
Private elite						
Liberal	7.6	30.6	61.8	7.6	41.5	51.0
Middle of the road	10.9	37.7	51.4	12.8	50.6	36.6
Conservative	6.6	38.1	55.3	8.9	56.1	35.0
Public flagship						
Liberal	16.7	44.4	38.9	17.1	51.8	31.1
Middle of the road	21.4	48.8	29.7	23.2	55.1	21.8
Conservative	13.6	51.1	35.3	16.6	60.4	23.1
All other types						
Liberal	26.2	45.1	28.7	24.9	50.8	24.4
Middle of the road	31.6	47.6	20.9	31.4	51.9	16.7
Conservative	22.4	50.6	27.0	24.2	57.4	18.4
Total	25.5	46.3	28.2	25.7	52.4	21.9

schooling with a high school degree than freshmen at public flagship universities, less likely to have fathers whose educational attainments peaked at some college attendance or a college degree, and more likely by a large margin to have fathers who went on to graduate school. The same general pattern holds for mothers. These findings for higher educational attainments (as one indicator of higher family background class status) are consistent with work conducted by many sociologists, demonstrating that children of better educated parents have a greater likelihood than other students of attending elite colleges.[34]

But how do conservative students stack up next to the general freshmen population? This is where our analysis gets interesting. The first notable pattern that shows up in table 2.7 concerns graduate school attendance of the parents of liberal versus conservative freshmen's parents. Somewhat surprisingly (given the impression that conservative families are more affluent than other families and so might be expected to have gained higher educational degrees in order to earn more income), the fathers and mothers of conservative freshmen at private elite institutions have *lower* rates of graduate school attendance or degrees than do the parents of the remainder of the freshman cohort at such institutions. For example, while 61.8 percent of fathers of liberal freshmen entering private elite colleges and universities have had at least some graduate education, a lower 55.3 percent of fathers of conservative freshmen do.[35] But even more interesting than this fairly small difference is to look at the *mothers* of conservative freshmen. These women have significantly lower educational attainments than mothers of the freshman student body at large, and the difference is driven mostly by the mothers of liberal students.

The pattern is somewhat different at public flagship institutions. Many fewer parents overall have graduate training compared to parents at private elite institutions. At public flagship schools, the fathers of conservative freshmen have gone to graduate school at rates similar to those for liberal students' fathers, with fathers of moderate students lagging behind. Interestingly, slightly more mothers of conservative freshmen at public flagship institutions also pursue graduate degrees than do mothers of moderate students, although the educational attainments of most mothers of conservative freshmen (77 percent) are at the level of some college or a college degree. In sum, conservative freshmen at private elite schools come from families with somewhat less impressive educational levels compared to other families at the same schools (particularly regarding mothers), while a similar but less pronounced pattern holds for conservative freshmen at public flagship schools.

Parents' Occupations

Another way to use the national survey to assess conservative freshmen's social class backgrounds relative to other freshmen is to look at the jobs their parents hold. Working from the 47 occupational categories that HERI uses to ask freshmen about their parents' ca-

Table 2.8. Comparison of Parental Occupational Prestige by Campus Type, Conservatives and Other Students, 2001

	Father			Mother		
	0–60	*61–70*	*77+*	*0–60*	*61–70*	*77+*
Private elite						
Liberal	18.8	36.2	45.1	33.5	33.0	33.5
Middle of the road	22.3	39.9	37.8	39.1	35.8	25.0
Conservative	21.5	41.1	37.5	40.3	35.3	24.5
Public flagship						
Liberal	30.9	34.9	34.2	44.3	34.1	21.6
Middle of the road	35.2	36.2	28.6	49.8	33.0	17.2
Conservative	31.2	38.1	30.7	47.0	34.6	18.4
All other types						
Liberal	37.9	34.2	27.9	48.1	33.2	18.7
Middle of the road	42.1	34.2	23.7	52.3	33.1	14.6
Conservative	38.8	36.1	25.2	49.4	34.3	16.2
Total	37.4	35.2	27.5	48.8	33.5	17.7

reers, we assigned prestige rankings to these occupations in order to compare them numerically.[36] Scores for the HERI occupational categories ranged from a high of 88 (physician) to a low of 23 (laborer).[37] Table 2.8 summarizes the distribution of these occupational prestige scores for all freshmen on both types of campuses. The overall picture that we gain from looking at the parents of all freshmen at the schools most similar to our cases is that parents of freshmen at private elite institutions have higher occupational prestige than public flagship parents. As with the educational attainments reported above, this also is consistent with social science research showing that students whose parents have more prestigious careers are more likely to attend more elite colleges and universities.

While this pattern has long been established for students in general, what can we say about conservative freshmen's parents compared to the parents of non-conservative freshmen? Breaking these scores down by freshmen's political views shows that conservative students' parents' occupational prestige scores follow the same general patterns we saw for educational attainments as reported in table 2.7, where at private elite institutions, parents of conservative freshmen rank a bit lower in prestige level than do the parents of other freshmen. For both fathers and mothers, the parents of conservative students are similar to the parents of moderate students, while the parents of liberal students are more likely to have higher-prestige occupations. Again, these findings are quite interesting in light of popular imaginings of who families of conservative private elite students must be—moneyed, successful, and firmly ensconced in the establishment. Yet despite these ideas, the national HERI results actually accord with our Eastern Elite conservative students' quite varied social class backgrounds. As we will see below, conservative students at Eastern Elite are generally *not* to the manor born (although one of our interviewees was), even though few come from the lowest social strata. In fact, hailing from slightly less elite backgrounds than their moderate and liberal classmates, we think, may have some effect on their selection of conservative styles—Eastern Elite conservatives may in some instances be making up for their class origins by taking on the mantle of civilized discourse. Meanwhile, at public flagship institutions, conservative freshmen's parents' slightly higher educational attainments do not seem to matter much, insofar as conservative freshmen's parents' occupations do not differ dramatically from what is seen in the social background of the overall freshman cohort. Conservative students at universities like Western Flagship are no more and no less likely than their peers to come from working-, middle-, or upper-class backgrounds.

Interviews

Our interview data also allow us to look at parents' highest level of education completed and parents' occupational prestige scores. But because our respondents were often quite good at eliding questions about their parents' social class attainments, we supplement our discussion of their backgrounds with information that goes beyond the measures in the national survey. One bit of additional information we provide concerns where our students came from—the region of the country they grew up in, and the size and cosmopolitanism of their hometowns—to get a deeper sense of their class characteristics. The second strand of information comes from our interviewees' discussions of their own feelings of affluence relative to their peers—what we might call their subjective feelings of class—a topic they discussed a bit more freely than their parents' specific attainments. When we combine these three different types of qualitative evidence about our respondents' social class, we find both fewer differences across the two campuses in terms of social class background than might be expected from the literature on elite private versus public institution populations and more internal variation on each campus than we would have guessed, given the consistency with which students engaged in particular dispositions and styles of political action on each campus.

Parents' Attainments, Students' Subjective Descriptions of Relative Affluence, and Their Hometowns

Because an unfortunately large amount of data is missing on parents' education, we must be cautious in our statements here. That said, from what we do see, the patterns for our Western Public and Eastern Elite parents do not look especially different from those we see in the national survey. As there, we find that the parents of conservative students at Eastern Elite have higher levels of educational attainment than the parents of conservative students at the Western Public campuses, particularly with respect to postcollegiate education.[38] Table 2.9 gives an overview of what we know about our interviewees' parents' educations.

Though we do not break out information here on what type of schools were attended by interviewees' parents, we do see some patterns in parents' educational paths that make some of the numbers that would appear comparable (for example, the number of parents

Table 2.9. Parents' Highest Educational Attainment

	Western	*Eastern*
High school degree or less		
Father	4	1
Mother	2	2
Some college or a college degree		
Father	8	8
Mother	10	10
Some graduate school or graduate degree		
Father	1	11
Mother	2	8
Data missing		
Father	6	4
Mother	8	4

of students at each school who attended some college or received a college degree) less so. Take, for example, these two quotations describing fathers' educations, the first from a Western Flagship University student whose father attended but did not receive a degree from a small Bible college and the second from an Eastern Elite University student whose father also attended Eastern Elite:

My dad, he never actually . . . well, some people can be skeptical about this, but he never actually went to seminary. . . . He's just kind of a self-learner, and he's always just taught us, "Hey, base everything that you hear off of the Bible and what they say." So he never went to school. (Samantha Hart, Western Flagship)

I think the general atmosphere in [the area where my father grew up] at that time was one of sort of high achieving suburbia where education was taken very seriously. So I think a lot of his classmates and students above and below him at his high school had gone to very good universities. He's very smart, so I think for him . . . that was the goal towards which you were pushed if you were in his high school. And just a public school there, but yeah. (Nate Quinn, Eastern Elite)

Thus, both in terms of level of education and in terms of the type of institution attended, we do find higher levels of attainment for Eastern Elite parents than for those whose children attended the Western Public campuses, in accordance with the HERI data. At the same time, it is important to note that at *both* schools we also see a spread—from those interviewees' whose parents received a high school diploma, to those who were first-generation college-goers, to those who pursued graduate degrees.

The internal variation within our Eastern Elite and Western Public samples is likewise reflected in interviewees' reports of their parents' occupations, shown in table 2.10. Although this table indicates that overall, there is not an extremely large gap between parental occupational prestige at Western Public and Eastern Elite, we do observe somewhat higher levels of occupational prestige at Eastern Elite, with Eastern Elite fathers and mothers having on average a score four points higher than their respective counterparts at Western Public. Among Eastern Elite fathers, in particular, we find the

Table 2.10a. Comparison of Parental Occupational Prestige Scores (Western)

	Range	Average	NA*	Data Missing
Fathers	43–71	61	0	9
Mothers	42–70	57	6	9

Note: Occupational prestige scores were calculated with the occupational categories used by HERI and the prestige scores developed by Ganzeboom, De Graaf, and Treiman (1992).

"NA" here indicates not missing data (shown in the far right column) but the number of individuals who have a prestige score of "not applicable." This scoring system gives a score of NA to responses of homemaker, unemployed, other, or undecided. In our data, all NA responses are homemakers.

Table 2.10b. Comparison of Parental Occupation Prestige Scores (Eastern Elite)

	Range	Average	NA*	Data Missing
Fathers	23–88	65	0	7
Mothers	23–85	61	4	7

Note: Occupational prestige scores were calculated with the occupational categories used by HERI and the prestige scores developed by Ganzeboom, De Graaf, and Treiman (1992).

*"NA" here indicates not missing data (shown in the far right column) but the number of individuals who have a prestige score of "not applicable." This scoring system gives a score of NA to responses of homemaker, unemployed, other, or undecided. In our data, all NA responses are homemakers.

full range of possible scores, and a nearly equal spread among Eastern Elite mothers. Also, in examining these numbers it is important to point out that our scoring system does not assign a number to homemakers, which means in our cases that the range of scores shown for mothers is only representative of women who worked outside the home.[39] Since many of our interviewees' mothers were not in the paid labor force, there are limitations to these scales.

Because of these limitations, it is important to supplement these measures with somewhat thicker descriptions from our interviewees regarding social class. One of these is through examining our respondents' discussions of their perceptions of their own class as compared to other students on their campuses. Although we do not have an abundance of data on this front either, we see some differences between Western Public and Eastern Elite—for example, more of our interviewees on the Western Public campuses reported they had to work at outside jobs while enrolled in college. One recent alumna of Western Flagship told us,

> I worked 20 hours a week all through college, so on top of school it was hard to do that. But that was another thing, I think, that helped me solidify my beliefs that I was working and I was like

getting a paycheck and I was seeing how much money is being taken out for taxes. And I was having to send myself on my own spring break trip. . . . I think that gave me a different perspective. (Stephanie Cohen, Western Flagship)

Though Stephanie went on to say "I'm definitely very privileged," and acknowledged her parents' help in putting her through school, she contended that other Western Flagship students—including liberals, who always insist that they are fighting for the little guy— "need to recognize that this is a privilege and they need to be grateful for it and they can't . . . hold it against others who can't afford to do what they can do" (Stephanie Cohen, Western Flagship).

Students who explicitly discussed social class and related it to their experiences and beliefs most often did so in the context of relative deprivation, as in Stephanie's comments above or in another interviewee's recollection that "I was from a single-parent family, I worked multiple jobs, and that very much defined who I was. I was in a sorority because I wanted to prove a poor girl could do it" (Kayla Shain, Western Flagship). At Eastern Elite, meantime, we heard almost nothing of hardship, even though a couple of our interviewees came from quite modest backgrounds. When one of our interviewees *did* raise the issue, her comment did not evoke her own social origins but rather the background of a less well-off relative (who, it should be noted, ultimately made good):

I haven't had any fiscal hardship in my life because I've been very lucky to grow up in a family with means. But for somebody like my grandfather who's quite a staunch conservative, I think his conservatism is almost, it's almost the opposite. It's almost informed by *having* been poor as a kid and having sort of gutted it out. So to me in some ways, I talk about having grown up as sort of a blessed person, but part of it actually—what I relate if I'm really being frank about it—so part of that is that in my family this idea that oh, you just pull yourself up by your bootstraps is very, seems very real. I mean that has happened in our family. (Molly Nash Downing, Eastern Elite)

The remainder of our interview data from both Western Public and Eastern Elite could be described as indicating mostly middle-class to upper-middle-class backgrounds, with only a few cases in the tails of the range.

A final way for us to get greater purchase on our interviewees' social class backgrounds is to examine where they grew up. To maintain our respondents' confidentiality, we break out data for states only to the level of census regions and divisions.[40] For those interviewees about whom we know not only the state (or states) where they spent their formative years but also the names of the cities or towns, we have aggregated data on what types of places these are, based on their geographic location and size. Tables 2.11 and 2.12 summarize this data.

Table 2.11a. Comparison of Region of Origin of Interviewees (Western Public)

Region	Division	Students
Northeast		0
	New England	0
	Mid-Atlantic	0
Midwest		5
	East North Central	4
	West North Central	1
South		5
	South Atlantic	4
	East South Central	0
	West South Central	1
West		11
	Mountain	10
	Pacific	1
Missing Data		2

Note: The totals do not sum to the total number of interviewees for each university system (22 for Western Public and 24 for Eastern Elite) as a few interviewees indicated they had spent considerable time in more than one place. Regions and divisions are based on those used by the U.S. Census Bureau. See http://www.census.gov/geo/www/reg_div.txt (accessed July 13, 2011) for a list of states included in each region and division.

Table 2.11b. Comparison of Region of Origin of Interviewees (Eastern Elite)

Region	Division	Students
Northeast		6
	New England	5
	Mid-Atlantic	1
Midwest		3
	East North Central	2
	West North Central	1
South		9
	South Atlantic	5
	East South Central	1
	West South Central	3
West		9
	Mountain	6
	Pacific	3
Missing data		1

Note: The totals do not sum to the total number of interviewees for each university system (22 for Western Public and 24 for Eastern Elite) as a few interviewees indicated they had spent considerable time in more than one place. Regions and divisions are based on those used by the U.S. Census Bureau. See http://www.census.gov/geo/www/reg_div.txt (accessed July 13, 2011) for a list of states included in each region and division.

Table 2.12a. Comparison of Type of Hometown of Interviewees (Western Public)

Type	Students
City	5
Small city	3
Suburb	4
Small town	4
Rural	2
Missing data	4

Note: Estimates of type of hometown were made based on the town's geographic location and its most recently available population statistics. Data are missing here for more interviewees than in table 2.11 because some students indicated which state they were from but not the specific town.

Table 2.12b. Comparison of Type of Hometown of Interviewees (Eastern Elite)

Type	Students
City	5
Small city	4
Suburb	5
Small town	3
Rural	1
Missing data	6

Note: Estimates of type of hometown were made based on the town's geographic location and its most recently available population statistics. Data are missing here for more interviewees than in table 2.11 because some students indicated which state they were from but not the specific town.

What is most remarkable in looking at the regions and divisions our interviewees come from is the sheer level of diversity. One might suppose that given the generous discounts on tuition for in-state residents, conservative students attending the Western Public universities would likely all be from the same state or, at least, region. And yet because Western Flagship is a public university that attracts a decent proportion of out-of-state students, we find that interviewees grew up in nearly every region of the country save the Northeast.[41] At Eastern Elite we find an even greater spread, with interviewees representing every census region and division. Though we have less data on specific hometowns (as many students named a home state but did not specify further), we likewise see a mix. We do not find a majority of Eastern Elite students arriving from cities, or the bulk of Western Public students coming from small towns or just the nearest metropolitan area.

In further examining our interviews, we find that region of origin came up much more as a significant issue for Eastern Elite conservatives than it did for those from Western Public. This is particularly the case for those who perceived themselves as being from areas of the country that the average Eastern Elite student would look down on. When Western Public interviewees in similar situations described their backgrounds, they did so in ways that suggested this was relatively unproblematic for them. Here a Western Flagship conservative from a very small rural town described her status as a college student relative to her milieu:

> A lot of people don't go to college, honestly. And a lot go to a community college. I'm trying to think how many from my class. My class had four people that graduated from universities. . . . And I think pretty much everyone else . . . some did like trade school. A lot are back in that area, though. (Christina Young, Western Flagship)

Though she now saw herself as different from the people she grew up with and did not want to move back (even though "I loved growing up there"), this young alumna did not characterize herself as taking any static from peers for her rural upbringing. By contrast, this kind of background seemed to be much more of an issue for Eastern Elite conservatives, as this small-town southerner described:

> So I've just been able to kind of see that part of America that I think a lot of my peers just by sheer where they grew up, what schools they went to, just have never really interacted with them; so they get uncomfortable when they see a Waffle House or a gun range or something and that kind of scares them. I don't, like it's not that foreign to me; I feel comfortable in that environment. (Staci Congdon, Eastern Elite)

Eastern Elite conservatives who came from "flyover country" thus generally appeared to perceive this as marking them as different from their elite peers. In contrast, regional origin did not appear to be a salient distinction on the Western Public campuses.

CONCLUSION

In this chapter we have moved through a tremendous amount of information—both national survey data, collected by UCLA's

Higher Education Research Institute, and our own interviews in our two university systems. Before we leave this behind, we think it useful to recap some of our key findings, comparing our evidence with the national survey and also looking within our interview data at how right-leaning students from Western Public and Eastern Elite stack up when contrasted with one another.

In terms of political identification on the national level, conservatives are the *least* represented of all three political identifications at either private elite or public flagship institutions, at right around 20 percent for each of these campus types. That said, throughout most of the time period that HERI has been administering its surveys, the numbers of both liberals and conservatives have been dwarfed by the majority of students who identify as middle of the road.[42] Looking at our interviewees—a group that of course only includes students who self-identify as right-leaning—we do find differences between Western Public and Eastern Elite universities. Though students on all campuses identified most frequently as "conservatives" (both prior to coming to college and at the time of their interviews), on the Western Public campuses we noted the development of libertarian political leanings among nearly half of our interviewees. We believe this speaks to the culture of not only the geographic region where the Western Public system is located but also the culture on the campuses, particularly Western Flagship's reputation for an "anything goes" lifestyle.

In terms of political identification, we were also able to dig into aspects of political identity that the HERI survey does not capture. In examining our interviewees' stated reasons for developing their political commitments, we find a similar range of reasons, including national events, conversations with family members, and students' reflections on their lived experiences. Further, in looking at the kinds of political *styles* that students recall being exposed to or participating in during their precollege years, we find a range on both campuses. Conservative students at Eastern Elite do not all seem to have arrived on campus already steeped in the culture of civilized discourse (some quite the opposite); likewise, Western Public conservatives were not born provocateurs. We believe the mix-and-match quality of our interviewees' precollegiate styles provides strong evidence for the power of the campus to develop political style.

Demographically speaking, whites and men are overrepresented among conservative collegians, both nationally and among our interviewees. When we turn to questions of religious affiliation, however, a more complex story emerges, both in terms of differences between Eastern Elite and Western Public and in respect to how our cases line up with the national evidence. Nationally, many conservatives identify as Catholic, and even more so at private elite institutions. We find this to be true of our Eastern Elite interviewees as well, and we contend that in many ways, Catholicism appears to be a good fit for the prevailing political ethos among Eastern Elite conservatives: traditional and intellectual. Interestingly, several of our interviewees described themselves as embracing their Catholicism more once they got to Eastern Elite. In contrast, based on the national survey we would expect to find large numbers of conservative interviewees identifying as born-again, particularly at Western Flagship. However, we actually had more evangelical Christian interviewees at Eastern Elite than on all the Western Public campuses. Though Western Public interviewees identified with many different faiths—most of them some variety of Christian—the most notable pattern we found on the Western Public campuses with respect to religiosity was the number of students who chose not to affiliate with any form of organized religion. Again, we argue that this speaks to many of the features of the Western Public system.

Last, in terms of social class background, what we find among our interviewees matches up well with the national data: in general, the parents of conservative students at Eastern Elite have higher levels of educational attainment and occupational prestige than do the parents of Western Public conservatives, and interviewees at Eastern Elite are less likely to speak of deprivation. Still, it is important to note that we find a range at both schools. Our Eastern Elite students were not all born with silver spoons in their mouths, nor were our Western Public interviewees all generically middle class. Moving still further beyond what is available from the HERI survey, we discovered that our interviewees lived in all parts of the country before attending their respective schools. Though we did not have any Western Public interviewees from the Northeast, every other part of the country is represented; Eastern Elite conservatives in our sample hailed from every census division. We find a similar spread in terms of the types of hometowns where interviewees grew up; conservatives at neither school were especially likely to have grown up in urban metropolises or in rural backwaters. Most are simply children of suburbia.

In spending so much time going through this information, we hoped to accomplish two tasks. First, as noted at the beginning of this chapter, we delved into the HERI survey to give a picture of who conservative students are at the broadest level, simply because this information is not widely available. This provides a point of reference for our data, but we hope it may also be a resource for others interested in examining conservative identification in higher education. Second, as may already be clear from some of our asides, we hope to dispel any stereotypes that might exist about what "type" of student those who matriculate at either of our schools must be, such as the idea that Eastern Elite undergraduates must be uniformly upper middle or upper class or that Western Public conservatives must be ardent members of the Religious Right. In terms of their origins, our interviewees in each of these university systems mainly failed to fit a single mold. Though there are some systematic differences (for example, higher parental educational attainment among Eastern Elite parents), we do not believe these differences are so great as to point to selection effects as the sole cause of the variation that we see in undergraduate political styles between Eastern Elite and Western Public conservatives.

And in many of the places where we do find substantial variation—Western Public's libertarian streak, for example, or the preponderance of Catholics among Eastern Elite conservatives—we think such variation points less to common origins among these students than to *common campus experiences*. As we will continue to argue throughout the book, we believe that the unique campus environments—not just the human inputs of those coming into it—matter for how students become different types of political actors. Before we go full-bore into this argument, however, there is one more piece of the puzzle that we need to fit into place. In the next chapter we look at the right-leaning, national-level organizations that sponsor conservatism on college campuses. Examining the types of political styles these organizations espouse, and how they choose to align with particular types of colleges and universities for their recruitment efforts, will give us a fuller picture of exactly what kind of conservative political organizing exists beyond the campus level, and thus what students may encounter when they finally get to college, which we'll see in chapter 4.

Chapter 3

Sponsored Conservatism

The Landscape of National Conservative Organizations

Now that we have more information about who conservative students are demographically and how they first come to embrace their right-leaning political beliefs, it is time to turn our attention to the organizations that mobilize undergraduates for conservative action—both to be young voters and supporters in the present and to take on political leadership positions in the future. In this chapter we look closely at three organizations specifically set up to advance the cause of right-leaning college students: the Young America's Foundation, the Leadership Institute, and the Intercollegiate Studies Institute. Although our story in other chapters concerns how students at Eastern Elite University and on the Western Public campuses interact with these national organizations, here we mostly analyze the three organizational players on their own terms. Once we grasp these groups' separate but integrated goals and can appreciate the distinctive modi operandi they employ, we will have a clearer picture of the spectrum of styles that are available as broad templates to conservative students on the college campuses we study.

The three organizations at the heart of this chapter provide an array of goods and services to conservative students. Among other offerings, they finance summer internships, give start-up funding to right-leaning clubs on campus, and grant fellowships in support of either students' undergraduate years or graduate programs, so long as students pursue "liberty-advancing research."[1] Some of these organizations also extend more down-home advice in addition to material benefits, such as providing online tips on dressing for job interviews—advising women, for example, that while "you don't have to dress like your grandmother," you *do* need to dress carefully because "Washington is full of seedy politicos with bad intentions."[2] In this chapter we explore the variety of offerings on hand from these organizations to see how the specific needs of the conservative student population are met, while also calling attention to the fact that these organizations work formally and informally with one another to build momentum for their recipients. As one young woman who had enjoyed internships at three national organizations put it, the foundations, fellowships, and internships made available to right-leaning students like her constitute "a spiral of exposure" to the conservative world (Erica Tanner, CPAC).[3]

While our main task in this chapter is to describe the overall mission and tactical operations of each of the three organizations we have chosen as exemplars, we also show that they can be categorized as one of two ideal types—and that these categorizations have consequences for whether students at Western Public or Eastern Elite will be interested in them. First, we classify the Young America's Foundation and the Leadership Institute as *populist* in orientation because they encourage students to be highly visible out on the quad, confronting their liberal peers and professors head-to-head with "aggressive" tactics, and they train students in "boot camp" on "effective techniques to organize and lead mass-based youth efforts."[4] In contrast, we categorize the Intercollegiate Studies Institute as relatively *refined* in orientation because its leaders urge students to contemplate conservative principles and to apply these to big questions—such as the nature of Western civilization and the fate of free markets in a pro-statist society—which are deliberated at a distance from party politics. We should point out that the types that we indicate here, populist and refined, are labels of our own devising and, like all "ideal types," are useful for analysis, if not for precisely capturing all the characteristics of the organizations that fit the type.[5] For example, even when we argue that the Intercollegiate Studies Institute should be seen to be more intellectual than populist, we also notice that staff and student members often signal that they have preferences in the real world of party politics.

Additionally, we demonstrate that no matter what specific services these different organizations provide to students or what style of conservative action they advocate (aggressive populism vs. more sophisticated contemplation), all of them—and virtually all other organizations besides these that mobilize conservative young people—coalesce around a common message. That message is that conservative students on campus—not by their own choosing but by the very nature of America's liberally skewed higher education system—are ideologically at odds with the political and social commitments of the vast majority of faculty members, administrators, staff, and other students in American universities and colleges. The three organizations we study here get this message of marginalization across to students loud and clear, whether their main stage is the didactic seminar, the strategic training session, or the full-blown megaconference.

Few people outside of conservative circles know much about these organizations. Although the important history of the 1960s era organization the Young Americans for Freedom (the original YAF) has been recounted in separate projects by sociologist Rebecca Klatch and historian John Andrew, there has been no good description written of late about the organizational world in which today's young conservatives participate.[6] While our student interviewees demonstrated an excellent working knowledge of the organizations that have been set up on their behalf—as surely do the staff members and leaders across the country who are employed to organize the events and materials that these organizations sponsor—this knowledge base is far from widely public. Occasionally a journalist will do the work of social scientists and fill the void, such as when the *Time* magazine writer John Cloud correctly pointed out in a 2006 article that the student right is "very old and very powerful, run not by gangly kids but by seasoned generals of the right."[7] But we think that much more should be done to provide information on how conservative organizations are set up to cater to youthful conservatives.

Before we begin to analyze these three organizations, though, we once again offer a couple of caveats about what we are studying and the limits of our purview. For one, we do not claim that the organizations discussed in this chapter represent the universe of groups aiding conservative college students—far from it. For example, readers might note that we do not include the College Republicans National Committee among our organizations, even though some of this generation's most consequential conservative leaders have emerged from that group, *and* despite the fact that many of our interviewees are involved with College Republicans on their home campuses. But since we look so closely at the work of local College Republicans clubs in subsequent sections of the book, and since very few of our interviewees said that the national organization had much of an impact on their local action, we have opted to leave that group off this chapter's agenda. For different reasons, we do not study David Horowitz's Students for Academic Freedom since the work Horowitz does critiquing college campuses is mostly a one-man operation (if an attention-grabbing one), and his speaking engagements are coordinated to a large extent by the Young America's Foundation. Nor do we cover in detail the Institute for Humane Studies, an organization in support of a freer society that seeks to build a pipeline for conservative academics and journalists; the Federalist Society for law students; the Clare Boothe Luce Policy Institute for women; the Heritage Foundation; or the remaining conservative organizations that together spend tens of millions of dollars on conservative undergraduates each year. But in choosing these three organizations—from populist to refined—and depicting at least some of the key aspects of their functioning, we highlight the largest and, we think, some of the most important groups mobilizing today's undergraduate population.

POPULIST ACTIVISM: THE YOUNG AMERICA'S FOUNDATION AND THE LEADERSHIP INSTITUTE

BATTLEPLANS AND NATIONAL CONFERENCES: THE YOUNG AMERICA'S FOUNDATION

A good place to begin investigating this organizational landscape is with the Young America's Foundation (or YAF), which since 1969 has grown to be the largest and richest organization aimed at cultivating the next generation of conservative leaders for the nation.[8] Using the motto "The Conservative Movement Starts Here," the YAF provides a slew of goods and services to right-leaning students in college and, since the mid-1990s, to high school students as well.[9] As one of our Western Flagship interviewees informed us of YAF's prominence on the right-leaning scene, "Young America's Foundation is great. Patrick Coyle at YAF. I mean, if you talk to any sort of connected student leader around the country, they've probably met Patrick" (Chuck Kelley, Western Flagship).

Although it largely flies under the radar screen of those on the left of the political spectrum, the YAF is well known among conservatives. The organization boasts national and regional conferences, seminars, a campus activism "battleplan," internships, educational materials (which include lists of the "dirty dozen worst classes on U.S. campuses," as well as the "top 10 conservative colleges"), a widely used lecture program, and an "activists rewards program," called Club 100, which entitles high-points-earning conservative college activists to an all-expenses-paid trip to the Reagan Rancho del Cielo in Santa Barbara, California—which, not coincidentally, the YAF purchased in 1998 for preservation and as an inspiration to generations of conservative youth.[10] The mission of the YAF is unabashed: to ensure "that increasing numbers of young Americans understand and are inspired by the ideas of individual freedom, a strong national defense, free enterprise, and traditional values."[11] Although this mission statement sounds a lot like the Republican Party platform, the YAF is a tax-exempt, 501(c)3 educational organization, which means that it is both not-for-profit and officially prohibited from lobbying for legislation, a status shared with the two other organizations we discuss in this chapter.

With assets reported at $41 million in 2008 by the liberal website Media Matters Action Network, the YAF has both received grants and made expenditures in the neighborhood of $15 million each year in the years 2006–2008 (2008 is the latest year for which data are available), benefiting from the generosity of such individuals and organizations as the Richard and Helen DeVos Foundation, the F.M. Kirby Foundation, and the highly recognizable conservative benefactors Charles and David Koch, the Bradleys, and the Olins, among others.[12] As of 2011, the organizations with which the YAF shares 14 or more such funders include the Cato Institute, FreedomWorks (the advocacy organization for low taxes, chaired by former House Majority Leader Dick Armey), and the Heritage Foundation.[13] In addition, the YAF's staff, advisers, and members of the board of directors are culled from positions of power both within the GOP proper and from the field of organizations that widely support conservative policies. Right-wing luminaries gracing different parts of the YAF's organizational structure include former attorney general Edwin Meese; the former governor of Virginia George Allen; Rich Lowry, the editor of the *National Review*; Tom Phillips, chairman of Eagle Publishing Inc. and founder of the Phillips Foundation; and the current president of the YAF, Ron Robinson, who is married to Michelle Easton, the founder and president of the largest organization aimed at conservative women students, the Clare Boothe Luce Policy Institute.[14] The YAF is a major player, indeed.

The YAF's Campus Conservative Battleplan and Marketplace

It is difficult to know exactly where to begin describing the activities of the YAF since each area is grand in scope, and all are deeply intertwined. But digging in first with materials widely disseminated online, we start with the organization's *Campus Conservative Bat-*

tleplan: Your Month-by-Month Plan to Activism on Campus. In the years since we first became aware of the YAF, we have seen a multitude of events marketed to students in this guide. Each month that is listed in the *Battleplan* offers a number of different activities tied to the time of year, such as commemorating 9/11 in September, with students encouraged to not "let the Left appropriate this day to promote its politically correct, multicultural agenda"; recrafting February's Black History Month so as to counteract university events that "reinforce the same tired, liberal message"; using April to draw attention to "April's Liberal Fools"; and marking December as the time to remind others on campus that "sadly, Christmas has become politically incorrect" (the guide reports that Christmas trees are no longer allowed on campus and that the term "holiday break" has replaced all references to celebrating Christ's birth).[15]

Given all of that to explore, we look in some detail just at March, which is Women's History Month. During this 31-day period the YAF focuses on the follies and dangers of feminism, as evidenced by this content on the website:

March: Activities This Month

Provide fresh alternatives to the feminist agenda during Women's History Month and help your campus decide who is the worst liberal in the country.

Activity 1—"Strong Women Shoot Back!"

Help educate and train young women to protect themselves with a firearm.

"Strong Women Shoot Back" is a breakthrough initiative offering a proactive alternative to the feminist program, "Take Back the Night." Feminists on college campuses hold their program, "Take Back the Night," which seeks to end violence and sexual assault against women. Their program typically consists of a march across campus, poetry readings, and speeches by victims of sexual assault. However, other than vocally denouncing violence and sexual assault, this "night" does little to help women protect themselves.

Make It Happen.
Through "Strong Women Shoot Back," women attend a demonstration taught by a certified instructor on the benefits of protecting themselves with a firearm.

The *Battleplan* then features a pull-out box advertising that readers can "Learn Real-World Examples of the Benefits of Gun Ownership" and noting that students should "Be sure your club members know the arguments in favor of gun ownership. The National Rifle Association (NRA) can provide you with many examples of how women have defended themselves with firearms."

The list continues with:

Activity 2—Women's Studies Burqa Day Protest
Expose your women's studies departments' failure to address atrocities towards women in the Middle East.

Make It Happen.
Select a day where your members dressed in burqas stand outside the women's studies department and/or student union building with signs and leaflets questioning the classes and programs offered.

Activity 3—Empowered Conservative Women Week
Introduce your peers to strong, conservative women including Michelle Malkin, Ann Coulter, Condoleezza Rice, Bay Buchanan, and others.

Still other actions are provided for the month, guiding students to visibly and audibly protest the damage done to college life by feminism.

In addition to the campus activism the YAF promotes in the *Battleplan*, the organization also has a storehouse of images and adages that can be used in conjunction with staged events. Picked up at conferences or ordered online, posters of celebrity conservatives like Sarah Palin, Ronald Reagan, and Ann Coulter are available, as are those that state "I Love Capitalism" and "Superstars of the Conservative Movement" (tagline: "No education is complete . . . until it includes us," under a group shot of participants in the YAF speakers program). Wall calendars, downloadable flyers, and bumper stickers are also available from the YAF's "Conservative Marketplace."[16]

What do these activities and images have in common, and why do they lead us to place the YAF solidly on the populist end of our spectrum? If it is not clear from the examples above, the YAF insists that conservative students are most effective when they use confrontational tactics that get under the skin of their political adversaries. In fact, the organization all but throws down the gauntlet on this point in one edition of the *Battleplan*, where the authors draw a clear distinction between the group's preferred mode of activism, which it calls "aggressive" conservatism ("constantly challenge leftist ideas"), versus a more temperate form of political action that it calls "passive" conservatism ("working for candidates, running voter registration drives . . . essentially a philosophy of accommodation").[17] The 2009 guide goes on to raise the stakes for the aggressive style by comparing it to the "Ronald Reagan Model of Campus Activism," stating that in the same manner that Reagan denounced "the Soviet Union as an Evil Empire," young conservatives also "want to follow the aggressive model—the Ronald Reagan Model—of campus activism.[18] Students are duly warned that "you should expect to be attacked by the Left if you choose to follow the strategy set forth in this guide," but that rather than "being intimidated by the opposition," students should welcome such attack and "view hostility as another opportunity to expose the Left's intolerance and hypocrisy."[19] Thus, according to the YAF, active, provocative confrontation—both for the ideas it advances and the sense of noble martyrdom that it can deliver to its enactors—is a good thing.

Our interviewees on the Western Public campuses in particular are quick to sign on to this worldview and stylistic commitment. We have already noted Western Flagship's Chuck Kelley's admiration for the YAF's vice president, Patrick Coyle, while a Western Satellite interviewee simply concurred, "Yeah, those are great organizations," in reference to the YAF and the American Conservative

Union, the latter of which organizes the annual Conservative Political Action Committee (or CPAC) meeting (Karl Hayes, Western Satellite). Still a third Western Public respondent made his embrace of the aggressive style, as promoted by the YAF, even clearer: "Once I got involved with the YAF . . . my goal and a goal of a lot of us from just coming in as freshmen was to make a splash and to do things that would get people's attention" (Bryan Carhart, Western Satellite). Even a small handful of our Eastern Elite respondents saw some utility in the YAF style. According to one of our respondents, a law student at a prestigious university at the time of the interview:

> Young America's Foundation . . . is more like activism-based, like they equip you to be able to counter people on campus, they give you posters, they have these big conferences as well. Some of my friends would criticize them. . . . But I think there's a place for them too. . . . Not everything has to be an intellectual argument. (Nicole Harris, Eastern Elite)

Still, while some Eastern Elite conservatives concede there is a case to be made for populist activism as promulgated by the YAF, most accept that it certainly should not happen on *their* campus.

Speakers Program and Conferences

Battleplans, flyers, and posters are not the sole purview of the YAF. The words written on the posters and in the guide are also brought to life for thousands of students each year in person. One way this is done is on students' home turf, when the student organizations bring conservative speakers to campus using the YAF's lecture program to "energize your club, challenge the Left, and offer your peers an opportunity to hear conservative ideas."[20] The second way this is accomplished is at regional and national conferences sponsored by YAF, where students have the chance to "learn conservative ideas and effective activism, meet and network with like-minded students, [and] interact with your conservative heroes."[21] Visiting the YAF's

Conservative Speakers page in July 2011 showed that the organization showcases no fewer than 79 lecturers on its roster (those whose
schedules are at least in part coordinated by the YAF) and who,
when taken together, can produce a bit of quizzical head-scratching
since speakers run the gamut from what we would label purely populist (for example, Ann Coulter) to a couple of intellectual outliers
(for example, Princeton University's Robert George or Harvard
University's Harvey Mansfield). Before describing a couple of these
events in greater detail, we provide more information on the people
who are enlisted to invigorate the student troops or, as President
Ronald Reagan referred to the attendees he addressed at the 15th
Annual Conference in 1993, the young "freedom fighters," who are
sorely needed on today's liberal campus.[22]

Conservative Speakers Program

When deciding which conservative speaker to bring to campus, students perusing the YAF's Conservative Speakers page can search the
program's offerings using three different search criteria—speakers'
names, speech topic, and price. Were a student group to select simply on top price ($20,000 and up), nine marquee stars populate the
next screen (at least as of July 2011), most of whom need no further
description, such as Ann Coulter, Ben Stein, John Ashcroft, Karl
Rove, Oliver North and, somewhat surprisingly, the aging rock star
Ted Nugent, whose topics are identified as "Second Amendment,
Environmentalism, Political Correctness."[23] For a few thousand
dollars less, students might invite Kenneth Starr, Rick Santorum,
Dinesh D'Souza, David Horowitz, or Ward Connerly, among a
large assortment of others.[24] Rounding out the list with the lowest
speaker fees are Harvard professor of government Harvey Mansfield (known for his old-school manner), Star Parker (a "former
welfare dependent" who is now a "conservative crusader"), former
Colorado congressman Tom Tancredo, and Phyllis Schlafly, once
one of the most highly visible names of the New Right but who at

this point in her career brings in only $1,000 to $3,000 for a speaking engagement.

While about 30 of the YAF's speakers can be reserved for the lowest price of $0 to $1,000, the real stars—the folks that students really want to bring to campus—are significantly more costly. We were interested in finding out not only how these high-cost speakers got on the YAF's list in the first place but also how student groups can afford to bring to campus speakers whose fees are well above universities' budgets for campus clubs. Our student and alumni/ae interviewees gave us some information on this—"Through Young America's Foundation there was quite often a substantial subsidized portion of that. If we could put up the $5,000, half of the $10,000 speaking fee honorarium, they would kick in the other half, or do whatever—give us free promotional materials or support" (Neal Thompson, Western Flagship)—but in order to learn the official details about this program, we posed a few queries to Roger Custer, then the conference director at the YAF.[25] On the issue of how the organization selects speakers to include on its roster, Custer was quite candid, saying that his staff looked for speakers whom "students can relate to easier than just like intellectuals and professors":

> We're trying to reach just the Joe Average student who plays video games or who goes to party on the weekends and who wouldn't necessarily come to hear a discussion by a prominent intellectual conservative, or it might not interest them as much as, say, somebody like Michelle Malkin who often appears on TV, or Ann Coulter, for that matter, who is more well-known. (Roger Custer, YAF)

Saying that other organizations like the Intercollegiate Studies Institute host professors, "or at least theorists," and "focus on *that* demographic," Custer relays that his organization is "really just trying to reach as many students as we possibly can" (Roger Custer, YAF). In other words, the YAF is trying to mobilize the average college kid with exciting, provocative content, not through intellectual or theoretical speakers to whom they may not be able to connect.

As for the question about funding, and how student groups can afford a speaker's fee in excess of $20,000, Custer said that while the YAF foots the bill for travel and accommodation expenses for campus speakers, it does not generally pay the honorarium. Ideally, according to Custer, "the students have to raise that money themselves"—which means that student groups have to hustle to come up with the resources for a big-name speaker. The organization encourages students to go to their funding boards and request financial support from their universities, since "often schools are spending a lot of money on the equivalent lectures on the left," creating an "unfair balance" between liberal and conservative speakers (Roger Custer, YAF). The conference director also told us that the organization encourages students to find "prominent conservatives in their community" who "might be interested in helping them improve the college through bringing conservative ideas" to campus (Roger Custer, YAF). This clearly was the case at an Ann Coulter event we attended at the University of California–Irvine in May 2008, where a cordoned-off section of the standing-room-only event was reserved for affluent Orange County conservatives.

All that said, if students cannot network quite enough in their community and are unable to pull in sufficient dollars, YAF will "usually kick in a little bit" to bring a speaker to campus, according to Custer. Using its vast reserves, the organization activates its "discount program," as one of our Western State interviewees, Conor Denning, called it, to help undergraduates bring the celebrity conservative speaker of their choice to campus.

National Conservative Student Conference

Hosting a conservative speaker at one's home campus clearly has benefits: It energizes the base by creating a collective experience of solidarity for the club that is sponsoring it and, at least in the case of the Coulter event we attended, in vilifying shared enemies.[26] But it is also expensive for campus clubs to host speakers, especially in cases where donors do not materialize. This is a prime reason why in addition to bringing conservative luminaries to students, the YAF also brings students *to it*—to the Reagan Ranch in Santa Barbara, to regional meetings, and to its biggest event of the year, the National Conservative Student Conference (NCSC), held every summer in Washington, D.C. While the NCSC is not the largest conference hosted for conservatives—that distinction is held by the CPAC meeting, which occurs every February for 6,000-plus attendees (about 2,500 of whom are students)—the NCSC is on the dance card of many conservative student leaders.[27] The following announcement described the 2011 NCSC's 33rd Annual Meeting in terms that are nothing if not confrontational:

Tree hugging. Gun taking. Wealth hating. Leftist loving. Sound like a nightmare?

The Details

For most college students, this is an accurate portrayal of their professors and peers and the left-wing ideas they espouse. You can learn the best ways to stand up for and advance conservative ideas on your campus just in time for the start of your fall semester! Don't miss this chance to be a part of the nation's largest and longest-running program of its kind. . . . **The National Conservative Student Conference!**[28]

For a nominal fee of $300 plus travel costs, students who are admitted to the conference can expect to spend six days and five nights, eating meals, attending talks, and networking with one another and their conservative role models.

The cost to students is substantially underwritten by the YAF and its contributors, according to Roger Custer, "because we want as many as possible to come." The 2011 conference that was taking place about the time we were writing this chapter did not stray much from past years, offering in its line-up the omnipresent Coulter and Bay Buchanan (sister of Pat), both of whom could be described as down-the-line populist. But as in other years, the roster also included a speaker or two from the more intellectual end of the conservative spectrum—in 2011, for example, Robert George from Princeton gave a talk titled "Social and Economic Conservatism: A Marriage of Principle." What this tells us is that the NCSC is predominantly a conference of the confrontational Right, but not exclusively.

Although attendees and conference organizers speak of the conference's allure in many different ways, Roger Custer argues that the best parts about it are less the "seeing and meeting the prominent conservative speakers" or getting to "go up to George Will and talk to him and shake his hand and get a picture and get your book signed" (Roger Custer, YAF). Instead, Custer thinks it's the "bull sessions" that students get to have with one another well after the official program has ended:

> And the students just talk about conservative ideas, often until 1 or 2 in the morning. And it's just a free-wheeling session and it's totally off the record, and they discuss what they're going to do on campus, similar experiences, but also the policy ideas and the philosophy, what they learned that day. . . . And they really enjoy that. Because often at their campus, they don't have a group like that. I mean maybe they will have 10 or 12 other conservatives, but they're not going to have hundreds of other ones. And they're probably not going to have the huge variety of other types of conservatives to discuss with. And it really is just a wonderful conference for them to get together and do that. (Roger Custer, YAF)

Interviewees who had attended the NCSC agreed. As one recalled, the conference "was a recharge for me in a big way. If you're working constantly in the trenches—especially in a small chapter—you start to get depressed and you wonder what the heck can I do. And YAF was a big eye-opener for me in the sense that there are a lot of other people trying to do what I'm doing" (Bryan Carhart, Western Satellite). The conferences that YAF organizes and funds can be a boost to Bryan and others like him in sustaining their conservative activism on their home campuses.

THE LEADERSHIP INSTITUTE: TENS OF THOUSANDS TRAINED AND STILL GOING STRONG

The second organization that falls on the populist end of the spectrum is the Leadership Institute (or LI), which was founded in 1979 "to increase the number and effectiveness of conservative activists and leaders in the public policy process" by identifying, recruiting, training, and placing conservatives in government, politics, and the media.[29] Although the president and founder of the LI, Morton Blackwell, may not have huge name recognition outside conservative circles, and although the organization he founded has net assets less than a quarter the size of the YAF's, Blackwell is a mover and shaker who has unquestionably altered the landscape of conservative political action in the nation.[30]

Since his early days in the 1960s as an undergraduate student at Louisiana State University, where he was active in the campus College Republicans and attended the 1964 National Republican Convention as the youngest elected delegate for Barry Goldwater, Blackwell has lived and breathed an aggressive style of conservative engagement (Morton Blackwell, LI). Exhilarated by his own successes as an activist, and realizing that he had a gift for training youth to become ardent participants and leaders in the conservative movement, Blackwell started an organization that has trained tens of thousands of young people over the past three decades to become strategists, media personalities, elected officials, and behind-the-scenes operatives in the conservative world. His earliest trainees, he said in an interview, included Mitch McConnell, the current Republican senator from Kentucky, and Terry Branstad, the current Republican governor of Iowa. Other big names followed, among them, per one of our interviewees, the former Republican governor of Colorado, Bill Owens (Victor Irwin, Western Satellite) and, according to the LI's own website, the videographer James O'Keefe, who in recent years has become an admired figure among many conservatives for his hidden-camera sting operations targeting the organizations ACORN, Planned Parenthood, and National Public Radio.

With stars like these, in addition to thousands of less visible trainees, the LI has clearly populated a healthy faction of the conservative movement. The organization's website variably claims to have trained 74,000, 94,000, and 97,000 young leaders, while in our interview with Morton Blackwell conducted in 2008, he put the number at 69,000.[31] Whatever the precise figure, the organization does this work with a staff of more than 50; has four separate program areas, including a training institute for would-be activists; boasts its own high-tech media and production studio; runs an online job services program; funds an interactive website that shares information on conservative clubs on 2,000-plus college campuses; and pays between 50 and 70 undergraduate field representatives per year to develop new conservative organizations on college campuses.[32] According to its online tax statement, the LI had contributions and grants totaling more than $8 million in 2010; cross-referencing this information with data from the Media Matters Action Network, its three most generous contributors are the F.M. Kirby Foundation (a family foundation located in New Jersey), the Castle Rock Foundation (a free enterprise foundation located in Denver and founded by the Coors family), and the Lynde and Harry Bradley Foundation (a large contributor to all three of the organizations working with conservative students that we discuss in this chapter).[33]

Like the YAF's, the LI's mission statement reads as if taken directly from the Republican Party platform, noting that it trains leaders to be "unwavering in their commitment to free enterprise, limited government, strong national defense, and traditional values"—the standard cluster of issues for the party's base.[34] The sense of being in a GOP stronghold is enhanced in person when one enters the organization's replica-colonial lobby in Arlington, Virginia, where on the "Lafayette Mantle" sit one presidential portrait of George W. Bush and another of the president with his wife, Laura. The main thing that deepens the feeling of being in the center of partisan politics, though, is the display on the coffee table. For there are assembled two clay elephants with an inscription that reads, "Two Types of Republicans." One of the elephants (the one on the left, perhaps not coincidentally) is sitting on its behind and looking like it's having a great time; but the point seems to be that this fun-loving elephant is a lollygagger and not to be taken seriously. The other elephant, seen only from the back, charges up a steep slate hill. This is an active and muscular elephant, an elephant that means business and takes no prisoners. It is this kind of activist, the artwork conveys, that the LI intends to develop.

Training Future Leaders: The Leadership Training Institute

If the mission of the LI is laser-focused—training conservative activists and decision makers in the manner of a charging elephant—the organization itself is extremely multifaceted in its approach to recruiting and educating young people.[35] In this chapter we explore three areas of the LI's work, beginning with its well-funded training institute.

In 2011, when we were doing the bulk of our background research on this group, the organization's namesake Leadership Training Institute advertised 41 distinct training areas—teaching these 41 topics almost 300 times throughout the year across the country—which covered a range of areas for young people interested in careers in politics and punditry. Officially, these training sessions are open to any applicant, regardless of ideology, and are nonpartisan—hence the LI's tax-exempt status (Morton Blackwell, LI). Session titles attracting future leaders include "Building Your Winning Coalition School," "Public Relations School," "Campaign Management School," "Public Speaking," "Youth Leadership School" ("nicknamed 'the boot camp of politics'"), and "New Media Workshops," in which trainees learn to "harness the power of internet technologies."[36]

These training sessions sometimes take place over the course of one day or as multiday sessions, and they are offered both online and in physical settings, either at LI headquarters in Arlington, Virginia, or off-site, often on college campuses.[37] When the training takes place in Virginia, it is held in the F.M. Kirby National Training Center, which, the website proudly informs, features six classrooms (each with "an integrated audio visual system") offering "enough space to accommodate 46 students during training."[38] According to the organization's 990 tax form, the training institute constituted more than $3 million of the organization's budget, making it the largest of the organization's areas of operation.[39] The training institute also has been known to conduct special training events for people beyond student age. One such event had LI instructors working with Dick Armey's FreedomWorks organization to school more than 400 Tea Party activists who were in town for a March on Washington in association with Fox News personality Glenn Beck's 9/12 Project.[40] According to the LI's website, Tea Party members were instructed in "grassroots techniques that will make them more effective 'online, on the ground, and on the Hill'"—basically providing to these noncollegians what the institute normally offers to students.[41]

CampusReform.org

CampusReform.org is quite a different kind of project run by the LI insofar as it compiles information about, and networking opportunities for, students on college and university campuses across the country. At the time we were conducting research for this book, the LI reported that there was information on 2,376 four-year colleges in its database.[42] Designed to help undergraduates "borrow and share activism and fundraising ideas, report leftist abuses on your campus, rate professors, and review textbooks," the website has numerous sections and subsections that produce an avalanche of information for students interested in getting active as conservatives in college.[43] For example, under its "Campuses" section, students can find out about both the state where their campus is located (their broader political context) and their own home campus—the latter of which is useful for determining whether any right-leaning groups already exist at their college or university. Students also have the option of clicking a button to start a new conservative organization. Visitors to the site can check up on "leftist faculty" who work on any given campus, the "biased textbooks" used in the classroom on that campus, "local reformers" who are working to help the conservative cause, and blogs about all of the above for that particular college or university.[44] Interested to see what was reported on at Western Flagship and Eastern Elite, we discovered that as of July 2011, CampusReform.org was either in a beta testing phase or simply not very popular—or perhaps we found evidence that students were not particularly concerned at the moment (at least during summer break) about the threat of radical professors—since only one "leftist faculty" member was listed at Western, and none at Eastern.

Under the "Resources" tab of CampusReform.org, students can choose to get more information on bringing a training session to campus, find out how to be a better publicist for a conservative group, and gain access to an electronic library of "Manuals and Writings," which include topics with such titles as "Conservative Outreach to 'Minorities,'" "How a College Student Can Safely Create Pain for a Professor Who Is Misusing His Bully Pulpit," and "Mrs. Manners: A Crash Course in Courtesy."[45] With this initiative, the LI attempts to provide a "one-stop resource, networking, and instruction center for conservative activists to take back their campuses from leftist domination."[46] To this end, the organization spent nearly $350,000 on the totality of CampusReform.org in 2010, according to the LI's 2010 tax filings.[47]

Campus Leadership Program

A third component of the LI organization is the Campus Leadership Program. Established in 1997, the Campus Leadership Program "is a very, very active program to assist conservative students in forming independent conservative student groups on their campuses," according to Morton Blackwell, and at the time of our interview in

the fall of 2008, the president reported there were 1,241 such campus groups "currently active and cooperating with us" (Morton
Blackwell, LI). As the LI website points out, conservative student
groups on campus normally exist in isolation from one another—
"independent, self-directed, and unaffiliated"—which, while having
some advantages (especially as concerns autonomy), also has disadvantages.[48] According to this website, it can be hard to effect change
locally when students don't know what other successful right-
leaning groups have accomplished. The Campus Leadership Program attempts to address this problem by "providing resources and
advice to local groups," even while honoring those campus groups'
self-determination.

The program structure is what we would call top-down but light-
handed, at least as it is described by Blackwell and others we spoke
with. It has eight regional supervisors located in the Virginia office—from their Internet profiles, most look young enough to be
only recent college graduates themselves—who provide information
and support to undergraduates on affiliated campuses. These eight
supervisors also oversee an ever-shifting corps of field staff, who,
with a small stipend, go out and recruit conservative students to
start new right-leaning groups of their own on their campuses. With
the idea that student groups can benefit from shared wisdom about
what works and what doesn't, and can be mobilized from above
with a little bit of wisdom and a fistful of cash, the LI devotes about
$2 million per year to this endeavor, according to its 2010 federal
990 form.[49]

Because there is not much information online about how this part
of the LI works, we sought to interview a couple of people on the
ground who are familiar with the Campus Leadership Program. One
of these sources of information, an interviewee at Western Satellite
named Victor Irwin, was working as a "field rep" for the program
when we met him, organizing students in his assigned region on their
home campuses, while also finishing up his own undergraduate degree. Our other source of information for this program is our Western State interviewee Conor Denning, who became aware of the organization when he received a call from a regional supervisor shortly

after the conservative newspaper he started, the *Western Sovereign*, got substantial coverage in the national right-wing media.[50]

We begin with the mobilization side of things, quoting at length from our interview with Victor, who described what recruitment and organizing work is like for the Campus Leadership Program:

> Basically, there were 70 of us. They send us all around the country to different schools. And we go in and we help students start conservative clubs and organizations. So I would go and either, I did a lot of Facebook kind of trying to find people that way, or I'd just set up a recruiting table, put up like a trifold, "Are You Conservative? Come Sign Up Now." And then I'd get them together and then kind of find a leader among them and get them to start their own little independent conservative groups. (Victor Irwin, Western Satellite)

Asked what he did if he found conservative-oriented campus groups already in place but as yet unaffiliated with the LI, Victor told us that the field reps were expected to put the officers of such groups in touch with the regional supervisors in the home office so that they could be part of the network of campus organizations.

Victor also clarified what it meant to organize nonpartisan conservative clubs—the "nonpartisan" part being a mandate from above. When we asked if he was mostly going to campus and organizing College Republicans clubs, he responded quite adamantly, "No, they have to be nonpartisan, so they couldn't be Republican." He continued:

> So it was like we could talk to the College Republicans. We would be like, "Hey, do you guys want to start like a pro-life club? Do you guys want to start a gun club? Do you just want to start another general conservative kind of thing?" But since they were with the Republican Party, because of the PAC status, we couldn't help them or else the IRS would come in and take away our [Leadership Institute's] nonprofit status. So that was actually kind of tricky, because you would talk to people and you're like, "Do

you want to start a club?" And they're "Yeah, like the College Re-publicans?" (Victor Irwin, Western Satellite)

At which point Victor would have to tell them, "Yeah, kind of, but not really, though."

Still later in the interview, Victor talked about the quality and quantity of support campus groups might receive from the Campus Leadership Program. Here we provide a longer exchange, which offers information on the types of material resources and on-site training that student groups can obtain from the LI:

> R: We give them like training, like I would kind of help them get started. Like we would write up a mission statement. And then we had some materials and like books and like bumper stickers and things that we would send to them.
>
> I: So what, if they were starting a gun club, then they would get bumper stickers about guns? Or if they were starting a pro-life [club], they would get bumper stickers about that? Things like that?
>
> R: Yeah. The fall semester was all just pretty much generic stuff, and then they kind of revamped it for the spring and made like specific stuff for those. But then there was also if you wanted to start like a free market club, there weren't really specific things for that. But we'd give them like, we had copies of like *The Law* from Frederic Bastiat, and *Road to Serf-dom*. And we had like a John Stossel DVD and a bunch of other stuff that we'd give them [and] I would pretty much, I would get them set up, and then I would move on.
>
> And then the Leadership [Institute regional supervisor], whoever was in charge of that region, like that full-time person there, they kind of take over and they would help them. It's kind of more up to them to kind of learn the stuff on their own. We were just kind of a tool to help them more with the activism, like if they needed ideas for an event we could help them out. Of if they needed connections, like if they were a

gun club, then we could try to get them connected with like the representative from the NRA or Gun Owners of America. (Victor Irwin, Western Satellite)

In other words, the Campus Leadership Program gets the ball rolling, and then does what it can to help it build speed.

Talking with a student on the other side of the benefits transaction—that is, the recipient—is also enlightening. In the case of Conor Denning and his newspaper the *Sovereign*, a field representative like Victor Irwin was not the instigator of funding from the LI. Rather, staff in the LI organization noticed that Conor was already doing commendable conservative work in his newspaper and had been successful at garnering national attention. Not only did regional and national staff at the LI contact him out of the blue, but Conor said they also immediately offered him $750 for use on his newspaper. And the gifts kept coming:

I can't say enough good about [the Leadership Institute]. I mean, I still get phone calls from them, "What else can we do?" They really see kind of the same problem that I do. They want to give students just a fair shot as far as either starting just a college group, an active group, or starting a newspaper. They have a Broadcasting and Journalism Center in Virginia. They have a whole complex. . . . I mean, just donors all over the country give to these organizations. If we needed $200 for a wienie roast, I'd call them up, [and] $200 is in the mail. It's really great! (Conor Denning, Western State)

Asked if financial resources were the extent of the benefits he has received from the LI, Conor responded that there was still more that he was grateful for:

They do a ton of workshops. Like when I was in LA, I went . . . they flew me out there, put me up in a hotel room, all meals paid for. I mean, it's just, I felt *bad*, like. . . . It was, it must have been like $600 or $700 bucks for a weekend. It was like . . . this was a Youth Leadership program, new leadership school. (Conor Denning, Western State)

As soon as Conor provided this information, he clammed up a bit, stating that the LI doesn't "like a lot of press exposure. . . . I don't know what I should be saying . . . they don't like a whole lot of in-depth detail about what they do."

Whether Conor is correct in his assessment of the LI leaders' desire for opaqueness, it is clear that at the most fundamental level, the organization's mission is to get young people organized, trained, and channeled into the world of conservative politics with an activist mentality. And through its multiple operations, it has done this many, many times over the past three decades.

A Last Note on the Leadership Institute

With as many as 97,000 activists organized over the years, including elected officials, strategists, and pundits, it is impossible to say that there is a *typical* LI alumnus/a, since different trainees and student members mobilized by the LI have followed divergent career paths. However, it would not be completely off-base to say that there may be *archetypal* LI alumni/ae and that one of these would be personified by James O'Keefe. O'Keefe, as we have mentioned already, is the hidden-camera impresario whose sting operations had him at one point posing as a pimp to catch ACORN members behaving badly and at another breaking into a U.S. senator's office.[51] While O'Keefe may not be a representative LI trainee—he is much more audacious and has received far more attention than others who have gone through the institute—it is clear he has taken the provocative and populist style taught at the LI and run with it, making himself a star for the cause. As a student he received seed money from the organization for his college newspaper at Rutgers University and enrolled in ten seminars offered by the Leadership Training Institute; upon graduating in 2006, he worked for the LI for a year, as a field representative organizing students and as an instructor in 75 training programs of his own, according to the LI's website.[52] His own advice to conservative students, according to an article on Politico.com, is not to just "respond to news, but actually create your own headlines. Make demands upon your professors. Make demands upon your university to actually change things. Don't just wait for something to happen and sit back and report on it."[53]

Although some LI leaders ultimately condemned O'Keefe and his colleagues for their operations, with a spokesperson saying they had "cross[ed] the line," "exposing yourself—whatever organization you're affiliated with, and the people that you're associated with—to a deserved and justified backlash," that condemnation was somewhat ambivalent.[54] Morton Blackwell himself blogged that "James left LI in 2007 because his priority was personally to organize taped stings against the left on hot public policy issues which relate to legislation, which was different from the training role of his job here."[55] But Blackwell also went on to herald O'Keefe as a "national conservative hero."[56] With these highly visible successes under his belt and a new organization called Project Veritas off the ground, O'Keefe can be seen to be innovating within a rich tradition—cultivated for decades now at the LI and the YAF—of the populist right.

THE REFINED WORLD OF CONSERVATISM: THE INTERCOLLEGIATE STUDIES INSTITUTE

While O'Keefe's star shines brightly (if somewhat ambivalently) at organizations like the YAF and the LI, his activities would likely induce shudders in the environs of the Intercollegiate Studies Institute (ISI), an organization that is on the more intellectual, or refined, continuum of conservative groups. To suggest that ISI members might cringe at the mention of O'Keefe's activities is not to say that those involved with this organization would not have appreciated it when the ACORN organization finally met its maker, or when the "liberal, taxpayer-funded" NPR suffered humiliation at the ex-LI videographer's hands.[57] Rather, what we are saying is that the *practices* that O'Keefe and his collaborators employ lie quite outside the imagined selves of those participating in the organizations that are known to be on the more civilized, philosophical, contemplative, and refined end of the spectrum.

The people who gather at various events under the ISI banner regard themselves as different: intellectual, more inclined to deliberative discourse, and not prone to overt political crusading. In an email we happened to receive from the ISI at precisely the time we were writing this chapter (July 2011, in the midst of the national debt ceiling debate), we were informed:

> One thing you won't see from ISI are urgent appeals regarding the newest bill before Congress, or the latest presidential outrage, or whatever the crisis of the political moment happens to be. That is not because we are unconcerned with the actions of government. Far from it—we believe emphatically that liberty depends on a well-informed and engaged citizenry, especially in the political arena.
>
> What distinguishes ISI, however, is a call to view the heated moment from a larger or, more accurately, a *higher* perspective. To see the truth of a situation, to gain the higher vantage, requires standing on the shoulders of the giants who came before us. (ISI email, dated July 2011; emphasis in the original)

From this "higher perspective," continues the writer for the ISI, one can think more clearly about how to respond when "the federal government is seizing more power, racking up crushing debt, attacking the free market, and encroaching on individual liberty and the family."[58] As one can see from the concerns listed in the email quoted here, it is not that the belief system at the ISI is different from the one embraced by the YAF and the LI (its ideological underpinnings, just as at the other organizations, concern the sanctity of free markets and keeping track of liberal outrages). The difference lies in the tactics that are advocated by the organization: seeking a loftier vantage point from which to pronounce one's views.

In a similar vein, during a lecture delivered to students at the National Conservative Student Conference in 2007, the ISI's executive director of academic affairs, Richard Brake, voiced concerns to the undergraduates in the audience that "conservative students have stopped reading the classics and are prone to 'sexy' activism."[59] Although Brake quickly acknowledged that "in this technological age" it is helpful to know the "politics" of mobilization and to "have a gut instinct" about what works well in a world that is now instantly connected, he also argued, "You need to know the classics . . . you need to know deep down why you believe what you believe."[60] Drawing a distinction, essentially, between confrontational political activity as promoted by the YAF and the LI and the classical education advocated by the ISI—or what we call populist versus refined styles of conservatism—this was an appeal for the latter: Become more learned in the classics (which your liberal professors are failing to teach you), and be a better conservative. While we do not know how many students at the conference genuinely connected with this appeal (the speaker received polite applause, according to the student we know who attended the conference, but nothing like the standing ovation the LI's Morton Blackwell had gotten just minutes before), we did discover that such a sensibility resonates with at least one group of our interviewees: Eastern Elite students and alumni/ae. According to data from our interviews, ten Eastern Elite interviewees, but only one Western Public student, even *mentioned* the ISI during our conversations with them. One Eastern Elite respondent spoke of the organization as "a bit more old-school . . . very philosophical" (Nicole Harris, Eastern Elite), while another characterized the ISI as "a fairly influential group among intellectually minded conservatives" (Henry Quick, Eastern Elite). From a more dismissive perspective, but still in keeping with the general theme, a third Eastern Elite student commented that the group is "all men," and they "all dress Brooks Brothers Republican to the nth degree" (Kyle Lee, Eastern Elite). In other words, there is an air of distinction that comes from being involved with the ISI, an image of seriousness and intellectuality, of sitting somewhere above the fray of day-to-day politics and of participating in an illustrious group of fellow intellectuals—even if a few students think the whole thing is stuffy and a bit affected.

This all makes sense, given the organization's origins. The ISI was established in 1953 by Frank Chodorov, a writer for *Human Events* and a handful of other conservative journals, and its first president was William F. Buckley, Jr., who, if well known for his *realpolitik* successes in helping to bring about the Republican electoral strategy of "fusionism," is also revered in conservative circles for his urbane style of conservative writing and debate.[61] Embodying erudition, Buckley must have seemed to Chodorov the ideal person not only to help cultivate "the best and the brightest" of the day's undergraduate population but also to redress the widespread image of conservatives, who in the 1950s and early 1960s were popularly perceived as paranoid and unsophisticated John Birch Society provincialists—that era's provocateurs.[62] Since its founding nearly 60 years ago, the ISI (which originally stood for the Intercollegiate Society for Individualists) has become a "behemoth," as one of our Eastern Elite interviewees opined (Vincent Long, Eastern Elite). With the lavish funding of several prominent foundations and donors (the Sarah Scaife Foundation alone has donated $7,250,000 since 1990, according to Media Matters Action Network), and with assets totaling $19 million in 2010, the ISI has grown into the most august, although not the largest, of the conservative organizations targeting college students.[63] Under its considerable purview, the ISI sponsors more than 300 events across the nation each year, including lectures, debates (for example, the University of Colorado ethnic studies professor Ward Churchill pitted against Dinesh D'Souza on the issue of Western civilization), student conferences, and summer schools.[64] The ISI also offers graduate fellowships, and claims to distribute more than "three million copies of ISI books, journals, and affiliated student newspapers on college and university campuses."[65] Its Collegiate Network funds more than 100 independent student newspapers across the country, including the *Harvard Salient*, the *Michigan Review*, and the *Irish Rover* at Notre Dame.[66] The organization also offers numerous other services and funding opportunities, ranging from an honors program that pairs about 25 students a year with faculty mentors across the country to a college guide that includes, along with other, more standard criteria (average SAT scores at any given college, student-faculty ratio), a "red, yellow, or green light" for each campus regarding how liberal to conservative that campus's politics are. (Not unexpectedly, red lights are given to liberal campuses like Hamilton "Just Say No to Western Civ" College.)[67]

Lectures and Conferences

With such a range of activities that might be explored, we find it useful to narrow our focus to the ISI's most visible offerings, its lectures and conferences (which are addressed in this section) and the Collegiate Network (taken up in the next). The lectures and conferences are designed to "instill an understanding and appreciation for America's founding principles," which are listed as limited government, individual liberty, personal responsibility, the rule of law, free market economy, and moral norms of Western civilization.[68] Lectures, according to the website, are given by "top scholars and nationally known speakers" who visit campuses across the country to talk about "both popular topics, such as affirmative action and core curriculum controversies, as well as perennial concerns, such as the nature of freedom and the best forms of government."[69] Perhaps helping to explain why the organization attracts "mostly men," per our Eastern Elite interviewee Kyle Lee, the ISI website states that lectures on the circuit "are rooted in fundamental principles and the enduring Western intellectual *patrimony*" (emphasis added).[70] Current lecture series titles include "Western Culture: Its Culture and Critics," "The Positive Role of Christian Social Thought in Public Service," and "The Worldwide Persecution of Christians."[71] There is also a "great issues debate series" called "Cicero's Podium" that, like the lecture series, "aim[s] to elevate and exemplify civil discussion" and "promote genuine intellectual diversity on college campuses."[72]

In addition, the ISI hosts conferences around the country in the format of half-day seminars, weekend colloquia, or weeklong intellectual retreats, at which students, faculty, and sometimes donors (such as at the conference we were invited to attend in June 2009 in nearby Rancho Santa Fe, California) are provided with "access to leading scholars who discuss and debate a variety of ideas."[73] In "Student Seminar: Conservatism 101," for example, held in April 2010 in Fresno, California, students exploring the principles of conservatism had "the opportunity to learn more about what constitutes a conservative library and how the Classics have shaped our modern understanding of conservatism . . . under the tutelage of historian George H. Nash."[74] At the ISI National Leadership Conference, on the other hand—held in Indianapolis in October 2009—topics were somewhat more down to earth:

> The global financial crisis has prompted Americans to question the very foundations of our nation's economic system. . . . Join ISI in Indianapolis . . . to discuss conservative reaction to the crisis and the viable solutions available. How do free markets fit into a broader conservative understanding of man and society? How does the present situation compare with past recessions? Can short-term government intervention be followed by a return to market freedom, or has an increasing reliance on federal intervention been at the core of the problem?[75]

At the conference we attended in Rancho Santa Fe, California, topics varied a good deal and included lectures by Professor Richard Gamble (Hillsdale College) on C.S. Lewis's *Abolition of Man* (a defense of natural law and the role of education in promoting it); by ISI's senior vice president and chief academic officer, Mark Henrie, on how teaching theology in college is more useful than teaching about Marxism, Freudian theory, and biology; and by then ISI president T. Kenneth Cribb, Jr., on the ISI's apolitical goal of providing assistance to young faculty—a goal that is said to be needed more than ever because the free market is under attack (field notes, Intercollegiate Studies Institute Conference, Rancho Santa Fe, California). Although these are not direct quotes from the small conference we attended, they give the gist of the content of such gatherings. As we documented in our field notes from the event, the students and donors in attendance savored the lecture comments.

Collegiate Network

A second key area of ISI activity occurs under the auspices of the Collegiate Network, a project established in 1979 by the neoconservative journalist Irving Kristol and the laissez-faire businessman and philanthropist William Simon. An initiative that has jump-started the careers of many an editor and writer, its first funded publication was led by student John Podhoretz at the University of Chicago.[76] The CN, as it is commonly referred to, was brought under the ISI umbrella in 1995 and provides financial and technical support to "independent" newspapers on campuses across the country. According to its website, in 2010 the CN awarded "more than $122,000 in grants to 42 member publications," with the average grant amounting to about $3,000.[77] Although this may not sound like much, such grants help to keep conservative newspapers going. In the case of Eastern Elite University's conservative paper, the *Searchlight*, for example, as much as 30 to 40 percent of the paper's budget comes directly from the CN, according to one of our interviewees who was a former editor on the paper (Vincent Long, Eastern Elite).

In conjunction with funding newspapers, the CN also hosts a series of conferences for their newspapers' editors and staff, where the topics of discussion are tailored specifically to students' journalistic needs (rather than the more philosophical issues analyzed at the general ISI conferences), such as "tips on layout and that sort of thing" from a designer at the *Weekly Standard* (Calvin Coffey, Eastern Elite), or, as a former CN staff member told us, hearing an "entertaining talk about life as a journalist and how you don't get paid much, it can be tough, you lose the tape to your tape recorder. . . . But how it really is a great life, especially if you like ideas" (Joe Lindsley, ISI). Describing a conference that had taken place in Charlotte, North Carolina, in the days following the 2008 elections, this same staff member described two equally important organizational goals of the CN: to improve these students' independent publications and to "encourage the best of them to consider careers in journalism."

To this second end—encouraging talented young conservatives to follow in the path of a Kristol or Podhoretz, rather than go into investment banking or management consulting or some other more lucrative career—the CN goes to serious lengths. Although it cannot offer the material rewards of these other career paths, it does boast yearlong fellowships and summer internships in high-profile media outlets. The fellowships come with annual stipends of $24,000–$30,000 and in 2010–2011 included placements at the *Weekly Standard, USA Today, The Hill*, and Radio Free Europe.[78] The summer internships pay stipends of $4,000, and in that same year, summer interns took up temporary residence at the *National Review, The Hill*, the *Washington Times*, and the *New York Post*, among others. During the fellowship period, CN offers "training and support," which includes an Intern/Fellow Training Workshop that offers "briefings with professional journalists," a Journalists Salon ("a small, private gathering for its yearlong fellows and alumni and friends" in Washington or New York), and an Alumni and Friends Reception "for all current students, alumni, and friends of the CN."[79]

Clearly, networking opportunities are a prime appeal of the media internship programs. In addition to its own numerous fellowships, in July 2011 the CN advertised an additional opportunity on its website, the Eric Breindel Collegiate Journalism Award, which is given to a young journalist who "reflects the spirit of the writings by Eric Breindel: Love of Country and its democratic institutions as well as the commitment to preserve the freedoms that allow such institutions to flourish."[80] Named for a storied editorial page editor of the *New York Post*, this award comes with a "cash prize of $10,000 and a paid internship" at one of three of Rupert Murdoch's News Corporation media outlets: the *Wall Street Journal*, the Fox

News Channel, or the *New York Post*. Given the conservative political stances of these media outlets, it would seem that while CN and the rest of ISI may be formally committed to nonpartisanship, this organization is and always has been an important socialization and training ground for the conservative end of both intellectual theory *and* action.

In Summary

The ISI is an organizational force in the conservative world—its leaders, staff, scholars, funders, and students are deeply sewn into the fabric of conservative politics and thought, and the organization has a rich and storied legacy—particularly for those who picture themselves on the intellectual end of the conservative spectrum. It is more William F. Buckley than David Horowitz; more Brooks Brothers than blue jeans; and more self-regardingly philosophical than political.

Yet at the same time, the ISI does not advocate intellectual conservatism alone, as if ideology existed in a political vacuum. Rather, the organization makes current partisan issues a focal point of discussion as well. As the email with which we started our section on the ISI demonstrates (the author referred to the "latest presidential outrage" in the Obama administration's third year in office) and as one of our interviewees revealed in his comments to us, the conservative principles discussed at ISI seminars and conferences are not divorced from political concerns in the real world. A description of the connection that the organization makes between ideas and action was formulated nicely by our Eastern Elite interviewee Henry Quick:

> They [ISI] seek to explain what they understand to be the principles of American civilization and Western civilization. When they get into the principles of Western civilization, that is when perhaps they become more intellectual as a whole. They try to evaluate the question, "Is Western civilization as a whole in crisis,

and if so, what does that crisis entail? How did we get here?" Not simply the *Weekly Standard* question of "How do we appeal to middle-class voters in 2010 or 2012?" but "Out of what debate did the American founding come," right? So they provoke you to read John Locke and Thomas Hobbes. They also promote a more vigorous engagement with the non-, *apparently* nonpolitical cultural aspects of Western civilization. So in that sense they're more philosophical, if philosophy is the pursuit of truth.

[But] they have in that sense a *political* aspect. "How can we explain that we don't want more taxes?" And they have what you might call a more contemplative aspect, which is "What is wrong, what happened, is anything wrong, what's the right diagnosis, and what are the shining aspects of the Western tradition to which we would appeal?" (Henry Quick, Eastern Elite, emphasis added)

For 50,000 students and faculty today, then, this organization stimulates the brains behind the politics, fortifying young conservatives with the educational content they believe they cannot receive on their college campuses—which are said to be lacking "intellectual diversity" and are "ambivalent if not hostile toward open intellectual discussion and debate," according to the current ISI president and CEO Christopher Long.[81] With the knowledge and social contacts they gain from being part of the ISI network, young conservatives are expected to continue to transform society in a more conservative direction long after they graduate. In one sense, the ISI is very much a different type of organization than the populist YAF and the LI. But in a deeper sense, all three organizations are part of the same game. Whereas the latter are focused on developing the rank and file of the next generation of conservatives—those who will serve in local leadership positions, who will be elected as party delegates, or who will act as fundraisers and policymakers for the GOP—groups like the ISI are developing the next generation of elite leadership. The two ends of the spectrum are mutually supportive, even while there is a recognized, if largely tacit, division of labor among these groups.

CONCLUSION

We have gone into considerable detail on these three student-centered conservative organizations because they are standouts on the organizational terrain. But in some regards we have only scratched the surface. Many other groups are helping to craft the next generation of conservatives, from the national College Republicans, which with a chapter on virtually every college campus is the conservative club of choice for thousands of students with political aspirations, to the Institute for Humane Studies (IHS), which through its program of targeting and funding promising young scholars throughout their careers "promotes a kind of change that is much more long-term and aimed at educating a whole generation of scholars that are more sympathetic to classical liberalism" (Jonathan Fortier, IHS). These organizations are the outgrowth of a concerted effort that began in the 1950s and 1960s with the founding of the ISI and the Young Americans for Freedom, and was further propelled forward in the 1970s when Lewis Powell (not yet a U.S. Supreme Court Justice) wrote a famous memo to the U.S. Chamber of Commerce arguing that conservative leaders must undertake a multipronged strategy to reverse the unbridled liberalism of American universities.[82] William Simon, in his role at the John M. Olin Foundation, helped lead the funding charge. Since these early days, the number of conservative student organizations has grown; their missions have multiplied and diversified; and tens of thousands of college students have passed through their programs. While other social scientists and journalists have documented the sophisticated organization of the political Right, in general, what they have not noted is how much of this organizational effort is geared to *college students*, on university and college campuses. As we have shown here, national organizations are spending significant amounts of money on the next generation of conservative voters and leaders, focusing particularly on the areas of media, politics, and government.

As we turn now to our case-study universities and a comparison of conservative styles that are used there, we bear in mind the discrete resources that these three organizations offer to students. As suggested earlier, while all of these organizations share a fundamental message—"You need us because your college or university is not exposing you to intellectual diversity"—they also articulate that message differently: in populist form to "Joe Average" students (Roger Custer, YAF) and in more refined form to the "the best and the brightest," as the ISI's website puts it.[83] The students and alums we interviewed were aware of these distinctions—Eastern Elite respondents even more so than Western Public interviewees. In crafting their conservative personae and activities on campus, students draw selectively from this larger national conservative repertoire.

Chapter 4

How Conservatives Think about Campus

The Effects of College Reputations, Social Scenes,
and Academics on Student Experience

What do conservative students discover when they get to campus? Certainly the arguments developed by the national organizations described in the last chapter—as well as by Fox News, the conservative blogosphere, and such books as Alan Kors and Harvey Silverglate's *The Shadow University* and David Horowitz's *Indoctrination U—* are intended to lead right-leaning students to expect the worst.[1] Critics accuse professors of politicizing the classroom when they should be exposing students to a canonical education in Western culture. They complain about administrators who, they say, mandate freshmen orientation programs and support libertine campus organizations that create a sexually decadent environment on campus. They condemn affirmative action admission policies, diversity requirements, speech codes, and what they see as an antipathy toward the military as wrong-headed and hopelessly "politically correct."[2] And while not all conservative commentators subscribe to a complete "indoctrination" model as per the David Horowitz title above, virtually all conservative critics argue that a hostile political atmosphere exists on American campuses that militates against diversity of opinion and has a chilling effect on speech and expression—a problem for all members of the campus but especially for conservative students, who, it is said, are all too frequently at the mercy of their professors.[3] Given the multiple sources of information delivering this unified message, we would not be surprised to learn that right-leaning students at institutions of higher education across the country might experience their college years as one of embattlement.[4]

Yet the intimation animating the conservative critique—that students perceive that their colleges and universities are engaged in a massive program of liberalization—is questionable on a couple of counts. This is not just because no real scholarship of student perceptions has yet been conducted but also because it ignores the fact that there is considerable institutional variation in the field of higher education, which makes any hypothesis of uniform student experiences—of *anything* on campus, including political indoctrination—doubtful. Students today find themselves in postsecondary education settings that encompass everything from elite Ivy League universities to the for-profit online degree programs that advertise during daytime television. Even among Research I universities of the type we study in this book, a tremendous amount of variation exists. While there is certainly a high degree of institutional similarity between, say, the Duke Universities and the University of Minnesotas of the world (both schools employ ladder-rank faculty with PhDs, both require undergraduate students to select a major, and both put an emphasis on research productivity for graduate students and faculty, among other similarities), there are simply far too many different ingredients in the mix for any two universities to be exactly alike or, more to the point, to be precisely similar in how students perceive them. The basic organizational structures of universities, like the types of housing that students live in or the way students are required to fulfill distribution requirements, make a huge difference in students' experiences and impressions of their schools. Less concrete aspects of higher education, as well, have an impact on students' perceptions: a university's reputation or standing in the wider world, the expectations the university places on its students for what it means to be a member of its community, the social scene affecting friendship networks, student clubs, and athlet-ics—each of these also plays a role in creating undergraduates' per-ceptions of their classes, their professors, and their political and social lives.[5]

Based on the assumption that specific campus organizational and cultural features shape students' experiences, this chapter delves into what conservative students say they find when they arrive on the Western Public and Eastern Elite campuses—and the degree to which students comment on their university's politics. Whereas chapter 2 introduced us to conservative college students both at the national scale and in our sample, and chapter 3 acquainted us with the broadest level of national conservative politics and organiza-tions, this chapter focuses on the campus level, as does the rest of the book. Following a brief overview of the two schools at the cen-ter of our study, Western Flagship and Eastern Elite, we go into ex-tensive detail on these campuses in three general areas. First, we look at the schools' reputations and characters, examining what our conservative interviewees said they expected to find on their college campus when they applied for admission and what their strongest considerations were in choosing to attend their university. Next, we turn to extracurricular aspects of college life, describing the social and residential scene at each school and our interviewees' percep-tions of the student body, and how this causes them to feel that they fit in or stand out uneasily as conservatives. Last, we discuss aca-demics. We go through the nuts and bolts of how several aspects of scholastic life work on our two primary campuses (such as registra-tion procedures for classes, and when and how students select ma-jors), and we examine how even these most basic organizational features of college life affect our students' experiences *as conserva-tives*. By examining students' interactions with this entire set of cul-tural ideas and structural arrangements on each campus, we find that being a conservative is a very different experience—in some truly remarkable ways—depending on whether a student goes to Eastern Elite or Western Flagship.

Yet despite these institutional differences, we also find that con-servative students at both of these universities hold some ideas in common as a result of understanding themselves to be in the political minority on their campuses. To varying degrees, interviewees at both universities described common disadvantages—and also benefits—of having opinions that go against the grain. We conclude this chapter with a discussion of the shared issues students say they face at their universities but that nevertheless result in a parting of stylistic ways on the different campuses—the subject of chapters 5 and 6.

WESTERN VERSUS EASTERN: AN OVERVIEW

Our comparison of Western Flagship to Eastern Elite leverages many dimensions of difference across the two university campuses.[6] Both are Research I, religiously unaffiliated universities, and both Eastern Elite and Western Flagship, the main campus in the Western Public system, have been identified in the conservative media and on the Internet as particularly (and problematically) left-leaning. However, in many critical ways these two universities are quite distinctive.

First, the Western Public system is a public, multicampus system that includes several campus locations throughout the state. Though our main focus is on its primary campus, Western Flagship, we also include data from interviewees on its other campuses—Western State, the land-grant university, and a smaller, commuter-oriented campus, Western Satellite. Both of these latter campuses are popularly considered by students, faculty, state legislators, and state residents to be more conservative than Western Flagship, which in addition to boasting a reputably "crunchier" student body is also located in a city known for its vibrant "blue state" politics despite being in a "red state" political landscape. The campus often is a political target for right-leaning politicians or other conservatives in the state: It is not unusual for Republican members of the state's legislature to deride the Western Flagship campus on the Capitol floor for being too far to the left of voters and thus undeserving of greater taxpayer aid, or for conservative alumni/ae to write letters to the local newspaper derisive of nearly everything related to the campus except the football team (and sometimes even the football team comes in for a dose of vitriol). It is also true that media pundits like Bill O'Reilly take shots at the university for being off-the-charts radical, and that members of the strong evangelical voting bloc in the state regard the campus with suspicion.[7]

Besides its reputation among conservatives for being liberal, Western Flagship is also notable at the national level for its recreational opportunities and sports.[8] Its Division I athletics program provides much of the school's national visibility, as does its reputation as a party school and the occasional misdeeds of its fraternities. The student body at Western Flagship (made up of 22,000 full-time undergraduates) is drawn primarily from within the state, with approximately 70 percent of the undergraduate population state residents. Women make up half of Western Flagship's undergraduate population (a greater percentage than that reflected by our interviewees), and 85 percent of the campus's students identify as white. Unsurprisingly, admission to Western Flagship is not terribly competitive (though it does get categorized as "highly selective" by organizations like the UCLA Higher Education Research Institute, or HERI, on the basis of median SAT scores), with only 20 percent turned away for admission.[9] Tuition is relatively low for state residents ($5,500 per year, not including room and board, and lower at the other Western Public campuses than it is at Western Flagship), and so while financial aid is not extensive—just 40 percent of incoming freshmen receive some form of assistance—a Western Flagship education is relatively financially attainable for state residents. Finally, although its students are not known in the aggregate primarily for their stellar academics, Western Flagship does boast a more elite honors college within the university, which offers highly competitive merit scholarships that encourage the most academically promising high school students to stay in the state for their college education. Outside the honors college, however, the student-to-faculty ratio is 18 to 1, and most classes taught by full-time faculty are large lecture classes, while smaller discussion sections are usually taught by graduate students. Adjuncts do a fair share of undergraduate teaching.

Eastern Elite University, conversely, is perceived not only by its students but also by the broader population as being an elite institution even among those in the upper echelon. The university's list of famed alumni/ae in numerous fields goes back virtually to the founding of the nation, and holding one of its highly coveted diplomas is considered by many to provide nearly limitless career opportunity. With a full-time undergraduate enrollment of just 7,000, Eastern Elite boasts an impressive student-to-faculty ratio of seven to one, and with nearly 23,000 high school seniors sending in applications each year for fewer than 1,800 seats, it is among the most selective universities in the country. Eastern Elite's high status and relatively small size—as well as its almost entirely on-campus social scene and generous housing—help create a largely cohesive community among its undergraduates.[10] All of these features have ramifications for how students perceive the university's administration, the professors who teach them, and the peers who live with them.

The Eastern Elite community includes substantial racial, ethnic, and regional diversity among the undergraduate population, which is typical of many of the most elite institutions in the United States.[11] Though the university is still majority white, drives for minority recruitment have helped Eastern Elite reach a 30 percent nonwhite undergraduate population.[12] The university has slightly more male than female students. In addition, the majority of students at Eastern Elite come from public schools, and 70 percent of incoming students receive some form of financial aid. While many of these students arguably hail from elite public schools, and Eastern Elite's high tuition plus room and board (about $50,000 per year) means many receiving funds are from the middle and upper middle class, these figures nonetheless point to the university's commitment to seeking out the best students regardless of their family's ability to pay out-of-pocket.[13] Even with all these other forms of diversity, however, conservative students are an ideological minority on Eastern Elite's campus.[14] Nonetheless, as we will see, Eastern Elite's elite status and sense of community seem to somewhat insulate these students from the negative effects of political difference experienced by students at Western Flagship and on other American campuses.

REPUTATIONS

Colleges' and universities' distinctive institutional reputations are important in determining both who applies and who is chosen for admission on certain campuses, and how undergraduates perceive themselves once immersed in the school. These institutional characters—what Burton Clark terms "organizational sagas"—simultaneously shape universities' reputations and serve to integrate students into campus communities during their undergraduate years and afterward, as devoted alumni/ae.[15] Though these reputations can be informal and based on shared lore or even gossip, they are also institutionalized in many ways, both by the schools themselves (such as in glossy brochures and information-saturated websites that are targeted to prospective applicants) and by outside interests (such as in college guidebooks or the various annual rankings like those published by *US News & World Report*).[16] These organizational sagas create a sense of the history of the university as a place, but they also implicate current students in the task of continuing to shape the legacy of the institution.[17] While it is true that each class of admitted students' tenure is short-lived—just four years or so—colleges and universities are not constantly pulled in different directions as students come and go. Instead, new students are incorporated into the university and invited to build on the reputations of their predecessors. For those who perceive themselves as fitting in with the university's character, there can be considerable benefits of community, camaraderie, and connections. However, for those who come to experience a disconnect between their own values and those of their university, college can be a more difficult time.

Though both Eastern Elite and Western Flagship are often characterized by critics as notoriously liberal, and though many of our interviewees—as prospective students—were well aware of these reputations, politics did not appear to loom large in their minds during the application process. Instead, other factors, such as value or academic rigor, appear to have been much more prominent in their considerations of which schools to apply to and attend. As one Eastern Elite interviewee put it, in a way echoing the conservative critique of higher education, "Where else are you going to [go]? If you want a great education, you're talking about the schools that have a predominantly liberal bent and, so, that was just kind of a given" (Staci Congdon, Eastern Elite).[18] While this interviewee and some of her colleagues (at both universities) mentioned that they had entertained the thought of attending campuses with political reputations more in keeping with their own priorities, the students we interviewed were attracted to the best school they could get into and, for some (particularly at Western Public), that their parents could afford. They liked the "brand" they were investing in, and they thought attending their presumptive best choice—whether it was Eastern Elite or one of the Western Public campuses—would pay off in the future. It is true that we may have missed talking with the most turned-off conservative students enrolled at each of these schools (because they were uninterested in doing interviews), and we of course do not have in our sample any hard-line conservative or religious students who decided at the time of college applications to avoid such liberal campuses altogether by choosing to attend a college more to their political liking. However, we can say that in terms of *our* interviewees' college decision processes—the conservative students who *did* choose to attend Western Flagship or Eastern Elite—neither the universities' political tenor nor opportunities for political involvement appear to have had much impact on their choices.

FUN BUT PRACTICAL WESTERN FLAGSHIP

As indicated by sources such as *U.S. News & World Report*, Western Flagship is known for football, fraternities, and most of all fun. Students generally cite the on- and off-campus party scene, as well as the numerous opportunities for outdoor recreation afforded by its location, as the school's best-known assets. Several of the conservative students interviewed for our study expressed their understanding of the place they were about to join as freshmen:

I guess I sort of liked the western atmosphere. But politics didn't have much to do with it. I thought I was going to come out to Western and be a Frisbee-playing, mountain-biking hippy. I still bike way too much, but the hippy part didn't happen. (Chuck Kelley, Western Flagship)

I didn't really know that Western was like, kind of more liberal. I knew that . . . at the time, it was like one of the top party schools. (Samantha Hart, Western Flagship)

Western Flagship's students are often stereotyped as laid-back and not especially academically oriented. Incoming students tend to gravitate either to athletics and recreation—with seven in 10 students coming from inside the state, many have followed its Division I teams their entire lives—or to the Greek system. As one interviewee characterized his expectations, "[Before I came to Western Flagship] I thought mostly of college students wearing [the school colors], going to the football game, and getting drunk every night. So my perception of [the city where Western Flagship is located] was just a college party town" (Neal Thompson, Western Flagship). And indeed, some interviewees described partaking in the party atmosphere once they arrived on campus.

At the same time that all of the students and alumni/ae we interviewed were highly aware of the school's reputation for fun and recreation, they often also cited the relatively low cost of tuition as a more salient reason for choosing the Western Public system. State residents receive a reduced tuition rate, and some of our interviewees had won prestigious merit-based awards specifically to go to Western Flagship or to attend a private or public university in the state. Explained one interviewee, "I was going to stay in state because I received a scholarship that was an academic merit-based full ride" (Christina Young, Western Flagship). Numerous interviewees talked about having decided to matriculate at one of the Western Public campuses to save their parents money or of working to support themselves during college:

> Western Flagship wasn't my first choice necessarily, it's the choice that made the most sense because it was an in-state school and it was going to be the most bang for your buck. (Stephanie Cohen, Western Flagship)

> Pure and simple was money. I can't afford on-campus housing for the next couple of months. . . . I am still living with my parents at the moment. (Bryan Carhart, Western Satellite)

Though our Western Public interviewees came from a wide range of socioeconomic backgrounds (as described in chapter 2), a sense of pragmatism prevails in many of their explanations for choosing to attend a Western Public campus. One interviewee had even accepted admission to a private out-of-state university before having what she described as "a crisis at the last minute" when she realized, "Why would I want to graduate with $150,000 in student loans when I could just stay in-state?" (Lindsey Nicholson, Western Satellite).[19]

Western Flagship's reputation is built not just around opportunities for recreation or for saving money, however. Western Flagship and the community in which it is located are noted—especially by hard-right conservatives—for their liberal leanings. As such, many interviewees recall having been warned about this by friends or family members, though most who chose to attend Western Flagship did not characterize *themselves* as having been especially worried by this aspect of its reputation. Said one alumna, "I don't know how many times I heard, 'Are you a Democrat yet?' or 'What are they doing to you at Western Flagship?'" (Christina Young, Western Flagship). Even the Western Flagship College Republicans president who was responsible for the successful 2004 Affirmative Action Bake Sale, quoted above, did not describe himself as especially concerned about the political atmosphere on campus before he got there:

> I literally thought I was going to go to Western Flagship. . . . I was going to be involved in the rec, the outdoor education pro-

grams, things like that. *That's* what I researched up on, not so much the politics of that. And some people said to me, "Oh my god, Western Flagship—very liberal." But I said I'm not going there for that, essentially. (Chuck Kelley, Western Flagship)

For most of our conservative interviewees, then, Western Flagship's reputation as a liberal campus was overshadowed by its low cost and plethora of recreational options.

THE AURA SURROUNDING EASTERN ELITE

Eastern Elite University is known above all for academics, having a reputation as an elite school even among elite schools, with a lengthy roster of famous alumni/ae in a myriad of fields. Conservative students entering Eastern Elite are keenly aware of its place within the higher education pantheon, as are their parents and peers. Said one student from a mid-sized city in the Northwest, "When I got into Eastern Elite all my friends and family were like, oh my goodness, you can't turn down Eastern Elite!" (Shannon Yaffe, Eastern Elite). Another student from the rural south explained,

> There is an incredible mystique to [it]. . . . It was like this wonderful place where everyone was really smart and talked all the time, learning these great ideas. . . . That is the image I had in high school, was that Eastern was the place of intellectual discourse and debate and all-night discussion. (Keaton Townsend, Eastern Elite)

Many Eastern Elite interviewees described themselves as in thrall to this "incredible mystique" and the opportunities presented by "attending one of the best schools in the nation" (Derek Yeager, Eastern Elite). Only one Eastern Elite student expressed a sense that, as an applicant, he did not find Eastern Elite *that* different from the other schools he had applied to, explaining that "they were all very impressive and it was certainly hard to judge, but Eastern Elite has its appeal and it was not too far from home. I certainly never had thought of it as the shining city sitting on the hill that I had to get to" (Drew Metcalfe, Eastern Elite). Drew's views are the exception, however, as most interviewees characterized gaining admission to Eastern Elite in terms that make it sound akin to finding one of Willy Wonka's golden tickets.

Eastern Elite conservatives cited numerous reasons for wanting to attend the school, with the most common being academics, their future careers, and, interestingly, their fellow Eastern Elite students. Although almost certainly not aware of the large body of formal educational research demonstrating just how highly consequential peers are for student success, these undergraduates shared a commonsense understanding that their fellow undergraduates were talented and exceptional people who were destined to follow the tradition of Eastern Elite alums and become leaders in their fields.[20] Students described anticipating building extensive social capital with their classmates:

> Growing up, I was always the odd one for actually studying, and it was great to be at a place where that was no longer an oddity but an expectation and a goal for people, that people wanted to do great things and make big changes. (Elizabeth Tennyson, Eastern Elite)

> There's something to be said for studying with these people and entering into that crowd. It's not for everybody. But . . . before I went to Eastern Elite I think I did fairly clearly think that that *was* what I should do, and that was sort of what I *wanted* to do. So it was more a matter of Eastern Elite's the best and I wanted to go to the best. (Nate Quinn, Eastern Elite)

Even one woman who described herself as initially worried that Eastern Elite students would be "stuck up" or "snooty" said any apprehensions were swept away when she arrived on campus for an admitted students' weekend. She explained,

I was just floored, just by the caliber of these people that we were surrounded by. They were just so amazing. I was like, "These are the peers that I would love to be surrounded with." . . . I just was really impressed with how approachable the students were and how they kind of blew away any stereotypes I had, just in what you hear of Eastern Elite. (Tabitha Lanier, Eastern Elite)

Interest in joining this special community of exceptional students and faculty thus appeared to be the main factor in our respondents' desire to attend Eastern Elite—that and the payoff their credential would bring later. Whether formally via its exceptional academics or informally by providing access to a pool of talented peers who are not only impressive now but who can be anticipated to have high profiles in the future, it seems that for these students, Eastern Elite's reputation is seen as well deserved.

The possibilities inherent in admission to Eastern Elite likewise mean that these aspects of its reputation outweigh characterizations of it among conservatives as a liberal, even godless bastion of left-wing, relativist ideas.[21] Though most interviewees said they were aware of this reputation, it mattered less in their decision making than did the other reasons for attending Eastern Elite. For some this seemed to be a general consideration in choosing colleges to apply to rather than one specific to Eastern Elite. As one student said, "My criteria was academic rigor and was not related to a political litmus test" (Calvin Coffey, Eastern Elite). Others, though, talked more specifically about weighing what they had heard about Eastern Elite's politics against its other virtues:

For me it was more of a, like what's the school's academic reputation that would bring me there? So my family is not overly political, my community is not overly political, it's not like I was thinking I'm coming from this small town [in the South] where everybody votes the way I do and how am I going to fare in this liberal faction of evil? . . . I've always had friends that are of different political beliefs. . . . Probably everybody has—like, you don't live in some cloister, and so it wasn't, the political bent of the school really wasn't something that factored into my opinion. (Staci Congdon, Eastern Elite)

Similar to most Western Flagship interviewees, then, Eastern Elite respondents did not seem to have been overly concerned with the campus's political climate in making the decision to apply or attend. At both schools, students wanted the best they could get—one of the world's best universities (Eastern Elite), a premiere public institution with a reputation for recreation and affordability (Western Flagship)—and they prioritized those respective criteria rather than the schools' suspected political tendencies. Though the liberal reputation seems to have been already assumed by our interviewees at Eastern Elite (they had, after all, been aware of the conservative critique in the national ether), esteem for the university's incomparable educational opportunities and the possibilities for making connections with outstanding peers and its alumni/ae network appear to have been more influential in their decision making. As one interviewee explained, though he had heard Eastern Elite was liberal, "I had sort of taken it with a grain of salt. Like, well, you know, whatever. I certainly wasn't coming to Eastern Elite—I should stress this—with some kind of a battle mentality" (Vincent Long, Eastern Elite).

SOCIAL LIFE

Though in theory, the purpose of college is to provide students with academic knowledge, increase their complex reasoning skills, and prepare them for active participation both in the public sphere and in the labor force, in reality, much of what goes on in the life of the campus does not occur within classroom walls. When students initially arrive as freshmen, it is not academics but the social aspects of college life that they encounter first—moving into dormitories, engaging in orientation activities, meeting other new students. In many ways, orientation begins students' informal education, what some have termed outside-the-classroom learning.[22] Then, through many ongoing informal interactions over the years in dining halls, dorms, apartments, or at social gatherings, undergraduates get a sense of what it means to be a student at their university—its shared norms and values and practices—and what is taken for granted as appropriate behavior among their peers. The college or university itself furthers this outside-the-classroom learning, not only by facilitating it in different ways (for example, by providing on-campus housing to a certain percentage of students or by funding a large variety of student clubs) but also by hosting nonacademic student events such as orientations, all-campus parties and festivals, and athletic competitions. In this way, we see campuses' organizational arrangements, or their structural features, creating opportunity spaces that implicitly encourage certain types of interactions among students while discouraging others. Though students can bend the formal and informal rules and can create new spaces for themselves, both formal campus structures and more informal peer group arrangements make some kinds of social life more easily accessible than others.

Undergraduates arriving at Western Flagship and Eastern Elite find themselves on campuses that are arranged in quite different ways. From their first encounters with their campuses and peers during orientation, students at Western Flagship and at Eastern Elite begin learning how their school works on the day-to-day level. Whereas Western Flagship students are plunged into a sea of fellow freshmen, swimming relatively blindly through university bureaucracies and impersonal crowds, Eastern Elite first-years are invited into a close-knit community that quickly builds a sense of "we"-ness. The differences between the social arrangements on these campuses contribute to the variance we see between Western Flagship and Eastern Elite conservatives' perceptions of their universities and their peers, and further, as we will see in the following chapters, contribute to their sense of what constitutes appropriate conservative styles of action on their campuses.

GETTING LOST AND FINDING FRIENDS AT WESTERN FLAGSHIP

Incoming freshmen arriving on the Western Flagship campus find themselves quickly swallowed up in the enormous size of the university. While freshmen arrive a week earlier than returning students for a welcome week of orientation activities where they can meet other first-year students, attendance is not required, and no one checks whether a new student participates or not. It's easy for freshmen to feel lost in the swirl of massive organized activities such as barbecues and pep rallies. For many students, the campus size makes finding a social niche early in one's college career imperative:

> I think in Western Flagship a lot of kids choose to identify with a sport or with the Greek system. . . . They choose to identify with a speech and debate team, a political organization. Because I think on a campus of that size, if you don't find somewhere to fit in, you're not going to meet people. (Lindsey Nicholson, Western Satellite)

> Well my freshmen year I had no idea, I didn't know anybody when I was coming here. . . . I was having trouble meeting people. I was in a dorm room where it was a lot of music and theater majors. And they were all extremely close from the beginning and I didn't really find a good niche in their group. So my mom and dad were like, "Go join some clubs, go try some different activities." And this one [College Republicans] was like, "Well, I know I'll have something in common with these people if I go to this meeting." (Brooke Gerson, Western Flagship)

As the first quotation implies, for many students the answer to a large campus environment is to turn to the Greek system. Though only 16 percent of Western Flagship students are officially involved in fraternities and sororities, a much larger proportion participates in that system's parties, and the social scene at the school revolves in large part around Greek events. This undoubtedly contributes to Western Flagship's broader reputation as a party school.

The conservative students we interviewed described varying degrees of fit with the wider undergraduate world at Western Flagship from their first year on. They characterized their peers as conforming to more or less two sets of stereotypes—the pot-smoking, laid-back hippies or the hard-drinking, party-hearty Greeks—which we see in interviewees' descriptions of the ways they personally did or did not fit with what they saw as "typical" Western Flagship students.

I'd say a lot, such as I drive a truck, I don't drive a Subaru [*laughs*]. So I get looked at for that. A camo hat most of the time, and I get looked at [for] that. Just things like that. . . . I don't enjoy marijuana like most kids do here. . . . And I'm not really a California guy like all the frat guys. I don't really fit in with *that* crowd. So I would say out of place in a lot of things. (Kurt Tatum, Western Flagship)

I mean, don't get me wrong. I hang out with them and all, and I listen to the same music as they do. I mean, besides politics and religion I fit in very well. I mean, I'm not a hippy, but I do fit in kind of well with them. I do all the same things that they do. If you're going to let politics overshadow everything that you do, then you're not going to have very many friends. So I don't mind them that much. (Kody Aronson, Western Flagship)

Like Kody, several other conservative students on the Western Public campuses described themselves as being friends with what they thought of as the great mass of non-conservative students at their university, an association that, in their formulation, was as often a matter of necessity as of choice:

I had no choice [*laughs*]. I mean, honestly, if I wanted only Republican friends I wouldn't have friends! (Brittany Urban, Western Satellite)

You know, I love it and I love the people I've come across. I have friends that are very liberal and I have friends that are conservative, more liberal than conservative because obviously the demographics tell us that.... [Without liberal friends] I'd be very lonely. (Kevin Sharkey, Western Flagship)

It would therefore be a mischaracterization to say that Western Public conservatives uniformly vilify their "liberal" peers. In fact, because of shared recreational and musical tastes, conservative interviewees reported that they had some social common ground with liberal classmates, although they also intimated that in a bid to keep the peace with their roommates or friends, they mostly did not talk about politics with them.

Despite these forms of sociability, Western Public, and especially Western Flagship, conservatives also reported feeling politically isolated on their campus. Though the student body at Western Flagship is not as homogeneously liberal as the above characterizations make it sound, there is truth to our interviewees' perceptions of being in an ideological minority. As we recall from chapter 2, UCLA HERI data on public flagship universities most like Western Flagship show that there are more self-identified liberals than conservatives enrolled in these schools (35.6 percent liberal compared to 20.1 percent conservative), though of course there are even more moderates than liberals (44.3 percent of incoming freshmen call themselves middle of the road)—so it is not clear whether our conservative respondents were assuming that middle-of-the-road students are also dyed-in-the-wool lefties. Whatever the precise basis of their calculations—though certainly the national conservative organizations' mantra of "liberal campuses" has a lot to do with it—our interviewees perceived that they were surrounded by liberals, and they said this was problematic.

Western Flagship conservatives reported feeling uncomfortable on campus, saying that they were both isolated and marginalized. One officer of the College Republicans said, "I know of a lot of students who are conservative who just don't speak at all. And they tell me, 'I'm just too intimidated because everybody's either going to look at me or think I'm an idiot or laugh at me'" (Hunter Devine, Western Flagship). Others told us that liberal students held ridiculous assumptions about them, engaged in ad hominem attacks, and made wild-eyed claims. One student reported,

> I don't want to say all of them because it's not really true, it's not as bad as it really sounds. But it's definitely there and you definitely feel it when you're further on the conservative side, I think. We're the big bad wolf.... At least that's the way I feel ... and I don't know why it is because, I mean, I'm not a bad person. I just have different views. The big bad wolf—we're *not* the big bad wolf. (Kurt Tatum, Western Flagship)

Another student recalled that "When I said that I supported Sarah Palin in one of my classes, another student called me a cunt" (Brooke Gerson, Western Flagship), and a recent graduate said, "I don't know how many times I've been called a fascist" (Neil Thompson, Western Flagship). Others who were visibly identified as "not liberal" said they are treated like foreigners on their campus, as per this ROTC cadet:

> R: There's also the people who have told me that I'm a "baby killer," which is like, "Okay...."
> I: Other students, you mean?
> R: Other students, yes.... Just the general anti-soldier statements. And the feeling that I am not welcome. (Eric Leonard, Western Flagship)

In these and other examples, right-leaning students at Western Flagship said they had a strong sense of being on the political margins of their university. As chapter 5 demonstrates, the confrontational style used by right-leaning students at Western Flagship is in part a bid to expressively counter what they see as the social stigma associated with being conservative on their campus.

Before we get to that analysis, however, it is important to look at the structural features of the campus scene that amplify conservative students' sense of being alone in a vast wilderness of liberals run amok. For one, the Western Public campuses offers few university-facilitated organizational opportunities (especially when compared to the abundance of such organizations at Eastern Elite) for students of differing political persuasions to sit down and talk with one another about their political ideas and beliefs. That leaves partisan speakers' events, students' political tabling to recruit members at the student union, and other relatively anonymous settings where liberals and conservatives can more or less sling mud at one another as the prime sites of idea exchange. It also renders conservative student groups the primary locations for right-leaning students to act and speak politically, meaning that when conservative students at Western Public do find themselves politically engaged— whether in an informal conversation or at a planned event—there is a much greater sense of hardened right versus left, or red versus blue, than there is a mutual recognition of shared experiences or affinities.[23] Conservative students share their war stories of marginalization with one another in these clubs and cement their sense of being outsiders.

In addition, conservatives' perceptions of being socially isolated are shaped by the residential situation on the Western Public campuses. For example, while all freshmen at Western Flagship are guaranteed on-campus housing, and 90 percent of them live in suite-style arrangements or more traditional dormitories with randomly selected (and therefore more heterogeneous) others their first year, upperclassmen do not have this housing option. Nor do students at Western Flagship say they would *want* it. Virtually no upperclassmen—save a small number of students who work as resident assistants—live in the dorms. Instead, they live off campus in less expensive apartments or Greek housing, where they no doubt come into less regular informal contact with classmates who have different ideological orientations. As studies of peer groups in both K–12 and higher education have indicated, when students are allowed to self-select into groups of their own choosing, the result is greater social homogeneity than when students are placed by others (such as teachers or administrators) into groups.[24] One well-known consequence of self-selected homophily is that boundaries between groups grow more rigid, with a stronger sense of the difference between who "we" are and who "they" are.[25] By extension, because so few students at Western Flagship live on campus, where they could get to know one another in more intimate settings, there emerge many strongly bounded, small, mutually exclusive groups—rendering students outside one's own group as a relatively anonymous mass. This creates ideal conditions for a fairly weak set of community norms for respectful political discussions across the ideological spectrum, potentially explaining both liberals' and conservatives' shots at one another. While conservative students reported that they enjoyed social lives with liberal-identified classmates, we saw little evidence that they had much opportunity to talk seriously about politics with those "on the other side"—likely ratcheting up the animosity on campus for both groups.

BECOMING ONE OF "US" AT EASTERN ELITE

Eastern Elite students encounter an almost diametrically opposed social experience from the moment they set foot on campus for orientation their first year. In terms of sheer numbers, there are many fewer freshmen—about 1,800 of them at Eastern Elite (out of a total undergraduate student body of 7,000) versus 5,500 freshmen at Western Flagship—but it's more than simply a matter of how many or how few students attend events. Each orientation week event thrown by Eastern Elite is specifically designed to make freshmen feel truly embraced. For example, during one event, new students watch highly adorned faculty, upperclassmen, and alumni/ae parade by just for them. Each year following orientation, the university surveys freshmen to find out what, if anything else, they could have done to make them feel even *more* at home. Freshmen are made to feel that they are being welcomed into a community that is now their own; Not just *theirs*, but *ours*.

Four-year on-campus housing continues the process of community-building. Historian Julie Reuben reminds us that dorm life has long been understood by elite university administrators to be a key feature in molding students' lives to the institution. She quotes an early Stanford University president Ray Lyman Wilbur, who in the first part of the twentieth century wrote that "when students are housed together there is developed a strong cooperative sense of loyalty and enthusiasm called 'college spirit' which has a profound effect upon the development of the character of the students and upon the welfare of the institution.'"[26] Thrown together seemingly randomly their freshman year, but allowed to select roommates for their subsequent time on campus, undergraduates at Eastern Elite are housed together all four years in college, which creates a sense of community throughout their college careers. Unlike at the Western Public campuses, at Eastern Elite it is unnecessary to live off campus. Yes, rental costs in the community surrounding Eastern Elite are more expensive, but on the whole, students *want* to remain in university housing.[27] Because of shared living arrangements and dining halls connected to dorms where most students choose to eat daily, undergraduates at Eastern Elite forge tight bonds with one another. With all this close contact within a relatively small student body, students at Eastern Elite, unlike those at Western Public universities, have a feel for one another. If you don't know the name, there's a decent chance you'll at least recognize the face.

Joining a conservative club is thus not as much of a social imperative for finding social connection as it is for right-leaning students at a larger school like Western Flagship. Nonetheless, Eastern Elite offers an impressive array of co-curricular activities and recreational opportunities, which the school's ambitious students take hold of with gusto. There are 300 official organizations on campus at Eastern Elite, 12 of which by our count are explicitly political. Eastern Elite's administration strongly maintains that the political ideology of an organization is never a factor in deciding its suitability for funding (and our interviewees told us they also believe this is true), so undergraduates on campus have rich opportunities to get to know a wide range of their fellow students well. Our interviewees expressed considerable enthusiasm for Eastern Elite's extracurricular programs:

I really liked the extracurricular climate here. I loved it. It's so vibrant and so alive. Everyone does some type of extracurricular activity. People love being active outside of just their schoolwork, although that does suck up a lot of time. But yeah, I really liked this campus most in an extracurricular sense. (Shannon Yaffe, Eastern Elite)

One thing I did like about Eastern Elite is they did get people, at least extracurricular that were into all different types of things. And in a typical weekend I could go to the football game, but then an a capella show and then a tap show. . . . People were all into different things and so there was no . . . one thing I really liked about Eastern Elite, there was no one dominant social scene, whereas I feel that, like at [another] school, like a lot of Greek life or something, then you're either in that scene or not. And I kind of like Eastern Elite because everybody could do their own thing. (Kingsley Griffith, Eastern Elite)

Although Eastern Elite has no Greek life, it does have a system of highly selective, invitation-only clubs that go back several generations and that are comparable to social fraternities in terms of both their means of admission and their social function on campus. However, the vast majority of students does not belong to or have much to do with these old boys' clubs. Ballpark estimates from a variety of sources put the participation figure at somewhere between 5 and 10 percent.[28]

Like their Western Public counterparts, Eastern Elite conservatives characterize the student body as politically left. And like Western Flagship conservatives, they are undoubtedly correct in their estimates of more liberals than conservatives on campus: as we saw in chapter 2, UCLA HERI data show that at private elite institutions like Eastern Elite, even more students than at public, highly selective institutions self-identify as liberal or far left; in 2001, that figure was 48.7 percent.[29] Despite being further outnumbered by liberals on their campus, however, and in stark contrast to Western Public students, conservatives at Eastern Elite University are generally more sympathetic to their peers. Rather than stereotyping them as stoners, partiers, or name-callers, Eastern Elite conservatives see their liberal classmates as being for the most part not especially different from themselves. For example, one woman who described Eastern Elite as liberal (but not as liberal as she had thought it might be) characterized her classmates as follows:

> I mean it's interesting because I think there is a lot of [*sigh*] limousine liberalism at Eastern. . . . This is actually changing in the lower classes here; they've really drastically expanded the financial aid here, and stuff like that. And in the freshman and sophomore classes, there are much higher rates of people on financial aid. But most of my friends are people who sort of went to private school in Manhattan. So even though they're basically all liberal, it's not like their liberalism causes them a whole bunch of kind of different. . . . Or there's not as much, there isn't as much attention paid to the normal sort of buzz words that are associated with liberal causes. Like there's not among my friends. (Molly Nash Downing, Eastern Elite)

Molly's distinction is similar to that made by conservative pundit Ross Douthat in his memoir of attending Harvard University, *Privilege: Harvard and the Education of the Ruling Class*, where he describes such students as "parlor liberals," as opposed to the type of liberal student akin to those discussed by Western Public's conservatives, which Douthat terms "street liberals."[30]

Other students describe this less as a difference springing from the type of student that Eastern Elite attracts and more as part of the nature of Eastern Elite itself:

> I think one is that there are just so many opportunities for bipartisan dialogue. . . . We analyze these political issues on a very academic level. I think, two, it's just so many activities going on. It's just the nature of the Eastern Elite campus. People are involved in opera, choir, or whatever. Politics is just one dimension of daily life. And I think it's an often forgotten dimension of campus life. And I think, third, it's just we come to the realization

that I'm not going to change *your* views and you're not going to change *my* views, so why try so hard to do that? So I have to think about that more, but also the fact that I'm friends with a lot of people in the Democrats ... I know everyone in the College Democrats. We go out for ice cream, we joke, we talk. After a while that civility just develops. (Kyle Lee, Eastern Elite)

Just as the structural features of the campus at Western Flagship have consequences for what it feels like to be a conservative student there, so too the organizational dynamics at Eastern Elite affect students' political experiences at their university—although we see this going the other direction. Several of the informal dimensions of Eastern Elite life described above, particularly the wealth of on-campus housing and dining, contribute to the way that "civility just develops." Even as Eastern Elite students self-select into student-run groups (as do those at Western Public), in a larger sense they are kept together as part of a larger college community. This spatial closeness both encourages more frequent interactions and discourages students of whatever political stripe from alienating students of other stripes. At the same time, more formal elements of Eastern Elite campus life also provide spaces explicitly for bipartisan political discussion. Its Center for Political Institutions invites well-known public figures from both sides of the political spectrum to address its membership, while also hosting informal debates between Eastern Elite students. In this way, the university administration demonstrates a commitment to fostering mutual understanding and allocating equal resources regardless of ideology.[31]

These institutional qualities produce distinctive results for Eastern Elite undergraduates who identify as right-leaning. On the one hand, their constant exposure to their peers and the openness of informal discussions means that unlike at Western Public, conservative students seem to have a relatively easy time finding and connecting with one another. As one student observed, "I think just kind of keeping your ear to the ground during conversations with friends, I kind of ran into people who I didn't realize shared my views just by kind of listening to conversations in the lunchroom and things like that" (Melissa Preston, Eastern Elite). This is different from the Western Public campuses, where several conservative students said they felt pressure to hide their views for fear of being considered a conservative "big bad wolf," and thus had a difficult time finding fellow travelers in informal social situations. One Western Flagship interviewee described this problem as conservatives on his campus needing a covert "handshake" (Eric Leonard, Western Flagship). Only one Eastern Elite interviewee expressed a similar level of discomfort, saying that

> I would definitely never, at say even a table with eight of my good friends in my dorm, I'd never say I voted for John McCain or something like that, because it just would. . . . I mean, one, it's just not really a socially appropriate thing to do. And two, I know that probably all of them didn't. (Staci Congdon, Eastern Elite)

This young woman's views are the exception rather than the rule, however—and she tended to keep her conservative views more on the down-low than most of our other interviewees. Nearly all other Eastern Elite conservatives characterized themselves as having more or less unproblematic relationships with left-leaning friends.

Further, for Eastern Elite students it seems that friendships with liberals are not only a question of numbers or convenience, as conservative students at Western Public often characterized them. Rather than talking about being friends with peers with different political views because they *have* to, Eastern Elite conservatives more often describe having left-leaning friends because they *want* to. One interviewee from a humble background explained at length the cosmopolitan virtues of having friends of varying political opinions:

> I think you have to have a lot of friends who aren't [conservative] if you're a conservative-view Republican, if you're a Christian. I mean, you're going to have friends who do not believe in the same thing as you do on Eastern's campus. And I mean that's good, that's a very good thing. I wouldn't want to have friends who are only like me. I mean at the same time I have my . . .

probably some of my best friends are in my Christian Bible study here, because we know so much about each other and we've grown so close. But my roommates are not, two out of the three of them, are not Christian. They're also my best friends here. I mean, there's not an overwhelming amount of Christians here [*laughs*], and so. . . . I mean what's the point anyway of only having certain kind of friends. That just defeats the purpose of Eastern Elite's diversity. (Shannon Yaffe, Eastern Elite)

Shannon's comment clearly echoes some of the Western Public interviewees' comments (basically: I'd be lonely here if I didn't reach out to people who don't believe everything I do), but in a larger sense, Shannon was saying something different. She said the social scene at Eastern Elite encourages all students, not just conservative ones, to mix, mingle, and meet as many different peers as they can.

From one perspective, this can be instrumental. As is pointed out to them from orientation through graduation day, Eastern Elite students are the cream of the crop and headed for great things, and thus their tenure as undergraduates can be seen as an extended opportunity for networking. The classmates they find common ground with today, including the liberal ones, will be the people they may be working with, in some fashion or another, tomorrow (a perspective we definitely do not see shared at Western Flagship). Even if Eastern Elite did not have such an outstanding reputation, the constant closeness that is forged by students' living, eating, studying, and socializing together generates bonds that make each student a visible member of the community. Unlike on the Western Public campuses, at Eastern Elite anonymity is not only not a given, it's hardly even an option.

ACADEMICS

Academics is the core mission of colleges and universities, at least officially, even if undergraduates in the aggregate are studying and learning less (by some measures) now than they did in the past.[32] But however much undergraduates are actually acquiring academic skills, students would not be able to enjoy the social trappings of the "college experience" without going through a course of study that provides the structure for their college years.[33] While the main purpose of classroom learning is enrichment—exploring the fundamentals in a field, gaining critical thinking and complex reasoning skills—college courses also teach students plenty that is not contained on the syllabus. Rather than simply looking at what is officially taught in the curriculum, we may also consider the university classroom or lecture hall as an interactional space where students continue to learn the values, norms, and informal rules governing life on their campus. The actions of individual faculty members and other students certainly play a role here, but so too do the organizational arrangements of the university. How students choose their majors, what classes students are required to take to fulfill their distribution requirements, and how individual classes are set up all have an impact on students' perceptions of their place within the university.

In chapters 5 and 6 we examine how conservative students actively negotiate the classroom environment; here we look at how academics "works" at Western Flagship and Eastern Elite. As with social experiences, students at these two universities encounter quite different organizational arrangements regarding their formal education. Western Public students choose majors before they even matriculate and are plugged into an impersonal registration system, while Eastern Elite undergraduates enjoy the freedom to explore different courses before deciding on a particular path of study. These differences in levels of attention to the individual student continue inside the classroom. As we will begin to see here, and explore fully in the chapters that follow, this variation in institutional arrangements furthers Western Public and Eastern Elite conservatives' divergent opinions of their professors, their peers, and even themselves. Classroom experiences also reinforce students' understanding of the campus climate and how to negotiate being politically conservative in such a place. What we find, in short, is that several seemingly little things—

organizational features not ordinarily recognized as having any impact whatsoever on politics—in fact can have major consequences for students' sense of fit with their campus.

IMPERSONAL BUREAUCRACIES AND POLITICIZED CLASSROOMS AT WESTERN FLAGSHIP

Though Western Flagship's reputation is not built primarily on students' intellectual endeavors, academic study remains an important component of day-to-day student life. As at most large public universities, however, academic arrangements at Western Flagship are largely impersonal.[34] This sense of being a number rather than a face begins even before students arrive on campus, as incoming students must choose majors before they have ever taken a college course. Although students can change majors later, this is more easily said than done, as between major requirements and the university's general education requirements, making a significant alteration in one's course of study can result in an additional semester or year needed at the university, putting a dent in one of Western Flagship's main appeals, its affordability.[35]

Further, unlike at private institutions, where students have a better chance of getting into classes they want, when they want them, or even have weeks to "try out" several different classes at the beginning of the term, students at Western Flagship face a depersonalized registration system with little room for negotiation. They end up in classes they don't prefer or hanging in limbo on wait lists for classes they need. At Western Flagship, students register for classes online before each semester, having received a registration time based on the last two digits of their student identification number. Priority registration times are given based on class standing, athletics, and academic honors, with all other registration times determined by lottery. There are no guarantees for majors, meaning again that students may wind up needing extra time to complete their undergraduate education as they wait for space in courses they need to finish their degree.

Most classes at Western Flagship are large lecture courses. This style of teaching, which predominates at public universities, can strongly depersonalize faculty-student relationships both in and outside the classroom.[36] Many students complain that the bulk of their undergraduate years is spent in large lecture halls that are fairly anonymous, where professors are harder to connect with, and in which every student knows his or her teaching assistant significantly better than the professor—that is, for the students who go to discussion sections or review sessions.[37] The campuses of the Western Public university system provide few opportunities for undergraduates to be in smaller, more personalized classes; in fact, the few organizational opportunities for being in smaller seminar settings, such as Western Flagship's honors program, are largely disdained by most undergraduates as being overly academic, "not cool," and a strain because they remove students from the ordinary swing of things on their campus, at least according to one faculty member at Western Flagship who works with the honors college (Kim Kellog, Western Flagship).

Like most universities in today's higher education world, Western Flagship requires students to fulfill not only the requirements of a major but also to get academic breadth through a core curriculum, which at Western Flagship covers the social sciences, the humanities, the natural sciences, math, and a "diversity" course. As is the case at most large public universities, the set core, or general education, classes are generally larger and reputably less enjoyable than classes taken for electives or for major requirements and, as other educational researchers have documented, are viewed by most students as something "to get out of the way" or as "jumping through the hoops."[38] This is different from the general education requirements at Eastern Elite, which allow students to choose individual seminars that fit these different distribution areas rather than take prescribed survey courses.

At Western Flagship, it is in the general education courses that many students first become acquainted with academic thinking on topics like economic stratification, gender inequality, and racial diversity, which means that it is also in the general education courses that many conservative students experience their most consternation with "liberal" concerns. As one alumnus described, other viewpoints are not included in this curriculum:

> I mean, if you look at the . . . and especially you're not going to get that in, you're not going to get any sort of contrary view in the Department of Education, a lot of the Philosophy Department, Ethnic Studies. Are you kidding me? Is there any curriculum at all in some of these Women's Studies classes about maybe feminism has backfired on the movement? Not even, I mean you could still teach a Women's Studies class that comes out on one side or the other, probably properly so, but when are you going to read more than *an* article by Christina Hoff Sommers that gets stuck into the reading curriculum so you can *mock* it? (Chuck Kelley, Western Flagship)[39]

While conservative students can try to avoid contentious material by choosing their majors carefully (as one student said of his field of study, "the engineering school is very . . . these are the numbers, do the math, and there's the answer"; Eric Leonard, Western Flagship), their inability to get out of general education requirements often means exposure to ideas they find disagreeable. This is not to say that they object completely to learning about topics like gender and race but rather that most claim the presentation of these areas is skewed and does not include alternative—usually right-identified—points of view.

What is ignited in conservatives on a campus with large class sizes, purportedly skewed core curricula, and an impersonal registration system is a more pessimistic view of professors and of the campus in general. While both campuses are home to a large majority of faculty who vote Democratic and identify as liberals, as Neil Gross's recent research has indicated, conservative students on the Western Public campuses are considerably more suspicious of their professors' motives in the classroom than are their peers at Eastern Elite.[40] This finding about Western Public students' higher suspicion levels of their professors also squares with research that demonstrates that students with less academic preparation and who have parents with lower educational attainments have more negative assessments of faculty.[41] As we saw in chapter 2, students at schools like Western Flagship in the aggregate have lower SAT scores as well as parents with lower educational attainments than do students at Eastern Elite, so Western Flagship students may share in a more generalized culture of complaint about "distant" faculty. It is therefore likely that both campus features and selection effects lead to greater criticism of faculty.

While both Western Public and Eastern Elite conservatives characterize faculty as personally liberal, Western Public interviewees are far likelier to contend that their professors bring those personal politics into the classroom, or to describe negative experiences they themselves or their acquaintances have had with faculty, such as feeling they had to wordsmith written assignments so as not to betray their views and receive a punitive grade. Describing an instance when a faculty member called her out for an editorial she'd written in the local paper, one Western Satellite interviewee said,

> I would say that the single thing that stands out in my mind is that professors completely control the atmosphere of the classroom. They control the discussion, they control where it goes and when it stops. And in this case it stopped before I had the chance to defend myself. And I would say that was probably on purpose. (Lindsey Nicholson, Western Satellite)

Besides faculty, graduate student teaching assistants (TAs) also come in for a good deal of criticism from Western Public students: many of our interviewees asserted that TA-led discussion sections were absolute nightmares, since graduate students (or in some cases advanced undergraduate students) were seen to be unrestrained by professional norms and thus comfortable forcing their liberal politics on a captive audience. One interviewee talked extensively about negative experiences with TAs:

> I would have teaching assistants that would like say really bad things about the Republican Party in my discussion section, and

that was hard. I was [like] "You're grading my papers." . . . I had a negative experience with a TA that just talked horribly about Bush or just about conservative viewpoints or things that were . . . we got into a lot of political discussions, and so when the person facilitating the discussion doesn't respect your opinion or your belief, that can be . . . that's really hard. . . . It was a hard semester because you really have to trust these people, to really share what you believe in those small-group discussions. And that's hard. (Christina Young, Western Flagship)

Students in the Western Public system thus more frequently accused faculty and TAs of politicizing the classroom, although even here most students said the majority of their campus experiences were fine. But where (as we will see below) Eastern Elite students regarded professors as serious scholars who would not think to sully their classrooms with ideological posturing, conservative students on the Western Public campuses were quicker to point to examples that they said revealed how faculty allowed politics to enter the classroom, as well as to occasions when their grades seemed to be at risk.

Western Public interviewees also pointed to particular incidents of faculty members visibly making them feel like social and political outliers. The student quoted above described a course in which the professor singled her out, asking her "Why don't *you* speak for the conservatives?" or "Why don't *you* shed some light on the other side?" (Christina Young, Western Flagship). In many other instances, though, students on Western Public's campuses recalled examples of faculty introducing liberal points of view or politically charged topics when these were not relevant to the classroom discussions:

And you know, if I'm taking a macroeconomics class, I want to learn about economics, not about how horrible the Bush administration is—all semester long. And for me, it is a complete turnoff. . . . I'm open to criticism and to hearing criticism about things that maybe I support. But when you only focus on those criticisms, there's a problem. For example, in the class . . . when we were starting to get into the early race for the presidential candidates, it was always focused on "Oh, let's talk about the Democratic candidates." Let's give some air time to the *other* guys, too. Like, this isn't even the foreign policy class or political science class. And I understand that they are intertwined to a certain degree with macroeconomics, but let's get to the core of the topic. (Kevin Sharkey, Western Flagship)

Actually, one of the better classes I've ever taken was the History in Rock 'n' Roll. The professor was intelligent, I mean very bright. It taught me a way to look at music and to look at ideas and dissect them and find out where is the original value in this idea. But I can't tell you how many times we got on the Iraq War or ... and I understand that certain songs have political meaning. But it was—I think he said that democracy is the worst form of government because 51 percent of the people decide. I don't know. These are valid points and they're okay. I don't know. I would just like something in a History in Rock 'n' Roll class, I would rather not talk about why democracy is a terrible form of government. But having said that, I've learned a ton. (Conor Denning, Western State)

Even when conservative students at Western Public schools find classes they enjoy, they are sometimes dismayed by faculty who they say use the classroom or lecture hall as a space to air political views. Other students point out that even when content is relevant to the course, it often has a liberal bent. For example, a few students mentioned the preponderance of readings by the liberal Princeton economist and *New York Times* columnist Paul Krugman in economics classes. As one Western Flagship interviewee characterized it, even in courses where professors were not cracking jokes about George W. Bush, "There's always this tone of, this subtle tone of liberalism that probably at any one point isn't enough to be objectionable. But it's so constant. It's like a constant that it gets on your nerves sometimes" (Hunter Devine, Western Flagship).

Thus, Western Public interviewees found their creeping concerns about the liberal campus to be confirmed in classroom settings. Our conservative respondents on the Western Public campuses described their professors and TAs as not simply liberal but as outspokenly so, bringing their personal political beliefs into the forum of the lecture hall or seminar room. Although we cannot adjudicate because we were not in the classroom with the students and alumni/ae we interviewed, it is possible that the depersonalized setting may in fact encourage this type of behavior by some instructors. When faculty do not know their individual students well, they may breezily assume that the students in the classroom *are* as left-leaning as the campus stereotype would have it, and shoot from the hip at Bush or Romney or some other conservative target. As one respondent commented, "They do stuff that hey, if I was more liberal I'd think that was funny and I'd laugh at that. But I don't think that's very funny" (Samantha Hart, Western Flagship). Or it may also be that in depersonalized environments, students are quicker to interpret faculty as more callous toward them. The more atomized setting may work both ways, distancing conservative students from their professors and bolstering their sense that faculty lord it over them as disempowered undergraduates.

In instances where conservative students talked about having more direct contact with faculty, this seems to have mitigated the divide:

> I found that in some of my classes actually I think the professors respected me more because they didn't really view me as a sheep. So I would start conversations with professors in the middle of class it seemed like sometimes. It was just me and the professor. And so I felt like I actually gained a little bit *more* respect from professors *some* times [*laughs*]. (Kody Aronson, Western Flagship)

Overall, though, given large class sizes, limited one-on-one time with faculty via office hours or other encounters, and some students' unwillingness to speak up or speak out, Western Public conservative students and alumni/ae often perceive their professors as outspokenly, inappropriately liberal and uninterested in hearing al-

ternative viewpoints. These organizational arrangements on the
Western Public campuses not only shape students' dimmer views of
their instructors but also lead many conservative students to want
to engage in provocative political behavior both inside and outside
the classroom.

ENDLESS POSSIBILITIES AND EXPERT
PROFESSORS AT EASTERN ELITE

Unlike at Western Public, students say that academics are a primary
focus at Eastern Elite. Small classes taught by full-time faculty—
with a few large lectures thrown in with high-wattage celebrity professors—mean that undergraduates receive a level of care from professors that is becoming ever rarer at American universities. Rather
than declaring a major when they enter, as many university students
are required to do, Eastern Elite undergraduates enjoy a model
more similar to that of a liberal arts college, where they may dabble
in different fields before committing to one major. Most Eastern
Elite students spend their first two years fulfilling general education
requirements, which they choose from lists of classes in several
broad subject areas (humanities, sciences, writing, and so on). Individual students thus develop their own directions, declaring a major
area of study only at the end of sophomore year. The sense that students are in control is furthered by the way course selection works.
Students enjoy a two-week "trying-out" period at the beginning of
each term when they may sit in on as many classes as they like in
order to decide which to enroll in. On top of that, enrollments are
not capped, so there is even less of a sense of urgency surrounding
which classes to take.

This wealth of educational opportunities provides yet more evidence for the abiding sense Eastern Elite University students share
with one another that theirs is a special campus, a world-class institution, with unparalleled faculty and boasting some of the smartest
students in the nation. Although they believe that faculty members
tilt significantly to the left of the political spectrum, they insist that
the vast majority of Eastern Elite professors are consummate pro-

fessionals—the expression "experts in their field" comes up with some regularity—who do not and indeed *would not* try to indoctrinate students, as per the conservative critique. Eastern Elite students and alumni/ae seem unable to picture their professors as condescending to any Eastern Elite undergraduates, including conservatives, as easy, impressionable targets. Additionally, almost to a person, the conservative students we interviewed were adamant that they had never been penalized for their political views through lowered grades. They didn't see themselves as victims nearly to the extent that Western students did.

These themes were articulated again and again in the interviews with Eastern Elite students. While our conservative interviewees acknowledged their professors' putative left-leaning political beliefs, at Eastern Elite they made a consistent distinction between professional demeanor and personal beliefs.

> If you go to a school such as Eastern Elite, you expect a level of seriousness from your professors. I certainly read a lot of accounts of *other* students who had experienced bias . . . [but that] really wasn't my experience in school, and I was grateful for that. . . . If you polled them, I'm sure most [faculty] probably voted for Barack Obama, and for John Kerry before that, but at least in the courses I took, that did not jaundice in any way their presentation of materials. (Evan Dooley, Eastern Elite)

> I mean you probably know this, but most of the Eastern faculty is very, very liberal. But I have not encountered overwhelmingly liberal faculty in terms of *classroom conduct*. For the most part the faculty that I have encountered . . . have been very willing to not announce their personal political beliefs. In fact, they don't want to. (Elizabeth Tennyson, Eastern Elite)

Eastern Elite respondents understood their professors to be both knowledgeable and professional. While they acknowledged faculty members' likely political leanings, they did not feel this impinged on students' experiences in the classroom. Although we do not have data to substantiate this, it is possible that there are some differ-

ences between Western Public and Eastern Elite faculty. Eastern
Elite faculty, who are highly selected and integrated into the elite
environment, where neither graduate assistants nor adjuncts deliver
lectures (as at less prestigious campuses) and where there are fewer
noncanonical arts-and-science departments on campus that recruit
faculty with weaker past socialization, may make it a greater point
than their Western Public colleagues not to let their politics intrude
into the classroom.[42] Whereas Western Public faculty may—like
their students—be affected by the more anonymous classroom,
Eastern Elite professors may be influenced by the seriousness of elite
education, as well as by the fact that they know their students at a
more personal level. The structural and cultural features of Eastern
Elite should be presumed to work to some extent on faculty as well
as students.

This is not to say, however, that Eastern Elite conservatives' reports of their classroom experiences were rosy without exception.
Some students felt that the atmosphere of mutuality and closeness
of the community can create problems when they lead to assumptions of ideological uniformity:

> It's very uncomfortable when there's a tacit understanding of a
> subject or idea . . . and suddenly you feel, like, yourself shrinking
> back. . . . And then when you add an authority figure to that, it
> just really does change it. I'm 22, and these professors are emi-
> nent heads in their field, and so you really don't feel like you
> could or should challenge this type of belief. (Staci Congdon,
> Eastern Elite)

Though this student clarified that she had suffered no "existential
crisis" over class content, her comment underscores one of the potential problems of a small community that, while based on some
amount of shared status, also contains within it a clear hierarchy of
authority. While Eastern Elite students find faculty members' behavior to be much less egregious than do their colleagues at Western
Public, as the above quotation suggests, their experiences in the
classroom are not entirely unproblematic.

Part of Eastern Elite conservatives' easier experience, however, may be explained by their avoidance of particular classes, majors, and programs—particularly those identified broadly with multiculturalism and ethnic/gender studies—and a tendency to choose more "conservative" courses of study. As described above, the university's registration policy enables undergraduates to try out various courses before they commit to them, which allows conservative students to more easily avoid classes or professors whom they might find distasteful. As one student explained:

But it's also, like, I've never taken a Critical Gender Studies class, for instance. If you take a Critical Gender Studies class you know what you're getting into. . . . And so maybe I have avoided those classes. . . . I think part of it is that a lot of the courses that I've taken have been kind of removed from those themes. (Molly Nash Downing, Eastern Elite)

Students can be particularly critical when they feel curricula stray too far from classical texts, especially in the humanities and social sciences, as this alumnus—a gay man who described himself as interested in the content of the course—reported:

I took a class on Intro to Gay and Lesbian Studies. . . . [The professor] gave us like articles about lesbians fisting gay men, and all this just like *shit*, that I would really take her to task on. I'd be like, "You could really have given us *Phaedrus* to read by Plato, or you could have given us Virginia Woolf instead of this fucking article about lesbians fisting gay men!" (Edward Ingle, Eastern Elite)

In other words, some interviewees seemed to be saying it was a real shame that some faculty choose to stray from time-honored texts and bring in tendentious and flaky content, but they were still experts in their field.

Eastern Elite students' ability to test-drive their courses—as well as the pooling of information among the conservative minority within an already relatively small and close-knit campus community where information circulates easily—helps them steer clear of course content they may find offensive or faculty members whom they consider politically unpleasant. Such avoidance is harder to accomplish at large, public universities such as those of the Western Public system, where course selection is more impersonal and tied to enrollment times and wait lists and where a greater number of majors and classes, as well as a larger student body, makes information sharing of this kind more difficult. Indeed, conservative students at Eastern Elite often hold up their choice of major as a reason they have not encountered issues with their coursework. Among our interviewees, economics, political science, and history were the most popular majors. Interestingly, however, these are also the three most popular majors among Eastern Elite students as a whole, implying that even within these relatively "conservative" fields, right-leaning students are unlikely to be among the majority. This tempers somewhat the conclusion that Eastern Elite conservatives' more positive experiences are solely the result of course selection.

To sum up, we find that Eastern Elite conservative students generally agree that they are not manipulated in the classroom. In both instances, their feelings seem to be very much connected to the idea of Eastern Elite as an exceptional institution, and of themselves, their peers, and their professors as being part of an elite intellectual community. This does not mean that Eastern Elite conservatives issue no objections about their campus. But for the most part, being at this nationally renowned campus seems to temper Eastern Elite conservative students' critiques. Students' belief in the Eastern Elite "brand" seems to mitigate their willingness to tarnish it by complaining too much about—or even *conceiving* of it as—a place where professors lack standards of professionalism.

SUMMARIZING THE DIFFERENCES

In some ways, then, the experiences of students at both Western Public and at Eastern Elite articulate with the conservative critique of higher education: there is a shared sense on both campuses that conservatives are in the minority. In other respects, however, there is considerably less convergence between right-leaning students on these campuses. On the whole, we see conservative students on the Western Public campuses describing experiences that echo more resoundingly with the complaints of right-leaning critics: They believe that the student body and the professoriate are overwhelmingly liberal, and that an atmosphere of ideological conformity prevails on campus. While Eastern Elite conservatives likewise describe their peers and professors as predominantly left-leaning, their experience of this seems to be much less problematic. Eastern Elite students say they embrace the experience of learning alongside their liberal classmates and report that professors' personal ideological commitments rarely impinge on the classroom experience.

We can attribute many of these differences to the varying formal and informal organizational arrangements of these schools. Not just conservative students but all students at these two different universities learn about their place on their campus from their experiences with the campus's academic and social characteristics. While Eastern Elite students come to see themselves as prized members of an influential and elite community, Western Public students have a more isolating experience, and seek to find their own niche within a bureaucratic system that often treats them as little more than a set of transcripts and a student ID number.

THE UPSIDES AND DOWNSIDES TO "MINORITY" STATUS

Still, amid these differences, we also find commonalities. Foremost among these is that both Western Public and Eastern Elite students characterize themselves as being politically part of a minority on campus.[43] This self-understanding has important consequences for students in both university systems, consequences we found—somewhat surprisingly—to be relatively consistent across them. First, conservative students at both the Western Public campuses and

Eastern Elite characterize being in the political minority as having been, in some ways, an empowering experience. Second, and simultaneously, our interviewees at both schools described being in the political minority as generating feelings and experiences of isolation and marginalization. There are thus benefits and drawbacks to being a conservative student on what are popularly considered to be liberal college campuses.[44]

HONING ONE'S ARGUMENTS

Among interviewees in both university systems, we were surprised to find extensive discussions of the benefits that conservative students enjoyed from being in the political minority on their campuses. In contrast to the conservative critique of higher education, students at both Eastern Elite and on the Western Public campuses described their minority status on campus as having positive consequences for their intellectual, emotional, and political growth.[45] Students and alumni/ae on both campuses pointed out that being in what they thought of as a liberal milieu motivated them to strengthen their convictions and sharpen their arguments:

> I'm really glad I did [go to Western Flagship] as opposed to a conservative campus, because this campus has caused me to challenge my beliefs multiple times and I've actually really . . . in the same way that a politician gets . . . like Ronald Reagan made it to the top in California, and that experience of getting through a really liberal election and a liberal state helped him for when he ran for president later. And I really have been able to fine-tune my arguments and my thoughts and my politics as a result of being around so many liberal people. It's really helped me more, I think, than had I gone somewhere where I would have probably become more extreme in my opinions, rather than more moderate. (Hunter Devine, Western Flagship)

> I've been kind of forced to define who I am and to define and to ground and base these opinions in intellectual thought. And it's

been good. I do feel like I'm on the spot a lot and I do feel like I always have to be a little bit on guard. And sometimes life gets a little stressful, and it's like, "Why can't we just stop talking about politics on dates" and "Don't make fun of me." But for the most part it's been very healthy. (Shannon Yaffe, Eastern Elite)

The degree of student consensus across campuses on this point is higher than on almost any other issue discussed in the interviews, a striking counterpoint to many critics' stated anxiety over the welfare of students on today's college campuses where "nobody dissents at all" (John Leo, Manhattan Institute).[46]

Even though being a campus conservative was often experienced as isolating, many interviewees found the experience enriching as well. Notably, several respondents at both universities claimed their minority status had given them a competitive advantage over their liberal classmates. Western Public conservative students castigated other undergraduates who simply drank the faculty's "Kool-Aid" (Conor Denning, Western State) and thus "can't hold an argument as well, [and] ... don't emerge from school being seasoned debaters" (Kayla Shain, Western Flagship). Eastern Elite students similarly characterized their time at the school as an "opportunity to really face the tough questions, because you're going to get those at some point in your life anyway" (Kendall Nelson, Eastern Elite). Other students expressed similar views:

I really sincerely feel that you become a much lazier thinker if you are part of the majority because you just aren't challenged that much. When you're in the minority you have got to do a lot of extra work. I read the newspaper every day, mostly because when you argue with people, if you can have a fact or statistic or an anecdote, that really strengthens your case. So it is kind of like you are studying for a pop quiz that could happen any moment. (Calvin Coffey, Eastern Elite)

Going to school in a place like Western Flagship ... forces conservatives to really be on their toes and to really know their issues.... And so it was always something that if I wanted to believe this or I wanted to support this, I had to be able to back it up. And I found that a lot of times I knew more about an issue because I *had* to. (Stephanie Cohen, Western Flagship)

In this manner, then, conservative students were able to transform their minority status on liberal campuses into a point of pride. This view also presents a point of commonality between interviewees on the Eastern Elite and Western Public campuses, despite their many other differences. Across campuses, these students drew strength from being in the ideological minority, and in spite of the trials they said they'd faced—the "pop quiz that could happen at any moment," for example—none said they would have had a better experience at a more conservative school. As one explained, "I'm not even sure if I would be happy on a conservative campus. There wouldn't be anything to do. Everything would be right" (Devin Daleo, Western Flagship).

ISOLATION AND MARGINALIZATION

At the same time that students offered assessments that being in the political minority generated benefits for them, conservative interviewees from both universities also described feelings of loneliness, isolation, and marginalization in both social and classroom settings. Virtually every one of our respondents referred at least once to the preponderance of liberal faculty and students they encountered in college, and the relative paucity of conservatives. Students from both Eastern Elite and the Western Public campuses talked about this feeling of being in the minority in similar terms:

> At Eastern Elite there is a kind of sense that people wouldn't necessarily talk in class if they were conservative, so there was kind of an underground feeling. (Kingsley Griffith, Eastern Elite)

> In a lot of respects Western Flagship has kind of polarized me because [being conservative is] almost like belonging to a secret

society. . . . I'm sure there's plenty of us out there in reality, but we're just kind of afraid to mention it because it's such a hassle. (Eric Leonard, Western Flagship)

When you were sort of conservative at Eastern, you were a part of this counterculture. And inevitably you just ended up . . . if you're the type of person who wants to discuss politics *at all*, you ended up in many more arguments than the average student, who probably is just kind of generically politically liberal. (Vincent Long, Eastern Elite)

These descriptions of being part of an "underground," "secret society," or "counterculture" demonstrate how conservative students on both campuses shared a sense of themselves as belonging to a minority, and that this can lead to closing oneself off or not openly expressing political opinions. "I felt the need to kind of shut up a lot, like not say anything because I didn't want to outcast myself," explained one Western Satellite interviewee (Brittany Urban, Western Satellite).

When they do not "shut up," students sometimes recall instances where they themselves or others of like mind had peers turn on them:

My roommate a couple, maybe a month ago expressed her opinion that she was going to vote for John McCain. . . . And she was sitting at the dinner table and for an hour a couple of people kind of berated her and said that she was denying children education and she was sending soldiers to their death. And she came back to my room crying because it was like a very traumatizing experience to have people who are your friends saying things like this. So I think that is kind of a decent example of what can happen if, in just a random grouping of Eastern students you announce that you were doing something that probably 90 percent of them weren't doing. (Staci Congdon, Eastern Elite)

It was fellow students. It was the fellow students who were attracted to Western Flagship that outside of the fraternities and the sort of ones who show up to drink and [participate in recreation], sort of the activists on campus are the far left progressive students, so that's who I eventually encountered pretty much on a daily basis. And they were the ones, the peers, were the actual pressure points in terms of applying those kinds of marginalization feelings. Once they know you're conservative or a Republican on campus, you're just a target. (Neal Thompson, Western Flagship)

Experiences of criticism or isolation like these can lead conservative students to feel uncomfortable speaking their minds even, as in the first example, among friends. This fits with other students' descriptions of having to watch out for politically sensitive areas. As another Western Flagship woman said, "Sometimes you have to avoid certain topics, but besides that you can still be friends because they're just topics" (Samantha Hart, Western Flagship).

CONCLUSION

Universities offer students many different possibilities for constructing their identities—both political and otherwise. However, a university's unique organizational arrangements make some outcomes likelier than others. Forging a different path may be difficult, given the practical limitations imposed by major requirements and tuition payments, to give two concrete examples. Describing a campus that is similar to Western Flagship in many ways, Elizabeth Armstrong and Laura Hamilton discuss the "pathways" that are available to students at a large midwestern public university.[47] Like Western Flagship, this campus promotes itself heavily around its Greek party scene and athletics, making these popular draws for affluent students who desire a fun, academically undemanding college experience. At the same time, however, as Armstrong and Hamilton point out, these emphases are not as appropriate for less well-heeled students who are looking for a practical education that will lead to secure employment. Carving out a unique path—as many of our engaged, conservative interviewees wanted to do—is difficult on a campus like Western Flagship, which is largely depersonalized.

At the other end of the spectrum, but in some ways no less confining, Robert Granfield's research looking at Harvard Law School in many ways echoes our findings about Eastern Elite.[48] Granfield describes how incoming law students, from varying backgrounds and with different ideological commitments and reasons for studying law, are socialized into what he terms the school's "collective eminence."[49] From orientation through to job interviews, these law students are told again and again that they are the best of the best, and that there is no need for them to compete with one another because there are spoils enough for all. As Granfield documents, this has consequences for these students' self-understandings and, further, for their career outcomes, as even those who enter with commitments to social justice and public law come to see themselves as candidates for only the very best jobs with large, white-shoe law firms.

Our findings about the cultural and structural features on these different campuses fit well with these other scholars' accounts of institutional campus features—although of course we extend their insights to the case of conservative politics. We find that conservative students share some perceptions and many ideological concerns across campuses, but that the distinctive features of each campus create different experiences with peers, faculty, and the university itself for right-leaning students. In both instances, however, the challenges these conservative students face are not challenges they face alone. Though one person's classroom experience, for example, may feel idiosyncratic or unique to that person, it is likely shared by another conservative student. And so, as this Western Flagship interviewee explained, conservatives on campus say they need to reach out to one another:

> You just feel like you're ideologically very lonely because you go to class after class where everybody's agreeing on things that you don't agree with. And sometimes you just don't have the nerve to speak up about it. And then you're walking down the street and

there are people protesting Bush and there's people protesting the Iraq War and there's people . . . and then there's professors joking about politicians that you admire all the time. And it just wears on you, it probably just wears on you. So it's good to have a few people who you're not afraid of saying, "Can you believe that Professor So-and-So blahblahblah." . . . It's good to get it out and off your chest and talk to other people. (Hunter Devine, Western Flagship)

Given their shared sense of being in the minority, and that in many ways, being politically conservative is not something that is encouraged at these schools, right-of-center students at both Western Public and Eastern Elite believe it is essential to find sympathetic friends with whom they can feel solidarity and from whom they don't feel the need to hide their thoughts or feelings. Conservative students do not believe they can fight all these battles or develop solutions to different problems they face—with professors, with peers, or with the university itself—on their own. Instead, they actively work to develop solutions to the challenges of their campuses and to create pathways of their own with the aid of student-run conservative clubs. As we will see in the following chapters, these provide right-leaning students not only with like-minded peers but also with an informal education in campus politics and what it means to be a conservative on campus—and, perhaps, beyond.

Chapter 5

Provoking Liberals and Campaigning for Republicans

Two Conservative Styles at the Western Public Universities

In this chapter and the following one, we provide answers to one of the central questions posed in chapter 1: What is it about university campuses—which are home to specific constellations of organizational and cultural structures—that make them such important influences on students' political expression? How is it that this influence can be so strong that what it means to *act like* a conservative student—even when ideological concerns are more or less shared across universities—can be so radically different from one campus to the next? Why does life at Eastern Elite University, for example, lead the majority of actively involved conservative undergraduates to settle into a "civilized discourse" style of conservatism while eschewing the confrontational style of activism so popular on the Western Public campuses? Conversely, at Western Public, why is "provocation" so dominant that we find little support for more deliberative discursive styles? In this same line of questioning, why do a handful of conservative students at Eastern Elite risk losing the respect not only of their liberal classmates but also of their conservative peers by using a style of aggressive conservatism we call "highbrow provocation," while at Western Public such a style barely

161

sees the light of day? And (to fill out the fourth and last conservative style we see in evidence at these schools), why do both the Western Public and Eastern Elite campuses have devotees of what we label a "campaigning" style, despite most conservative interviewees' sense that this form of political action is, quite frankly, lame? Finally, what role do the national conservative organizations like the Young America's Foundation (YAF), the Leadership Institute (LI), and the Intercollegiate Studies Institute (ISI) play in this mix? How do the unique forms of expression promoted by the organizations get funneled through groups of conservative students on different campuses?

In these two chapters our answer to this question is simple: it's complicated. Accounting for students' variable uses of these styles is complex because a variety of inputs, on campus and off, matter. At the campus level, not only do general university culture and organizational structures prove important for shaping the styles of conservative students, so too do the interactions that occur inside the specifically right-leaning campus clubs, such as the College Republicans and conservative campus newspapers. While we find that the conservative clubs are the central organizational settings where right-leaning students come together and share their ideas of appropriate political discourse and style—and are the places where they also actually put their ideas into action—the interactions that students have in these clubs already are deeply suffused with the ideas that they have gotten from being a member of the campus at large. That is to say, what it means broadly to be a *student* on a particular campus centrally shapes undergraduates' interpretations in right-leaning clubs of what it means to be a *conservative student* on that campus.

In fact, the university as a whole and the conservative clubs at a more specific level act something like nested organizational cultures, or, in the evocative image that Neil Fligstein and Doug McAdam use to describe fields, Russian matryoshka dolls.[1] Open up the campus level and look at what is considered to be appropriate student expression there, and you see elements of the larger university-wide repertoire refracted in its lower-level parts, like the conservative clubs. It is only once we have located these campuswide structures and meanings—where, for example, Western students place an emphasis on fun and pragmatism, while Eastern students put a premium on being members of a special intellectual community—that it makes analytical sense to interpret the experiences of student members of the conservative clubs that are nested within that larger campus environment. All of this is to say that the formation and maintenance of conservative styles lies inextricably with both levels of campus culture, and always in the context of the larger world of conservatism to which students are exposed. Once we understand the distinctive culture found on the campuses and in the clubs, we have a much easier time understanding how the ideas and tangible resources offered by the national conservative organizations fit comfortably or uncomfortably at different universities.

To show the influence on conservative styles of the different campus organizational and cultural features we just described in chapter 4, we move through a significant amount of evidence in chapters 5 and 6—with most of our findings about Western Public (focusing particularly on Western Flagship) in the former and most of our findings about Eastern Elite in the latter. The chapters have similar templates. We first explore how students "perform" conservatism at each of the two primary case-study universities, offering a good number of examples of the dominant and submerged political styles used in different clubs on each campus. Then, having gotten these descriptions on the table, we seek explanations: *Why* do students use these particular forms of conservative political style and not others? We get our answers to this question in two ways. First we look at students' own accounts of why they use some styles and not others—what methodologists call the "emic" account of action—where we favor allowing students to speak for themselves. When they provide their own analyses of the situation, conservative students at Western Public, for example, provide explanations that are heavy on finger-pointing at liberals. Later in the chapter we put on our "etic" hats, using the social scientist's tool kit to probe more deeply into how students' accounts are influenced by the structural and cultural environments of their campuses. Together, the emic and etic methods of analysis tell us a good deal about the styles of conservatism prevalent in each of our university systems.

Finally, after discussing how students use these styles in the explicitly political sphere, we shift our focus to look at how students adapt these styles to other parts of their lives, particularly in their classroom behavior but also as they begin to think about their career plans. Examining how students transpose these styles from mostly on-campus politics to other social experiences provides evidence for our argument that such styles, while worked out in small-group settings on campus specifically for politics, provide solutions to their "problem" of being a conservative on the wider "liberal campus."

WESTERN FLAGSHIP COLLEGE REPUBLICANS: PROUD TO BE PROVOCATIVE

We begin this analysis with the College Republicans clubs in the Western Public system, with a particular focus on the Western Flagship group (whose Affirmative Action Bake Sale was briefly described at the beginning of chapter 1), which is by far the most vibrant and active of all right-leaning clubs on the campuses of the Western Public university system. Although annual changes in leadership lead to some variation in the degree to which the club chooses to stage controversial events from year to year, the Western Flagship College Republicans club has an unmistakable inclination toward provocative action. This group generally strives to be a visible, vocal, mediaworthy presence on campus both during and outside of their planned events. Even those conservative students who are reluctant to put *their* bodies and reputations on the line for provocative action say that the eye-catching, polemical style of the group is important on a campus like Western Flagship.

Before explaining why this style captures the imaginations and commitment of many conservative students at Western Flagship, it is first important to get a fully fleshed-out understanding of what the provocative style precisely is, and what it feels and sounds like to engage in this style. The following extended quotation gives some of the flavor of what one highly energetic former club president, Chuck Kelley, was able to accomplish during his year at the helm of the Western Flagship College Republicans—though this description is far from the only one that illustrates the clear reverence among conservative students for this form of expression. Although we have abridged the excerpt for readability's sake, it still provides a long laundry list of actions that are aimed (and highly successful) at goading the Left:

Well, we had a bunch of events. . . . We brought Ann Coulter to campus. . . . I thought this was innocuous, [but] we had a form [on our website]. . . . It was the Liberal Bias Button. Click the button and it would send us a report . . . "My professor said *this* in class. Oh my god." . . . And all these reporters were calling us about the stupid Liberal Bias Button. So that was good. And we also had these t-shirts—and I can't lay claim to this because we got the design from [another College Republicans club], but they weren't really using it. It was this great t-shirt. It's this big elephant going crazy on the back of it and it's got like its leg up. And a big star on it, and it says "Join Us Now or Work For Us Later" [*laughs*].

And I would *literally*, I would go out[side] during periods [between classes], and I would just stand there, especially early in the semester. . . . I'd just stand there. I'd say, "Are you tired of your communist professors?" Blah blah blah. And people would either come up and yell at me, or they would go, "Oh, can I have [a flyer]? Can I have a few more?" in whispered tones. So we would do that.

But those were the promotional things. The events we would do? Geez. We had Second Amendment Day, which was out at the [student union] to *demand* that the university [allow guns on campus]. And I would say incendiary things like, "I blame the next campus rape on the [university system administration] for not repealing the gun ban." . . . We got good media coverage out of it. . . . We did Conservative Coming Out Day. I'm sure you can figure out what that's a parody of. . . . People would say, "Oh, I always knew there was something different about me," and "I would sneak into my dad's car and listen to Rush Limbaugh when no one was watching." We did that. We did Free Market Earth Day where we barbequed and celebrated tasting animals. Celebrating the Bounty of the Earth I think is what we were calling it. We did that on Earth Day. (Chuck Kelley, Western Flagship)

In addition to all of these events, designed to get under the skin of his purportedly humorless liberal targets, it was also Chuck and his clubmates who staged the first Affirmative Action Bake Sale at Western Flagship—an event that was repeated with just as much enthusiasm, if somewhat less success, a couple of years later under the auspices of another College Republicans president. When asked about his inspiration for staging the Bake Sale and what reaction he had been anticipating, Chuck told us about a Bake Sale he had heard about "in California," and told us that he loved the event because it perfectly illustrated how liberals "just can't control themselves in some of these situations," as well as how the Western Flagship administration refuses to protect the free speech of conservatives:

It was funny. A lot of them had white tape, they got like white duct tape at Home Depot, and they put it over their mouths as a symbol, of course, of the white oppression that was silencing them. Whatever! But they couldn't control themselves! So a lot of them would take the tape off and yell at us, and then they'd stick the tape back on! [*laughs*]. And they would stand there . . . and they created like a ring around our table and they weren't letting people through.

I went to the administration and I said, "Look . . . I have no problem with them being here, I *want* them here. But at the same time, you have to at least allow people free passage into and out of this area." And [the administrator] goes, "There's nothing I can do about it. I'm sorry." And I had one of those moments where I just had no words, because I've been back and forth with these people, and the university talks out of both sides of its mouth. *Free expression of ideas?* BS! That's not what the university stands for. (Chuck Kelley, Western Flagship)[2]

In this extended quotation, Chuck describes the types of activities and attitudes that fall under the style we are calling provocative and explains what is so appealing about it. According to Chuck and his colleagues, the provocative style lays bare the absurdity of liberals. It exposes the hypocrisy of administrators. It shows how conservative students are the *real* aggrieved party on campus even though it is always other groups (blacks, Hispanics, women, and non-Christian religious groups) who claim oppression. The style always gets a reaction. And therefore it is really, really fun—at least for those who are not on the receiving end of it.

Lest we give the impression that the era of Chuck Kelley—a school year that was marked by boundless energy and many plates in the air at once—was the start and end of the provocative style at Western Flagship, we look to other interviewees' descriptions of the attention-grabbing activities they were involved in both before and after Chuck's leadership. A subsequent president of the Western Flagship College Republicans—a student named Kody Aronson, who described himself as also "extremely opposed to" affirmative action—reflected on the Bake Sale his cohort of Western Flagship College Republicans put on three years after Chuck's. This Bake Sale was not as masterfully coordinated as the earlier event, not least because Kody ended up creating quite a stir on campus when he inadvertently hit "reply all" on an email that included some particularly indelicate statements about one specific student of color at Western Flagship who he assumed was a beneficiary of affirmative action. Despite the scandal that the email created, Kody insisted that "we didn't do [the Bake Sale] to piss off the black kids." Instead, he said his group used the provocative style to get a point across:

It provoked [the Black Student Union] the most. They felt like they were being directly attacked, and they organized a silent protest, but they weren't very silent about it [*laughs*]. They were very, very upset about this. And we weren't trying to just provoke them. We did want them to take note of the fact that we were opposed to affirmative action. But we weren't trying to, like, make them feel oppressed or anything. I'm sure some of them *did* feel that way, but that's because they didn't understand the message. *But that's not our problem.* (Kody Aronson, Western Flagship, emphasis added)

In Kody's telling, such a provocative event is intended to forcefully elucidate Western Flagship College Republicans' opposition to a hated policy. But if it rubs people the wrong way, which was not part of the club's original intent, then hey, liberals need to develop a thicker skin.

While affirmative action is a supremely hot-ticket issue at the 85-percent-white Western Flagship campus, it is not the only political issue around which Western Flagship College Republicans stage controversial events. Under different leadership in the 2007–2008 school year, members of Western Flagship's College Republicans agreed that they might take a break from more domestically oriented issues and instead foreground the topics of national security and antiterrorism in their large-scale events. At the time of our interview with Kevin Sharkey, then the Western Flagship College Republicans' vice president, the club was a few days away from hosting an event called "Why We Want to Kill You"—a speaker's forum that featured two purportedly reformed Muslim terrorists warning about the murderously dangerous Islamic world.[3] Given that the event's speakers had earlier "appeared on national news with Fox and Bill O'Reilly," Kevin knew this would be "a very controversial event" for his left-leaning classmates and the community where Western Flagship is located, "who feel that the Bush administration and that this country are the demise of the world, and [who] are just, in my opinion, very anti-American" (Kevin Sharkey, Western Flagship). But controversy was part of the point, since his audience "had to be" provoked out of their liberal complacency to see the dangers of "Islamo-Fascism":

We knew that it would incite stiff opposition by the left radicals around here as well as in the Muslim Student Association. But it was something that *had* to be done, it had to be spoken. . . . People are *offended* that we're representing terrorists in this fashion. Well, that's how terrorists are representing themselves! I don't *care* if you're offended! Quite frankly, if this is how they're going to represent themselves, then what's the problem of them showing up on *my* poster in the same fashion? (Kevin Sharkey, Western Flagship)

Kevin concluded his remarks with a healthy dose of exasperation: He held his arms up, looked to the sky in disbelief, pursed his lips, and shook his head from side to side while stating, "I'm *over* our society becoming a P.C. environment. . . . Why can't people speak their minds?" "Speaking their minds" on terrorism using the provocative style, this student and other members employed the same tool used by other Western Flagship College Republicans in previous years for their anti–affirmative action campaign and transposed it to a different issue area. From these examples, we note that though specific issues may change annually, the provocative style remains a ready tool that conservatives use to make their point about the "politically correct" atmosphere on the Western Public campuses.

CONTEXTUALIZING THE WESTERN FLAGSHIP COLLEGE REPUBLICANS

While Chuck's, Kody's, and Kevin's examples show clearly that the Western Flagship chapter of College Republicans dependably used the provocative style around the time we collected our data, this form of conservative expression actually goes back much further than the 2000s. Since at least the mid-1980s (which is the earliest we heard about it; it may go back further still), Western Flagship College Republicans and other campus conservative groups and individuals at Western Flagship have used the style to stake several sorts of claims.[4] We discovered that it also extends to other right-leaning groups on the Western Flagship campus as well as to College Republicans chapters on other Western Public campuses, and it is further reflected in conservative students' activities quite apart from their partisan conduct, such as in their interactions with faculty. Each of these uses of the style deserves attention.

First up is to look at how the provocative style has been used in other right-leaning, issue-oriented student clubs on the Western Flagship campus. Many members of these smaller organizations also participate in the larger Western Flagship College Republicans club, but students' involvement in the single-issue clubs gives them the opportunity to promote causes that are not priorities for their campus chapter of the College Republicans. Given these groups' overlap in membership, as well as their ties to populist national organizations like the YAF and the LI, it is unsurprising that within these issue-oriented groups we also see a reliance on the provocative political style. For example, Western Flagship's chapter of the national initiative called Students for Concealed Carry on Campus was begun with funds from the LI's Campus Leadership Program, while the Western Flagship for Life club is supported by a larger anti-abortion group based in the state's capital.

During the time we were conducting our research, the Concealed Carry group sponsored an event called Empty Holsters week, during which students who owned (or at least supported) legal firearms wore empty gun holsters in plain view to draw attention to a state law that prohibited them from bringing their weapons onto the campus. Concerns about Second Amendment rights and "preventing another Virginia Tech" abounded during the week (field notes, Empty Holster Event). Though a few interviewees said most students on campus did not even notice the holsters they wore, the event drew considerable preemptive attention from Western Flagship's administration, as this conservative student explained:

> The campus sent out like kind of an all-call email to everyone around campus saying "Don't worry, they're not crazies." . . . So for them to put out an email, I mean it's . . . kind of like a joke. Are people really going to freak out when they see a leather

pouch? . . . . Why do you have to send out an email about that?!
. . . And I don't know why they would. I think it just comes along
with the territory of going to Western Flagship. (Kurt Tatum,
Western Flagship)

While this group's main activity during the week was tabling to get
signatures on petitions demanding that lawmakers allow registered
concealed weapons on campus, the visual presentation of the empty
holsters—where guns *should* have been—certainly raised hackles at
this university. Perhaps by design (we could not confirm this with
Concealed Carry organizers), the event drew a liberal counterpro-
test similar to the one that mobilized against the Bake Sale.

Student-run pro-life organizations at Western Flagship also use
the provocative style. According to our interviewees at both Western Public and Eastern Elite, abortion is an issue that College Republicans groups on many campuses tend to shy away from as too
divisive within their own membership, where fiscal conservatives
can clash with social conservatives.[5] At Western Flagship, students
opposed to abortion are more active in two different groups, Western Flagship for Life and Choose Life, which at the time of our interviews were both relatively new. Both of these fledgling organizations take a similar approach to spreading their message on campus,
although one is more provocative and gets more attention. The
Choose Life club distributes literature, invites pro-life speakers to
campus, and holds fundraisers, in addition to more visible actions.
One Choose Life member recalled, "We did a chalking, where we
chalked a bunch of hearts, thousands of hearts on campus and num-
bered them as kind of a Valentine's Day thing, the number of fetuses
that are aborted every day in this country" (Isabel Stricker, Western
Flagship). The Western Flagship for Life club, however, had outdone
that with a more provocative event the previous spring, posting
large images of unborn fetuses in a prominent location on campus.
The event drew crowds and incited counter confrontational actions,
with other students yelling "fascist!" at student organizers and one
opposing student depositing a pile of wire hangers on the group's
table. Although one of our interviewees involved in Western Flag-

ship for Life deemed the club's action too confrontational, a freshman member of the Western Flagship College Republicans who had not yet entered college at the time of the event championed that pro-life group's provocative style:

> They had a lot of graphic pictures, but I think that sometimes people need to see those kinds of things. They need to be exposed to that. There were a lot of people protesting the whole thing. And I just think that, that kind of stuff, I think it needs to happen on a campus like this. (Brooke Gerson, Western Flagship)

For this student, events like the one put on by Western Flagship for Life are not only justified, they are necessary.

Lying on the opposite pole of conservative ideology from social conservatives at Western Flagship are its avowedly libertarian students, who have not had an easy time getting a club going on campus but who have found that using the provocative style has bolstered what little success they have had. Although the Western Public campuses boast a considerable number of students who have become more libertarian-leaning since coming to college, it appears that getting them organized is a bit like herding cats since, as one Western Flagship College Republicans member commented,

> Libertarian groups are never successful because they're all libertarians! [*laughs*]. And that may sound like a joke, but it's truer than you know. They really have a tough time keeping things together sometimes. (Hunter Devine, Western Flagship)

Corresponding to this interviewee's description, campus groups espousing the ideals of unfettered markets and limited government intrusion did not appear to be particularly robust—or at least they were not at the time of our data collection, which was prior to the rise of the Tea Party.[6] Western Flagship's law school has a Federalist Society, which holds meetings and hosts speakers at events that draw a few undergraduates, but this does not appear to be a substantial presence.

A Western Flagship Objectivists group, devoted to the teachings of Ayn Rand and her followers, seemed to be making greater headway, but only by moving away from its roots to host more provocative events with broader appeal. One of the Objectivists group's organizers said that his original vision had been to "bring in speakers to talk about the ideas, and also to host discussions . . . but we had sporadic attendance between maybe four people and eight people. And it just got to the point where not a lot of people were showing up" (Keith Newton, Western Flagship). This group found greater success when it set those original, more discussion-oriented intentions aside and put on splashy events that, members admitted, were not always entirely relevant to objectivist philosophy. For example, at one point the club hosted the Danish newspaper editor who commissioned the Muhammad cartoons that caused considerable political outrage in 2005; another time it aired a film highly critical of environmentalists' efforts to curtail the mining industry (a hot issue in this western state). The failure of holding small-group discussions and the turn toward more controversial public events testify to the dominance of the provocative style at Western Flagship.

In addition to working well in student clubs that are identifiably conservative, the provocative style also is effective when it is used by conservative students in other campus organizations that are ostensibly nonpartisan. For example, some conservative students who had succeeded in getting themselves elected to the student-run Funds Board at Western Flagship used provocation to advance their goals in campus governance activities. At Western Flagship, the Funds Board has authority for doling out many hundreds of thousands of dollars each year to undergraduate groups.[7] Perhaps not surprisingly, the Funds Board has the reputation among campus conservatives for being not only bloated (as almost any governmental body would be, according to fiscal conservatives) but also for being politically biased, whereby liberal groups are thought to garner resources much more easily than conservative organizations. When conservatives find a way of getting elected to the Funds Board (which some of our interviewees say occurs mostly through their classmates' failure to care enough to fill out a ballot at the beginning of the year), contentious "meetings would go until 2 a.m.," reported one alumna (Kayla Shain, Western Flagship). Conservative student representatives would gleefully gum up the funding process in order to promote fiscal conservatism, according to another alumnus. "My shtick, as a student government representative. . . . One night we were presented with this [huge] budget. I voted no on every single funding issue that came before us. 'No, No, *sorry*, no! [*laughs*]. No, No, No!' " (Scott Dickey, Western Flagship).

As we can see from the examples above, even while the provocative style has a long legacy on the Western Flagship campus, it also has a good bit of elasticity. Sometimes the style is used to press a point home (such as how resources are meted out to campus groups), at other times it is used to articulate a position on domestic or even international issues (such as affirmative action or "Islamo-Fascism"). On occasion the issue for which it is marshaled displeases even those *within* the conservative clubs, such as when libertarians within the Western Flagship College Republicans expressed chagrin at the anti-gay message of some of their clubmates' proposed Straight Pride Rally ("We *do* . . . accept people who are gay"; Kody Aronson, Western Flagship). But at other times the provocative style appeared to build solidarity among all conservative factions when students united against a common enemy, such as the purportedly P.C. administration.

The success of provocation at Western Flagship also varies depending on leadership in right-leaning groups. For some periods the provocative style can be outrageously and skillfully deployed by a charismatic leader like Chuck Kelley, who swelled the membership ranks of the Western Flagship College Republicans during his year at the organization's helm. But the style can also seem clunky, even ham-fisted, as noted earlier when Kody Aronson mistakenly cc'd the supposed beneficiary of affirmative action on the email he sent to his fellow Western Flagship College Republicans during the second Bake Sale. Whatever the particular moment or the specific issue, or whoever happens to be the head of a club in any given year, the provocative style is a piece of institutional culture at Western Flagship; it can be easily drawn on from the cultural repertoire in place on campus. Another way to put this is that at Western Flagship, opportunity spaces abound for provocative actions. It is not the only style that is included in this repertoire, as we show below when we discuss the campaigning style, but it is undoubtedly the dominant style.

WHY PROVOKE? WESTERN PUBLIC INTERVIEWEES' OWN EXPLANATIONS FOR THEIR STYLE

Why do Western Public's conservative students, particularly those on the Western Flagship campus, throw themselves into the provocative style in many different contexts? What is its cultural, emotional, cognitive, and strategic appeal? As we learned in chapter 3, national conservative organizations like the YAF put a lot of money into promoting the use of such an activist style, and we might also note that many members of the national GOP over the past two decades (but especially in the new millennium) have given the style prominence in their own actions. Republican congressman Joe Wilson from South Carolina, for example, displayed something akin to the provocative style when he shouted out "You lie!" during a major address on healthcare delivered by President Barack Obama; Sarah Palin used crosshair symbols resembling a rifle scope to indicate which Democratic congressional districts should be targeted in the 2010 elections; in 2011 congressional Republicans threatened to default on the national debt if their demands were not met.[8] Conservative journalists like Michael Lind, meantime, bemoan the "collapse of intellectual conservatism" at the hands of the "conservative masses" across the country.[9] The provocative style is in many respects a national style.

Nevertheless, the populist, provocative style is not prevalent on *all* college campuses, so the question is an important one: Why is the provocative style the conservative tool of choice at Western, and how does it fit with the extant cultural repertoire of action at this university? When we put the question directly to conservative students, or when we interpret their less direct comments on this topic, we find several interesting things. Although all are interrelated, the sections below provide a range of reasons, in students' and alumni/ae's own words, for why undergraduates on the Western Public campuses choose to provoke. In the first part of this analysis we give a rundown of students' own stated reasons for why they use the provocative style (the emic account), and later in the chapter we bring in our own etic point of view to show how a few cultural and organizational features of the Western Public system, and especially of the Western Flagship campus, shape the development of particular kinds of political selves.

SURVIVING MARGINALIZATION, HAVING FUN

As illustrated in chapter 4, when conservative students were asked to reconstruct what they had expected to find at Western Flagship as incoming freshmen, they reported that they and their parents had anticipated that their future campus would skew liberal. Even if they didn't anticipate it being problematic, most still shared a sense that they would have to confront something of a liberal presence when they got to school. Reflecting back on that time, most of our interviewees said that their 18-year-old selves had, if anything, underestimated reality and that their experience in college proved to them that Western Flagship *is* really liberal, conservative students *are* in the minority, and it *is* a lonely place for anyone to the right of the typical "Che Guevara t-shirt-wearing, granola and patchouli"– loving Flagship student (Neil Thompson, Western Flagship).

Although we know that moderates, not liberals, predominate on campuses most like Western Flagship and that the patchouli-scented caricature Neil campily provides above is an overstatement, conservative students' sense of marginalization came through loud and clear in their accounts of their treatment on campus. As noted in earlier examples, various of our interviewees recounted that they had been called a "fascist" and a "cunt," said they had been made to feel like "idiots" and "the big bad wolf," were put on the spot to "present the conservative side" of issues in class, and were forced to encounter stares and name-calling when wearing a military uniform for ROTC or an empty holster to show their support for gun rights. As yet another student recalled, "In classes, people will call you Republican Nazis and yadayadayada" (Eric Leonard, Western Flagship).

Discussing reports of this treatment among themselves in conservative clubs, where their sense of isolation and alienation is shared and nurtured, many interviewees said that the provocative form was a natural style to turn to at Western Flagship and that a certain rebelliousness in orientation toward others was essential in the face of what they considered to be ill conduct. An older alumnus told us at some length:

> From the moment I get there [to Western Flagship], it's, you're bombarded with the "White males are the source of all the problems in the world," and how I'm to blame for this even though there really isn't a racist bone in my body. . . . But they put it in racial ideological terms from the second you get there. And it does cause you to look at it and think about it.
>
> I had the reaction that, you know, "I've never propagated a racial crime against anyone." So initially I was awakened to this ideological thing that I never wanted to be part of and didn't seek out. And I'm naturally a rebel, and that's kind of who I am. I think that's who a lot of students are. And so I rebelled against what I saw as the prevailing orthodoxy which was this left-wing, race-conscious, politically correct view. (Scott Dickey, Western Flagship)

This is the same interviewee who funneled his "natural rebelliousness" into the avid use of the blanket veto on the Funds Board, as well as into changing his political affiliation from Democrat to Republican and joining a fraternity where he felt he might find more like-minded classmates.

For conservatives who feel isolated going against the liberal grain, joining right-leaning organizations that build group solidarity through fun, provocative action can provide what they see as a lifeline, as this former Western Flagship College Republicans president described:

> There are some kids who are just oddballs, and College Republicans definitely attracts a lot of the oddballs. And so they kind of forge friendships within the group. . . . This was the way to make some kids happy because some kids really were as isolated as it gets on this campus.
>
> If you come onto this campus as a black student, you've instantly got a group of friends in all the other black students. You come on the campus as a white conservative male, you're just another fish in the big pond and you have to find the other fish, and it's really hard to do. (Kody Aronson, Western Flagship)

Conservative organizations thus provide a haven for students who regard themselves as isolated rebels or as outliers in other ways, and who see their situation as considerably more dire than it is for students of color (who, it should be observed once again, are a smaller minority on campus than are self-identified conservatives). While not every conservative student may individually feel confident enough to take the heat for staging confrontational actions, meeting other students in these organizations who are willing to put themselves on the front lines and confront their liberal campus community with elbows jutting can provide a sense of strength.

Going beyond merely "surviving" marginalization on campus, many Western Public students cited another reason for embracing their identities as renegades and pouring themselves into a commitment to provoking. For these conservatives, provocation in itself is simply *fun*:

> The best part about standing up in front of a group, people that are protesting you or . . . calling you names, whatever, is that besides believing you're on the right side of the issue, it does give you a charge, gives you a certain energy. And, you know, it's fun! . . . You're standing up for what you believe in and you're not

backing down just because someone else tells you that you're wrong. (Karl Hayes, Western Satellite)

Just as the YAF's *Conservative Battle Plan* and related websites encourage right-leaning undergraduates to do, Karl has taken on the "activist mentality."[10] Continuing on, he reported, "If you wake up and come to school in the morning and someone calls you a bigot, you know you're going to have a good day." Clearly, this student felt he was far to the right on the political bell curve—even on the reputedly more conservative Western Satellite campus—but he credited his insurgent streak with keeping him from shriveling up and becoming merely resentful of the liberals he perceived as running the institution. For Karl, as for other conservatives on the Western Public campuses, the provocative style can function as an expressive, sometimes joyous self-preservation technique on what they see as their radicalized campuses.

GETTING ATTENTION *ON* CAMPUS

The expressiveness contained in the provocative style also serves another key purpose, according to our interviewees: being provocative gets attention from campus insiders, including peers, faculty, and administrators; as well as from campus outsiders, such as the surrounding community, the media, and potential donors).

Getting peers to pay attention to conservative issues is an uphill battle, as our interviewees described most Western Flagship students as ranging from self-satisfied liberals who refused to recognize other political points of view to politically apathetic party-down hedonists.[11] Either way, conservatives said, you have to grab their attention. Referring to the problem of his classmates' pleasure seeking, one of our conservative interviewees claimed that the provocative style is necessary on a campus where "there's a zero-sum game" among the causes Western Flagship students *really* care about: "Recreation, partying, enjoying being young, being happy, dating, sports, working out, and you have to go home to your family every once in a while" (Scott Dickey, Western Flagship). Conservative clubs have to make bold actions to break fun-loving Western Flagship students out of their politically apathetic routines.

On the other hand, when Western Flagship peers are perceived not simply as complacent bystanders but as aggressive, fly-off-the-handle, liberal activists, the provocative style remains the weapon of choice—but in this case, conservative students say they use it to fight fire with fire, making this style a tool with many purposes. According to our interviewees, liberal students on campus are not merely satisfied to benevolently support progressive causes. Rather, say our respondents, they are obnoxious, oppressive, and provocative themselves, using "swoop and swarm tactics" to get their liberal points across, such as reportedly wearing Ku Klux Klan hoods to a speech given by the black affirmative action critic Ward Connerly (Neil Thompson, Western Flagship) or relentlessly heckling the speaker David Horowitz during a lecture about professors as radical indoctrinators (Kayla Shain, Western Flagship).[12]

Western Flagship College Republicans perceive that they can always expect an equal—or in some cases, outsized—reaction from left-wing student groups to *any* of their public events, and in such a context, they argue that they need to stage provocative events so as not to be completely overwhelmed by their opponents. One student interviewee, recounting the Concealed Carry group's Empty Holsters event described above, said that liberal students regarded the conservatives as "Oh my God, these freaks":

> They set up this little booth and they had t-shirts. And it was kind of funny. They actually did a little, they actually came over to our area about five feet away, and they all *lay down and pretended they were dead*. And I was like, "Really? Are you serious?" . . . Ironically enough, it just brought us more attention because I'm like, "Hey, prevent massacres like this on campus!" (Eric Leonard, Western Flagship)

Asked whether his liberal protesters were interested in engaging in "substantive discourse" with him about his position on concealed weapons and his argument that they would deter school shootings, Eric said, "They mostly came over to our booth and died is the extent of their discourse. And various . . . 'Stop the killing,' 'Guns are evil,' 'I'm afraid of weapons'—that sort of thing" (Eric Leonard, Western Flagship). In such an environment as this, our conservative respondents rhetorically wondered, what are they expected to do *but* be confrontational?

Another interviewee, reflecting on the Affirmative Action Bake Sales that were sponsored on campus, said, "There was like a lot of talk on campus about it, [people saying] 'I'm shocked that Western Flagship is allowing it.' But I can't believe people were shocked. I mean, Western Flagship allows so much ridiculous behavior on the *other* side, you know?" (Stephanie Cohen, Western Flagship). In such cases the provocative style is called for, conservatives say, since in effect it is simply a response to *liberals'* provocative style. Our Western Public interviewees said that they had learned to expect liberals' exaggerated responses to their actions, that they planned their events accordingly, and that they even counted on their events to bait liberals into making what conservatives consider to be laughably moronic statements. "Angry liberals," one interviewee stated, "tend to be conservative activists' bread and butter. I mean, College Republicans will do silly, stupid stuff, often very purposefully, to get people's emotions to come out" (Bryan Carhart, Western Satellite). Such action is very much in keeping with organizations like the YAF, which encourage young conservatives to lay traps for the Left.

But inducing peers' responses is not the only sort of attention the provocative style is meant to stimulate on campus: Faculty attention, too, is the rightful target of the provocative style, some of our Western Public interviewees said. Remember that Western Public conservatives are particularly prone to viewing their professors as politically biased toward the Left. One College Republicans member described an encounter with a Western Flagship professor before the 2008 election that was problematic:

We had a booth set up in the Student Union dining area just to try to get new members. And I've had faculty walk by and say,

"You damn Republicans have done it to yourself and you guys are going to get it good." We don't need to hear this from *you*! I know you're a faculty member. I know who you are. This isn't that small, or that large of a university that you can just hide and not expect to be known and recognized. But that's, you know, kind of the attitude that you get. (Kevin Sharkey, Western Flagship, emphasis added)

This kind of direct confrontation with a faculty member again relays the message to conservative members of campus that the provocative style is not only acceptable but *essential* on a campus like Western Flagship University.

GETTING ATTENTION *OFF* CAMPUS

In addition to on-campus audiences, Western Public students also practice provocation for the benefit of audiences off campus. One additional factor that our interviewees said encourages provocative action at Western Flagship is the community that surrounds the campus. Western Flagship is located in a mid-sized city known to be far outside the mainstream of the state's politics—it is affluent, crunchy, and decidedly liberal. The surrounding community earns from right-leaning critics the moniker "the Moscow of the West," and conservative politicians in the legislature as well as students on campus point to the power of the "remnants of the 1960s" (Kevin Sharkey, Western Flagship) who vocally and visibly show up at campus events to protest anything they see as having even the slightest soupçon of conservatism. According to conservatives, the city is comical in its politics, such as when "it spent $50,000 to relocate a colony of, like, 12 [gophers] that got the plague and died after their relocation" (Stephanie Cohen, Western Flagship).

We mention the town because conservative students say it affects their lives on campus and their style of politics in two ways. First, they say it is yet another liberal cross they have to bear, which can only be countenanced through absurdist theater or by going further right to balance the liberals' far left. Second, conservatives see the community as *comprising* the faculty, and the faculty as *typical members* of the larger community. They feel surrounded on all sides by people with liberal politics. This makes the provocative style, in their estimation, a necessary tool. As one student put it,

> I mean, it really, it has a lot to do with the community. And I would go to speaking events, be it a liberal speaker or a conservative speaker, and it was always kind of the same people there, always kind of hanging out in the same crowd, saying the same beliefs. *And the professors were right there with them....* Professors that I had were in that circle, and I realized that it's a community. It's, they're all like-minded individuals and they pay lip service and they do a great job of doing it, but at the end of the day they have their beliefs, and they look down on people who don't share those beliefs. (Kody Aronson, Western Flagship, emphasis added)

Not far removed from national conservatives' plaint that liberals disdain those who "cling to guns and religion," right-leaning students at Western Flagship think that outside community members— aligned with, and including, the liberal faculty—are arrogant and condescending toward them.[13] This is yet another factor contributing to conservatives' justification for trying to cut through liberal bias using a confrontational style.

In addition to students' critiques of faculty and the community, conservative students also expressed a high level of suspicion about the university administration. Particularly at Western Flagship, students believed that the funding practices of their university were stacked against them, such that they had to fight much harder than liberal clubs for monetary resources to bring their preferred speakers to campus and to organize other activities. They described even nonmonetary allocations (such as the locations to which student groups were assigned space for setting up tables in common areas) as unfair to conservative groups and causes, and funding for such events as a pro-life rally as a series of hurdles to surmount. As such, conservative students said it was often necessary for their groups to find high levels of outside funding to augment what they received from the administration—and a productive way to do this, they found, was by hosting events that drew the attention of the media, which helped them garner financial support from regional and national organizations.[14] It perhaps comes as no surprise that Western Flagship College Republicans have teamed with the YAF several times to bring speakers in from that organization's lecture program.

With the prevailing idea that there's no such thing as bad publicity, Western Public campus conservatives in clubs like the College Republicans go for broke trying to catch the media's gaze—which they often do. The provocative style is like catnip to Fox affiliates and the local newspapers, said our interviewees, and conservative clubs try to serve up "suitably controversial" events on their campuses to get good coverage (Neil Thompson, Western Flagship). Talks over the years by the YAF-affiliated pundits Ann Coulter and Michelle Malkin have received heavy media coverage not only in campus newspapers but also in the larger metro-area newspapers and radio outlets, as did events such as the Bake Sales and the Empty Holsters week described earlier. The organizers of the "Why We Want to Kill You" forum even hoped to gain national media attention "regarding this bias that we're getting around town. . . . Bill O'Reilly loves Western Flagship so much, [and] I'm hoping that he will give us a little bit of equal air time and quash some of these smears against one of our speakers" (Kevin Sharkey, Western Flagship). Others weigh in that any event's success can be measured by the amount of column space it receives in the local papers.

Making a splash in the community and in the media can also bring further benefits: Attention-grabbing events, reported a handful of our interviewees, are especially desirable because local conservative politicos love them and are willing to back the provocative style with money. Chuck Kelley, the mastermind behind the original Affirmative Action Bake Sale at Western Flagship, talked about the utility of the provocative style for raising money for the Western Flagship College Republicans while at the same time raising his own profile among those who are highly connected in his state. Chuck revealed, "I would go to the [local] County Republican Men's

Breakfast, and I would go down there and I would do my dog-and-pony show. All of the old men down there would go, 'Oh my God, it's great!' And I would collect business cards and they'd pass the hat, and I'd come out of it with $300 bucks in twenties" (Chuck Kelley, Western Flagship).

The business cards come in handy for later as well. Chuck continued:

> Every job that I've had since college I got because I was Chuck Kelley, the guy who did the Affirmative Action Bake Sale at Western Flagship. . . . And that's what I told people who are going to be [Western Flagship College Republicans] president. I say, "It's a lot of work, you have to do it right. But if you want to go on, even if you just want to work in business, do you know how many rich business people there are in [this city] who like the College Republicans?" I mean, get involved with these people, because . . . if you can be perceived as somebody who brings a conservative message to evil Western Flagship and all the social-ists up there, you can have any job you want! (Chuck Kelley, Western Flagship)

Chuck's own career is proof positive of the quality of his advice—which is to play up conservatives' harrowing marginalization on campus even while collecting donations from organized right-leaning groups for conservative student activities. He is now a well-known local pundit himself, having impressed the then sitting Republican governor of his state, who, following the Affirmative Action Bake Sale, encouraged him and other club members in a handwritten note, "Keep Up the Good Work!"[15]

CAMPAIGNING: THE SUBMERGED STYLE OF CONSERVATIVE ACTION IN THE WESTERN PUBLIC SYSTEM

Despite its status as the dominant mode of conservative expression in their university system, the provocative style is not equally em-braced by all right-leaning students on the Western Public cam-

puses, either as a self-styled method of self-preservation, or as a way
to indulge predilections toward rebellion, or as an attention-getting
boon to one's future political career. The most recent Western Flagship College Republicans president we interviewed, for example,
was elected to his position when he offered the membership of the
club a more placid approach to campus politics, one that privileged
electoral participation—or what we call the "campaigning style"—
over the combativeness of the provocative style. College Republicans, he insisted, "exist to help the Republican Party, volunteering
and doing phone banks," walking precincts, and engaging in other
types of institutionalized politics, not to inflame members of the
campus community or otherwise attract attention (Hunter Devine,
Western Flagship). While some might imagine that conservative political activism on any campus would be centrally about campaigning, this submerged style was seen only within some iterations of the
Western Flagship College Republicans and is not especially visible
in other conservative student groups on the Western Public campuses. Institutionalized politics in the manner of campaigning is actually *peripheral* at Western Flagship, as it is also (although to a
somewhat lesser extent) at Eastern Elite University.

Recounting that he had "nearly just quit College Republicans because I got so fed up" with the internal politics of the organization,
the recent Western Flagship College Republicans president, Hunter
Devine, decided to "stick around" the club for one more year only if
he could win the leadership role and do things his way (Hunter
Devine, Western Flagship). He intimated that his interest in leading
the campus group was at least in part to lay the groundwork for his
own future career in state politics. Unlike Chuck Kelley, who saw
punditry as his future, Hunter wanted to run for office, and this rendered provocative action personally problematic. Asked about some
of his members' and predecessors' interests in the more confrontational style, Hunter reflected:

> It depends on the situation. If you're trying to get ratings, or
> you're trying to get attention, then you should do something pro-
> vocative because . . . like in the past, the College Republicans did

an Affirmative Action Bake Sale that always gets a lot of attention because it's really controversial. . . . And I've been thinking
about it. I don't know if it's worth it. . . . While it may be beneficial in the short term, it makes me nervous because it certainly
leaves a bad taste. It's good for the fringe, but it's not good for
the growing independents of the country. They're tired of it.
(Hunter Devine, Western Flagship)

Mapping out his own ambitions as a future candidate palatable not
just to the conservative base but also to swing voters, Hunter calculated that the provocative style was not advantageous.

Not surprisingly, the mild-mannered, play-by-the-book campaigning style (and the leaders who advocate it) received a good bit
of backlash from previous leaders and some current members of the
club, who did not pull their punches expressing their dissatisfaction
with this alternative conservative style. One past president of the
Western Flagship College Republicans club stated that if it were
possible as an alumnus, he would get the club's current president
removed from office (Kody Aronson, Western Flagship). The provocative style, he and others insisted, is much better suited to their
campus than the campaigning style.

Such condemnation notwithstanding, Hunter's campaigning
style attracted a sufficient number of advocates among conservatives on campus to elect him to the post, and these students reported
that they could appreciate a less contentious role for the group,
which, for better or worse, serves as the face of conservatism on the
Western Flagship campus. One of our interviewees, a young woman
who said she did not like "being yelled at" for her political stances,
claimed that she was glad to have fellow members in the Western
Flagship College Republicans club who were "intense about politics, really passionate about the McCain campaign, really passionate about the election" (Brooke Gerson, Western Flagship). She reported that she enjoyed belonging to Western Flagship College
Republicans because it gave her a "direct route into working on
the [presidential] campaign, but on the same note [not feeling]
pressured really to do it" (Brooke Gerson, Western Flagship).

Other interviewees also expressed satisfaction at using less "super-confrontational" tactics than Bake Sales or Conservative Coming Out Days (Isabel Stricker, Western Flagship), arguing that such tactics were just not their preferred mode of expression.

Yet while the campaigning style wins advocates among those with aspirations toward elected office or with less stomach for being yelled at, the conservative style of provocation often seems more exciting, more authentic, and more productive, even to those who do not enjoy being on the front lines. As a subordinate style on their campus not only in the sense of being less dominant or common but also of being less esteemed or enthused over, campaigning creates ambivalence for those who settle into the relatively lackluster style. Although Brooke Gerson, above, is on record for enjoying direct get-out-the-vote activities for local politicians, she also thinks that the provocative style has a credible role to play in college conservatism:

> The Bake Sale, I thought it was; I guess I don't know how to put it. I thought it was very provocative. I don't know if I would have participated in it. Because I don't like being in the spotlight for things like that. I like kind of keeping that private. But . . . I mean for the people that do it, I think *sometimes these things have to be done*. (Brooke Gerson, Western Flagship, emphasis added)

Likewise, another of our interviewees, a sophomore member of the Western Flagship College Republicans who also had been made aware of previous years' Bake Sales, said, "I'm more inclined to say yes than no," when asked if he thought such an event should be used on his campus. Although he tended more toward the "yes" camp, Devin also added that if "you do something provocative," it is important to "explain why we're doing this, what we're doing this for, why we believe there's an injustice, and how we're going to solve it" (Devin Daleo, Western Flagship). For this interviewee, the heavy-hitting confrontational style is a door-opener, a way to start a more reasoned conversation with one's adversaries. Devin may be right or wrong about the potential for greater access being achieved through combative tactics, but from his perspective, it is not a problem to provoke if it helps begin a solutions-oriented conversation.[16] The provocative style, even though not his preferred style, may be crucial to getting points across on his campus, and it certainly is more exciting.

One gets the sense from these two students—and even from the interview with Hunter, the recent Western Flagship College Republicans president who was worried that the provocative style would leave a bad taste in people's mouths—that conservative students at Western Flagship are always at least potentially able to be mobilized by the provocative style, and that a socially skilled actor, if so inclined, could tap this omnipresent piece of institutional culture.[17] If these more recent students had been around during Chuck Kelley's tenure, for example, perhaps they too would have been out on the quad getting their cash registers knocked over by protesters at the Affirmative Action Bake Sale. It may take a charismatic leader to successfully lead members into a full embrace of a style they are familiar with, if perhaps also ambivalent about. But whatever the case, the cultural tropes for the style are always available at Western Flagship. As we see in the next section, the university's organizational arrangements also create opportunity spaces that make these solutions the most readily accessible for conservative use.

FURTHER EXPLAINING THE PROVOCATIVE STYLE'S DOMINANCE ON WESTERN PUBLIC CAMPUSES

We have now described at length both the feel of these two conservative styles at Western Public and our interviewees' own explanations for why such styles do and do not make sense on their campuses, particularly the provocative style. In a nutshell, conservative students who are active members of right-leaning organizations say that the expressive style of provocation is a necessary component of simple survival at universities like theirs, where liberals run the show and conservatives have to fight back with every weapon at their disposal. As we have seen, this style links up well with the repertoire of conservative actions promoted by national organizations like the YAF and the LI, as well as with the depiction of victimization that these organizations paint. But is that the end of the story? Do students use the provocative style simply because they perceive their campus to be liberal and because national organizations advocate a persecution stance, accompanied by a bid for the "activist mentality"?

Actually, the emic understanding offered by Western Public interviewees is insufficient for explaining their widespread use of the provocative style since there are students and alumni/ae at Eastern Elite, too, who say they are political outliers at their college and who also use the broader discourses advocated by well-funded national organizations but who, as we will see in the next chapter, are more likely to strongly disdain the provocative style and to identify with the greater refinement of the Intercollegiate Studies Institute. This means that if the eyebrow-raising, rabble-rousing, populist style flourishes on the Western Public campuses, and especially at Western Flagship, it is because it is a part of a shared cultural repertoire on campus and is likely embedded in much of Western Public students' organizational, lived experiences. As sociologists interested in how organizational contexts affect shared meanings, we want to know how the institutional features at Western Public, and particularly at Western Flagship, shape a culture of provocation.

Reflecting back on our earlier description of what academic and social life is like at Western Flagship, we can see that the provocative style, with its emphasis on trying to ensnare liberals and capture media and donor attention in the process, fits in well with the very zeitgeist of Western Flagship as a larger institution. While it is always a fallacy to say that a university means a single, unitary thing to all people who belong to that community (it means, of course, many different things to many different people), there is an undeniable, accepted social construction among the undergraduates of Western Flagship about their university. It is a large state university with a reputation as a party school and a campus where recreation is the dominant shared understanding for what it means to be a college student. This reputation suffuses all the way down to the level of politics on campus, as evidenced in the entertainment that can be had in provoking one's adversaries.

The university's distinctive blend of fun (the party and recreation scene) with pragmatism (being at a school that doesn't break the bank) fits in well with the dominant style of provocative conservatism, which mixes pleasure (getting a rise out of liberals) with business (getting students to acknowledge the presence of conservatives on campus, getting a lot of bang for your buck with events, and paving a path to one's future political career in this western state). This emphasis on pragmatic fun shows up in the everyday practices and ideas of Western Flagship's conservative students in a number of ways, from the attention-grabbing media coups and "dog-and-pony shows" for local potential donors (Chuck Kelley, Western Flagship), to electing "sociable," "charismatic" people to be the "face of the organization"—someone who fits "the mold of the typical Western Flagship student" (Kody Aronson, Western Flagship). For example, Western Flagship College Republican leaders blend fun and practical considerations when they try to keep the club's "weird factor" (unappealing members) out of the public eye, working behind the scenes as "foot soldiers," while relying on more enticing "conservative girls" to work the recruitment tables (Chuck Kelley, Western Flagship).

We find that the blend of fun and pragmatism also contributes to a sense among Western Public students that college represents a liminal stage in which anything goes, and a wider range of political behavior is acceptable than in other social arenas. Echoing the opinion that college-age conservatives should not just do the routine bidding of the national or regional Republican Party but instead should be having the time of their lives pushing the political envelope, a Western Satellite student explained, "The function of a lot of College Republicans chapters is that we are the ones who are crazy enough— and don't have as much to lose—to make points that the national Party really can't afford to make" (Bryan Carhart, Western Satellite). Thus, conservatives at schools like Western Public choose to take advantage of their status as uninhibited college students to get away with hosting controversial speakers or provoking professors and administrators. Besides, having fun at liberals' expense can attract the kind of attention they desire—from the media, from donors, and from their more socially acceptable peers on campus. This kind of politicized provocation fits in well with Western Public conservatives' understandings of themselves, both generally as *college* students, more specifically as fun-seeking *Western Public* college students, and most centrally as *conservative* Western Public college students.

In addition, the provocative style works well in a fairly atomized campus environment. Where classes are mostly lecture format, dorm life is limited to first-year students, highly bureaucratized systems create a sense of depersonalization on campus, and few organizations foster bipartisan dialogue, Western Public conservative students tend not to feel as strongly integrated into a campus community as their counterparts at Eastern Elite, and they are more likely to develop fairly grim assessments of others' interest in being civil toward them. This, in turn, makes the provocative style seem more like a fully warranted tool. Our interviewees reported that other students would rather stage "die-ins" than engage in a rational conversation with them about gun control, would prefer to abridge conservatives' freedom of speech by getting administrators to shut down their events before they even begin, and are more likely to shout insults at them than to calmly talk about the basis of their political positions. Administrators and faculty were perceived to be little different. In all the evidence we collected, we found scant commentary from our Western Public interviewees that politically active conservative and liberal students have much formal or informal substantive interaction that is fundamentally respectful in nature. It is true that conservatives reported that their social lives included liberal friends ("my whole life my friends have been really liberal"; Brittany Urban, Western Satellite), but on the whole, political discussion seems to be limited when it comes to interactions between avowedly left-leaning and right-leaning students—that is, those who care about politics enough to discuss them seriously. Formal structures that support such conversations do not appear to be in place at Western Flagship or on the other Western Public campuses. And so while it may be true that conservative activists hang out with liberal friends, they may not know liberal activists who care to really push them on their ideological principles. Whatever the particular formulation, our conservative interviewees were quite clear that there is not much significant political exchange across ideological lines on campus. Where such is the case, a confrontational style can prosper since neither side takes the other particularly seriously.

Furthermore, on a campus and in a community where conservative students feel they are in a significant minority and where there are few easy avenues for sociability with the other political side, explicitly conservative organizations become significant spaces for creating shared meanings—in this case, a sense of camaraderie built largely on perceived mistreatment. One interviewee described the Western Flagship College Republicans as "an oasis, like an island of conservatism in the big sea of liberal Western Flagship" (Hunter Devine, Western Flagship). Another young woman discussed the benefits she received from participating in the same group:

> We all talk about how professors are crazy in class and stuff like that. Every single meeting we get to tell, somebody stands up and tells a story about what happened in a class this week with a professor. So I mean it's not—the group itself is serious but we don't take ourselves too seriously; which I liked about it. (Brooke Gerson, Western Flagship)

In these examples we can see that conservative students sometimes seek out College Republicans and other groups for socializing, but once there, they find mutually agreed-upon definitions for what they are experiencing on campus as conservatives, as well as ready-made solutions for what to do about those experiences. Not to belabor the point, but when groups such as these are the primary locus for political discussions, more deliberative forms of discourse are unlikely to take root. In sum, the large size of the student population, the fact that 75 percent of students live off campus, the sense of depersonalization that comes from the institution's large class sizes and registration policies (among other organizational features), and the general cultural ethos of combined fun and pragmatism that pervades the institution all create a fertile opportunity space for provocation to flourish.

POLITICAL STYLES IN OTHER SETTINGS: CLASSROOMS AND EVENTUALLY CAREERS

More evidence for the durability and dominance of the provocative style can be found by examining its uses in other areas of students' lives. Though developed within explicitly politically oriented organizations such as the College Republicans, we also see the conservative style of provocation being transposed to other settings. This adaptability is evidence that the strategies of action that are incubated in the small-group settings of these clubs are then also taken by individuals and applied to other challenges they face. In this way, we continue to see this political style as a group solution to the perceived problem of being a conservative student on a liberal college campus. Here we look at how these ideas about what kind of political action and language are appropriate for student groups are brought into two other areas of student life. First, we examine how Western Public students use the styles picked up in these student organizations to deal with what they see as the overwhelmingly liberal environment they confront in the university classroom. Then we move on to look at how a reliance on the provocative or the campaigning style interacts with students' career aspirations after graduation.

NAVIGATING THE LIBERAL CLASSROOM

As with ideas about appropriate political action in the clubs, we also find two types of reactions to the classroom. Unsurprisingly, we find that many Western Public conservative students use confrontational tactics in tackling situations that arise inside the classroom—certainly much more so than Eastern Elite students do. Though in many cases these are the same individuals who are most committed to using the provocative style in their student organizations, we find that others who express *less* commitment to this style for their clubs sometimes take a *more* combative approach with regard to academics. That said, Western Public students do not uniformly engage in provocative behavior in classes: We also see numerous instances of students taking a sort of "grin and bear it" approach, saying that they keep mainly to themselves and do what needs to be done in order to accomplish the task at hand, usually with the goal of earning a good grade. They may say they *wish* they could be more confrontational with their instructors and peers in class, but they pull their punches. While we cannot see this as an exact parallel to the style of campaigning, there is a sense still of both being ways of "working within the system."

Fighting Fire with Fire: Confrontational Classroom Tactics

One way that conservative students on the Western Public campuses attempt to combat the perceived liberal atmosphere in their lecture halls and sections is to counter faculty/instructor bias by clearly voicing their disapproval. Similar to how many Western Public conservatives see provocative behavior by their organizations as necessary to provide a counterpoint to the campus at large, some students describe being outspoken in the classroom as an important intervention:

> I mean, I think that professors have an obligation to be fair and to teach truth. And if truth is only a liberal side then I would like to see the definition of "truth." . . . I was the most outspoken student in the classroom because, frankly, I mean, there's another side. There's another side to economics, there's another side to the Iraq War, there's another side to terrorism. And so I just kind of took it upon myself. One, I really relished in trying to get the

professors *riled up*. I mean, it's just kind of like a *gotcha* thing. I don't know. But two, it was almost my obligation I felt to say the whole classroom is *not* Democratic. There are other people with different views here and we have a brain. We can decipher different ideas for ourselves. (Conor Denning, Western State, emphasis added)

Students characterized this as alerting not only professors but also fellow students to their presence. Another student talked about sitting in the front row of a political science class where the professor would go on long anti-Bush tirades just to engage in "yelling matches" with him and provide a conservative response. She was especially proud of the time she proved him wrong, subsequent to one of their classroom bouts: "And I went the next day on . . . Lexis-Nexis and found an article about it and brought it in and gave it to him. I waited until the end of class, I was nice about it, but yeah" (Brittany Urban, Western Satellite). Here this student followed up her more vocal confrontation with the professor in the classroom with a later private moment after class—but it should be pointed out that a heated verbal exchange in class originally took place.

Others engage in similar behavior but use tactics that are more under-the-radar than in-class confrontation. One interviewee told of a professor who taught 9/11 "Internet conspiracy theories" in the classroom and "always insisted on referring to Jesus Christ as, and I quote, 'the radical Palestinian Jew,' and never by his name" (Bryan Carhart, Western Satellite). This student brought a tape recorder to the professor's class with the intent of passing the recordings along to the YAF. Though this plan did not pan out because the recorder malfunctioned, it clearly was an attempt at playing "gotcha" on a still more disputatious scale—one supported by the LI's CampusReform.org website and the YAF, as well as others such as David Horowitz's Students for Academic Freedom.

Still other Western Public students discussed engaging with faculty one-on-one rather than having confrontational exchanges with them in front of the whole class. Though not as outwardly provocative as the behaviors described above, individuals who are willing to directly confront professors fall much closer to the provocative end of the spectrum than those who aim, if not to please, then to appease. For example, one young woman gave an account of calling out a professor for comments made during class:

> Just this past semester, I'm taking a class on the American Revolution and my teacher went off on this huge tangent about health care and how people that don't believe in it sit in their houses with tin foil on their heads, and think that the government . . . and I was just, I was so irritated by that . . . I just went up to him after class and I was like, you know, that's really insulting to say that we're so stupid that we just don't get it. I mean, the people that are at these town hall meetings are my parents. They're my grandparents; they're my aunts and uncles. They're my neighbors. I know them personally. I know they're not crazy. And to say that we're all totally nuts and sleep with tin foil on our heads and everything like that was just extremely insulting. . . . And he kind of was just like okay, well, I mean that's how I feel about it. I was like, you are a sixty-year-old man, have a little class. (Brooke Gerson, Western Flagship)

Though this student did not interrupt the lecture in order to point out the offensiveness of the professor's remarks, her willingness to confront the instructor in such a way is still notable—particularly in comparison to Eastern Elite interviewees' reports of their classroom conduct. That said, what allowed Brooke to do this comfortably was not just the taste for confrontation supported by student organizations at Western Public but also the classroom features of large state school campuses: given the lecture class size, this student was unconcerned about facing consequences for her behavior. As she mentioned, "I don't think my grade will be jeopardized just because he doesn't know exactly what my name is, or anything like that" (Brooke Gerson, Western Flagship).

Grade retaliation is a concern that Western Public conservative students do not take lightly: Several of our interviewees were adamant in telling us that they thought grading issues arose with regularity, particularly in the social sciences and humanities, where essay assignments made grading more subjective. One student commented that in his freshman writing class on environmental issues "there's less red on your papers—definitely, definitely" when students write essays from a liberal viewpoint (Kurt Tatum, Western Flagship), while another student commented wryly that at least "the math department is pretty unbiased" (Hunter Devine, Western Flagship). So in addition to issues arising within the interactional setting of the lecture hall, Western Public conservatives assume they will also often find themselves graded more punitively because of their views.[18] One way to confront this problem is post hoc: reviewing as a group assignments that receive harsh marks from a professor, and keeping copies of them in the College Republicans office:

> I've seen term papers that came back with bad grades that we reviewed in College Republicans. We had faculty reviews and they came back saying no, this is actually a good paper. The criteria [were] met. And there would be comments written on the sides saying like, "Well, why this, if Bush said this." Like something to that effect. We have copies of them in the office and I'm sure they still have them. There were some pretty blatant things, and I consider it *persecution* when a student's getting a bad grade because of something that they wrote, especially if they followed all the criteria of the assignment. I can understand if they didn't follow the criteria and they got a bad grade. That's one thing. But it's completely another thing when they *only* got a bad grade on a paper or a test because of something they said or because of things they say in class. Because I know that a lot of students, conservative students, are very outspoken. So the professors know who they are. (Kody Aronson, Western Flagship)

Western Public conservatives—already more suspicious of faculty than Eastern Elite students are—prepare themselves for the worst and assume grade bias in advance.

In another example, one student told of choosing to write a research paper on a conservative topic for a teaching assistant whom she presumed, from comments in class, to be liberal. Before handing the paper in, the student gave it to a family friend who is a high school teacher to read. The interviewee explained:

> So I sent her the paper because I was like if I'm going to turn this in I want to make sure it's really good. [And] if it's not, like if I get a bad grade on it, I can kind of fight her on it. And she sent it back to me. She said, while I don't agree with you, it's very well written. You make good points, you have good sources, so I don't see why you shouldn't get a very good grade on this. So I turned it in and I got a C– on it or something like that. And I went into [my TA's] office hours, I was like hey, you know, what's the deal on this? What should I improve on for the next paper? I never really said like what topic didn't you like in it, I just wanted to know what I could do for the final. And she just kind of shut me down, wouldn't really tell me what to do. (Brooke Gerson, Western Flagship)

Thus, for many Western Public conservatives, the best way to individually respond to the liberal environment of the classroom parallels to some extent the way that groups such as the Western Flagship College Republicans confront the liberal environment of the campus in general: assume that you are likely to be on the losing end of the battle in the classroom and try to fight back with a range of strategies. Styles of action or language nurtured within the group setting are taken by individuals and adapted to situations they must face on their own. In this way, being a part of student-run organizations helps these conservative students minimize their sense of being isolated or marginalized not only when they are actually with the group but also at other times, by giving them ways of behaving that they believe are more effective on their campuses.

Keeping Mum and Getting A's: Working the System

Just as in campus politics, however, for some students adopting the provocative style in the classroom is not seen as a feasible option. For these conservative Western Public students, sometimes engaging contentiously with their liberal professors, teaching assistants, and classmates is not worth the trouble. While some students described this more as choosing one's battles wisely, others simply felt silenced by what they saw as the academic liberal majority:

> From like the professor side of it when you're sitting in class, and they say "Oh, some people think that abortion should be banned even on first-stage embryos, or whatever, oh, isn't that just the stupidest thing you've ever heard?" You know, I'm a pretty strong-willed person, so I don't take those kind of things personally, but you sit there and wonder, well, is it worth it? Should I raise my hand? Should I question it, or should I just let it slide and move on to the next thing? (Isabel Stricker, Western Flagship)

A recent alumna said:

> I think, because I didn't feel comfortable. I didn't feel like it was a safe environment in my discussion sections. Even though [the other students] were my friends, I was not close to my TA, and so a lot of times I just wouldn't say what I was thinking because I knew that it was going to be mocked by her, perhaps, or . . . I just didn't feel safe so I didn't. I didn't talk. (Christina Young, Western Flagship)

Despite knowing that they have conservative peers who will support them, if not in the classroom itself then behind the scenes at organization meetings, for some Western Public students actively fighting the liberal tide in classes is simply too much. Though it may be unsatisfying and make them question their commitment to the cause, some students decide to stay silent and simply get through the class rather than create a stir.

Western Public conservatives discussed varying levels of discomfort associated with this type of avoidance strategy. While some, like the young woman quoted above, "don't take those kinds of things personally," others said they were forced to extremes to tolerate their coursework. One Western Satellite student described wanting to pursue a double major in political science but found herself unable to bear the faculty's overall liberal stance. "So I dropped it to a minor, took another class, and I was like, oh, this is terrible. So I took a year off. And my total credits from summer school right now, I'm doing one political class—one political science class in the classroom—and two online because I absolutely cannot take it" (Lindsey Nicholson, Western Satellite).

Conservative students who lack a taste for confrontation in the classroom have similar concerns about grading biases as their more outspoken peers, but unsurprisingly show quite different strategies for dealing with them. One interviewee, who widely promulgated the provocative style in his role as vice president of the Western Flagship College Republicans but who wanted to ensure a high GPA for applying to graduate school, told about learning to take an alternative tack in some classroom settings:

> In the classes, we usually find there are three or four of us who are on the right, and everybody else is on the other side. And for me as a student looking back, I'd raise some questions that would come up. Sometimes I would just be disgusted because I would almost fear for my grade being affected [if I spoke up]. I had one [conservative friend who] did great on all her assignments and she challenged her professor . . . who I think is one of the heads in political science group. And because he was very anti-Bush administration, very anti-neo-conservative, her grade suffered. She got a C– on her grade. And it didn't quantitatively add up, and she let it be. She didn't fight it. But that kind of told me, hey, I need to be careful in certain classes. (Kevin Sharkey, Western Flagship)

Assuming similarly that grading was not meritocratic, other conservative students described more actively courting liberal faculty's favor by adjusting their coursework to fit what they believed faculty wanted to hear. One young woman told of giving an in-class presentation challenging the writing of the feminist author bell hooks—a presentation that appalled her professor—only to have her grade raised later when she decided to recant her earlier critique.

Still another interviewee—one who practiced the provocative style in his role as Western Flagship College Republicans president—spoke of securing a good grade in a course by preemptively assessing his professor's politics:

> The first class I took at Flagship was with quite possibly one of the most liberal professors I've ever had. And I wrote a paper supporting the feminist movement because I figured it would get me a better grade in the class. And it did. I got C's on all the tests I took in that class that year, and I got an A in the class after I wrote that paper [*laughs*]. . . . It was a sociology class on gender and society. I don't remember the professor's name, but she was a nice professor. I liked her. But I knew where she stood and I knew what I needed to do to get a good grade in the class. But I completely didn't believe what I was writing but it worked, you know. (Kody Aronson, Western Flagship)

For some Western Public conservatives, in some classes, students say keeping their politics to themselves and getting a good grade takes precedence over confronting their professors or their peers. Though it may not be as fun or attention-getting as taking on the professor, it gets the job done. As one student explained, "I do try to please the professors when I'm writing, and sometimes that means hiding some of my own *real* opinions. . . . You do have to be careful on tests and papers. You've got to get a grade. That's why you're there" (Hunter Devine, Western Flagship).

Variability in Approaches

Just as we saw the student-run conservative organizations at Western Public working together to develop new strategies and draw on the legacies of the provocative style (and in some instances the campaigning style), so too in the classroom we see evidence of individual Western Public conservatives engaging in behaviors that fit with these styles. This is not coincidental: we argue that what we are seeing here are the fruits of the collective problem solving that takes place during the small-group interactions being transposed by individuals to new situations, all within the opportunity spaces created by the organizational environment of the university campus. The ways that the group finds to manage the liberal campus become resources that individuals can draw on as they make their own ways through their schooling. At the same time, when these individuals bring their experiences back to the group, it allows for continued fine-tuning and adjustment of these styles.

These styles predominate inside the classroom much as they do outside of it with the clubs because in many ways they are suited to the campus environment. All of the elements of how education is arranged at Western Public, such as large class sizes and impersonal registration, make confronting professors, on the one hand, or harboring suspicions about them and simmering quietly on the other, "reasonable" options for conservative students. Interestingly, in instances where the institutional features are mitigated—one-on-one in office hours, or in smaller seminar classes—we see a considerable change in conservatives' tone and behavior:

> Well, first and foremost, I would say interact with faculty as much as you can. So don't necessarily go in with the persecution complex, try to, and you may be persecuted some, but don't assume that you will be. I found a lot of people are at least willing to talk in a reasonable manner if you approach it that way. And go and talk to your professors outside of class and tell them what you're thinking and try to be very respectful of where they're coming from. You might learn something. (Isabel Stricker, Western Flagship)

> I've probably been most vocal about my political thoughts in [my senior seminar]. And I think that's because it *is* our senior seminar, it *is* designed to create dialogue and dissecting different issues. But even those people that don't agree with me, we smile

at each other, we say hi, we engage in dialogue beyond just what we're talking about in class. And I feel that it's a comfortable environment. (Kevin Sharkey, Western Flagship)

Given that small courses are getting ever harder to come by at public universities and that faculty's office hours are limited, options for Western Public students to have small-group discussions remain limited. Still, these examples imply that when some of the organizational features of the campus are altered or minimized—and, quite simply, look more like those at Eastern Elite—the routinized political styles no longer work as well. At the same time, this tells us that these styles are well adapted to business as usual at Western Public.

That said, large class sizes, core curricula requirements, and depersonalized class registration alone cannot explain all the animosity that leads to Western Public conservatives' inclination to provoke, since not all large state universities with a predominance of such features have such discontented conservatives. In fact, at least one study has found that politically conservative students across higher education institutional types tend to be just as satisfied with their professors—and are just as likely to have personal relationships with them during office hours or in research settings—as their liberal classmates.[19] For further evidence that distant relationships with professors do not always lead to the "gotcha" mentality among conservatives: when we did interviews with conservative students at our own large home institution, UC San Diego, we heard less of a consistent preference for politically provocative action. This bolsters our argument that the campus features of Western Public are only one factor in students' perceptions of faculty and the classroom; also necessary are elements of institutionalized culture that make confrontation seem appealing. But this is clearly a two-way street: The cultural features need the structural prerequisites as scaffolding, but the structural features are understood in particular ways only through the use of well-established cultural precepts.

Also of interest is the way that, while these styles are developed within the student-run organizations and then transposed to day-today situations by individuals, there is not a one-to-one relationship between those students who engage in more provocative behaviors within the groups and those who do so within the classroom. While many of the Western Public interviewees who espouse campaigning as a political style are the same students who choose to keep quiet in the classroom or say that they write what they need to in order to get an A, this is not always the case. For example, Brooke Gerson, who is quoted extensively above as a *classroom* provocateuse, is not totally sold on the more glaring activities that the Western Flagship College Republicans engage in. At the other end of the spectrum, Kevin Sharkey—who discussed being cautious about how he conducted himself in the classroom and wrote palatable answers to exam questions—was the main organizing force behind the "Why We Want to Kill You" event. These seeming mismatches do not weaken our argument. Instead, they show that the styles of political action developed within the conservative student organizations are accessible even to those who do not subscribe to them as the best methods for the organizations. This is strong evidence of individuals picking and choosing among the cultural materials available to them.

PLANNING FOR CONSERVATIVE CAREERS WITH A LOCAL HORIZON

Our best evidence for how these different styles might be deployed throughout the life course comes from students' descriptions of their career aspirations—or, in the case of the graduates we interviewed, the career paths they were already on. Conservative college students encounter multiple ideas about being conservative, promoted by a range of significant actors: from their families to the national conservative organizations to their campus clubs. By interacting in these different settings, conservative college students build up specific social networks and political styles, all of which help set expectations about the plausibility of certain career paths. The choices that individual students make, the cultural repertoires they tap in to, and the settings in which they find themselves appear to lead to the replication of certain types of career outcomes for conservative students in the different universities we studied. Of note, we see this as recreating particular forms of elite and nonelite political leadership in the larger society.

Western Public students expressed interest in a range of jobs after graduation; however, there are certain commonalities among them. The conservative students we talked to were particularly interested in working in local politics or policy (only two expressed interest in national-level politics) and in working with local media (none described a desire to work for national-scale media). Remaining at a regional level brings with it certain issues, particularly with regard to pay. Western Public graduates pursuing this path generally have to juggle more than one position in order to stay solvent, as this young man explained about a local libertarian think tank:

> I had originally thought that if you got a job at a think tank, that's your job, just like a normal person. You get your paycheck and everything. And then when you talk to these people, these think tanks don't really seem to pay well, so a lot of them work multiple jobs. . . . I just turned in a résumé with . . . one of the state senators. . . . I was talking to him and I was saying I assumed that he's not going to pay very well for a staffer. But work for him and work for [a local think tank] at the same time. They'd both be in [the same city] and I could do maybe research for one while I'm doing staffer things for him, and it would actually work out fairly well. (Victor Irwin, Western Satellite)

Personal finances, on the other hand, did not come up as an issue in any of the Eastern Elite interviews, regardless of the individual's class of origin.

Further, when Western Public students rely on their mostly local networks to obtain jobs, this leads them into certain types of careers, in the sense that who they know can only get them so far. This can be seen as part of what keeps many Western Public students more locally oriented, as in this alumna's story of how she found her postcollege job:

I graduated and I was looking for jobs and I contacted a couple people that I worked with [at the state senate minority (Republicans) office]. And I was thinking, okay, campaign season's coming, so maybe I could do something related to campaigns. And I asked a few friends that I had from that internship, and they sent my résumé . . . to our friend . . . who works down the hall. And he does some campaign work, but he didn't have anything. And he said, oh, what about [this local political website]. It's writing. I met with Chuck Kelley, and I think probably after one lunch with him I was really sold on what they were doing, and it's been working well ever since. (Stephanie Cohen, Western Flagship)

This type of story is common to Western Public students in that they generally seek out positions by way of contacts they made in internships or through campus organizations rather than more impersonally through an alumni/ae network or a national organization like the Heritage Foundation. At the other extreme, some students find positions through completely impersonal networks (for example, job listings on the website ConservativeJobs.com).

Even among students who have spent time working in Washington, D.C., or who have been exposed to national organizations, by far the biggest commonality among Western Public conservatives is this desire to stay within the state after graduation:

After studying in Washington, D.C., and [seeing] how Congress works, I don't know if I'd want to start at the back of the line and be there for forty years before I can really influence policy. And so I think I might run in the state, . . . maybe as like a state legislator. And who knows, maybe one day run for governor or something like that, someday. (Hunter Devine, Western Flagship)

If I go to D.C., I could only see myself there for like four or five years. All my family is here. Everything I like is here. I think D.C. would be a lot of fun for a while, but I've been to D.C. I don't know if I could live there for four or five years. (Karl Hayes, Western Satellite)

As mentioned by the latter student, family is often another consideration for Western Public undergraduates. This comes up in respect to both their families of origin and the future families they hope to have. In contrast, the issue of staying close to family did not come up in a single Eastern Elite interview, and the prospect of future families arose in only a few.[20]

On the whole, Western Public students maintain less of a national horizon than did our Eastern Elite interviewees—in part because the Western Public university system doesn't construct them as players on the national stage, but also because they see opportunities for their future political engagement as much greater on the local scene. Their somewhat lower social class standing relative to Eastern Elite students may have something to do with their preference for sticking closer to home, but not always: Hunter Devine, the interviewee who thinks he might run for governor someday, is the son of a father with an MD degree from a prominent medical school in another state and a mother with a PhD from an internationally prestigious university. The conservative students and alumni/ae we interviewed on the Western Public campuses wanted to stay in the state not just because it was familiar but because it seemed to offer the best political opportunities for them.

What does any of this have to do with the provocative or campaigning styles used while conservatives are undergraduates at Western Public? Significantly, several of our interviewees believed that the confrontational style they used during their college years would be useful to them once they entered the wider world—even including those who envisioned careers in national politics or policy:

I think that this has helped me, and I looked at it. . . . I did look at it from the strategic points, saying hey, how can this help me get to where I want to be, and at the same time help educate others about the issues? . . . And it *has* been instrumental. (Kevin Sharkey, Western Flagship)

Well there's not much for a college student to lose [in being provocative]. It's not unheard of for college students to do stupid things. . . . I'm proud of what I've done. There are a number of people who've done much quote-unquote "worse stuff" than I've done in college that are now in Congress. And I'm sure that people will be more than happy to know that I was organizing issue events in college rather than getting high and/or drunk. So I don't think that's a big paper trail. Have I written a lot of provocative columns? Yes, and that comes with being anybody who's ever worked in any form of media. (Bryan Carhart, Western Satellite)

For the first student quoted above, staging provocative events relating to his key interest of national security (the "Why We Want to Kill You" event) had put him in touch with people on the national level who work on these issues. Meanwhile, the second student's provocative actions had already paid off for him: at the time of our interview he had attracted considerable attention from national conservative organizations, including being awarded a prestigious fellowship from the Phillips Foundation and a high-profile fellowship at one of the premiere conservative D.C. think tanks. Others at Western Public reported that their combative stance toward nonconservatives put them in good stead in the local market.

However, other Western Public students see the need to adapt to a different style in order to achieve success outside of campus. One Western Satellite graduate explained:

I want to be seen as a well-respected person who's established as ... center-right. You're fair, you go after people on both sides if the issue is wrong, but you tend to lean more towards the right side of the spectrum. And so I'd like to be established in the [state] community as someone who is well respected in that regard. . . . And if things continue the way they are, I think that I have the potential to be a name in [state] politics. And what excites me about that is being someone in the political minority, especially in [our state], . . . who can offer a well-respected perspective. (Lindsey Nicholson, Western Satellite)

For this interviewee, provocation has its limits, and adopting a more civilized tone appears to be the key to success in the local political arena. Others more invested in the campaigning style as undergraduates, such as Hunter Devine, do not seem to feel such pressure. At the same time, however, his future aspirations to elected office appear to have put the brakes on any proclivities toward provocation that Hunter may have harbored.

CONCLUSION

Students at Western Flagship go to a large state university with a reputation for being a party school, and where fun predominates as the overriding logic for what it means to be a college student. An understanding that college is a time where anything goes underscores the social, academic, and political lives of undergraduates here and on the other Western Public campuses. As we saw above, conservatives at Western Public for the most part are confident that regardless of their future paths, they will be able to write off their exploits as the folly of youth on an as-needed basis. In this way, they actively draw not only on conservative national discourses that favor confrontational, populist conservatism but also on popular ideas about college life in the United States. These understandings suffuse campus and college clubs.

On the academic front, students on the Western Public campuses are suspicious of their professors' motives in the classroom—certainly more so than are Eastern Elite students. Attending large state schools, our interviewees mostly did not know individual professors well, and there was a low level of esteem for the faculty in general. Large class sizes—a hallmark of state universities—contributed to this level of disregard. Disregard in the case of conservative students breeds contempt, which breeds a willingness to goad liberal professors—at least more so than at Eastern Elite. Socially, Western Public conservatives likewise have darker assessments of their liberal classmates' potential to be fair and nonjudgmental interlocutors in discussions of political ideas than do Eastern Elite students. Because so few undergraduates at Western Public universities live on campus, where they could get to know one another in more intimate settings, there is a fairly weak set of community norms for friendly and respectful political discussions, and Western Public conservatives feel quite marginalized on their campus. Even though middle-of-the-road students actually predominate on campuses like Western Flagship, conservatives perceive themselves as cast adrift in the swirling social currents of their liberal milieu. Conservative students at Western Public schools talk at much greater length than their Eastern Elite counterparts about feeling marginalized on campus.

For Western Flagship conservatives, the broader liberal environment of their university and the community that surrounds it—as well as the campus organizational features of large classes, off-campus housing, attenuated funding for campus organizations, and relatively little contact with faculty—helps to make a provocative style of conservatism appealing to many of these students. Conservatives on the other Western Public campuses actively look to their counterparts at Western Flagship, and especially the Western Flagship College Republicans, for cues. Their interest in actively opposing the liberal environment, as well as their distrust of the mechanisms that are in place to make student voices heard, frequently leads conservatives at Western Public campuses to link up with national conservative organizations, which are thrilled to lend monetary and ideological support. Someone, they say, needs to provide an opposing point of view within what the students perceive as their overwhelmingly liberal environs. Best to connect with highly visible organizations like the YAF and the LI.

Our interviewees' future aspirations also appear to contribute to the dominant conservative style of provocation. Students on the Western Public campuses who join clubs like College Republicans learn to share ideas about their activism with an eye to heated state-level politics, not the bigger stage of national politics. In addition, virtually all the students who plan for careers with a policy bent want to be in partisan environments; their years of provoking liberals make them uninterested in working across the aisle. Explained one student, "If you're a diplomat you have to represent whoever's in office. And I'm just too much of an opinionated cuss to deal with that, so it probably wouldn't be a good fit" (Bryan Carhart, Western Satellite).

These aspects of the Western Public campuses, and particularly Western Flagship's undergraduate structures and campuswide cultures, combined with students' beliefs that they will have partisan political careers and that being in college is supposed to be a "fun" experience, help make the provocative style of conservatism appealing. College, Western Public young conservatives say, is not a time to be cautious about the future, or refined and palatable to the opposition. As we will see in the next chapter, this attitude stands in sharp contrast to the Eastern Elite model of conservative action.

Chapter 6

Civilized Discourse, Highbrow Provocation, and a Fuller Embrace of Campaigning

Three Conservative Styles at Eastern Elite University

When we arrived on the East Coast in the fall of 2008 to complete our interviews with Eastern Elite University students and alumni/ae, we had more or less wrapped up the first phase of data collection at Western Public. Because we had found the provocative style to be so dominant in our first case-study—and also knew it to be a favored form of expression in much of the Republican Party at large—we expected to find it would have at least *some* presence at Eastern Elite. We were thus unprepared for just how dissimilar conservative styles at Eastern Elite actually were from those at Western Public. While more than a few of our Eastern Elite respondents hailed from families quite similar to those of their Western Public peers, and though the university they attended is likewise located on a campus and within a community popularly known for its liberal leanings, Eastern Elite conservatives shun the provocative style as, well, *beneath* them. By this they mean not intellectual enough, overly populist and partisan, and, after all is said and done, not really *conservative* in style—if conservative is taken to mean either measured in temperament or evocative of an older tradition.

In place of the in-your-face style of provocation, we found Eastern Elite students engaged in three different modes of expressive action, only one of which is used with any regularity at any of the Western Public campuses. First, there is civilized discourse, which is by far the dominant style of conservative expression at Eastern Elite. Second, the campaigning style has a greater presence at Eastern Elite, with the Eastern Elite College Republicans in particular working on local, regional, and national campaigns at the behest of the national GOP or the College Republicans National Committee. Finally, we discovered a third style at Eastern Elite that has only the smallest inkling of existence at Western Public, a style we call highbrow provocation. In this chapter we use much the same blueprint as we did for Western Public to make sense of these three styles, first using the emic analytical method to discuss our interviewees' own explanations for why certain forms of political expression are preferred or disdained in their clubs and on their wider campus, and then laying out our etic analysis of how a variety of organizational arrangements at Eastern Elite influence students' ideas and behavior.

EASTERN ELITE COLLEGE REPUBLICANS: A CIVILIZED PRESENCE

Civilized discourse is the form of expression at Eastern Elite that conservative students use and philosophize about most frequently, no matter which of the right-leaning clubs they belong to. More than any of the other styles we witnessed on any of the campuses we studied, civilized discourse is built around students' sense of "who we are" as Eastern Elite undergraduates, as well as their impressions of what membership in this university community portends for their future careers and roles in society. As such, this style is deeply symbolic, speaking to issues of the core identity of what it means to be a student at (and later a graduate of) this prestigious institution, and of finding one's niche in the country's most privileged social strata. At the same time, it is also highly pragmatic, with an ever-vigilant

Eastern Elite eye on how such a style will be viewed later by high-status future employers, graduate programs, or fellowship committees whose members might be interested in how a student conducted him- or herself while in college. Interestingly, those who use the campaigning style at Eastern Elite are committed to using a civil tone in their activities, and even those interviewees at Eastern Elite who practiced the more contentious style of highbrow provocation—with the intent of goading other students into recognizing the politically correct follies of their campus—insisted that they too were fundamentally civil members of the community. This explicit commitment to the appropriateness of civil exchange pervades the Eastern Elite campus, even if in practice there is a good deal more affront made to others than some students would like to admit. Given the premium that is placed on calling one's own political style civil, we begin our analysis of Eastern Elite conservative political expression by looking in depth at the purest form of "reasonable debate"—the civilized discourse style.

COLLEGE REPUBLICANS AND OTHER
CONSERVATIVES IN SUPPORT OF CIVILITY

Of all the interviewees we spoke with at Eastern Elite, members of the university's chapter of the College Republicans were the most avid proponents of the civilized discourse style. Since the Eastern Elite College Republicans is the largest conservative club on campus—with membership in the hundreds, not the tens—its style is clearly the modal form of active conservatives' expression on campus, if not always the most noticeable (the conservative newspaper, the *Searchlight*, often wins the visibility contest).[1] Past and present leaders of the Eastern Elite College Republicans sounded quite similar to one another when they described the type of political action they feel works best on their campus. Said one, "I think good events are events that are intellectually stimulating, that influence the people that are [at Eastern Elite] that may not be Republicans, that will cause them to question their beliefs or their political views" (Derek

Yeager, Eastern Elite). The types of events Derek refers to as "intellectually stimulating" included bringing speakers to campus, such as
a top George W. Bush administration strategist in the waning days
of the 2008 election, and at another time a highly visible elected
black Republican. Since the latter politician was African American,
Derek reached out to an African American men's club at Eastern
Elite, whose members agreed to cosponsor the visit—an example of
working with a nontraditional ally to get his speaker heard. Likewise, the College Republicans under Derek's leadership made it a
point to work collaboratively with the College Democrats to gain at
least some recognition for ROTC on their campus—an issue that
this leader thinks is not purely Republican.[2] The emphasis in Derek's work is to be reasonable, to spark considered debate, and in
doing so, to spread conservative ideas on campus.

In addition to preferring formal events with intellectual content,
Derek—who is no stranger to partisan politics (in fact, he interned
for the same chief Bush strategist he had brought as a speaker to
campus)—wanted to have informal, courteous conversations with
any and all of his liberal peers, not just those in political clubs, especially when certain issues threatened to reach a fever pitch. Recalling an incident in which a "firestorm" about abortion had arisen on
an Eastern Elite student listserv, Derek thought that the written nas-
tiness had gotten out of hand, and he attempted to tone it down
through reasonable face-to-face exchange:

> I [wrote on the listserv], "Look, this is ridiculous. If you actually
> have something to say, I'll go down to the dining hall. Come
> down and talk about it." So I brought my computer down to the
> dining hall to work on some things, and a dozen people showed
> up. We had a great conversation about it in a very civil, respect-
> ful, intellectual way. So I'm not afraid to engage these issues in
> an intellectual manner. I welcome it. (Derek Yeager, Eastern Elite)

This, according to Derek, is the way contentious politics ought to be
handled at Eastern Elite. He did not want to protest for his issues
outside the student union or play gotcha with liberal "opponents,"

as College Republicans do at Western Public. Derek wanted to talk reasonably with his liberal peers.

Another student who was a member of the Eastern Elite College Republicans (and also a discernibly mellower editor of the conservative newspaper than the previous person in charge) did not deny that he sometimes felt overwhelmed by the sheer number of liberals who tried to engage him—not infrequently with barbs—in political contests. But Calvin Coffey contended that rather than "not taking the other side seriously," as his Western peers might do, he was inclined to check out books from the library and do research on the Internet in order to fashion better arguments for his position, which he attempted to deliver in a calm, reasoned manner (Calvin Coffey, Eastern Elite). "You can't be nasty, and they have to respect you because you have done the extra work" (interview, Calvin Coffey, Eastern Elite). Calvin went on to say that this level of research had its costs—it could be aggravating to have to do this much work on top of an already demanding academic load, just to defend one's political position—but that engaging in this form of discussion made him feel as though he had integrity and was better prepared in the intense intellectual environment at Eastern Elite:

> It is kind of the thing where you feel better about yourself because you listen to the other side, and then you can argue with it. And that makes you feel good because you have considered something else, and you feel smart because you have got that engagement. As opposed to maybe you don't feel so proud of yourself if you are confronted with another view and you have nothing to say, and you just get frustrated. (Calvin Coffey, Eastern Elite)

Political discussions at Eastern Elite, at least ideally, have to be built on facts, respectful dialogue, and sometimes, according to our interviewees, being the cool-headed person in the room who tamps down the tension that arises in political debates—something they say they have to do when they are so often outnumbered. Calvin and Derek, both of whom were elected to lead their respective conservative clubs, believe strongly in civilized discourse, as we see clearly through these statements of affirmation.

Of course, another way to understand what the civilized discourse *is* is to distinguish it from what it is *not*. One of the things the civilized discourse style most decidedly is not—and all Eastern Elite interviewees were very clear on this point—is the *provocative* style, which they saw being deployed on other campuses across the country by students affiliated with such national organizations as the Young America's Foundation (YAF), the Leadership Institute (LI), and David Horowitz's Students for Academic Freedom. Almost to a person—again, even among those who practiced the Eastern Elite version of highbrow provocation—conservatives at Eastern Elite condemned such a style and its proponents for being "populist" (Drew Metcalfe, Eastern Elite) or "not as thinking" (interview, Nicole Harris, Eastern Elite). For this reason, Eastern Elite students put a good deal of distance between their form of conservatism and what non-Eastern Elite students do.

True, a few of our interviewees at Eastern Elite did have relationships with organizations like the YAF—and when they did, these students were quick to say diplomatic things about the benefits they derived from those relationships, such as receiving financial help to bring select speakers to campus or appreciating the national conferences, which are fun to attend. But they were even quicker to add what they *didn't* appreciate about events such as Catch an Illegal Alien Day and the Global Warming Beach Party, both of which are associated by reputation with national conservative organizations like these.[3] Darren Norton, a president of the Eastern Elite College Republicans, specifically questioned the provocative style advocated by YAF, during which critique he also made clear why he supported a more "reasonable" way of being conservative at Eastern Elite:

> I disagree with a lot of [the Young America's Foundation's] tactics. I think that even the emails that I get from them, that are directed at conservative students who are on their email lists—I'm uncomfortable with some of the things that they propose and some of the things they say. I think that sort of goes back to the

mentality of, 'What is the best way to create change on campus?' Is it to be basically a caricature of yourself and try to get that very visibly done, or is it to try to work sort of, I guess you could say, within the system in more reasonable ways to try to soften the image of people towards Republicans, and then come at them with what your ideas are.

Darren went on to say that he enjoyed a good argument, but not when it involved "screaming at the top of your lungs at someone":

I like debating when I can get my message across in a way that I can feel like people are respecting [me]. It is no fun for me to have people walk by and leer or gaze at me or yell at me that I am bigoted or whatever it is, because I'm not. . . . I would rather argue with them in a more reasonable level to say here is why I'm not and here is why we can agree to disagree, but I will not respect you calling me something that I am not. (Darren Norton, Eastern Elite)

The difference between Darren's comment here and the sentiment expressed by Karl Hayes at Western Satellite in the last chapter ("If you wake up and come to school in the morning and someone calls you a bigot, you know you're going to have a good day") could not be more pronounced.

A past editor of the conservative newspaper the *Searchlight* concurred with his classmates in Eastern Elite College Republicans that the populist provocative style—as it is practiced at other schools and sponsored by certain national conservative organizations—is not a good fit with his university. He recounted, "I just thought Young America's Foundation . . . some of its emanations on certain campuses . . . strike me as really kind of needlessly belligerent and unthoughtful" (Vincent Long, Eastern Elite). There is a consensus at Eastern Elite—even among those conservatives who *themselves* get accused by others of being needlessly belligerent in their conservative newspaper articles—that proper conservatives should not aim to stick it to liberals with no intellectual basis for the taunts, nor should they propagate cartoonish versions of right-leaning positions. Reasoned argumentation ought to play a role in how conservatives get their issues across on this campus.

There is one more thing we should add here about what is contemptible about the type of provocative style practiced on other campuses, according to our interviewees at Eastern Elite University. In addition to calling this form of expression anti-intellectual, Eastern Elite conservatives also voiced concern that the provocative style is not suited to conservatism *in general*. In explaining why he opted for a style of highbrow provocation rather than provocative activism, another past editor of the *Searchlight* said, "A proper conservative stance involves great concern with politics but some distance from its possibility of success, right?" (Henry Quick, Eastern Elite). Yet another student related this interpretation of the intellectual roots of conservatism to the type of conservative presence that is acceptable on campus:

> I mean, there's something inherently radical about that [kind of activism] and not quite with the conservative aesthetic. . . . I mean, we bring in speakers and they're provocative as far as being a conservative at Eastern is provocative. *But it's nothing for its own sake*. It's in order to have a good discussion about some issue that would otherwise be ignored at school. (Drew Metcalfe, Eastern Elite, emphasis added)

Drew's concern, which underscores the type of elevated discourse drawn on by Eastern Elite conservatives, is not seen among students at Western Public. There the predominant focus is on confrontation and eliciting emotional reactions rather than on demonstrating that one is committed to meaningful, content-driven conversations with peers.[4] This, we hasten to add, is not because we think students at the Western Public universities are not bright enough or capable of having substantive conversations with their liberal classmates. Rather, it is because that style of discourse is not widely shared among conservatives on their campuses—as it is at Eastern Elite—

for all of the cultural and organizational reasons we laid out in the previous chapter.[5]

As such, the Eastern Elite College Republicans focus on working within the norms of civilized discourse in order to create a conservative presence on the campus. They host speakers and debates, often cosponsoring these with other groups. In especially stark contrast to Western Flagship, the Eastern Elite College Republicans often put on not only debates but also social events with the Eastern Elite College Democrats, including a popular annual bowling night. This constructs a space where conservatives are able to get considerable airtime for their views and, in collegial discourse with others, have their views openly challenged. As we will continue to see, unlike their Western Public peers, Eastern Elite conservatives do not construct their fellow students primarily as narrow-minded combatants or as apathetic drones who can only be snapped out of their complacency with a shock to the system (although Eastern Elite interviewees did at times touch on some of these themes). Instead, Eastern Elite conservatives tend to view their fellow students as classmates they should act respectfully toward because, first, they made it into Eastern Elite University, so they must be gifted and talented to some extent, and second, they are the people with whom Eastern Elite conservatives will very likely be wandering the same corridors of power at later points in their lives.

CONTEXTUALIZING THE EASTERN ELITE COLLEGE REPUBLICANS: OTHER CONSERVATIVE GROUPS ON CAMPUS

Unlike at Western Flagship, where the College Republicans are by far the largest and most visible conservative presence on campus, at Eastern Elite many right-leaning student groups vie for attention.[6] Given the relatively small number of students active in conservative clubs on campus, there is considerable overlap in membership between these clubs, but they still provide unique outlets for Eastern Elite conservatives to engage different aspects of their political identities. Further, in contrast to the Western Public campuses, Eastern Elite has a few nonpartisan organizations to which conservatives gravitate, as well as a university-sponsored nonpartisan political institute. In examining these different groups, we see the norms of civilized discourse cropping up again and again. That is not to say, however, that none of the other groups at Eastern Elite attempt a style other than civilized discourse. Still, right-leaning groups that experiment with more provocative styles seem to learn quickly that this does not work well for Eastern Elite's campus.

We saw this most clearly with single-issue clubs. Like their colleagues across the country at Western Public, the College Republicans at Eastern Elite mostly avoid social issues such as abortion as too divisive for their membership, and so conservative students who are especially committed to them tend to be members of both groups. Participants in the pro-life group (a contentious issue in any forum) reported that they had to learn the style of civilized discourse for use on their campus. For example, one member of this club told us that the group had once experimented with more provocative actions, but that through trial and error its members had learned to conform to the expectations of others on their campus:

> I remember freshman year our posters would be like, "Life starts at conception and ends at Planned Parenthood." And we'd have blood splatters. Or we'd have . . . even some less controversial, in my mind. . . . It was of [a picture of] a fetus developing, and the fetus would be saying different things, like "I want to be an [airline pilot] when I grow up." . . . I actually designed those posters [*laughs*]. . . . But those were like *crazy*. People *hated* them . . . tore them down and defaced them. But I learned from that experience, and when I [became] president, we totally changed it. (Kyle Lee, Eastern Elite)

This student went on to say that the group started different kinds of campaigns—raising funds for baby supplies and for pregnancy counseling—during which he and his colleagues worked across the aisle not only with the Women's Center on campus but also with the "crazy feminist organization" at Eastern Elite (Kyle Lee, Eastern Elite). Another member of the pro-life club echoed Kyle's recollection, recalling that early on "we were doing a lot of things which were intentionally controversial . . . and were just not very well received, and were not very well conceived either" (Melissa Preston, Eastern Elite). In other words, the pro-life group—many of whose members had used tactics like this when they were in high school— didn't like the controversy they were creating, and dumped those tactics for the civilized discourse style that seemed more appropriate for their campus.

Eastern Elite conservatives are also highly involved with groups that are not explicitly political, such as religious groups, a finding that departs somewhat from what we saw on the Western Public campuses.[7] As we laid out earlier, a large number of our Eastern Elite interviewees are devout Catholics, and many of them were involved in a Catholic student group at their university. Though not outwardly political in nature, this group appeared to have overlapping membership with more or less every other major student-run conservative organization on the Eastern Elite campus that we studied— the College Republicans chapter, the *Searchlight*, the pro-life group, and an abstinence group. One reason for this may be the wider perception students described that on the Eastern Elite campus, religious in some sense equals conservative:

> A lot of the people who might be considered Catholic conservatives because of their positions about faith and about these kind[s] of social conservative issues are, like me, not conservative on a lot of other areas. And what's interesting is that just in the current way that people get labeled on campus, those people get put in the conservative box, even if that might not necessarily make sense. (Kris Nagle, Eastern Elite)

Thus, given Eastern Elite's liberal bent, students involved in this group tend to be considered conservative by others, even if they do not self-identify as such, as when, for example, they have commitments to social justice.

Though the Catholic students' group is less organized around holding events for others on campus and more focused on creating a community of faith, we also find evidence of a taste for civilized discourse here. Kris described the club as a place where he could have political conversations and debates with "people who, even though they certainly had questions and certainly had doubts and didn't think they had everything resolved, were not willing to give in to the temptation of relativism" (Kris Nagle, Eastern Elite). At the same time, though, others (in this case, a member of the *Search-light*) criticized the Eastern Elite Catholic group as not civilized, or at least rational, enough: "It's very much an emotionalist, very modern type of [religious organization] … and I don't mean this to sound elitist in any respect, but very anti-intellectual" (Drew Metcalfe, Eastern Elite). Kris likewise allowed that for some, the Catholic club is insufficiently conservative, saying that "people who fall into the kind of Catholic conservative mold" contend that the group "is basically a mainstream, tolerance-promoting, sell-out organization, and they are very opposed to aspects of, have a very ambivalent relationship towards it" (Kris Nagle, Eastern Elite). For many Eastern Elite Catholics, however, the group seems to provide a forum for discussing and debating ideas with the structure of Catholic theology as a brake on an "anything goes" personal moral code.

The other student-run organization that a large number of our Eastern Elite interviewees were involved with and where civilized discourse is prevalent is the school's mainstream student newspaper, the *Manifest*. Numerous students from all of the right-leaning groups take advantage of the opportunity to write for the *Manifest*, either as members of its staff (writing regular articles or op-ed columns) or submitting opinion pieces as representatives of other student groups. For these students, the *Manifest* presents an excellent opportunity to get public airtime for the conservative point of view. A few interviewees described themselves as having been, at various points in time, "the token conservative on the op-ed page" (Evan Dooley, Eastern Elite). Another said,

I write for the *Manifest* just to get the conservative point of view on national politics, because it is so rarely presented. I asked one of the editors, and maybe he just doesn't remember, but it seemed like every day there was some other position or column just bashing Sarah Palin: "Oh, she is a religious nutcase. She is just dumb. She is just a pick to help get women." It was like every day. I asked him, "Was there any other column in the election that defended her [besides mine]?" He couldn't think of one. (Calvin Coffey, Eastern Elite)

Widely read and with a storied past—the paper's long list of illustrious alumni/ae can make it seem like a farm team for the *Washington Post* or the *New York Times*—the *Manifest* offers conservative students a public forum for their views. Though outnumbered by liberals, Eastern Elite conservatives say they do not have trouble getting their stories or letters printed. Or at least no more trouble than it ordinarily takes, as the *Manifest* puts its staff members through a lengthy and cumbersome tryout period. Some students thus come to prefer other outlets, such as the conservative newspaper, as this alumnus relayed: "The *Searchlight* was great because you could write whatever you wanted whenever you wanted to, as opposed to the *Manifest*, which is very rigid and time-consuming and annoying" (Kenneth Lambert, Eastern Elite). Still, many conservative students' desire to use the *Manifest* as an outlet for thoughtful political expression presents a substantial contrast to Western Public. None of our interviewees on any of the Western Public campuses talked about publishing an op-ed piece in their mainstream campus newspaper as a worthwhile endeavor, even if they appreciated having their political exploits noticed and written about by *other* media writers—and despite several of our interviewees now having careers in which they write extensively as political pundits or regional think tank fellows.[8]

Perhaps one of the strongest bastions promoting civilized discourse at Eastern Elite is an organization that is run not by the students (though they are heavily involved in it) but by the university itself. The Center for Political Institutions is a high-profile university organization that brings important political figures (politicians, but also journalists, lobbyists, and others) to campus. Eastern Elite undergraduates get to hear speakers give talks, participate in Q&A

sessions, and, in the case of students directly involved with the center, have dinner and engage more informally with these high-status guests. Though conservative students report that a greater number of liberal figures are invited to speak at the center than conservatives (since students get some voice in who is asked to visit, and liberals represent a greater proportion of the students involved), individuals from both ends of the political spectrum participate. In getting to "meet and speak with these amazing minds," Eastern Elite students are encouraged to engage informally but respectfully with prominent individuals of all political stripes (Elizabeth Tennyson, Eastern Elite). Thus, the environment of the Center for Political Institutions not only provides lessons in civilized discourse, it also (again) reinforces the sense of distinction inculcated in Eastern Elite undergraduates. We see this as being in marked contrast to the lack of such forums at Western Public.

WHY CIVILIZED DISCOURSE? EASTERN ELITE INTERVIEWEES' EXPLANATIONS

Eastern Elite conservatives offered several interrelated yet analytically distinct reasons for why they opted to engage in civilized discourse. First, civilized discourse is the style that best suits Eastern Elite as a whole (although we have already provided evidence on this score, there is more to come). Second, the civilized discourse style creates a way for Eastern Elite conservatives to manage their minority status on campus in a way that lets others in the university community know that conservatives not only "are here" but also are "not crazy." This style, furthermore, is a tool used to persuade others to seriously consider their points of view, and maybe even someday to support conservative policies. If this is not a real possibility at the present moment, when Eastern Elite students are young and practically de facto liberal, according to our interviewees, then perhaps it can be realized at some point down the road, when these students have had a little more experience, as well as some fat paychecks to protect from the IRS. Somewhat similarly, civilized discourse allows conservative Eastern Elite undergraduates to craft political identities that are appealing to people beyond the campus, particularly political and media elites. And finally, civilized discourse is a style that is seen to fit well with the kinds of career networks these students expect to be part of in the future. While Eastern Elite conservatives may draw on one of these motivations over others, depending on the circumstances, all of these add up to students' stated preferences for civilized discourse. We look at Eastern Elite students' own explanations for the style first, and then provide our structural and cultural analysis of these self-descriptions.

WHAT'S BEST FOR EASTERN ELITE

As should by now be clear, a strong sense of Eastern Elite's importance as an institution colors the interactions of Eastern Elite conservatives at every level. This understanding of being part of a special, influential community helps explain the supremacy of civilized discourse as the dominant style of conservatism at Eastern Elite, despite its being at odds with the prevailing styles in current Republican politics, the conservative style on other campuses, and the tone of discourse within the best-funded and most visible national conservative organizations serving right-leaning undergraduates. One Eastern Elite College Republicans leader explained that the civilized discourse style is best suited to the type of student found at this university, in contrast to others:

> Whereas a lot of the Republican message on other campuses . . . is structured around these big eye-grabbing, attention-getting things, because you have 60,000 students to try to get a hold of, who are more interested in the fraternity party that is going on on Friday night. . . . At Eastern, the way that you get to students is much different, because people are willing to go to a discussion seminar with an eminent academic, or people are willing to come to a speaking session . . . with a big-name speaker. You

don't have to sort of be out on [the quad] protesting in order to get people's attention. I think that gives us the ability to make a more nuanced and supported argument than some other people on other campuses. (Darren Norton, Eastern Elite)

Eastern Elite students understand that a markedly different conservative style often is deployed on other campuses to gain attention, but conservatives at Eastern Elite have the *luxury* of adopting a different tone because their fellow students are receptive to messaging in this mode. Eastern Elite conservatives seem to share with their peers a sense of what Robert Granfield calls the "collective eminence" that gets created on the most selective college campuses, where being a member of the Eastern Elite community grants everyone a certain level of status and consideration, or what the Intercollegiate Studies Institute calls being the "best and the brightest."[9] As one interviewee explained, "It is very difficult to generalize about Eastern students because the only thing you can really say about them is that they are at Eastern for a reason, at least most of them are. Most of them are smart and accomplished" (Derek Yeager, Eastern Elite). Such intelligent, accomplished peers can appreciate a more civilized tone.

Using the civilized discourse style, then, is part luxury. But it is also part *obligation*, as several of our interviewees implied. Being a member of such an elite community carries with it the expectation of a certain level of behavior, and so being a conservative at Eastern Elite requires a more refined mode of political expression, even if it is not always exactly as much fun as the alternatives might be. When we asked one former Eastern Elite College Republicans president if he would ever be interested in staging a provocative event like the Global Warming Beach Party, he told us that "there is a significant amount of our membership that is excited about those kinds" of events, but noted that his group simply could not stage them:

Those kinds of things have been going on for a while, and they don't seem to do much. If anything, especially at Eastern, they alienate people. . . . Maybe if I could be here for ten years and do what I'm doing right now, to try to bring academic discussions and more reasonable things [to this campus about conservatism], then once people *don't* have such a bad impression of Republicans at Eastern, maybe *then* you can start doing some of these bigger protests to draw attention. But I think right now it is counterproductive. (Darren Norton, Eastern Elite)

This is interesting. While the civilized discourse style clearly reigns supreme at Eastern Elite, it is not a simple case of the style coming naturally to its users. For at least a significant portion of the Eastern Elite College Republicans membership, Darren said, and even for some leaders of its clubs, the provocative style of conservative politics has appeal—and it should be remembered that for some, this was the style of politics they engaged in before matriculating at Eastern Elite. Still, despite this imagined flirtation with someday trying bolder methods on campus, conservatives at Eastern Elite come to realize that they must be responsive to the special environment of their elite university. The civilized discourse style becomes habituated, but it also always exists somewhere at the level of strategy. Another way to think of this is that while there are ample opportunity spaces at Eastern Elite for the civilized style, only very limited space exists for alternatives.

As we have already documented, this aligns with Eastern Elite students' understanding of themselves as part of the Eastern Elite community, and of themselves and their peers as significant within the wider scope of U.S. society, both currently and in the future. The university looms large in students' minds, as this interviewee aptly illustrates:

And there is something still about this institution and its history and its tradition, the fact that so many people have come before and this is not something that's been formed overnight. You're part of a grand tradition, not just of excellence but of things specific to Eastern. . . . This institution is not something that comes and goes. It's older than this country, it's something very sturdy. And there's something to be said for that. (Drew Metcalfe, Eastern Elite)

Thus, for Eastern Elite conservatives, the identity of being a college student—and having college as a liminal space prior to adulthood in which to enjoy a more ribald form of conservative behavior—is decidedly trumped by their identity as *Eastern Elite* college students. It would seem that Eastern Elite conservatives are unwilling to compromise their cultural and social capital within their august community in order to engage in what they consider to be lowbrow forms of provocation, even if sometimes some of them might be tempted to cut loose.

CREATING A CONSERVATIVE PRESENCE ON CAMPUS

As told to us by several students and graduates of Eastern Elite University, conservatives can have a hard time getting respect on their campus. While they may express less concern than their Western Public conservative peers that they are treated poorly by others, Eastern Elite interviewees articulated some distress that their professors and classmates simply assumed they didn't exist. When it is "discovered" that conservatives do attend this prestigious private university, Eastern Elite students described instances of surprise ("people realize that there are actually people who support this other view here at Eastern Elite, of all places"; Keaton Townsend, Eastern Elite) and haughtiness ("To be honest, a lot of people, when they find out you are religious ... they will somehow think that you're stupider than they are"; Kingsley Griffith, Eastern Elite). This sense of marginalization makes coming together in right-leaning clubs important, and it gives Eastern Elite conservative students the sense that it is all the more important to create a modulated presence on campus. As one interviewee explained, "I think because we feel like we're under attack or something, we have to do more. We're not the status quo. So you have to go above and beyond" (Nicole Harris, Eastern Elite). Going "above and beyond" in this case doesn't mean becoming more provocative, as it does at Western Public University, but striking a more deliberative stance.

Beyond just gaining some recognition for their existence, conservatives at Eastern Elite also told us they were interested in persuading fellow members of their exclusive college community to take their conservative ideas seriously, perhaps even consider adopting those ideas as their own. Civilized discourse is the tool of choice for creating a convincing conservative presence on campus:

> But I think we also wanted to remain visible. We wanted to remain a visible presence because we were a minority in terms of political beliefs. We wanted to keep people thinking okay, they're there and they have a voice and they're significant. So whether it be postering for a specific meeting or a specific speaker . . . I think one of the other things we tried to do is bring in a lot of speakers and bring in a lot of panelists, I guess, and try to get people more familiar with our viewpoint. (Elizabeth Tennyson, Eastern Elite)

In fact, this desire to familiarize other students with conservative ideas is one of the main reasons some conservative students cited for disliking the highbrow provocation of the *Searchlight*—the content and tone of the conservative paper are damaging because they turn off politically liberal or moderate students, making them believe conservatives are reactionary nuts. For example, one former Eastern Elite College Republicans leader, describing why he declined to cosponsor a controversial speaker with the *Searchlight*, said, "That's what drives people crazy, is when you bring people like that [in this case, former Pennsylvania senator and later Republican presidential candidate Rick Santorum] on campus" (Kyle Lee, Eastern Elite).[10]

On the whole, though, civilized discourse is seen by most Eastern Elite conservatives as being the best way to make their presence known on campus, and to build a space for conservative ideas. Much of their interest here seems to stem not only from an interest in promoting conservative ideas among their peers now, but of potentially creating positive memories of conservatism that these peers can draw on in their future roles as influential and affluent members of society. Two former Eastern Elite College Republicans leaders described this as an important goal for the group, and a reason for avoiding more confrontational behavior:

> I think we sort of take as a given that most young people are going to be liberals. We are not going after this goal of converting the Eastern community, and suddenly causing 90 percent of Eastern students or faculty members to identify as conservatives. It is not going to happen. But what we do want to say is when the liberal student graduates and goes and gets a job . . . and they get their first paycheck and they see a huge chunk taken out by taxes, and then they come to the next election and they're trying to decide who to vote for, we want them to not think of the Republicans as those crazy dudes on campus who were just lunatics. . . . We want them to say, "You know what? Republicans on campus may have had things right. They seemed like reasonable people. I understand where they're coming from now that I have to pay taxes." (Darren Norton, Eastern Elite)[11]

> I say the ultimate goal, number-one goal, *is* creating more Republican voters, *is* having people ten years down the road—it doesn't have to be the next election—ten years down the road, think, "Hey, the Republican Party I remember on campus, was not that crazy. I remember that they had black people, Hispanic people in the club. They're not the white southern Texan society as you would see on television." (Kyle Lee, Eastern Elite)

As another former Eastern Elite College Republicans president explained, "A lot of these people are going to be very influential in their futures, whether in business or medicine or teaching or politics, whatever. So I felt that if I can help to influence them now politically, then there is a chance it will have a great impact later on" (Derek Yeager, Eastern Elite).

Other times, the desire for civilized discourse seems to stem more from a serious philosophical concern—that is, with the goal of getting people to truly engage in ideas, not just to eventually vote out of self-interest, as the comments from Darren, Kyle, and Derek above imply. One very serious alumnus said he believed that by holding one-on-one discussions with sometimes spiritedly adversarial classmates, he could at least persuade peers that his positions were not irrational—a first step to getting people to consider his fundamental core principles on their own terms:

When I'm in a large group of people, and the topic turns to politics, you'll very often hear people railing against conservatives or talking about how crazy or bigoted or irrational conservatives are. And "How could anyone ever even think about voting for John McCain?" sort of thing. And that's actually very common. . . . When I'm talking to somebody one-on-one, I find that they are much more respectful. It's not always the case: Every now and then the conversation starts with a bit of outrage on their part, which actually is fairly common. But what I found is that usually I can do enough to at least show them where I'm coming from. I think there's this prevailing attitude that you can't hold conservative positions and still be a rational human being [*laughs*]. And I think that once you sort of break that stereotype, once you've demonstrated to them that there are actually good reasons for what you believe, even if they don't agree with them, they'll usually at least respect you. (Kendall Nelson, Eastern Elite)

This interviewee said this was even true of conversations about his pro-life positions: if he laid out his arguments calmly and steadfastly enough, his liberal conversation mates might concede that he had made some valid points. As he put it, they might be persuaded at least enough to grant that rather than thinking pro-lifers were "a handful of crazy religious extremists who were trying to impose their religion in a theocratic manner on the rest of the country," they could now "at least understand that there are rational arguments for why one might believe this" (Kendall Nelson, Eastern Elite). According to this young man, sustained, reasoned, dispassionate discussion was the way to achieve such possibilities with his liberal peers.

MAKING CONNECTIONS OFF CAMPUS

Finally, Eastern Elite conservatives' interest in civilized discourse is related to persuading others off campus not only in the future (as when they imagine their peers heading to the voting booths) but also in the here and now. For Eastern Elite College Republicans, this mainly means powerful figures in the national Republican Party or policy-oriented organizations. In this way, right-leaning students are able not only to potentially leverage Eastern Elite's considerable reputation but also to keep their politics front and center. One young woman commented, "If you're thinking about it strategically, there's also good connections. I mean, think about it. If you're in the conservative movement and you're from Eastern, like, you've got a leg up on everybody else" (Nicole Harris, Eastern Elite). Though Nicole somewhat guiltily admitted this "isn't necessarily the best way to think about" her participation in the Eastern Elite College Republicans, others were more willing to plainly lay their instrumentalism on the table, noting the prestigious internships and jobs that former club members had gone on to hold. Commented one former chapter president, "We have a student who just graduated this past May who was involved in the Eastern College Republicans who now's working at the [Bush] White House. We have had other students in the past who have gone on to be involved in campaigns and things like that" (Derek Yeager, Eastern Elite).

Conservative students at Eastern Elite believe that, should they desire it, they can and will have a voice in the higher echelons of political power, and that they will be part of fostering new ideas in the party. Right-leaning groups at Eastern Elite offer a unique forum, as the university's elite status allows undergraduates to gain access—even before graduation—to powerful individuals in politics, business, and media. Creating an appropriate space for networking among the Republican Party's past and future elites becomes an important part of the Eastern Elite College Republicans' mission, which according to one leader is:

> being part of the broader discussion . . . as to where the Republican Party goes from here. Bringing in speakers to talk to young Republicans in our club about what they believe about the Republican Party and how they think it should be structured and what they believe is important going forward. (Darren Norton, Eastern Elite)

Politically minded conservatives at Eastern Elite expect to be part of national conversations about where the Republican Party is headed. Practicing the civilized discourse style now while in college paves the way for their participation in a way that other political styles will not—in their estimation, it is better suited not only to a more elite character but also to opportunities for bipartisanship. Provocative styles might work for pundits on Fox News or fringe members of Congress, said our interviewees just after the 2008 election, but it can get one only so far. For the kinds of career paths envisioned by Eastern Elite interviewees—nationally recognized newspaper columnists, Supreme Court justices, even U.S. presidents—provocation simply will not do. That said, civilized discourse, though dominant, is not the only political style we found evidence of on Eastern Elite's campus.

SUBORDINATE STYLES ON THE EASTERN ELITE CAMPUS

We saw at Western Public a bright line that divides conservative students when they use one or the other political style. First, there are those in the majority who use the provocative style and think campaigning is for losers. Second, there are those who use the campaigning style who worry that provocation, though often necessary and certainly exciting on campuses like theirs, isn't "worth it" because it turns off mainstream students (Hunter Devine, Western Flagship). In the Western Public system, these conflicts over conservative expression primarily take place within the confines of the same organization, for example, the Western Flagship College Republicans, and are usually only palpable during times of transition, such as when new officers are being elected to lead the club, or when a particularly notable event takes place in the wider world.

At Eastern Elite, we also found plenty of evidence of clashes taking place between conservative students, but this campus's internecine battles are a bit more complicated. First, whereas the champions of the provocative style at Western Public express little desire to be viewed as working within the norms of civilized discourse or campaigning, at Eastern Elite *all* of our interviewees, no matter which of the three political styles they used most regularly, claimed that they and their organizations *were* involved in civil discourse with other members of their select community. No one—not even those who used the highbrow provocation style to write acerbic observations of the waywardness of their "politically correct" campus—wanted to label him- or herself as needlessly or violently provoking anybody else at the university. So if one asks right-leaning Eastern Elite students themselves about their political style, all of them will say that they subscribe to being civil members of their community.

Second, whereas at Western Public the dominant provocative style is widely shared by conservatives across a variety of organizations (College Republicans, conservative members of student government, the gun rights group), on Eastern Elite's campus, conservative students intentionally split into different clubs that sponsor different styles. Most conspicuously, the dominant style of civilized discourse and the subordinate style of campaigning are used widely in the Eastern Elite College Republicans club, while the subordinate style of highbrow provocation is used at the conservative newspaper, the *Searchlight*. While conservatives on the Eastern Elite campus may employ somewhat different language to talk about these divisions, three interviewees captured more or less the same thing when they described the boundaries in the following ways:

- There are those who are "activist" and those who are "contemplative" (Henry Quick, Eastern Elite, a past editor of the *Searchlight*).
- There are those who "do things" and those who "sit and think" (Darren Norton, Eastern Elite, president of Eastern College Republicans).
- There are those who "campaign" and those who "write" (Calvin Coffey, Eastern Elite, College Republicans member and editor of the *Searchlight*).

In other words, there are symbolic and practical boundaries that separate all the people who may self-identify as "civil" into different groups and styles.

Finally, one more complicating factor deserves attention. As tempting as it may be to simply map styles according to the boundaries between conservative campus clubs at Eastern Elite, this is not possible since there is a good deal of shared membership among conservative groups. Students self-select into different groups based on those organizations' styles, their own political commitments, and their motives for being conservative. For example, former Eastern Elite College Republicans president Kyle Lee also took an active leadership role in the Eastern Elite pro-life group because he knew abortion was too contentious an issue for the College Republicans. And while some practitioners of highbrow provocation abandon the Eastern Elite College Republicans because they see the group as too pragmatic, others, like the most recent *Searchlight* editor Calvin Coffey, continue to attend College Republicans events to enjoy the social aspects of that club. There is membership overlap among these clubs, despite visible stylistic differences that demarcate them. With this complexity in mind, we now set about looking at the subordinate styles on this campus, turning first to the campaigning style and then to highbrow provocation.

THE CAMPAIGNING STYLE

In the Eastern Elite chapter of the College Republicans, participation in electoral politics is energetic—much more so than at Western Public, where only a few students mentioned being involved in political campaigns. According to our Eastern Elite interviewees,

> There were a lot of campaign trips, as I recall, to New Hampshire. New Hampshire campaign trips were almost weekly.... And there were people who put up signs in their windows, and we'd go door-to-door knocking on dorm rooms to talk to them about College Republicans, but not necessarily about a particular candidate. Almost all of the canvassing was in New Hampshire ... sometimes Pennsylvania. (Elizabeth Tennyson, Eastern Elite)

> I spent my fall doing mostly Republican stuff. We went to New Hampshire, we campaigned downtown. I was doing so many hours a week of Republican stuff. It was like such a relief to me when November 4th passed. It was like, oh my goodness, I can breathe! (Shannon Yaffe, Eastern Elite)

As the quotations above attest, students at Eastern Elite who are interested in the world of party politics have a viable outlet at their university. They can join the Eastern Elite College Republicans and engage in the real world by making road trips to targeted precincts, knocking on doors, working in their candidates' local offices, making calls from phone banks, and bolstering their personal profiles within the Republican Party. Several of our interviewees have now completed internships with prominent politicians or talking heads, and at least two seem destined to run for public office themselves, according to their Eastern Elite College Republicans clubmates.

Eastern Elite College Republicans leaders are in the forefront of arguing that working for political campaigns is a reasonable enterprise for college conservatives, and that this style fits well with their university's sensibility—especially since a good number of the nation's most prominent politicians at the federal, state, and local levels once passed through Eastern Elite's hallowed halls. That said, interviewees also reported that the style nicely leavens the regular work of being a college student at Eastern Elite without diluting a student's commitment to being involved in serious matters. It is an activity that is not only ends-oriented insofar as it gets Republicans elected (campaigners "do things"), it is also inherently social—a plus at Eastern Elite, where conservative students can feel somewhat isolated. It socializes students to the practicalities of the political world, in part by encouraging them to figure out ways to seek alliances and coalitions with other groups on campus—perfect preparation for those with future political aspirations. As such, it is a style at Eastern Elite that lends itself to engaging in civilized discourse with others, insofar as students who campaign are asked to explain candidates' positions and to be representatives of their party. As a subordinate style at Eastern Elite, it is highly aligned with the dominant style of civilized discourse. Campaigning adds a layer of practical activity on top of what members are already trying to do: convince folks to think about conservative ideas, have good debates, and so on.

But campaigning is not for everyone, and especially not for those who work on the conservative campus newspaper, the *Searchlight*. *Searchlight* club members reported as much, describing bewilderment at the Eastern Elite College Republicans' activities:

> I was involved with the College Republicans my first couple years: I believed that would be the only perceived avenue to talk or discuss politics, would be through the political process. But I found that not really to my temperament or. . . . I don't really *like* activism, I don't like campaigning, I don't like the dirty work of trying to enact what you hope to see as best for the country. (Drew Metcalfe, Eastern Elite)

> They work on campaigns, they try to get people elected, they're working for a political party. That doesn't appeal to me. . . . I

mean, I think some people enjoy doing political stuff, and I'm not saying it's not useful. It's very useful, and some people should do it. It has to be done. There was just no sense in which that appealed to me. . . . I just didn't want to engage in any sort of practical activity. (Nate Quinn, Eastern Elite)

Thus some Eastern Elite students, particularly those involved with the conservative newspaper, take a dim view of the campaigning style. Nobody comes right out and says that their classmates who engage in routine political action are being exploited by the Republican Party—as some Western Public conservatives clearly proclaimed about any "ass-kissing," play-it-safe, campaign-minded peers—or that campaigning is the *wrong* thing to do. Still, as one *Searchlight* alumnus put it, "I didn't want to participate in [state] politics while I was at Eastern. I don't know who would! That was always one thing that baffled me" (Vincent Long, Eastern Elite). While some Eastern Elite conservatives find working in the GOP's political trenches fulfilling and part of the territory, to others it is an absurd proposition at best.

HIGHBROW PROVOCATION

Right-leaning students who work on Eastern Elite's conservative newspaper, the *Searchlight*, tend to think about what it means to be a conservative at Eastern Elite in a much different way from those who canvass neighborhoods on behalf of political candidates. As another alumnus explained, "I don't like campaigning or anything like that, but I always like an argument" (Kenneth Lambert, Eastern Elite). While those engaging in the subordinate style of campaigning align quite uniformly with civilized discourse, the writers and editors at the *Searchlight* are doing something different: They are stirring up the pot on campus using a style we call highbrow provocation. It is here that we see Eastern Elite students assembling more of their own alternatives and generating greater within-campus variation, although with a template that has been in elite conservative circles for half a century—as celebrated in William F. Buckley's *National Review*, for instance. Not coincidentally, it is also a style that has been institutionalized at high-status private East Coast universities for decades, such as at Dartmouth College, where the conservative *Dartmouth Review* launched the careers of Dinesh D'Souza, Laura Ingraham, and, at a somewhat lesser marquee status, Hugo Restall and James Panero.[12] Despite the style's exclusive pedigree, when students at Eastern Elite engage in highbrow provocation they are met with considerable opposition. This comes not only from the larger campus community (made up of moderates and liberals) but also from a group of students who might naturally be presumed to be their allies: other conservative students on campus, who regard the style as divisive. Intra-conservative conflict is alive and well at Eastern Elite University.

It is important to begin this section with a clear illustration of the highbrow provocation style. As much as we would have liked to provide an example from an article published in the *Searchlight* itself, in our Google age such a move could easily reveal the identity of the Eastern Elite campus. So, to give an initial overview of this style, we turn to Dinesh D'Souza, who in 2007 wrote about his political days at Dartmouth in an edited volume called *Why I Turned Right* (other contributing authors include Rich Lowry, David Brooks, and Heather MacDonald).[13] Although we should expect there to be certain institutional differences between Eastern Elite and Dartmouth that would create some variation between the campuses' respective conservative newspapers (for example, Dartmouth's reputation for being a more conservative campus than Eastern Elite), the paean to the style of conservative writing and socializing at Dartmouth that follows accords quite well with the highbrow provocation style we discovered at Eastern Elite. Further, while institutionally different in some key ways, both these universities have enough cultural and organizational features in common (selective admissions, a pipeline to national organizations like the *National Review*) that conservative students can easily pick up on this more broadly available elite style. This is from what D'Souza wrote in his contribution, "Recollections of a Campus Renegade":

> I joined the *Dartmouth Review* for two reasons: one aesthetic, and the other intellectual. The first was that I found a style and a *joie de vivre* that I had not previously associated with conservatism. The best example of this was the paper's mentor, Jeffrey Hart, a professor of English at Dartmouth and a senior editor of *National Review*. . . .
>
> Hart's most controversial column about Dartmouth was called "The Ugly Protesters." He wrote it during the time of the South Africa Protests . . . Hart said he was puzzled by the intensity of the protesters. What possible interest could they have in events so remote from their everyday lives? Observing the protesters, Hart noted their unifying characteristic was that they were disheveled. Not to mince words, they were, as a group, rather ugly. Exploring the connection between their demeanor and their political activism, Hart arrived at the following conclusion: They were protesting their own ugliness! Hart's column caused a sensation on campus.[14]

We can certainly see in D'Souza's illustration of his advisor's writing what is provocative about this style, but we can also see glimmers of what is highbrow about it, too: the wordplay used to find what is farcical about politically correct others and a position of superiority of the writer vis-à-vis his subject. As we will see below, such an attitude resonates with *Searchlight* writers.

In another couple of paragraphs D'Souza provides further description of this style's highbrow nature, this time concerning its foundations in intellectualism:

> The second reason I joined the *Dartmouth Review* was that I was greatly impressed by the seriousness of the conservative students. They were passionate about ideas and argued vigorously about what it meant to be a conservative, and what it meant to be an American, and who was a liberally educated person, and . . . whether journalism could be objective, and whether reason could refute revelation . . .[15]

In other words, the style of conservatism celebrated here is intellectual. Finally, D'Souza praises the élan of this kind of conservatism—its ability to outshine all others, which has everything to do with appreciating and participating in the traditions of elite culture. He writes:

> I remember some of those early dinners at the Hart farmhouse, where we drank South American wine and listened to recordings of Hemingway and Fitzgerald, Robert Frost reading his poems, Nixon speeches, comedian Rich Little doing his Nixon imitation, George C. Scott delivering the opening speech in *Patton*, some of Churchill's orations. . . . There was an ethos here, and a sensibility. . . . Here was a conservatism . . . that was engaged with art, music, and literature; that was at the same time ironic, light-hearted, and fun.[16]

From the earlier segments of D'Souza's excerpt above, we can see that like the provocative style at Western Public, the highbrow provocation style has a flame-throwing quality to it (ugly, misguided protesters!). But instead of sponsoring in-your-face events like Conservative Coming Out Day as Western Public students might do, highbrow provocateurs choose to grab the attention of their opponents through the written word and with bemused high self-regard. From the latter parts of D'Souza's recollection, we see that this style of comportment refers not only to the tone and content of what is written but also to the ways that conservatism is performed in interactional settings—like listening to Robert Frost poems together with their mentor at Dartmouth while enjoying bottles of wine. Right-leaning students at the *Dartmouth Review*, according to this account, learn a very particular style of conservatism on their campus—a kind of to-the-manor-born gentleman of ideas style.

Leaving behind D'Souza's written word now for our own interviewees, we are struck by the similarities between the accounts of this style, beginning with the *Searchlight* staff's flair for embracing old-world elite conduct. We heard of the annual badminton games that the *Searchlight's* editors and writers host (complete with cock-tails), and we witnessed (and heard snarky comments from others about) how the newspaper writers dress for class in up-market but old-fashioned apparel—think well-worn houndstooth jackets over lambswool V-necks and button-down shirts. One Eastern Elite alum-nus described the *Searchlight* as "a very self-conscious world of peo-ple who dress in a kind of dandyish fashion or who are kind of into *Brideshead Revisited*, and I think even then it actually seemed faintly ridiculous" (Sam Tuan, Eastern Elite).[17] As such, one editor we interviewed (Calvin Coffey) said he mostly tried to avoid such haughty traditions, but the point is this: the style of highbrow prov-ocation helps create an identity of elite conservative culture and su-periority for those who embrace it.

The highbrow provocation style, of course, does not stop with lifestyle choices. It is equally about content. Past editors at Eastern Elite portrayed the substance of the *Searchlight* in a manner that clearly echoes the Dartmouth description, as in the following ac-counts by two past editors:

> Well, the *Searchlight* for at least ten or fifteen years has loved the ironies of campus life. It likes to point them out as absurdities, as long as absurdities do not become too dangerous. So the way that contemplation can be paired with provocation is through awareness of the amusing character of the whole situation. (Henry Quick, Eastern Elite)

> It generally means criticizing the most absurd things that go on at Eastern. . . . [We] treat things with a lot of irony and levity and humor. And especially easy targets, but also very central to what makes all of these things so absurd sometimes, things like politi-cal correctness especially, and some of the more absurd aspects of multiculturalism. (Drew Metcalfe, Eastern Elite)

Whereas D'Souza's mentor ironically wrote about South Africa di-vestment protesters in the 1980s, issues that have been given the highbrow treatment in the *Searchlight* over the past decade include how environmentalism has become a pagan religion to faculty and students and how Muslims, women, and African Americans have been pandered to and coddled by an overly sensitive university administration.

Other topics, such as feminism more generally, also come in for skepticism in the *Searchlight*. One issue of the newspaper in the mid-2000s contained a positive review of *Manliness*, a book by the well-known conservative professor Harvey Mansfield of Harvard University that addresses the issue of social sex roles, arguing that the two sexes have fundamental, essential differences that ought to be celebrated and maintained in the social world, not socially engineered away through changing cultural mores or social policy.[18] The *Searchlight* editorial, while stating that the paper's staff did not fully endorse all of these views, posed a hypothetical question stemming from them: What *has* been lost when demands for rights erase traditional social distinctions and the social harmony that accompanies these norms? In keeping with this line of thought, the paper at another time tweaked gender politics on campus by wistfully referring to an era before the university was coed—halcyon days when men were men and college "girls" were rightfully thought of as eligible brides-to-be.[19]

In some sense, then, the *Searchlight* is focused on provoking liberals, slaying their sacred cows (feminism, gay rights, multiculturalism) and questioning their values. However, if this were the group's only interest, this would simply be provocation—albeit in newsprint rather than live on the quad. Just as with the *Dartmouth Review*, we add the "highbrow" modifier to point out *Searchlight* conservatives' other central concerns:

> We do a lot of more *philosophical* type of things. And I'm not talking about really high level, "what is the origin of government" type of philosophy, but more pieces that aren't necessarily related to [specific] events, is what I mean. Sort of cultural musings on a specific topic. . . . [I see it] as more cultural commentary about campus life, about being a college-age student in our modern culture. That's sort of what I feel I'm most interested in, and

where conservatism has its most appeal, I think, and also the best arguments. (Drew Metcalfe, Eastern Elite, emphasis added)

Another past editor noted:

I always like to think of the *Searchlight* as, you know, the kind of yeah, intellectual—this sounds so arrogant—but *intellectual conservatism* as opposed to a party-based, Republican-bound conservatism. . . . And to be honest, the *Searchlight* . . . we *wanted* to provoke and start debates and whatever. But it was also a way to just get together and amuse ourselves. (Vincent Long, Eastern Elite, emphasis added)

As we can see from these quotations, in some ways the style of the *Searchlight* is a hybrid style. By lampooning liberals and amusing themselves, the paper's editors share elements in common with their provocative peers at Western Public. At the same time, though, the paper's arch, philosophical tone, as well as its medium—the printed page, rather than face-to-face confrontation—shows that some of the norms of civilized discourse still hold.

What do non-*Searchlight* students think of this style? It should probably come as no surprise that neither the editors' notions of themselves nor the content they include in their newspaper sits well with others on campus. In cases where the *Searchlight* incurs the wrath of non-conservative groups, such as African Americans, gays and lesbians, or Muslim student groups, campus administrators have been known to step in and arrange for campus dialogues between adversarial groups. Naturally, this is seen by the *Searchlight* staff as overly solicitous toward those other groups. At other times, direct retaliation comes in the form of student-written op-ed pieces that take the *Searchlight* to task in the campus's mainstream paper, the *Manifest*.

But as we mentioned before, some of the most emphatic critics of the paper's highbrow provocative style are Eastern Elite conservative students practicing the dominant style of civilized discourse. A substantial number of conservatives we talked to at Eastern Elite (even including some who had at one time been writers for the *Searchlight*) expressed concern or condemnation for the newspaper. These students felt that the paper's style is detrimental to the conservative cause at Eastern Elite. One current student said,

> I read their articles sometimes and I think, first of all this is something that, to the extent that you're trying to promote a conservative message, even when you're trying to promote a message that I agree with, the tone that you've taken seems so blindly partisan that it's never going to appeal to or reach out to anybody who doesn't already agree with you. And so that definitely bothers me. . . . It just doesn't seem productive. (Kendall Nelson, Eastern Elite)

A former Eastern Elite College Republicans president and *Searchlight* writer (who has since turned his back on the conservative newspaper) mocked the editorial staff for believing in "returning to an eighteenth-century, French Catholic-inspired theocracy. . . . It's to a point where it's unbelievable! And that's bad for the conservative movement when people start thinking you are a joke" (Kyle Lee, Eastern Elite). Still a third, an alumna who had also been involved in both groups, asserted,

> I understand why the *Searchlight* is hated. It sets forth unabashedly some very contentious ideas. . . . They're not concerned about gaining members. They're like an intellectual group of people. It's not like they're just trying to shock people. But I think a lot of people can't get over the fact that they are saying some provocative things. (Nicole Harris, Eastern Elite)

Thus, while the *Searchlight*'s style of highbrow provocation provides a good enough fit with the dominant style at Eastern Elite for the paper to have a sustained presence on campus—one past editor insisted that his staff were "sensible people" (Drew Metcalfe, Eastern Elite), while another argued that, after all, "one person's provocation is another person's irony" (Henry Quick, Eastern Elite)—there remains enough dissonance for Eastern Elite conservatives practicing this style to have strained relationships with other conservatives on their campus, and, as we shall see, to have future career aspirations that are distinctive from their more mainstream Eastern Elite conservative peers.

EXPLAINING THE CIVILIZED DISCOURSE STYLE'S DOMINANCE AT EASTERN ELITE

At Eastern Elite, then, we find three styles of conservatism: civilized discourse, highbrow provocation, and campaigning. While one of these styles, campaigning, shares many features with the same style on the Western Public campuses, the other two styles are particular to Eastern Elite, in the same way that the populist brand of provocation is particular to Western Public.[20] Having examined the tenor of these styles in depth, and our interviewees' own accounts of why they use them, we now turn to our cultural and structural examination of why these styles are part of the cultural repertoire at Eastern Elite, and specifically why we believe civilized discourse dominates as the prevailing logic of Eastern Elite conservatism. After all, even those students who gleefully pen invective editorials for the *Searchlight* claim that they are being civil, and they seem to fancy themselves part of a noble, civilized tradition. Why is the claim to civility so important for Eastern Elite conservatives? What allows civilized discourse to be so persistent at Eastern Elite even while it is now a highly unpopular mode of expression at the national level—both among conservative organizations and within the GOP itself—and also in the Western Public system? To explore these questions, we consider once more the institutional dynamics of the university setting—from housing to course registration to institutional ethos—that are in place on this campus.

CAMPUS-LEVEL FACTORS INFLUENCING THE TASTE FOR CIVILIZED DISCOURSE

The civilized discourse style fits well with our descriptions of Eastern Elite conservatives' sense of their university as a special place, and of their peers and themselves as insiders at this highly selective institution. While students at Western Public draw on a broader, perhaps more media-sensationalized discourse of what being a "typical college student" is supposed to be like, for Eastern Elite students, identification with their campus community—and an understanding of themselves and their campus as uniquely exceptional—discourages strong identification with that fun-loving imagery.[21] The idea that college is a time when "anything goes" and that provocative behavior can be written off as youthful indiscretion is mostly not seen among our Eastern Elite interviewees. Instead, living up to the expectations of the Eastern Elite community—both in a practical sense on campus, and also symbolically in the wider world—is more important.[22] Civilized discourse provides the most effective tool for creating a conservative presence on campus while managing the obligations inherent in being an Eastern Elite student.[23]

It is important here to remember how fully integrated into their campus community Eastern Elite conservatives feel as compared to their peers at Western Public. While it is true that our interviewees said they seek out right-leaning clubs as necessary outlets to truly express themselves—or, as one of our interviewees put it, the conservative clubs she belongs to "support me and . . . make me feel like oh, I *am* sane, I'm *not* retarded" (Shannon Yaffe, Eastern Elite)—the confluence of organizational settings and cultural meanings on the Eastern Elite campus as a whole combine to make conservative students feel like part of a larger, more important club: their exclusive university. Eastern Elite has an almost unparalleled reputation as an elite institution. Students think of themselves as among the best of the best. One alum remembered being told at an orientation that "when Eastern Elite students first come as freshmen, 80 percent think that they're not as smart as the average of their peers and, then, when they are all seniors, 80 percent of them think that they're smarter" (Kris Nagle, Eastern Elite). It should be remembered that social closure at schools like Eastern Elite is the successful accomplishment of a long-term project of high-status schooling in the United States—students in any one cohort are disinclined to turn their backs on processes that have been in place for centuries, and that work to their tremendous advantage.[24] When students believe that their current classmates may well be the future leaders of the country, doing embarrassing things that appall them while in college just doesn't make that much sense. Using reasoned discourse to coax them in the direction of seeing your views as viable does. As a consequence of these campus characteristics and others (an extensive freshman orientation, many campus traditions that bring all students together at different points in the year, and so on), Eastern Elite conservatives feel they are part of the university's deep and manufactured special community. Such community, we argue, is a kind of natural governor to students' envisioning themselves as overly marginalized, and this sense of community rules out the provocative conservative style.

In fact, the influence of the campus seems so strongly to favor civilized discourse that aside from the use of the two submerged styles inside conservative clubs proper, there is little evidence that right-of-center students transpose either campaigning or highbrow provocation to other settings on campus. Unlike at Western Public, where we see echoes of both provocation and campaigning in other social experiences—most centrally, students' interactions with faculty—at Eastern Elite, neither highbrow provocation nor campaigning (nor, really, any talk of partisan politics at all) makes its way into academic settings, according to our interviewees. Pushing this further, we think that the cultural repertoire that makes civilized discourse "appropriate" at Eastern Elite is so powerful across all levels of this campus that it rules out conservative students' other options in situations beyond their clubs. To support our claim that this strong institutional culture of civilized discourse actually limits students' agency to transpose their submerged styles to other settings on campus to a greater extent than at Western Public, we first look at Eastern Elite conservatives' classroom experiences, where civilized discourse drowns out all alternatives, before turning to the influence of different political styles on our Eastern Elite interviewees' future plans.

MUTUAL RESPECT IN THE CLASSROOM

Unlike at Western Public, where we saw political styles nurtured in the conservative student clubs being brought into the classroom, at Eastern Elite this relationship is more difficult to distinguish. While

Eastern Elite conservatives certainly do understand themselves to be politically in the minority on their campus—with faculty, peers, and the university's administration seen as left-leaning—unlike at Western Public's campuses, Eastern Elite conservatives do not view themselves as *embattled* and their professors or classmates as frequent verbal assailants. They report that they do not fear grade retaliation and that they do not use the classroom as a forum to air their political beliefs. Instead, Eastern Elite conservatives seem to comport themselves almost as if by an unwritten code of conduct, to which all other members of the Eastern Elite community, regardless of status or political affiliation, likewise adhere. We do not see, for example, anything resembling the style of highbrow provocation being practiced in the classroom.

Is it, as our informants contend, that all of their political styles are, at base, civil, and so we are seeing that manifested here? Or is it that there is a lot of social engineering on this campus and that the campus-level structural features of Eastern Elite—its small class sizes, excellent student-to-faculty ratio, and exalted reputation— basically socialize students to the standing institutional culture so much so that they foreclose the possibility of other types of actions within the classroom, including, possibly, political debate itself? If we find the latter—that the institutional dynamics at Eastern Elite nearly rule out certain avenues of conduct, we have a real irony here, though not one that would particularly surprise cultural sociologists. While it is appealing to think of culture as enabling all kinds of action, at Eastern Elite we see the potentially constraining aspects of a highly unified elite culture—even as that level of culture opens up so many other avenues of opportunity. The reigning cultural repertoire that generates civilized discourse at Eastern Elite makes it much harder for conservative students to be expressively political outside their clubs.

Unbiased Professors and Respectful Peers

Eastern Elite conservatives view their professors as experts in their fields, and they speak of their classmates as highly respectable people—even if they say they are also overwhelmingly liberal—who are likely headed for success, as they themselves are. Thus in general, our Eastern Elite interviewees reported much more positive classroom experiences than their Western Public peers, even while acknowledging the probable politics of those who surround them:

> I think the professors here at Eastern *are* liberal. There's no doubt about it. They probably *all* supported Obama. . . . But I think here we learn to approach in an academic way . . . our classmates are much more civil compared to a lot of the—I don't want to say state schools—or other schools, we're more civil about it. (Kyle Lee, Eastern Elite)

> Generally, what people have told me is that classes . . . tend to be addressing nonpartisan issues, and where they are addressing partisan issues, they have done so in such a rigorous academic way that it is very nonpartisan or bipartisan, and they see both sides. So I have not really heard other people at Eastern give me any specific horror stories. Certainly there is a general grumble that "People are so liberal here" and that "Professors are so liberal and it is a shame." (Darren Norton, Eastern Elite)

Likewise, in the rest of our interviews: although some criticism was voiced, we heard very few "horror stories" from Eastern Elite conservatives, and among these, no incidents of alleged grade discrimination, as we had heard at Western Public. As one interviewee explained, "I think generally speaking, [our] faculty is too high quality to let [politics] really get in the way" (Drew Metcalfe, Eastern Elite). Eastern Elite conservatives generally depict their professors as unbiased, expert educators who are not only uninterested but generally *above* the notion of indoctrinating their students. Said one alumnus who now works at a prominent conservative think tank in Washington, D.C., "There were certainly a diversity of views presented. I never felt in any way that a professor was bringing their own agenda or politics into the classroom" (Evan Dooley, Eastern Elite). Even in cases where course content tilts leftward, Eastern Elite conservatives say it is generally presented in an evenhanded manner: "I mean, the book [used in a course] might be 'liberal,' to use quotation marks for those of you listening in [*comically addressing the transcriber*], but I have never thought that it was force-fed down my throat" (Keaton Townsend, Eastern Elite).

This review of professors' evenhanded approach similarly permeated Eastern Elite interviewees' discussions of students' classroom conduct, both their own as well as that of their peers. Unlike at Western Public, we heard about extremely few incidents of classmates injecting politicized content into the classroom, aggressively or otherwise. In these rare instances, it seemed cooler heads prevailed:

> But there were certainly a number of more vocal students who were far more vocal even than I was, who would just ramble about a very liberal point. And oftentimes the professor would have to say, "Okay, moving on." . . . So at that point those are the people that I just thought it's not really worth setting up a big fighting word match here. It's just not worth the classroom time, that's not what this class is supposed to be about. And when someone would go and rail on about a candidate or an issue for a while, I just felt like *that was not the appropriate forum for that type of dialogue.* (Elizabeth Tennyson, Eastern Elite, emphasis added)

Whereas a Western Public conservative might see such an incident as incitement to argue or as a sign to stay quiet, at Eastern Elite there is the sense that this kind of behavior is more broadly just inappropriate, and that professors keep their classes under control. For the most part, it seems that all members of the Eastern Elite University community, both students and faculty, regard the classroom as an unacceptable space in which to grind one's political axe.

Leaving Politics at the Door

This point comes across clearly in Eastern Elite conservatives' descriptions of their own active separation of their personal political beliefs from their conduct in the classroom. Rather than trying to be active antagonists or feeling pressured into silence, most Eastern Elite interviewees said they purposefully chose to keep politics apart from classtime. Even those Eastern Elite conservatives who were among the most politically visible on their campus characterized themselves as leaving their political beliefs outside the classroom door as a way to perform the role of serious Eastern Elite student effectively:

> I never, ever tell professors oh, I'm a Republican, because I don't think it matters. Because I view academia as totally separate from politics. And I've taken American politics classes, I know the way to balance a budget is not to do a flat tax, it's not to do a progressive tax or a regressive tax. I know how to do it. In a very academic setting, I've learned the best way to do it, and it's neither the Republican way or the Democrat way. But when I leave that classroom and head over to my College Republicans meeting, I put on my College Republicans hat, and I'm like, "Yes, the flat tax balances those books!" (Kyle Lee, Eastern Elite)

Although this candid statement about the disconnect this student crafts between politics and academic learning is somewhat startling, Kyle insisted that the two could be thought of as separate spheres and that, in a sense, he should protect the classroom from his political ideas. Another student also discussed detaching politics from academics:

> ... we, obviously, starting a group like [the Eastern Elite abstinence group] we certainly had no problem with speaking out and raising our voice, but I think there was definitely a sense that the classroom was not a place to do it And so I think, with the exception maybe of some of the classes that we were avoiding, maybe there was sort of a truce in that regard between the students and the faculty. (Kris Nagle, Eastern Elite)

These interviewees' descriptions of wearing different hats depending on the setting, or of an informal truce existing, fit well with many of the characteristics of Eastern Elite as a campus. Because of its small size, students and faculty are generally known to one another, and most students do not want to be combative in the classroom. Beyond simply putting the brakes on provocative behavior, however, Eastern Elite's prestigious faculty, small classes, and close-knit community help promote the idea of the classroom as an exalted space. It thus becomes an almost sanctified realm that would be tainted by the intrusion of politics—something that both conservative *and* liberal Eastern Elite students need to learn. Partisan views do not belong here:

> I would say it's important to know the appropriate venues for that type of thing. I think that some people can be very tempted to pull it out in the classroom. And I would caution against that, not only because I think that it's not the appropriate venue but from what I've heard—and again this is just hearsay—but I've heard that some professors can react negatively to that, whether it be from a liberal or a conservative student. (Elizabeth Tennyson, Eastern Elite)

Further, she continued, if one did interject political content into the classroom, it had to be done with caution: "If you're going to go about it, go about it diplomatically and try to pose your viewpoint as more of a suggestion of an alternative versus 'I'm going to push you on this point and be argumentative and combat you and say no, you're wrong'" (Elizabeth Tennyson, Eastern Elite). One way to view this description is that the political style of civilized discourse is being brought into the classroom. However, when this is additionally premised, as Elizabeth describes above, on the idea that interjecting *any* political content into the classroom is inappropriate, this connection becomes murkier. From this view, it appears campus-level characteristics already overshadow anything learned in the conservative clubs.

However, we can also look at this in a different way, examining why Eastern Elite interviewees believe other forms of political behavior in the classroom—like highbrow provocation—are negative. Unfortunately, we have few instances of respondents discussing this, perhaps because it happens so rarely. Only one interviewee, Kyle Lee, described a concrete example of what he viewed as the wrong way for conservative students to make their presence known in class:

> They're the ones that are like, in a talk in political theory class, saying, "Oh my god, Tocqueville was right. Women should be chained to their beds." I'm like, yo, that is the wrong way to talk about it. People are telling me that you said that in your class! People think we're [conservatives are] crazy. I might think, I might agree with you, yeah, men and women have biological differences, traditionally women's role is this, men's role is this. [But] that's not how you approach it in the classroom! So I think part of being conservative is being smart about communicating your ideas. (Kyle Lee, Eastern Elite)

This fits with Eastern Elite interviewees' broader understanding of provocation as simply un-*conservative*, that being conservative in and of itself implies a cautious, measured approach. That said, other than Kyle's description, we did not hear of any other instances of what could be termed highbrow provocative classroom behavior. Generally, the Eastern Elite conservatives we talked with were satisfied with their classroom experiences and felt the classroom should be a place of nonpartisan, depoliticized content.

Classroom Complaints

That is not to say, however, that Eastern Elite students voice no complaints about academic life. Though we heard far fewer stories about impolitic professors or classroom insults than we did in the Western Public university system, some Eastern Elite students cited specific instances of what they considered to be inappropriate incidents:

> For the last half he just blasted President Bush and blasted his policies, and then ended the lecture without taking any ques-

tions. I thought, "Well, that is just ridiculous." I had my question all prepared for why he was wrong and I wanted to point that out. So I went up to him afterwards to talk to him and raised my point. He said, "Yes, that's a good point." I just wish I would've had an opportunity to ask that in front of the other three hundred or four hundred students sitting in there who walked away without having [the professor's] views challenged at the end of that lecture. . . . . I thought it was a bit odd that he made it his policy to take questions every ten to fifteen minutes throughout every lecture the entire semester and he just chose that twenty- to thirty-minute block of lecture to be the one part that he didn't take questions on. (Derek Yeager, Eastern Elite)

But I noticed in a lot of my lectures, before the election there were a lot of Sarah Palin jokes. . . . Oh, by faculty. And so it was just, again, a tacit assumption [of consensus in the room]. And you know, everybody laughed, they were funny jokes, but you would never have heard, and I have never heard, a joke that would be made to the Democratic Party or to the liberal opinions made. But offhand I can remember four or five different Sarah Palin comments made in three of my classes. And one is a science class; it's not like they were even relevant. (Staci Congdon, Eastern Elite)

Though Eastern Elite students on the whole described their professors as unbiased and the classroom as generally neutral territory, there are reports that liberal bias does occur. Interestingly, when students say such incidents crop up, it seems they do not *automatically* apply the principles of the civilized discourse style and try to start a deliberative exchange with their professors. For example, in considering how to do well in classes where the professor makes Sarah Palin jokes, Staci continued, "Well, first thing I'm going to do is *not* walk up to him and say, 'I support Sarah Palin,' because it's just, you know, that's just something that you learn when you're like six. Like if you want to make people happy, you say what they say" (Staci Congdon, Eastern Elite, emphasis added). Having a faculty member breach what appears to be an overarching norm of civility can, it seems, sometimes lead Eastern Elite students to interject their own politics into the classroom (as Derek described), but more commonly it can resolve them to keep their personal politics quiet (as with Staci)—solutions we also saw in play on the Western Public campuses.

Eastern Elite conservatives can mitigate their chances of being confronted with liberal ideas or outspoken faculty and students by opting out of classes they feel are likely to have content they find disagreeable. Undergraduates at Eastern Elite have considerable leeway in choosing individual classes and in determining their overall course of study.[25] Some students acknowledged this may be a relevant factor in their lack of difficulty in the classroom. One of our Eastern Elite interviewees, Molly Nash Downing, said she "avoided classes" in departments such as the Critical Gender Studies program, thereby dodging potential trouble, and another interviewee sounded a similar note:

> Educators at Eastern usually are very professional people. There's not an intention to introduce bias into *any* classroom that I've ever been in. And one thing about that is also that, had I been in certain classrooms, I probably *would* have been [offended and unhappy]. But if you're a conservative you know not to take offerings in Critical Gender Studies or something. (Vincent Long, Eastern Elite)

However, the most popular majors among our interviewees were the same majors that were most popular among Eastern Elite undergraduates as a whole. Though avoiding classes in ethnic studies or on gender and sexuality probably does insulate Eastern Elite conservatives somewhat from content they find displeasing, they are hardly self-segregated into some kind of conservatives-only bubble. On the whole, then, Eastern Elite conservatives' rosier descriptions of classroom life likely cannot be attributed solely to an aversion to certain fields of study or faculty members. As one commented, "I don't think I avoided anything because, 'Oh, that's such a liberal person, I'm not going to take that class'" (Kingsley Griffith, Eastern Elite).

Eastern Elite conservatives' most consistent critique of academics at Eastern Elite is actually of academics itself, much in the same vein as the negative evaluations given to college curricula by national organizations like the Intercollegiate Studies Institute, the National Association of Scholars, and the American Council of Trustees and Alumni. Many right-leaning students feel that Eastern Elite's curriculum is insufficiently rigorous, allowing for too much freedom on the part of students to choose courses of study and incorporating too many niche areas rather than focusing on a traditional Western culture canon. As one student described, "I mean, education is not sort of the institutional, broadly-shared top priority at Eastern Elite. It's sort of, 'Some people are going to get really interested in some things and like them, and other people want to do activities or this or that, or just want to hang out or want to do athletics. Okay, do your own thing'" (Nate Quinn, Eastern Elite). Some linked this to what they saw as their peers' careerist orientations, and Eastern Elite's role in helping its students "make the most of their potential and opportunities," as one interviewee stated darkly (Drew Metcalfe, Eastern Elite). This student continued, "There's no necessary practical benefit in studying a Great Books curriculum. It's not going to get you a job in finance, it's not going to get you into law school, it's not going to get you into med school"—though he himself, incidentally, was graduating with a job lined up in finance (Drew Metcalfe, Eastern Elite).

In general, conservative students' concerns about the curriculum are less about politics and more about the quality of their educations:

But the other thing I would say is I would be really wary of—and I don't know if this would be termed "political" conventionally, but it is political—of academic faddishness, especially if you go into humanities-related fields. Now I don't know if you go into chemistry or math or other hard sciences. I mean I don't know that, like, that that's really a major issue. It may or may not be. But when I look back at my own academic work, I did a lot of work with canonical texts, but I also did a lot of work with what

I would call *crap*. And I can just tell you that I got so much more out of reading *Wuthering Heights* or the *Symposium* or the *Phaedras* then I got out of reading some *crap-ass like contemporary shit* that was assigned to me by a professor. We all know how the deal works. Every professor has done his monograph and is off on some really marginal writer or artist or whatever because they carve out their little niche. (Edward Ingle, Eastern Elite)

I feel like a lot of my educational experience here has been very, like I often . . . I often sort of feel like I'm majoring in, like, cocktail party talk. I just sort of have read all this French history and literature and it's lovely, it's so lovely. And it's so nice that someone's paying $50,000 a year for me to read these lovely books. But a lot of it is sort of . . . like it's not coherent as a philosophy and it's kind of a smattering of a lot of stuff. (Molly Nash Downing, Eastern Elite)

Molly here partly disparages the academic content of her education even while she undoubtedly will make use of it at future upper-crust social occasions.[26]

Overall, then, while Eastern Elite conservatives do voice complaints about their classroom experiences, those complaints are very different in nature from what we heard at Western Public. While some say that there are a few professors who bring unacceptable content into the classroom, liberal or otherwise, it seems a few bad apples do not spoil the bunch for these right-leaning undergraduates. Most Eastern Elite interviewees describe their academic experiences as positive, productive, and relatively depoliticized.

Online Discourse: The One Eastern Elite
Setting Where Civilized Discourse Fails

We have argued that the campus-level variables contributing to civilized discourse at Eastern Elite are so palpable that conservative students lack opportunities to transpose either their campaigning or their highbrow provocation styles into other campus settings, such as the classroom. But there is one place at Eastern Elite where, it seems, the gloves do come off. Just as at Western Public, we see the dominant style diminished in some kinds of classroom settings (in small senior seminars, for example, where students can get to know one another more personally and the provocative style falls away), so it seems that, given the right environment, Eastern Elite students can lose their civilized demeanor and become quite confrontational. The one space where we heard of this kind of "uncivil" behavior happening at Eastern Elite is on email listservs, which exist for the university's different dorms, and also for many of its organizations. Though postings on the listserv are not anonymous (since students must subscribe using their official Eastern Elite email addresses) or completely private (as the emails could be forwarded to outsiders or posted on the web for all to see), the listservs, which are used by all students, offer Eastern Elite undergraduates the ability to say whatever comes to mind without having to say it directly to anyone's face.

As such, one student reported, "People think they can say whatever they want and it gets very offensive. People get very offended and people lose their inhibitions"(Keaton Townsend, Eastern Elite). Likewise, emailing to a list rather than to a single person seems to lead to statements being made that would never fly in the classroom, face-to-face in the dining hall, or in any other Eastern Elite setting:

> People can be very vicious ... in the sense of the sort of comments that people would not make to your face. Most of the things that I'm thinking about were emails, not to me in particular, but on lists.... To the point that there was one student who was saying things about motives [of people] who were pro-life and the fact that they should be resisted and things like that, that were threatening to the point that I had the dean of my dorm come up to me at breakfast to make sure that I was okay.... It was very vague language, but I think it was intended to frighten. (Melissa Preston, Eastern Elite)

Another student reported an especially intolerant 24-hour round of email exchanges on his religious listserv concerning whether Catholic supporters of gay marriage should be able to take the Eucharist, in the course of which some participants—liberal, moderate, and conservative—expressed concern over the tone of some of their classmates' entries.[27] And as we recall from earlier in the chapter, Derek Yeager put an end to the flaming barbs during one listserv exchange about abortion when he asked people simply to come meet him face-to-face in the dining hall.

Though the listservs are obviously not related to classroom content, they do point to the overwhelming influence at Eastern Elite of the university's prestige and the weight that being a member of that community exerts. The minimal amount of depersonalization inherent in the listserv format seems to create just enough opportunity space to allow Eastern Elite students—conservatives and liberals alike—to temporarily shed the Eastern Elite mantle of civilized discourse and be flippant, provocative, or even cruel. "I can only imagine if they were anonymous how ugly the discussions would get," one student noted, "because people are quite bold as is" (Staci Congdon, Eastern Elite). While Eastern Elite's extraordinary reputation and exceptional academics in the main create many opportunities for students, they also limit the possibilities for other types of behavior. We see this further when we examine Eastern Elite conservatives' expectations for their future careers.

CAREER EXPECTATIONS ON A NATIONAL SCALE

Most Eastern Elite conservative students approach their political engagement mindful of actions that they learn are appropriate to the Eastern Elite community and that they think will not compromise their reputations as civil and cosmopolitan members thereof, or as qualified applicants for future graduate programs or jobs. At Eastern Elite, the local campus environment—with its perceived greater intellectual demands and its promise of prestigious occupations in the nation's most important power centers—moves controversial actions off the table of acceptability and even feasibility. Even those students who come to college with a background in listening to AM conservative talk radio become well schooled in the style of civilized discourse. And the conservative undergraduates who choose high-brow provocation over civilized discourse, while aware that they are pushing the envelope on their campus, comfort themselves by putting a great degree of mental distance between what they say they are doing and what they understand "populist" provocateurs are doing on other campuses. These styles are both informed by and have an impact on conservative students' career aspirations:

> People coming out of the *Searchlight* they, frankly I think they tend to be much more likely either to go into academia or go and write, whether that's in the *Weekly Standard* or *National Review*, or frankly even in more mainstream sources. Whereas the College Republicans, it's frankly a much larger group as I said than the *Searchlight*, and frankly you see a lot of them going to law school. You do see a lot of them going into business, a few of them going and working on campaigns back in their home states, and things like that. (Vincent Long, Eastern)

Indeed, among the students and recent alumni/ae we spoke to, Eastern Elite conservatives who adopted the submerged style of high-brow provocation were more likely to aspire to high-status careers where their identity as conservatives, per se, was explicitly relevant—for example, becoming journalists at national-level conservative publications. In contrast, students practicing civilized discourse hoped for careers in which they might be able to make use of their passion for politics (for example, in the legal world), but where political affiliation is not definitional to the position.

Eastern Elite students draw on their considerable cultural and social capital to launch themselves into high-profile careers when college ends. Not only do they generally boast considerable résumés and networks of contacts via internships, but in adopting a more civilized political style they have also learned a strategy for working more comfortably and successfully in bipartisan environments. No

Eastern Elite interviewee expressly stated an interest in going directly into politics, although as noted before, at least two seem destined for political careers according to their classmates. Of those interviewees who articulated interest in particular careers (or in the case of graduates, who were already engaged in those careers), ten were interested in law, six in business, four in national media, five in earning a PhD, and one in the military. Traditionally, large numbers of Eastern Elite graduates work in finance (in the 50 percent range for graduating men, according to the *New York Times*, at least in 2008), and this was true of several of the recent alumni interviewed.[28] However, given the economic climate at the time of the interviews, the overall proportion of students saying they would like to have financial careers was lower than would otherwise be expected. Still, unlike the Western Public undergraduates we spoke to, not one Eastern Elite interviewee communicated concern about financial hardship, even those who came from families who were not affluent. Perhaps the greatest commonality that we saw across the board with regard to Eastern Elite interviewees' career aspirations was their certainty of their own future success.

Much of this can be related to the school's excellent reputation. Recent Eastern Elite graduates are forthright about the extent to which the Eastern Elite imprimatur opens doors for them on the job market. Eastern Elite students have a strong sense of themselves and their peers as future leaders, and this is borne out in descriptions of the Eastern Elite alumni/ae network:

> That's not to say that doors are closed to people who didn't go to Eastern, but it's certainly great because there are so many Eastern alumni, and when you have that instant connection with someone it's just I guess another little bit of an advantage. (Elizabeth Tennyson, Eastern Elite)

This young woman had already seen this work for her, as she had gotten an internship the previous summer via an informal encounter with an Eastern Elite alum. "We had a lot to talk about, just knowing 'Oh, what dorm were you in, where did you live, what did you major in?' We know all the terminology," she explained, and the conversation led to a request for her résumé, and later a job offer (Elizabeth Tennyson, Eastern Elite).[29] Another student likewise recalled how he wound up working for a high-profile conservative publication:

> I wasn't really looking for a job. . . . And then I got an email . . . from the assistant to the editor of [a national conservative magazine] who wrote me an email saying [that an Eastern Elite professor] says you're really sharp and just graduated from college. Would you like to come interview for a job? . . . Frankly it really amazed me. I certainly feel that—guilt is too strong a word—but you certainly do feel some degree of embarrassment when, if you have friends who are searching for jobs and then all of a sudden, you're getting invited to apply. But yeah, I mean it's not I feel entirely undeserved. (Vincent Long, Eastern Elite)

Sharing "terminology," and knowing the same places and names on campus—not to mention having faculty who recommend one out of the blue to elite media outlets—creates a sense of insiderness and inclusion among Eastern Elite alumni/ae, and so these types of "invitations" are not, it seems, uncommon.[30]

However, this aura extends even to those who are still undergraduates at Eastern Elite:

> There's something to be said for the value of studying with other people who are generally quite intelligent and capable, and the sorts of people who are going to go on to do the jobs which are generally considered to be appropriate for the most intelligent and capable people. There's this elitist aspect to that and there's also this sort of self-selecting—quote-unquote—"We are the elite, therefore we should do these jobs." (Nate Quinn, Eastern Elite)

Even before they reach graduation day, Eastern Elite students understand themselves to be part of a special group. This interpretation is reinforced not only on the campus level but also in the wider world as Eastern Elite students go out and form relationships with national organizations, obtaining internships and, later, jobs. In the case of one national conservative organization, there is actually a fellowship reserved specifically for Eastern Elite students. Though several Eastern Elite conservatives critiqued their peers for being nakedly careerist ("it's a sad fact of life but on the very day—well, even before the very day—that people enter Eastern Elite, they're thinking about their careers afterward"; Vincent Long, Eastern Elite), none were too dismayed when their own connections paid off.

Eastern Elite conservatives thus tend to focus their career aspirations on high-level positions and on the national stage. This type of scope is where the Eastern Elite interviewees' plans present the strongest contrast to those of the Western Public students. Significantly, not only the *types* of careers that interest students are different between conservatives on each campus but the *levels* at which they see themselves working are as well. Eastern Elite students—with only one exception—were completely uninterested in jobs that put them on the local level:

> I worked for my congressman's campaign back home after my freshman year. Did not enjoy that at all. . . . Being on the lowest rung of the totem pole in a campaign is awful. Maybe at the very highest levels it's very interesting, but it's certainly not well suited to what I like. (Drew Metcalfe, Eastern Elite)

> I don't want to be a politician, but [work in] some sort of think tank where I'm working on policy. That's what I'm interested a lot in. I think I'll be in D.C., not back in [my home state]. I don't think I'll ever live there again. (Nicole Harris, Eastern Elite)

The first statement is particularly noteworthy for being so clearly the opposite of the dynamic between national versus local politics described by Western Public students, who felt that local politics are where the action is and, indeed, that it would be in *Washington* where they would have to "start at the back of the line" (Hunter Devine, Western Flagship). Similarly, Eastern Elite students who express interest in working in media (or alumni/ae who already do) do not appear to even consider local media as an option, whereas this is a popular path for Western Public students.

Even though some of our Eastern Elite interviewees criticize peers who they feel are overly careerist, they keep an eye on their futures while they are undergraduates. In this way, the style of civilized discourse serves them strategically, not only by helping them learn to work well with non-conservatives but also by reining in potentially provocative discourse or actions. Eastern Elite conservatives who are committed to highbrow provocation seem to recognize that having such statements "on the record" could jeopardize their future careers, and so rather than aspiring to the judiciary or running for office, they focus their ambitions on careers that are either explicitly political (working for conservative think tanks or media outlets) or that are ostensibly devoid of political content (such as finance). For the majority who practice civilized discourse, this more palatable political style can be an asset. As one student described:

> From a practical point of view it kind of depends if I have any aspirations of working in government or becoming a judge, to be perfectly honest. You don't want too many extreme, or what could be considered extreme, political positions. . . . It's also sad that you have to think of that now in some sense, just because, especially the confirmation process has gotten so brutal and they bring up everything. So the more neutral you are, the easier it is. (Kingsley Griffith, Eastern Elite)

Thus, while the style of civilized discourse that dominates Eastern Elite opens many doors, it closes others. Though Kingsley, for example, felt strongly about banning abortion, and had in his youth participated in vocal, visible protests, his potential for activism around this issue while a student at Eastern Elite was circumscribed by his future career ambitions.

CONCLUSION

As we have seen in the last several chapters, conservative students at Eastern Elite and the Western Public universities exist in a larger political environment that is home to an overarching political logic—the Republican Party's and the ubiquitous conservative media's current loyalty to movement conservatism—as well as a variety of ideological and stylistic positions beneath the level of that one dominant logic.[31] Students on both campuses are aware of, and selectively draw on, this complex set of widely available discourses to craft their political identities, but in so doing they are both enabled and constrained by the distinctive cultural practices and ideas shared locally on their campuses, as well as by the organizational structures that create the daily rhythms of their lives (large or small class sizes, on- or off-campus housing, and the like). Some of the national discourses get all but ruled out by the local practices on the home campus, so much so that particular conservative types can be seen to dominate cohort after cohort, while other styles of conservative identities are unable to gain much traction. This is true at Eastern Elite, where the reputation and much more tightly integrated feel of the campus deter students from engaging in the provocative style so prevalent among conservatives on the Western Public campuses. What we find is variation across these campuses in what is considered to be appropriate and legitimate conservative identity and action, informed by students' understandings of themselves as college students, their involvement in campus clubs and other organizational settings and, equally important, by their participation in national organizations and their sense of what they are likely to be doing in their future careers.

When interviewees state their own ideas for why such differences across campuses exist, we typically hear their theories about individual characteristics and motivations being of utmost importance, as expressed here by an Eastern Elite student who said that "the types of people who come to Eastern Elite have been in a culture where they have had a certain seriousness to them, and they bring that with them here" (Calvin Coffey, Eastern Elite). It is their up-bringing, their early socialization, their *habitus* (in the French soci-ologist Pierre Bourdieu's terms), that leads to different styles at schools like Eastern Elite than at schools like Western Flagship, our interviewees would argue. And surely elements in students' back-grounds—particularly their social class background and their self-selection in applying to and subsequently choosing to attend differ-ent types of universities—have an important effect.

But we contend that paying attention to the institutional cultures found on these campuses provides more explanatory power about these styles than we could get by looking at background factors alone.[32] In particular, social class origins cannot account for the consistency of the differences seen between these campuses. As de-scribed in chapter 2, the conservative students and graduates we talked to at both schools varied substantially *on each campus* in terms of their class backgrounds, as indicated by parents' occupa-tions and education levels. They also came from many different re-gions of the country and described differing levels and styles of po-litical engagement prior to matriculation—from watching Fox News and listening to conservative AM radio to picketing abortion clinics to having dinner table conversations with their parents about the news of the day. Though we cannot know everything about our subjects' lives before they entered their universities, what we do know shows that each university's students are not so homogeneous a group that either social class membership or institutional self-selection processes would be the only elements at work here. We argue that the campuses themselves are a significant factor in the development of different types of political—even *citizenship*—style, and thus argue against the position that we are simply seeing the re-production of political elites via the self-selection of students from privileged backgrounds toward elite campuses. Instead, we can make a strong argument for campuses serving as a significant orga-nizational mechanism in encouraging the production of different kinds of political selves.

Chapter 7

Conservative Femininity

In the last three chapters we have used the comparative case method to show how cultural and organizational features at each of our universities—in combination with our interviewees' precollege experiences and national organizations' formulations of conservatism—create notable differences in college-age conservative styles. One way to describe what we have found is that students and student groups "pull down" discourses and practices from the widely available national cultural repertoires for what it means to be conservative, while they also "build up" local-level innovations in relatively consistent ways, such that dominant and submerged political styles remain in place on campuses regardless of the precise membership in right-leaning student organizations in any given year.[1] In a nutshell, we argue that campuses matter for the political development of young conservatives.

Although the present chapter maintains this basic orientation, we have something a bit different up our sleeves here. Our first objective in this chapter is not only to study the variation in conservative ideas and practices that occur *across* campuses but also to look more closely *within* our cases to see if there is meaningful variation among student conservatives at each university. We have already paid some attention to the phenomenon of within-campus variation, of course, demonstrating that certain students gravitate toward a university's dominant conservative style while others take up submerged forms. Even so, we have not yet adequately examined why individual students, or clusters of students, on either campus might display different styles from one another, or to what extent this might link up with their allegiance to different political issues. Is there any type of systematic variation that we can see in students' choices of issues and styles, or are differences in commitments simply the result of individuals' personal tastes and preferences?

This brings us to our second objective, which is to explore one particular dimension of social experience, gender, to see how it influences college-age conservatism. When we use gender as a filter to analyze our data, we find that women interviewees weigh in on a set of topics that barely seem to occur to conservative men, issues such as how career aspirations and family desires must be balanced, what appropriate physical presentation looks like for conservative women, how liberal feminism creates personal dilemmas for young people, and even how college students should conduct themselves in the areas of dating and sex.[2] While in other respects women and men in our sample align quite closely on conservative bread-and-butter issues such as shrinking the government, ensuring strong national security, and even for the most part opposing abortion rights, many of our women interviewees clearly think about a set of issues that men do not. As a result, these interviewees seem to wrestle with their gender identities within a larger conversation about conservatism in ways that don't appear to animate men.

We begin our consideration of gender and conservatism by looking at the set of national-level ideas found in politics and the media that we call "conservative femininity." We argue that these prominent ideas provide touchstones for how undergraduate conservative women should appropriately "do gender," both in college and in their future lives, and we see that understandings of conservative femininity are shared to a large extent by women at both Western Public and Eastern Elite Universities.[3] That said, we are interested not only in the extent to which ideas about conservative femininity are shared across campuses at Eastern Elite and Western Public but also in how they vary. And what we have found is that when it comes to what it means to be a college-age conservative woman, ideas vary quite a bit.

A NOTE ABOUT TERMINOLOGY

Before going further, it will be useful to explain our focus on femininity in this chapter. We are not in any way arguing that gender is something that only women have or do; indeed, while the sociology of gender's roots lie in explicating femininity, there is now several decades' worth of a rich sociological literature examining masculinity.[4] Looking in particular at the literature on gender and interaction, sociologists have found that both men and women are constantly enacting gender even in situations where gender is not manifestly being called to account.[5] Arguably, then, the men who made up the majority of our sample were, in various ways, "doing" masculinity in their interactions on campus, their interpretations of the local and national political spheres, and even their interviews for this research. However, in going over our data, we find that masculinity remains relatively invisible and unremarked upon. This is as true of the male interviewees who identified as heterosexual as it is of those few who described themselves as gay; it is true for whites and men of color, for men of all class backgrounds, and—perhaps most notable for our purposes—for men on both campuses. While this absence of discussion does itself constitute a finding about our subjects' takes on masculinity, this silence does not make for rich data.[6] In contrast, nearly all of our women respondents actively discussed the role of gender, both personally and politically, in their lives. We found, as we describe below, the shared use of national discourses, but also diverging local manifestations, and individuals who were attempting to forge their own paths of conservative femininity. Given this issue's prominence both within the national sphere and within our data, it seems appropriate to focus on it, even if it means giving short shrift to an analysis of conservative masculinity.[7] Again, though, we must emphasize that this does not mean we see gender as an identity, a set of cultural resources, or a constellation of issues with which only women grapple.

We should also briefly note our intentions when we discuss feminism and femininity, two terms that are open to numerous interpretations, meanings, and possibilities. Though we did not ask our interviewees to describe in depth what, precisely, they meant when they talked about "feminists" or described someone as "feminine," we can make inferences based on context—both the contexts of the interviews themselves and also the broader context of the national-level conservative discourse. Though there are numerous strains of feminism, and the precise definition of each is frequently contested, when our interviewees referred to feminism (and so when we ourselves do here), they seemed most frequently to be invoking some version of late twentieth-century, Gloria Steinem– or Betty Friedan–style, second-wave, liberal/mainstream feminism. This is certainly what is seen most often in our other data sources—for example, when a college student characterizes a professor as a "NOW feminist."[8] Likewise, when our interviewees talked about femininity (and so when we do here), there appeared to be some consensus around the American ideal famously characterized by R.W. Connell as "emphasized femininity," the complement and counterpart to hegemonic masculinity.[9] We have tried to be relatively consistent throughout this chapter in the characteristics and components we attribute to each term but acknowledge that it would be virtually impossible to be either totally comprehensive or perfectly precise.

THE NATIONAL DISCOURSE OF DIFFERENCE: CONSERVATIVE FEMININITY

A robust discourse about gender exists within conservative circles, with many right-leaning intellectuals, media pundits, and politicians promoting the idea of "natural differences" between men and women and weighing in on women's social roles.[10] Such normative frames of reference have long been a staple in American conservatism, but

since the 2008 presidential election, and particularly since John Mc-
Cain's announcement of then Alaska governor Sarah Palin as his
running mate, the conservative woman has become a staple of both
the mainstream media and the blogosphere. Though women have
long played important roles in conservative movements in the United
States, Palin's sound-bite-ready self-descriptors (such as "mama griz-
zly" and "hockey mom") and not infrequent public gaffes (such as
her inability to name a specific newspaper she read when queried by
Katie Couric) made her something of an overnight media sensation:
while the former played well in right-leaning outlets, the latter provided joke fodder for *Saturday Night Live* and *The Daily Show*.
Palin arguably launched the mainstream media's discovery of the
conservative woman, and the search was on for more—and more
quickly appeared, from Tea Party insurgent Christine O'Donnell to
2012 presidential candidate Michele Bachmann to numerous
daughters of the right, including Meghan McCain, John Huntsman's daughters, and, naturally, Bristol Palin.[11] This groundswell of
vocal, visible conservative women has reignited debates around
work-life balance, the treatment of women who run for political office or who otherwise hold elite public positions, and whether any
woman—no matter her ideological orientation—can claim the title
of feminist.[12]

Though her star has since faded, Sarah Palin's momentum and
media interest were nearing their zenith at the time of our data collection. And while there certainly have always been prominent
women in the conservative movement who worked outside the
home—in many ways, this was a necessary part of their participation—Palin was among the first to explicitly declare women's right
to have careers as well as children. While just ten years ago Michelle
Easton, founder of the Clare Boothe Luce Policy Institute, touted
her campus appearances with posters reading "What does a woman
REALLY want? Husband. Children. Picket Fence," many conservative women now contend they can have all that *and* a satisfying career, ideally one that furthers movement goals.[13] Though at the 2007
National Conservative Student Conference organized by the Young
America's Foundation (YAF), Easton announced that though she

was "a conservative, a lawyer, a politician, a patriot, and a woman," she was emphatically "not a feminist,"[14] within just a few years Palin was among the vanguard of conservative women claiming the mantle of feminism.

In all, the ascendance of conservative women within right-leaning circles has brought with it a combination of ideological moves, merging core conservative principles with an ardent critique of feminism and a passionate dedication to conventional femininity.[15] Although this broad strategy embraced by the women of the Right has gained considerable steam in recent years, it had emerged well before the Palin era. For example, nearly a decade ago a *New York Times* article about young conservatives in America gave this quotation from a student at Bucknell:

> "There's the old stereotype of the WASP-y country-club wife or the Bible-study mom from the Midwest," Kasic says. "But that's not what conservative women are anymore." Kasic, instead, points to "stiletto conservatives" like [Christina] Hoff Sommers and [Ann] Coulter. "We have role models now," she says. "Hip, strong women who exude the message: 'I don't need hand-holding just because I'm a woman.' Kasic herself plans to be a working woman when she graduates ("I'm no soccer mom," she laughs; "I don't even like kids"), but she respects women who choose a different path—to be homemakers, like her own mother. "Conservatives are inclusive in a way that liberals are not," she says, voicing a central theme of the Independent Women's Forum ethos. "We say that women can be executives or stay-at-home mothers."[16]

These "stiletto conservatives"—and more recent examples, like Monica Crowley, Michele Bachmann, and Nikki Haley—are often held up as proof that women can "have it all": an important and influential career without sacrificing the family or feminine appearance dictated by emphasized femininity.[17] This type of persona is also institutionalized by organizations such as the Clare Boothe Luce Policy Institute and the YAF. As Palin's and others' forays into both national GOP and Tea Party politics have made clear, this style of rejecting feminism and reclaiming femininity not only plays well in the media, it also energizes many other right-leaning voters. And as we'll see below, for many of our women interviewees, this national version of conservative femininity resonates with their own actions and ambitions.

In examining our interviewees' responses to these larger national frames positing the "natural difference" between men and women, we find that women at both Eastern Elite University and the Western Public campuses make similar use of national discourses about rejecting feminism and reclaiming femininity. While it is important to note for the moment that women on each campus do modify the discursive strands within this larger set of ideas to fit their situations on their particular campuses, in many ways women at Western Public and Eastern Elite adopt several of the same cultural strategies to connect their identities as women and their identities as conservatives. It is to these similarities that we first turn our attention.

SIMILARITIES ACROSS CAMPUSES: PULLING DOWN NATIONAL DISCOURSES

REJECTING FEMINISM

One common thread in women's interviews across both campuses is a strong distaste for mainstream feminism, which our interviewees stated as a concern that feminists do not speak for *all* women's interests, and *most certainly not their own*. Several of our women interviewees described feeling barraged by feminist doctrine on their college campuses. One Western Satellite interviewee told of an early brush with feminist pedagogy:

> My freshman year, I remember, my first class, it was a literature class and [the professor] was saying how we're surrounded by phallic symbols—the Washington Monument and this and that.

And we live in a patriarchal society and women have nothing this and that. And it's shown even in our building structures. And I remember like calling my mom and [saying], "Mom, did you know that—?" I didn't know any better. And she's like, "You can't always listen to what your teachers say." And I'm like, "But she's my teacher, she knows." Luckily, I met somebody that taught me better. But I think that's what ends up happening is when these smart people are telling you all this stuff, why would you not believe them? (Brittany Urban, Western Satellite)

This concern is hardly confined to the classroom, or even to their college campuses. Though they often discussed these ideas in terms of their experiences as college women, reflections on their future plans often seemed to lead these young women either to reject feminism outright or to reframe it for themselves in a way that better fit with their ideological commitments. Here, two Eastern Elite women explain their identification as feminists, which they contended differs significantly from mainstream feminism:

People have accused me of I'm co-opting the term and I'm trying to subvert it. Well, sure: why not? It doesn't have to mean . . . I mean, what feminism *really* means is advancing women, right? A feminist is somebody who believes that women . . . well, I don't want to say this to come off as women need more help or anything than men, because I don't like that view of women as victims. I believe I support policies that help women. They help men, too, but they help women. I think you can be a feminist and be pro-life and be okay with somebody else being a stay-at-home mom, or you yourself being a stay-at-home mom. (Nicole Harris, Eastern Elite)

I consider myself a feminist as well—maybe in a slightly different sense of the word than what is often kind of portrayed, but I see this message as something that is really promoting an empowering message, really encouraging not just women but men as well, but people, [to] really just make decisions based on what is best for them. To not be afraid to do so, and to empower them and give them the courage to do that if that is something they want. (Tabitha Lanier, Eastern Elite)

These quotations reflect several commonly held beliefs among our women interviewees from both Eastern Elite and Western Public. First is the idea that feminists derogate women who opt for child-rearing over careers. Second, interviewees believed that conventional feminist dogma demands women have *more* rights than men rather than simply equal rights; as one Western Satellite woman explained, "I consider myself not to be too much of a feminist because I don't believe in like special privilege" (Lindsey Nicholson, Western Satellite). Last, there is the contention that feminism is, overall, a narrow ideology, limiting women's choices rather than enhancing them and ascribing the interests of a vocal minority of women to all women.

These sentiments from both campuses strongly echo the national conservative critique of feminism, implying that what we see among the college women in our sample constitutes a clear case of drawing directly from national-level discourses to make sense of their lives. Many of our student and alumnae respondents abhorred the expectation that they would agree with feminist doctrine purely on the basis of their sex and level of education. This was particularly true of "women's issues" such as abortion, marriage, and work-life balance. Instead, the women we interviewed relied on their beliefs as conservatives—particularly valuing traditional marriage; two-parent, heterosexual households; and women's labor in child-rearing—to claim an experience of womanhood that falls outside the bounds of liberal feminism. Their status as conservative women allowed our interviewees to generate counterarguments that not only helped them make sense of their own beliefs but also turn the tables on liberal feminists by claiming that *feminists*, not conservative women, are being narrow-minded. However, as we will see in a later section, this shared overarching view of feminism is manifested in different ways at our two case universities. Before we get to this point, though, we turn our attention to a second major element of conservative womanhood that young conservative women on both of our campuses take from wider conservative discourses.

RECAPTURING FEMININITY

At the National Conservative Student Conference (NCSC) organized by the YAF in 2007, a young woman from a small college in Maryland told the following anecdote during a question-and-answer session with Michelle Easton, head of the Clare Boothe Luce Policy Institute:

> I had a NOW feminist professor at my school . . . and she showed a movie on the women of Samoa and said that we should want to be like these women—women who are half naked and feeding their children on camera. . . . They don't have to wear bras or clothes, so they were supposed to be empowered women. Well, I don't think so. . . . I transferred out of the class, but before I did I said to my professor, "Any woman with no Victoria's Secret within ten miles is actually the persecuted one."[18]

Her story drew appreciative applause and much laughter, but it also brings up another theme that appears throughout interviews with women at both Eastern Elite and Western Public, which again taps into the broadest level of the conservative critique of feminism. In describing their own aspirations and talking about others they admired, our interviewees expressed considerable respect for women they felt had achieved success without compromising their conventional femininity. In this we see an extension not only of their rejection of feminism but also an articulation of what these women believed liberal feminists wanted to take away from them. Admirable women are beautiful, well-dressed, and unambiguously feminine, in addition to being successful as mothers, wives, and professionals. In contrast to this conservative version of feminism, liberal feminism and conventional femininity are viewed as incompatible. Again, this can be viewed as a specific manifestation of the overall contention that liberal feminism is a narrow ideology barring women from truly exploring all of their options. This aspect of the national critique also came up among women interviewees at both Eastern Elite and Western Public, as the data below attest.

Because many of our interviews took place during or just after the 2008 presidential election campaign, it is not surprising that the area where this issue surfaced most was in discussions of Sarah Palin. This finding is consistent across campuses, with women at Eastern Elite describing positive views of Palin just as much as women on the Western Public campuses. Though every single woman interviewee who had positive views of Palin also expressed having become at least somewhat disappointed about her qualifications or overall performance over the course of the presidential race, this did not entirely disqualify her credibility in their eyes. These interviewees' remarks are typical of our women respondents' comments about Palin:

> I liked Sarah Palin, I still like her. I hope she runs again. I think she definitely brought a new, fresh breath of air to the campaign. Especially as a woman, it's kind of obvious, I guess, to me that people really don't want to see a woman in power. But I think it's a little different, I think when you think conservative you think old men, and she was just this young, spunky woman, and it was new and cool. . . . I mean, if you kind of look at Washington, there aren't very many great beauties there. And Sarah Palin definitely is a beautiful woman. . . . I don't know, it was just—it was very interesting how they treated her because of that. And I don't know, I really like her. I identified with her, I like how she handled the whole situation. (Brooke Gerson, Western Flagship)

> [Palin's speech at the 2008 Republican National Convention] was delivered well, you didn't see an ounce of nervousness, which is, aside from some of Hillary Clinton's speeches, I think that it was just a really solid example of a female getting to the podium and giving, I mean, almost like a kind of Bill Clinton-esque speech in that it was folksy. You know, there were moments where it was very talking to Joe Six-Pack kind of thing,

but it worked. . . . . I felt like it was nice to see how a female could work the room, could make good old boy jokes, but instead they were sort of good old girl jokes. . . . . Kind of like, "I could have a beer with him," I think women felt like "I could have a . . . whatever women have with . . . [a] cosmopolitan? . . . with her," she brought out [a] female [version of that], a quality that males have exploited for so long. (Staci Congdon, Eastern Elite)

Even while interviewees were disappointed with some of her abilities, and certainly with the outcome of the campaign, they were thrilled to see a strong woman who was also conventionally feminine achieve such prominence. As another Eastern Elite woman explained in regard to Palin:

There is just that like . . . "Yeah, I'm a woman and I am not going to try to hide it or try to. . . ." When you are playing in a man's world, you can try to play like a man, or you can be like, "*No, I'm a woman. I am bringing this in.*" (Tabitha Lanier, Eastern Elite, emphasis added)

This interest in her femininity formed a large part of our women interviewees' acclaim for Palin across campuses.[19]

This contrasts with men's views of Palin on both campuses. On the whole, men disliked her and characterized themselves as voting not so much *for* the McCain-Palin ticket as casting a vote *against* Obama. Those who described pluses did so in different terms than the women, focusing primarily on Palin's stance on various issues and her effects on McCain's poll numbers, as here:

I stumbled upon Sarah Palin doing research to see who might be vice president in 2008 and thought I had a really good candidate, somebody who was very much in line with my views on the economy, on oil, on a vast range of subjects. And somebody who's very articulate in many of the same ways that Reagan was, very media savvy, knew how to communicate conservative ideology in a way that people understood and liked it. (Bryan Carhart, Western Satellite)

I wanted to give her the benefit of the doubt when she was first brought on to the ticket. I was really willing to tell people that I was talking with, who just were lambasting [McCain] for that choice, "Give her a chance. She may, maybe she's just nervous in front of the cameras, like maybe she has a lot to offer." But I just felt that throughout the course of the campaign her inexperience was painfully apparent. And I think that it would just have been a total disaster if she had, for whatever unfortunate reason, had to assume the presidency. (Kendall Nelson, Eastern Elite)

Only two men, both at Eastern Elite, mentioned aspects of Palin's personality or personal life. One described how his extended family, which included a cousin with special needs, empathized with Palin having a son born with Down syndrome. Another interviewee was the only man on any of our campuses to highlight Palin's gender, albeit in the context of criticizing her incompetence in a snarky way that none of our women interviewees began to match:

A part of me *loved* the fact that oh my God, a woman, this Westerner, a hunter, came on the ticket. This is such a different image of the Republican Party as espoused by George W. Bush and Karl Rove. She's just sexy, different. But a part of me is just like, Oh my gosh, she's an idiot! . . . I can do a better job than she can! And she can't even memorize those statistics. God, why is she so dumb? So I think I had mixed feelings about it. But at the end, I was much more confident in her than Obama. So I voted very confidently for McCain-Palin. (Kyle Lee, Eastern)

Further, none of the men on any of the campuses claimed to personally identify with Palin in any way, nor were they interested in discussing her appearance. We could interpret this as an effect of the men being interviewed by a woman, given the concerns in the media throughout the campaign about whether women candidates were being judged for their policy views and statements or for their ward-robes and haircuts. However, considering the interviewees' general lack of interest in P.C. attitudes and their willingness at times to comment on the attractiveness of the opposite sex (for example, a Western Flagship interviewee discussing the usefulness of having good-looking women working at the recruitment table for the College Republicans), this is probably not the case.

While men ignored it, women interviewees' concern with femininity makes sense in light of their anxiety about feminism threatening to narrow their own range of possibilities. Conservative women on both campuses do not want to surrender any advantages at their disposal, and having to give up attributes that they consider to be unique to women seems to them to close off options (just as they argue that feminists' emphasis on careers forecloses the option of being a stay-at-home mom). One very confident Western Satellite interviewee described the advantages of a feminine self-presentation at length:

> I: So do you say in conservative politics there is *not* a kind of macho culture?
>
> R: Well, there is, but I think that that almost gives me a bit of an advantage.
>
> I: How is that?
>
> R: Well, you show up at these functions . . . and you're the smart girl who is really cute and fun to hang around, and there's just this natural gravitation.
>
> I: But do they actually listen to what you have to say?
>
> R: Oh, yeah. I mean, it's hard to identify what variable makes me charismatic. It could be the fact that I'm young, a college student, a Republican, a woman. I don't know. . . . So it's hard to pin it down. But I don't think it has much to do with being a woman. I mean, there's definitely . . . you catch more looks, but I'd say that's *productive*, especially considering the macho white male sort of environment. So I think it works in my favor [*laughs*]. (Lindsey Nicholson, Western Satellite, emphasis in original)

This both fits with and extends discourses found at the broadest level of conservative femininity's rejection of liberal feminism. Conservatives argue that women and men are naturally different, and they charge that feminists want to erase those differences, thus reducing women's choices.[20]

To sum up the previous sections, women interviewees at both Eastern Elite and Western Public utilized similar elements from discourses of conservative womanhood that reject feminism and recapture femininity. Most notably, they did this while men mostly just ignored these issues. This finding showcases both variation *within* campuses, insofar as women prioritized some issues that men did not, as well as similarities among women *across* campuses, in that our women interviewees at both Western Public and Eastern Elite expressed concern about many of the same issues brought up by charismatic politicians and pundits. However, this is hardly the end of the gender story.

DIFFERENCES ACROSS CAMPUSES: BUILDING UP LOCAL STRATEGIES

Even while they look to similar discursive elements found on the national level, we find that women at Western Public and Eastern Elite use these discourses of rejecting feminism and recapturing femininity to different ends in response to the specific cultural and structural features on their college campuses and in their campus clubs. Every university presents unique challenges and opportunities for women as conservatives on campus; thus, even while our interviewees shared many of the same beliefs about gender and commitments to gender-related issues, these beliefs and commitments did not always translate into action in the same ways at the different universities. Instead of a shared vision of conservative womanhood, we see the construction of certain ideas and practices at the campus level—some of which might actually seem quite alien to members of the other university. This is seen both in women's interactions with their campus environments and in their anticipation of (and others' expectations of) their futures.

CAMPUS LIFE AT EASTERN ELITE: ADVOCATES FOR TRADITION

Eastern Elite sophomore Shannon Yaffe arrived for her interview looking every inch the all-American college coed, with long wavy hair and a big smile, dressed demurely yet flirtatiously in jeans and a cute corduroy jacket over a short cotton camisole that revealed a slice of her midsection. But Shannon, as she made clear right away, was not your typical college woman.[21] Though she enjoyed her classes and her professors, she had considerable concerns about her undergraduate peers—and about what she saw as her university's enabling of their lax morality and the silencing of her voice. Shannon was the leader of an abstinence advocacy group at Eastern Elite which, though Shannon herself was an evangelical Christian, used secular arguments to attempt to persuade students to delay sexual activity until marriage. She described a recent dust-up with the Eastern Elite administration:

> There's a required sex program . . . that is mandatory and freshmen have to attend it. And it's just kind of skits and blah, blah, blah about the college hookup culture and what to expect. . . . [Our conservative group members] have historically handed out flyers while students enter the event. And they just say "Ten Reasons to Wait," and they list these ten reasons, because in this event students are definitely expected to be having sex. And I think there's a certain . . . I mean these freshmen aren't necessarily walking on campus saying, "Oh, everyone has sex here." I think after this event they're all forced to go to, it just gives you the wrong impression on college life.

Her displeasure evident, she continued:

> And this fall right before I came [back] to school . . . , the dean emailed us and he was like, "You can't flyer outside the event this

year because we don't want students"—these were his exact
words—"we don't students to be inundated with too much information." I'm like, these are Eastern students! I think they can
handle two opposing viewpoints! (Shannon Yaffe, Eastern Elite)

While Shannon may not have fit the mold of the "typical" college
woman, in many different ways her concerns were shared by the
other conservative women in our sample from Eastern Elite. In con-
cordance with rejecting feminism, these interviewees felt strongly
that groups claiming to represent women's interests—including the
university's administration—were not representative of *their*
interests.[22]

The facts that Eastern Elite *has* a mandatory sex education program in the first place, and that a dean would then bar the abstinence group from providing commentary on the content of that
program, are just two of the features of the campus that strongly
colored our women interviewees' rejection of feminism as a narrow
ideology, and shaped how conservative women navigated social expectations at their university. At Eastern Elite, much of the critique
was based around conservative women's perceptions that the campus climate was overly permissive and morally relativistic.[23] In particular, women described an "anything goes" approach to sexuality
that they found troubling. Even the one respondent who was the
least concerned of those who discussed mainstream social life, and
who characterized herself as a participant in that social milieu ("I
mean, I haven't like gone through college being a virgin"), explained
how louche she also perceived the campus to be:

I guess it's hard for me now in my senior year of college to look
back on the things that were surprising to me because I've become so used to them. But a lot of them were things like . . . it's
also hard to think about them in terms of liberalism and college.
At least I think it's just hard not to conflate liberalness and college. So it was really shocking to me to be living in a dorm where
there were condoms given out in every freshman dorm. And it
was very surprising to, like, to have this sort of transgender task

force. . . . These were all things that seemed very weird to me [*laughs*]. But now they're totally, yeah. (Molly Nash Downing, Eastern Elite)

While this interviewee has been vocally critical of the tactics of the abstinence group on campus, overall her stance aligns with those of other women interviewees who expressed concern with campus mores and an interest in recapturing a more traditional vision of femininity.

In support of our argument that conservative ideology is in some respects experienced differently by men and by women at Eastern Elite, we found that campus social mores were not an issue on the agenda for most Eastern Elite men. Conservative men we interviewed criticized everything from the university's political climate, to the administration's stance toward the military, to the weaknesses of the core curriculum, but for the most part they did not discuss *social life* at Eastern Elite. Only two Eastern Elite men discussed social expectations about sexuality as an issue and took part in related campus groups.[24] For most conservative men in our sample at Eastern Elite, however, these issues did not appear to cause concern.

Thus, since most students populating conservative campus clubs at Eastern Elite are men, and most Eastern Elite conservative men are uninterested in women's issues, Eastern Elite women looking to be active in these areas have to look outside the primary conservative groups on campus.[25] As a result, many of the conservative women at Eastern Elite rely heavily on conservative student-run groups—particularly the pro-life group, the abstinence group, and campus Catholic groups—to provide a base of moral support and an alternative to mainstream campus social life. Tabitha Lanier, who founded the Eastern Elite abstinence group, described her motivations for starting the group:

In terms of sex and relationships in college campuses there is so much from the other side and it just seems like there were no young voices even kind of proposing or even talking about [abstinence] as a real option in terms of institutionally and also just in terms of what you see at parties or with friends. It just felt like there was something that was missing. (Tabitha Lanier, Eastern Elite)

These women's status as conservative fellow travelers who meet in small, supportive organizations provides a useful strategic base for their rejection of feminism and their refusal to be spoken for by other individuals or groups on their campus. Their choice to opt out of mainstream campus culture and beliefs defines them as conservative; at the same time, their identification as conservatives in high-profile campus organizations makes their "dropping out" of the campus social scene interpretable to both their conservative and non-conservative peers. In some sense, they draw on elements of conservative femininity to mitigate potential tensions brought on by their rejection of many of the expectations of being a "typical" college student.

While they often describe their experiences on campus as difficult and ostracizing, participating in student-run groups gives these women a social safety net that helps them find friends and remain strong in their convictions. As the woman quoted above explained, "Sometimes just knowing that one other person believes something, that can make you strong enough to stick with something that you truly believe in" (Tabitha Lanier, Eastern Elite). Their status as conservatives allows these Eastern Elite women to in some way fit in on campus. Even if they are somewhat socially isolated, their actions become comprehensible to others. Beliefs and behaviors that are seen as uncharacteristic of college women generally make sense for *conservative* college women. Rather than simply being oddballs or prudes, these women are conservatives.[26]

CAMPUS LIFE AT WESTERN PUBLIC: FIGHTING IDEOLOGICAL CONFORMITY

Despite similarities across campuses in rejecting feminism and seeking to recapture femininity, in contrast to their peers at Eastern

Elite, almost no Western Public women conservatives whom we interviewed used these two tools to critique social mores on their campuses (though as we'll see below, these discourses did crop up in their discussions of the future). Few discussed the vagaries of social life on campus with us, and just one woman reflected at length on dating and sex. Her comments sound much more similar to those of women at Eastern Elite (and at other schools where there are abstinence groups) than to those of her peers on any of the Western Public campuses:

> I think there is a lot of pressure for people my age and younger to be sexually active. And I think that it isn't always the healthiest or best thing for anyone. But I particularly, I think girls and how they handle themselves, that issue is close to my heart. And I feel like girls are under a lot of pressure and they often make decisions that aren't necessarily the best for them. And that just breaks my heart, so I am particularly interested in that issue. I myself have made decisions that I think have not been the best for me, so. . . . (Isabel Stricker, Western Flagship)

But Isabel is the exception. Despite a large evangelical presence in the university population at large, abstinence is just not much of an issue among students who are active in conservative *political* clubs on the Western Public campuses, though it may be among those students who confine their conservatism to religious activities. Even a Christian woman interviewee at Western Flagship who described herself as having grown up "living a biblical Christian life" characterized herself as having become *less* concerned about traditional social issues like sexuality since coming to college:

> I haven't really changed positions on anything. I've just become more open-minded on those types of things. . . . I think that's more of I realize that there's just not, I'm not caught up in my own religious conservative role anymore. So I'm more like oh, that person doesn't believe the same things that I do but that's okay. They have their own opinion and that's fine. (Samantha Hart, Western Flagship)

As we will see in a moment, we think that this kind of laissez-faire attitude may owe much to the libertarian streak in conservative politics on the Western Public campuses.

The gender-related issues that *do* arise as concerns at Western Public come across in terms of the ideological conformity these interviewees describe on their campuses around social issues directly affecting women. For example, one Western Flagship woman remembered an incident earlier that year surrounding her anti-abortion activities:

> I stood in the [student center] and passed out literature about [our event] to try to generate attention and we got . . . a few positive responses and even some people saying, "Wow there's a pro-life organization on campus, I can't believe that. I'm kind of an underground pro-lifer, this is great." Which tells you something about the atmosphere on campus, that people feel like they have to be underground about their pro-life views. But . . . a lot of very negative responses as well, a lot of hostility from people. . . . Like people picking up flyers and throwing them on the ground in front of us. And kind of yelling out stuff like "Oh we hate women too." And stuff like that. (Isabel Stricker, Western Flagship)

Notably here, handing out literature to promote a speaker coming to campus is one of the least provocative actions engaged in by the pro-life groups on the different campuses (both at Western Public *and* Eastern Elite), which vary in their approaches to creating visibility for their point of view.[27] On the whole, though, even those issues that are often seen to be aligned with women's conservative activism appear to be less salient for Western Public women. As we already noted, Isabel is a bit of an outlier among the Western Public women interviewees.

The only other area where campus concerns relating to gender arise is with the conservative women at Western Public who actively take issue with the Women's Center on the Western Flagship campus. In contrast to women at Eastern Elite, however, the concern here is not strictly a case of rejecting feminism, as it would be were they to espouse a belief that the center arrogantly tried to speak for all women. Rather, these interviewees expressed displeasure with the center as an arm of Western Flagship's overall liberal agenda, in which liberal feminism is but one of many noxious positions taken up by the organization. One interviewee, a Western Flagship alumna, went "undercover" and participated in events at the Women's Center in order to publicize what she saw as the absurdity of their programming and ideology. She later sent another interviewee, a recent graduate of Western Satellite, to continue this work. Interestingly, none of their criticisms of the Women's Center related directly to issues of sex or gender. Instead, these interviewees focused on other projects the Women's Center pursued related to racism and other forms of discrimination. Criticism of the Women's Center seemed to be another extension of critiques of the overwhelming liberalness of the Western Public campuses in *all* issue areas—a critique made by virtually every one of the Western Public interviewees—and not a focused attack based on gender-related issues alone. One woman characterized the ideological conformity of the liberal atmosphere at Western Flagship as creating a "bubble" around left-leaning students: "There were all these activists on campus but they were like preaching to the choir, you know. It's like they're just sitting in their safe little bubble on campus saying, like, you know, like 'Here's an issue, here's an issue'" (Stephanie Cohen, Western Flagship). What might be considered "women's issues" are just one of a wide array of topics that Western Public women interviewees criticized as the outlandish domain of the university's Women's Center.

This focus on liberal conformity and hypocrisy similarly shaped Western Public men's comments. While as at Eastern Elite, Western Public conservative men generally do not discuss topics such as the Women's Center, the Western Public men we interviewed did express concern about the ideological narrowness of their campuses, and as with the "undercover" work described above at the Women's Center, they took similar delight in calling out and critiquing liberals for their gender-sensitive stances. Chuck Kelley, the originator of the Affirmative Action Bake Sale at Western Flagship, related at length an experience he had had as a conservative member of the liberal-run student government, an incident he said showcased the disingenuousness of its members' gender political correctness:

[My friend] who at that time was running the College Republicans and she was doing all *that* stuff, she gets in an elevator with the—get this!—[chief justice of the student government court]. And he is, *he* is the chair of [Western's chapter of one of the national reproductive rights organizations]. You would think a woman would have that job, but whatever. I'm all for gender equality [*laughs*]. So anyway, he gets in there. . . . She's just standing there, according to her story. She comes and tells me this later. He's on the elevator with her in the student union, where you run into all kinds of people you do battle with. And before he gets off the elevator, he looks at her and he says "You fucking cunt" and walks off the elevator because, you know, for pissing them off. Well, she of course doesn't take much offense at this because she realizes he's crazy. But she walks down to me dutifully and goes, "You would not believe what your chief justice just said to me." And of course I said great!

So I get out my university letterhead and I say "Dear Justice whatever. I heard horrible news. I want to make sure, I want to hear your side of the story." And send it to him. Nothing. So I send him another one next week after not hearing back from him. "This is horrible, people shouldn't be treating women like this, you're representative of our government, and I'm going to have to ask you for your resignation if I don't hear from you." So I sent him another letter. "I'm asking for your resignation. I can't fire you but I'm asking for your resignation. This is horrible. You run a pro-women student organization on campus." And of course all this goes into my memory bank of *these people are crazy*! They're insane! So finally, so the next week I come and see the agenda for the legislative meeting for that week, where we sit there and plead with them. And what do I see but articles of impeachment—against [*me*]! (Chuck Kelley, Western Flagship)

Western Public conservatives, then—both men and women—express concern over gender-related issues mainly as a way to point out the "insanity" of the general ideological climate on the Western Public campuses rather than looking at these issues as problematic, either for themselves or for their peers. Like many of the events staged by conservative groups on the Western Public campuses, the point is more to poke fun at the absurdity of liberal sensitivity around areas like gender than to take seriously ideas about appropriate gendered behaviors, and perceived contradictions between feminism and femininity, in the way that some students at Eastern Elite do.

Despite their different articulation on each campus, then, animosity toward feminism and an embrace of femininity are vibrant on both Eastern Elite and the Western Public campuses and are used to critique distinctive elements of the campus climate. These pieces of conservative femininity were also used by women interviewees to discuss their hopes for the future, as they navigated conflicting expectations about education, work, and family. The women interviewees' uniform refusal to be spoken for by feminists or others purportedly interested in the advancement of women continues, while at least for Eastern Elite women, their interest in reclaiming femininity shifts in focus from campus morality and sexual reputations to issues of family and career. In doing so, they not only legitimate their own choices but also advance the conservative critique of feminism as narrow in scope.

CAREER PLANS AT EASTERN ELITE:
DEFYING HIGH-PRESSURE EXPECTATIONS

Conservative women at Eastern Elite University are particularly attuned to the expectations of those around them regarding their future achievements: Attendance at such an elite school brings with it enormous expectations for elite careers. More so than for women at Western Public, conservative women at Eastern Elite feel they are combating normative expectations not that women be oriented toward family and child-rearing but that Eastern Elite-educated women have to pursue high-powered careers *above all else*. One interviewee explained:

> I've heard people here say, and I think you find still a lot of people who say, like "That's a waste of your degree. You go to Eastern and you're staying at home. What are you doing with your degree? It's just a waste." I think that's a terrible thing to say. I mean first of all if you're a feminist, you think women should be able to do whatever they want. But they think you're only making that decision because you're oppressed, which I don't think is appropriate. That's not true. (Nicole Harris, Eastern Elite)

While this interviewee stated that she herself did not necessarily want to be a full-time, stay-at-home mother, she emphasized the importance of family throughout her interview, citing considerable admiration for women who are "able somehow to balance everything" even if "they're not having their cake and eating it too necessarily" (Nicole Harris, Eastern Elite).

Though recognizing that having a career and a family might be difficult, conservative Eastern Elite women generally want to do both, and they malign liberal feminists and campus critics for attempting to cut off their options. Another interviewee expressed this by saying she felt feminism should be "encouraging and empowering women" to "go for what they desire," regardless of what those desires are. She explained, "In terms of work, yeah, go and get that graduate degree if you want to get that graduate degree, but also if you would rather just take a couple of years off and raise your kids, do that" (Tabitha Lanier, Eastern Elite). Professors, non-conservative campus groups, and other Eastern Elite students were cited as examples of people and organizations that proffered a narrow, liberal version of feminism, seen as discouraging and disempowering to their goals of putting family equal to (if not above) jobs. Eastern Elite women who opted to emphasize the importance of family perceive themselves as having to remain on the defensive against these campus-level norms privileging a career orientation for women. Rather than making their future families fit in at the edges of their careers, these women expressed a desire to make their jobs work with their families. For example, one Eastern Elite woman described not wanting a political job that would force her to live in Washington, D.C., or New York in terms of not wanting to raise children there. "It wouldn't be because of the politics, it would be more because I don't want to raise a family in a big city," she said. "I was brought up playing outside. I don't know where people play here" (Staci Congdon, Eastern Elite). Feeling as if they would face enormous disapproval from the rest of campus if they made decisions about their families that would jeopardize their careers, Eastern Elite women use conservatism to fight for more traditional feminine concerns.

CAREER PLANS AT WESTERN PUBLIC: FORGING YOUR OWN PATH

Expectations for women in the Western Public university system are different from those faced by women at Eastern Elite: They see less of a prescribed career path before them. Nonetheless, our Western Public interviewees likewise emphasized their interest in "having it all," with children and a career. Compare, for example, the following quotation from a Western Satellite woman with the quotation in the section above about choosing between a graduate degree and raising children:

> I used to want to get a PhD to teach, but I realize that I don't want to spend that much more time in school because I want to have a family. I'm going to need to stay home with the kids for a couple of years and everything. So I don't think I want to do that. . . . And I honestly think I can read a bunch of like Austrian economic books and almost learn more than I could going to a school. (Brittany Urban, Western Satellite)

For Western Public women interviewees, there was less of a sense that one *had* to succeed at the highest echelons of one's career, and by extension, there was no one true way to succeed within a given arena—including taking time away from school and the labor force to do just that. In fact, according to this interviewee, one's intellectual and political curiosity might be better satisfied in a self-directed fashion than through an accredited graduate program. In contrast to the Eastern Elite interviewee who discussed making child-rearing work with academia, the Western Satellite woman above describes a path that does not necessarily have to include institutional legitimation.

Particularly in their willingness to consider alternative formulations of success, the Western Public women appeared to open themselves up to a greater number of possibilities, with less status threat for not conforming to high achievement. Another interviewee weighed her options:

> The only way I'd be happy staying home when my kids were little would be if I had a lot of contact with other adults through like Mom groups or something like that. Like I could not be just like at home with kids all day by myself. And so part of me thinks that I'll really want to be home with them when they're not in school, and part of me says I'd want to do teaching. . . . So I could do something like that. Or I just might decide I *don't* want to stay home. That is something I *always* thought I would want to stay home, and within the last year or two I thought, I don't know if I really want to do that. (Christina Young, Western Flagship)

This interviewee described some guilt that would arise around such a decision: "I don't know if it's an expectation of my family because no one has really said that. But my mom did it and her mom did it, and people where I come from do that" (Christina Young, Western Flagship). This contrasts not only with the expectations for Eastern Elite women in content, but also in emphasis. Whereas according to our Eastern Elite women interviewees, expectations are clearly laid out and reiterated by faculty and peers, on the Western Public campuses there is much less of a school-specific template that women seem to think they are expected to follow.

Generally, these interviewees did not have the concerns that Eastern Elite interviewees did about peer approbation for their life choices. They shared with the Eastern Elite women the relative lack of concern about potential negative consequences thereof, again underscoring that choosing children over a career, or children and a career, is not their problem—it's narrow-minded feminists who need an attitude adjustment. Or perhaps the work of feminists has mostly been done. Asked whether she believes she will face extra barriers to her career aspirations as a woman, one Western Satellite interviewee said, "I wouldn't say because I'm a woman I [will] face any additional barriers. And maybe I'm naïve, but I really like to think our society has evolved to a point where not only does race not matter but anything there in between" (Lindsey Nicholson, Western Satellite).

ACCOUNTING FOR THESE DIFFERENCES

Though women at Eastern Elite and Western Public are familiar with similar discourses from the broader society's version of conservative femininity, we also see systematic differences in the campus-level issues they see as most pressing and how they pursue them. In general, Eastern Elite women appear to contend with greater levels of conflict around femininity than their peers at Western Public— they feel they face considerable deprecation for embracing conventional femininity and for rejecting liberal feminism. As undergraduates, they feel out of step with their peers' social lives and morals, as well as the university's relaxed take on *in loco parentis*. In terms of their careers, Eastern Elite women appear to feel that they face more pressure than their peers at Western Public to follow a particular path to success. These diverging experiences can be traced back to institutional differences and how these flavor the expectations generated for women on each campus.

EXPLAINING EASTERN ELITE: THE INFLUENCE OF RELIGIOUS IDENTIFICATIONS AND TOP-TIER EXPECTATIONS

There are many potential explanations for Eastern Elite University women's greater concern with reclaiming femininity on campus and rejecting feminism in their career ambitions—for example, the school's extremely self-contained (and thus far from anonymous) social scene—but we believe two aspects of the campus contribute the most to their issue commitments. One is the stronger religious identifications found among Eastern Elite interviewees than among Western Public respondents, and particularly among the Eastern Elite women in our sample. The second and perhaps less surprising answer is the enormous sway of the high pressure, high status environment of Eastern Elite. Gendered expectations appear to be yet another area where the status of being an Eastern Elite student trumps other potential influences.

Religion

In contrast to Western Public women, all the Eastern Elite women in our sample identified with a particular organized religious tradition.[28] This likely contributed to their perceptions of themselves as out of step with the rest of the campus; Eastern Elite conservatives, both men and women, perceive Eastern Elite to have a secular campus culture that looks down on religion. As one Catholic man explained, "[Campus liberals] certainly like to say religious conservatives are backward-looking from the medieval ages. That was a big case with Sarah Palin. They liked to talk about evangelicals and fly-over country and that sort of thing" (Calvin Coffey, Eastern Elite). Conservatives who make their faith a central part of their lives thus have to contend not only with political alienation but also potentially with social derision based on their spiritual beliefs. It leads some students to practice their faith quietly, as this Catholic woman said:

Like I attend church and I try to keep myself informed on religious issues, but I wouldn't try to convert somebody. . . . I would never lie to someone about where I'm going Sunday morning, but I'm also not going to announce that I am headed to church and you should come with me. It's just kind of living the values but not necessarily putting them on a billboard or announcing them. (Staci Congdon, Eastern Elite)

The sense conservative students have of their peers as being skeptical of religion is a major reason why, for example, the abstinence group put a nondenominational face on their activities, focusing on physiological and psychological rather than faith-based arguments about premarital abstinence. This also fits well as an explanation for why Eastern Elite women might be particularly vocal around issues such as abstinence and abortion: Participating in these groups provides a secular—and thus more legitimate, in the eyes of their peers—outlet for issues of both personal and religious importance to them. Further, these groups provide a space for networking with like-minded peers, as there are fewer religiously affiliated student organizations on the Eastern Elite campus than at, for example, Western Flagship.[29] Last, this may help explain Eastern Elite women's strong avoidance of "typical college" expectations, which contain elements of secularism and a rejection of organized religion that are directly antithetical to these interviewees' beliefs.[30]

Communal Pressures

Avoiding the expectations of "typical" collegiate behavior is also strongly related to Eastern Elite conservatives' conceptions of themselves as Eastern Elite University students. Eastern Elite undergraduates, both men and women, find themselves part of an exalted community, with which they identify to the nearly total exclusion of the broader status of being a typical American college student.[31] We believe this is a major reason why Eastern Elite women appear to work much harder than their Western Public peers to distance themselves from the "typical" expectations for the college woman.[32] Particularly notable in this regard is how outspoken and involved Eastern Elite conservative women are, creating and joining organizations devoted to women's issues and developing extensive critiques of the campus culture.

This intrigues in light of the larger trends in political style that we observed in our two cases. The dominant style at Eastern Elite of civilized discourse involves politeness, distance, and an interest in bipartisan discussion. And in some ways, the conservative women in our Eastern Elite sample do reflect this. However, many of the interviewees' absolute commitments to their views—particularly around issues such as abstinence and abortion—led them to be considerably more outspoken about their beliefs and to engage in more provocative actions to further their causes than the average Eastern Elite interviewee.[33] Though still less provocative than the average Western Public respondent, the strength of Eastern Elite women's convictions is notable, as here:

> I've always been a person, certainly up through the end of high school, who was the kind of person people knew to be a person of integrity and a person of responsibility. I think just the fact that I live my life in a way that I did what I was supposed to do, and not what I wasn't supposed to do, kind of built that up. And then on leaving home, my first year in college, [abortion] was not something I thought about much and then after that, I'm not really sure what really got me . . . maybe it was just being in an environment that was more politically liberal and [abortion] was a cause that I cared about the most. So that is what I got involved in. (Melissa Preston, Eastern)

Here the change is described as occurring during the undergraduate years. Though Melissa characterized herself as having always been a "person of integrity," it was feeling challenged on campus that led her to translate her beliefs into more than just acting as an example, to becoming a visible and vocal advocate.

Thus the campus environment at Eastern Elite, by promoting secular values and by being an elite community, creates opportunity spaces for conservative women to leverage conservative femininity in specific ways. In maintaining their religious commitments, these women have a vested interest in recapturing conventional femininity. At the same time, Eastern Elite women understand that the stakes are high—expectations of them both as Eastern Elite undergraduates and as Eastern Elite women push them toward high-status careers—and so they find resources in the discourse of rejecting feminism to craft different paths for their futures. Further, recognition of their own visibility (some of these undergraduates' organizations have received extensive coverage not just from campus or local but from national media) means that for some of these women, simply living their beliefs would not be enough. In battling the strong cultural currents on their campuses, Eastern Elite conservative women have a virtual mandate to be articulate, ardent advocates for their viewpoints.

UNPACKING WESTERN PUBLIC: THE INFLUENCE OF LIBERTARIANISM AND LIFE OUTSIDE THE SPOTLIGHT

As at Eastern Elite, we can consider plenty of possibilities for why conservative women in the Western Public university system are less worried about campus mores and see their future lives as no one's business but their own, such as the lesser interest in organized religion we mentioned above (as compared to the strong influence of Catholicism's moral order at Eastern Elite). But in thinking hard about all of the different factors that make up the Western Public campuses, we find two sticking out as stronger candidates than the others. First, libertarianism is alive and well on the Western Public campuses. This type of political identification, virtually absent at Eastern Elite, is prominent both on the Western Public campuses and in the region where the schools are located. Next, and strongly related, Western Public's less elite status and the Western Flagship campus's considerable similarities to the "typical" college campus encourage a more relaxed attitude toward both campus life and future careers.

Libertarian Politics

Looking at our women interviewees only, we find considerable differences in political identification between Eastern Elite and Western Public women. The sharpest divergence comes from the five Western Public interviewees who described themselves as libertarian or "libertarian leaning."[34] Though there are not student-run libertarian groups on any of the Western Public campuses, several interviewees, including four of the women, worked for local or state libertarian organizations. Libertarianism's emphases on personal freedom and government nonintervention make it difficult for these interviewees to take a firm stance against abortion or premarital sex—the type of social issues that strongly concerned Eastern Elite women—as this exchange demonstrates:

> **R:** Abortion is a different issue for me because I consider life to be at conception and so I don't think there's any way that can give a person the right to murder another person. And to me that's what abortion is.
> **I:** Could you ever vote for a pro-choice candidate?
> **R:** For a pro-choice candidate? You know a lot of libertarians are probably pro-choice. I think that they're kind of on the cusp on that issue. And yes, because again I don't think that the government should have any say really in that whatsoever. I would prefer honestly for it to just be states that vote, each state gets to vote on it. But that's really my own personal belief and that's the way I think about it. (Brittany Urban, Western Satellite)

On this and other issues, we often found Western Public women (and libertarian men, as well) wrestling to reconcile their personal beliefs (for example, believing abortion is giving a person the right to murder another, as in the quotation above) with their ideological commitments (as a libertarian, staying consistent with the belief that the government should not be involved with regulating personal decisions, and so being willing to vote for a pro-choice candidate).

These commitments may have been another reason so-called "women's issues" were of less concern among Western Public women. Given their political positions, it would seem hypocritical for them to appear to be arguing for any sort of special rights or privileges for women, or even simply to identify strongly with women as a particular group. As one interviewee explained:

> I don't necessarily agree that, you know, just because you're gay like you needed to be treated any differently or you need to be protected. Or just because you're black that you should be handled with special gloves. I don't want someone to look at me and be like, "Oh, you're a woman, and what is *that* like?" I don't look at someone who's gay and say, "Is that hard? Is that weird?" (Stephanie Cohen, Western Flagship)

This type of political identification thus discourages affiliation with identity politics, not only in the sense we would commonly think of them (for example, attempting to claim specific rights as women, such as the right to choose to terminate a pregnancy), but also in avoidance of redefining identity (as in Eastern Elite women's strong interest in standing up for traditional femininity and creating a different type of collegiate womanhood).

Typical College Student Identification.

The laissez-faire attitude encouraged by libertarianism likewise fits in well with national-level ideas of the "typical" college experience, which resonates strongly on the Western Public campuses. Western Flagship in particular echoes many of the attributes believed to be part of the typical college experience—a large, attractive campus; an extensive Greek presence and party scene; Division I sports; relatively less emphasis placed on academic achievement—and the fact that most Western Flagship students actively partake of this.[35] While many Eastern Elite students participate in this kind of activity as well (if they did not, the Eastern Elite abstinence group would arguably have little reason to exist), the physical characteristics of the Western Public campuses and their less elite status mitigate the consequences of opting out of these social mores. Given the campus's small student body and relative containment, Eastern Elite students' social lives are highly visible and far from anonymous. Choosing not to embrace campus social life holds higher stakes for Eastern Elite women, and so they need to be more vocal in their explanations for themselves and their advocacy for others.

In contrast, students on the Western Public campuses are relatively spread out and do not share a unified social milieu. Students who choose not to engage in the frat party scene at Western Flagship or hit the strip of bars near the Western Satellite campus are not faced with fear of any particular sort of social censure. While the trappings of the typical college experience are right at hand, the libertarian "live and let live" ethos prevalent in the region means that, at least in this part of campus life, difference might be encouraged rather than discouraged (we recall that in political areas, Western Public conservative students allege there is stifling conformity). As a result, women at Western Public are allowed a wider range of acceptable social options and can make whatever lifestyle choices they like without causing a wrinkle in the social fabric of their peer groups. In fact, only select members of their peer group would even know about their choices.

Campus norms where "anything goes"—whether justified by libertarian political ideology or by a reliance on the "typical" collegiate repertoire—help explain why campus social life is of less concern among Western Public women, and why conservative femininity seems to be of less utility in this area of their lives. While we did have one interviewee who was closer to her Eastern Elite peers in this regard, most conservative Western Public women we inter-viewed adopted a relatively easygoing attitude toward sex and so-cial life in general. For example, the interviewee who earlier had described herself as moving toward a more "live and let live" out-look during college further explained, "A lot of political things like abortion and gay marriage and the big topic things. Those are, I'm pretty set in. But again, I feel like it's okay if you *don't* think the same way I do. I haven't really changed my mind in them, but I just kind of become more 'That's okay'" (Samantha Hart, Western Flag-ship). Samantha's views stand in contrast to the earlier quotation from the young woman at Eastern Elite who felt her undergraduate experiences had made her *more* visibly active around her value commitments. Instead, Western Public women described coming to hold attitudes that can be characterized as "not for me, but okay for others."[36]

The Western Public campuses, then, construct different types of opportunity spaces for conservative women, making certain ele-ments of conservative womanhood more appealing than others. Given their campus's resemblances to the "typical" college and their commitments to not intervening in others' lives, Western Public women are much less constrained in how they construct their gen-dered selves in college. They likewise find their use of ideas about conservative femininity in their larger lives unproblematic, describ-ing themselves as facing no outside pressure around work and fam-ily choices as Eastern Elite women did. Though Western Public women do take up the conservative critique of feminism, it is in a much more abstract sense; comparing themselves to feminists gen-erally rather than citing others in their lives as sending these mes-sages. With less of a sense of themselves as influential and likely to wind up as widely recognized opinion leaders, and often with strong commitments to libertarian ideals, Western Public women do not feel the need to extensively justify their choices, though they cer-tainly (and articulately) could. Living outside the spotlight, they can just be college students, or career women, or mothers. The strongest expectations they have to live up to are their own.

CONSERVATISM AS A GENDER STRATEGY

Cultural sociologists have long been interested in how women manage the "competing devotions" of work and family life, or the "double binds" of class and gender expectations.[37] As practitioners of the
national-level set of ideas we're calling conservative femininity, the
undergraduate and alumnae women we interviewed attempted to
use these cultural resources to develop creative solutions to conflicting expectations in their lives. Being conservative helped our interviewees find strength, particularly when they perceived themselves
as out of step with the cultural mores present on their campuses.
Conservatism allowed them to resolve these conflicting expectations not only for themselves; it also may have provided some degree of legitimation from their peers. While some of their views
might not "make sense" in light of expectations for what *women*
will think on an issue, they are interpretable as what *conservative
women* would believe. This does not always mean that their views
were accepted on their campuses, particularly when they conflicted
with expectations of the "typical" college student. It does, however,
mean their beliefs are viable in light of others' expectations about
conservatives.

The conservative women in our sample were thus able to use
their political beliefs to manage conflicting expectations during
their undergraduate years, and surrounding their plans for the future. Whether this will continue to serve them in the same way in
the future, if they will be able to "have it all," remains to be seen.
But it did seem they were likely to remain committed to conservatism, as this Eastern Elite interviewee described:

> I think I will always be an advocate and I'll always be one of the
> few who are very confident in presenting this information and
> for not hiding my beliefs and for saying, well, "This is who I am
> and these are my opinions and if you don't respect me for it, then
> like I don't feel a great need to have you in my circle." I have seen
> so many girls hurt and I just like think there's so much I could

say to them that for me to remain silent is just like kind of evil. So I see myself always being a proponent, if not in a professional or career-type setting, then always at a personal level. (Shannon Yaffe, Eastern Elite)

Likewise, the ways that they made use of discourses from the national level demonstrates that these women are plugged into a larger, vibrant dialogue about conservative womanhood. The floodgates having been opened, women are likely to continue to expand their presence in local and national politics.

At the same time, the campus-level innovations these women are constructing are not just helping them navigate campus life—they are also beginning to be incorporated by national-level organizations. In particular, some of the strategies we witnessed our Eastern Elite interviewees using during their college years in the early and mid-2000s are now being formalized by national conservative organizations focusing on college-age women. Conservative organizations aimed at women, such as the Independent Women's Forum and the Clare Boothe Luce Policy Institute, provide support for young conservative women's discontent with campus life, with such initiatives as the IWF's "Take Back the Date" and CBLPI's "Sense & Sexuality."[38] Others, like the Network of Enlightened Women and the Love & Fidelity Network—both of which originated on college campuses through the work of conservative undergraduate women—now provide ready-made plans to help conservative women set up organizations on their own campuses and learn the key talking points on their core issues.[39]

Examining the local variation on campuses provides an example, then, not only of how practices are built up at the local level of the individual campus but also for considering how leaders in outside organizations might appropriate these strategies for use at the national level. Local solutions are starting to be pulled up to a broader level, where they can then in turn be used by other women on other campuses. Further, where we can draw comparisons to the views of male interviewees, we can see differences in how individuals' experiences of gender lead them to adopt different strategies for making sense of themselves and their social worlds. This explains some of the within-campus variation we witnessed among conservatives at both of our case study schools.

Even while we find here that individuals' characteristics and experiences do matter for how they develop political identities and styles, we still see a strong impact of the campus. Though Eastern Elite and Western Public women draw on many of the same elements of conservative femininity and deploy these discourses in similar ways as *women*, we also see that they exhibit substantial differences, in many ways acting as *Eastern Elite* women or as *Western Public* women. These translate into both different political issue commitments, with Eastern Elite women more highly focused on social issues like campus mores and abortion and Western Public women bringing these in mainly as examples of widespread liberal hypocrisy, and divergent political styles. And so while we do discover systematic differences between our women and men interviewees in the area of gender issues, we continue to find evidence of the role of college campuses in forging individuals' political identities.

Chapter 8

The Theory behind the Findings

*How Studying College Conservatives Extends Our Understanding
of Higher Education, Politics, and Culture*

Over the past half century—through the eras of Barry Goldwater,
Ronald Reagan, George W. Bush, and today the Tea Party—conservatism
has dramatically reconfigured American politics. In the
words of the political scientist Stephen Skowronek, since the 1960s
"a conservative insurgency has pushed its way to power, transformed
national discourse, realigned political conflict, and brought
new priorities to the fore."[1] Given the enormous consequences of
this shift, historians, social scientists, and journalists alike have
scrambled to account for the roots of this change.[2] Some scholars
have focused on the movement's standout elected political figures,
demonstrating how conservatism may be a multifaceted and evolving
entity but is also imprinted with the DNA of its most visible
leaders.[3] Other authors have focused on the intellectuals of the
movement who during the late twentieth century managed to combine,
through a process called fusionism, the long-standing conservative
threads of anticommunism, pro-libertarianism, small-statism,
and moral traditionalism, in part by hitching the movement to a politically
reinvigorated evangelicalism and creating a new conserva-

309

tive base.[4] In a related vein, a handful of scholars have traced the emergent organizational sector that has engineered these major realignments, focusing in particular on the conservative think tanks, foundations, advocacy organizations, and media that have shaped the political field.[5] Still others have analyzed the demographic and regional shifts that created new opportunities for conservative Republican victories, such as the huge population growth that began in the western Sun Belt in the 1950s, which gave rise to "suburban warriors" who waged "tax revolts" and who are now the most vocal proponents of enhanced border security.[6] The list goes on, with researchers studying a variety of populations under the conservative umbrella—sometimes fringe, sometimes not—including creationists, African American Republicans, antipornographers, and right-wing women.[7]

While this research base is far-ranging and hugely informative, there are two things that have generally been left out of its purview. First, in most of the work that has been written about conservatives, there is a clear focus on *ideology*—how the conservative movement has grown through the marriage of social conservatives with free marketers, for instance, or how disagreements about foreign policy separate the hawks from the realists—to the general exclusion of a focus on conservative *styles*. As we argue throughout our book, however, while the students on the two campuses we studied are not as different from one another on their core issues or ideological positions, their stylistic inclinations are worlds apart. Style matters, and researchers to date have not adequately addressed this point. Second, while researchers and journalists have examined all manner of organizations that have emerged to advance the conservative cause, they have been mostly inattentive to two types of organizations that develop *the next generation of conservative leaders*: first, the more focused organizations like the Young America's Foundation and the Intercollegiate Studies Institute, which explicitly target right-leaning students; and second, and more important, the heterogeneous (and ostensibly apolitical) educational organizations—colleges and universities—that prepare students for their future social roles. On two fronts, then, our book examines what other scholars have overlooked: the fascinating stylistic differences that distinguish conservative politicians and pundits in the political culture at large, and how the roots of these styles can be found in large part in college settings. While we cannot make a causal claim that today's conservative battles in Congress and other political venues are the direct outcome of young conservatives' experiences as students (we would need a different kind of study to do that), we are at least analyzing the ties between these extremely important settings—conservative student clubs, and college and university campuses, on the one hand, and national organizations on the other—where these styles develop.

Because we find universities to be slighted in the literature, but also so central to the formation of expressive political styles, in this concluding chapter we broaden the focus from our case materials to lay out a conceptual framework explaining how we think this educational process of "becoming right" works more generally. Rising above the data and thinking more abstractly about how education shapes conservatism is good not only for better understanding disparate right-leaning styles in the larger conservative world but also for shedding light on how liberal students or moderate students or even radical students might learn to act "appropriately" like liberals or moderates or radicals as they go through college.[8] We also contend that the model of college culture and structure that we describe here is general enough to be useful to scholars studying other aspects of students' lives besides politics, whether those students are found to be developing identities and expressive styles that are religious, academic, party-oriented, civically engaged, artsy, or careerist. The learning of group styles by means of shared culture and organizational features on campus is far from limited to the production of conservative selves. As we lay out our analytical framework for understanding the empirical findings in our cases, readers might well consider how this model can be used to understand a large variety of group and individual identities that develop in college, and what universities' distinctive influences on those identities may be.

UNDERSTANDING HIGHER EDUCATION'S ROLE IN DEVELOPING POLITICAL SELVES

THE COLLEGE EFFECTS LITERATURE: ITS SCOPE AND ITS LIMITATIONS FOR UNDERSTANDING POLITICAL STYLES

Sociologists have long been interested in higher education's role in influencing students' attitudes, values, and behaviors (political and otherwise), and the bulk of scholarship on this question—known as research on college effects or, when about politics in particular, research on political socialization—uses a social psychological framework that makes the individual student the unit of analysis.[9] Using either national-level datasets like the HERI data we used in chapter 2 or campus-level survey data collected at individual colleges and universities, college effects researchers measure college's net impact on a range of student political ideas and behaviors, from their level of political participation (for example, whether students vote or discuss politics) to students' self-reported political ideologies (which they are asked to identify on a continuum from left to right), to whether education has made them more liberal on issues of race, gender, and sexuality (this is known as the "liberalization thesis").[10] In their meta-analysis of three decades of research on these questions, two of the scholars most centrally associated with this approach, Ernest Pascarella and Patrick Terenzini, argue that the existing body of research unquestionably demonstrates that higher education positively influences political engagement and participation levels, and that college-educated members of society have greater knowledge of, and more active commitments to, the political process. Students at both Western and Eastern, this research would predict, should be more inclined than other people their age who do not attend college to be more opinionated about politics and to become involved in political activities, regardless of whether they are liberal, moderate, or conservative.

Recent scholarship, however, has questioned whether attending and graduating from college actually does have significant effects on political awareness, once one controls for precollege experiences. Some scholars have argued, for instance, that differences in political sophistication and in students' decisions to be involved in politics "are already in place before anyone sets foot in a college classroom."[11] In fact, this newer body of research contends that the most important factors contributing to college-age political activity are all the things that students bring with them to college in the first place, including their inherent cognitive abilities, their interest in politics during high school, and their parents' political ideas and social position. Whether students attend a Western Public campus or Eastern Elite University, or for that matter any college at all, according to this research, is mostly irrelevant to their adult political ideas and interests since their predispositions have already been set in earlier life experiences. Taken together, these findings have caused some in the higher education field to doubt the significant, discrete influence of college on students' political ideas and activities.

How does this newer research square with our findings that campuses are places where conservative political discourses and styles are developed, shared, modified, and sustained over time—so much so that enrolling at Western Public or Eastern Elite will not only increase conservative students' political participation overall but will also largely shape how they choose to *act like* conservatives? Some might interpret these researchers' findings as casting doubt on our argument, since the bulk of the action in their explanations resides in family homes or in students' individual minds. Not surprisingly, based on the evidence we have presented in the past seven chapters, we do not subscribe to this conclusion. While we indeed did find that our interviewees' individual attributes and precollege experiences were important inputs to their college-age politics (as described in chapter 2, especially), it is a mistake to conclude that universities do not significantly shape college students' political development. One can think of the performance of political styles, such as we found, as a qualitative dimension of political experience that the college effects literature simply has not considered and which, quite frankly, it was never built to describe. This largely quantitative, social psychological approach cannot depict the types of interactions that students have on their distinctive campuses, or how students make sense of those experiences and decide to use one conservative style over another. While this literature *can* measure something about individuals' ideological positions on a left-to-right spectrum, as well as their levels of civic engagement, it has ignored the more expressive, symbolic components of constructing a political self in interaction with others—such as the way students talk about professors' politics or decide between playing "gotcha" with liberals versus having polite discussions with them. In short, quantitative studies such as these cannot provide a thick description of students' political styles while they are in college or in the years beyond.

MAKING HIGHER EDUCATION STUDIES MORE SOCIOLOGICAL: CULTURE, POLITICS, AND ORGANIZATIONS

Taking a different tack than these large-N studies, scholars in a more organizationally minded branch of higher education research have worked to direct attention away from the individual student as the unit of analysis and toward the campus environment and its subenvironments as the key objects of study. This scholarship has been enormously useful to us as we have examined how students at Eastern Elite and Western Public "become right." Viewing university students as operating in a series of interrelated formal organizational arrangements and informal small groups, researchers such as Burton Clark, Martin Trow, and Kenneth Feldman have long provided a more institutional account of the influence of college on student identities. These scholars study campuses as "arena[s] of social interaction in which the individual comes into contact with a multitude of actors in a variety of settings, emphasizing that through these social interactions and other social influences the identities of individuals are, in part, constituted."[12] Mainly using single case studies, this research shows how college settings affect students' understandings of themselves and their worlds, and how these understandings are colored by specific organizational experiences. The upshot of this institutional branch of higher education studies is that students—as they interact with one another in a variety of college-level organizational structures—learn how to be active, creative, and even appropriately behaving members of their college or university community. A key take-away message from this body of work is that researchers should be paying attention to university and college education at the *campus organizational* level of analysis, not privileging individual student-level impacts as the college effects literature does. The campus level of analysis is complex, constituted by multiple groups and interactional settings. It is in the confluence of these local settings that meanings are shaped.[13] Clearly, this research stream tells us things the college effects literature cannot.

But this is not to say that we should let the institutional branch of the higher education literature rest on its laurels. Indeed, this area of research, too, can benefit from reinvigoration—specifically through a closer examination of how group *politics* are socially constructed, and by comparing groups of students on different campuses to one another. Although rarely written with higher education in mind, research analyzing cultural repertoires and groups' political styles is an excellent first step.[14] In an article titled "Culture in Interaction," for example, Nina Eliasoph and Paul Lichterman study the "recurrent patterns of interaction" that arise from a group's shared assumptions about politics, civility, and other American cultural ideals—assumptions that help group members figure out how they should participate appropriately in their clubs and associational groups.[15] Members of one group may use a style aimed at "avoiding politics" as a way to remain sociable with one another, while members of other groups risk personal injury by adopting grassroots styles that include strikes and demonstrations, or get under the skins of their elders in the Establishment by staging absurdist political theater.[16] The point that Eliasoph and Lichterman demonstrate so well is that action is not made from scratch for every new event by free-wheeling individuals unmoored from common beliefs about their world. Rather, political action is the result of shared understandings about the larger world held by people in interaction who know each other well, and who talk about the ideas and practices that are most appropriate for their group setting. These shared understandings and practices concerning what politics should look like are durable over time and constitute the elements that make up the cultural know-how of a group's members. Applying these insights to our case of conservative students, we see that for an Affirmative Action Bake Sale to occur on a college campus, not only must a political distaste for the policy of affirmative action be shared by students, but these students must also assume that a no-holds-barred practice of provoking liberals is appropriate for expressing political opinions on campus. While both of these conditions were met at Western Flagship, only the first (distaste for the policy, but not the style of provocation) obtained at Eastern Elite. Comparing these different campuses, we can see how culture in interaction produces different kinds of conservative styles.

HOW AND WHY CULTURE VARIES

Another set of issues regarding culture, organizations, and politics concerns how strong and lasting these cultural understandings are on a given campus, how thoroughly they filter in (and filter out) political ideas from the larger world of right-leaning politics and thought, and how decisively they shape students' ideas and actions both individually and in groups. Basically, what we are talking about here from a theory standpoint is the question of the *determinative* power of campus culture on politics. For example, if a Western Flagship conservative student transferred to Eastern Elite, could he convince his new classmates to set aside their styles of civilized discourse and highbrow provocation and stage an Affirmative Action Bake Sale?

When stated in its strongest form, sociologists take local culture to be very powerful, and long-standing cultural practices and meanings are thought to largely determine action.[17] As Neil Gross discusses in relation to Charles Tilly's work, for example, the cultural repertoires available to political actors consist of "scripts for political performance that become institutionalized, sedimented in actors' expectations, and in the structure of institutions and inter-group relations."[18] If these scripts are not exactly seen to be written in stone, then at least they are etched in repeated practice, leading to their institutionalization in something like a canon of action. To put this another way, groups of people in local settings have shared understandings of the rules of the game, and, as Tilly points out, such rules get transposed into other settings and used in subsequent activities.[19]

While we find the general gist of these formulations appealing—culture matters and has enormous power—our study indicates that culture's force is derived somewhat more through a broader variety of interactions than such a conceptualization portrays and is itself variable in its power. First, there is clear evidence that the strength of culture—its power to direct consistent discourses and action—varies from campus to campus, depending on a large number of factors. At some higher education institutions like Eastern Elite University, where there is a centuries-old set of traditions and a highly articulated organizational saga about what it means to be a member of this august community—not to mention organizational features such as four-year dorms that keep students in close proximity to one another—the force of coherent culture on campus is strong, in part because it is more consistent and uniform. The demands for what constitutes appropriate behavior from an Eastern Elite student *can* rule out a good deal of action that might be defined as illegitimate if it does not align with long-standing local cultural ideas and practice. As we recall, conservative students at Eastern Elite were adamant during their interviews that the provocative style is *not* a viable option for use on their campus, and that if they had used it once (as some did to oppose abortion), they wouldn't again. However much fun the *Searchlight* writers have when they point out the follies of political correctness on campus, they still insist they are *not* borrowing from the playbook of the Young America's Foundation. So if that Western Flagship transfer student tried to talk his new classmates into being provocative in a populist way and put on a Bake Sale, our best guess is that he would not be successful.

At Western Flagship, on the other hand, where there is a larger student population but a much smaller percentage of undergraduates living on campus, less of a developed concern about a common identity, and fewer levers of opprobrium when people step outside the norm, the power of culture to shape action may not be quite so strong. As noted in chapter 5, the Western Flagship College Republicans did, after all, elect Hunter Devine president of their club—a student who contested the provocative style in its purest form and opted more for the campaigning style. If an Eastern Elite student transferred to Western Flagship, we suspect, there's a pretty decent chance that he or she could find a few conservative classmates who would be willing to engage in civilized discourse. There is, of course, a certain irony to these observations about the varying constraining effects of culture on these campuses: At Eastern Elite, where opportunities for self-realization are celebrated, a stronger cultural repertoire may actually *decrease* students' opportunities to innovate politically, whereas in the Western Public system, the possibilities for less endorsed action may be more open. As we can see from these two comparative cases, it is important to think about the strength of university culture to shape political identities and expression not so much as a *general* question but as a *specific* one, tied to institutional features like student body size, dorm life, and the reputation of the campus. Culture is variable in its strength to filter in and out particular actions.

HOW STRONG *IS* CULTURE?

There is another reason we should be careful not to overstate the determinative effects of cultural systems in university settings. While we know that shared local campus culture strongly shapes Eastern Elite and Western Public conservative students' assumptions about appropriate conservative styles, as we look at young conservatives in university settings, we find that much of what students know and do, and *think* they know, is in flux and far from perfectly consistent.[20] This is a point in the lifecourse, after all, when culture is quite unsettled and people are in high personal development mode, which means that students actively discuss and chew over different meanings and models of action, finding them to be lacking at times, brilliantly fitting at others, somewhere in between, or perhaps even ambiguous and confusing.[21] In chapter 2 we noted that the students we studied did a significant amount of fine-tuning of their ideological identifications during college—students who were simply "conservative" in high school became "crunchy conservatives," for example, or "Catholic conservatives" or "fiscal conservatives." Whatever assumptions conservative students may have at any given point during their precollege and college years, those assumptions are likely to undergo at least some revision as they participate with one another in a variety of types of campus organizations, or as they surf the Internet or talk to friends at other universities about their college experiences.

We also should not forget that while much of the campus stays the same from year to year—its built environment, the professoriate, and so on—the composition of student clubs has enormous turnover. New students join, other students quit, and some leaders attempt to take their groups in different directions in an effort to distinguish themselves on campus or burnish their résumés as innovators. It is important to look at how the parts of campuses that largely stay the same—classroom settings, the university's reputation—intersect with the parts of campus life that undergo yearly or even semiyearly changes, such as individual leadership and membership in conservative clubs. While overall we would argue that the dominant cultural repertoires of conservatism on these campuses prevail, it is not because students accept them routinely or without reflection; instead, they interact with a shifting cast of characters, some of them highly charismatic in their appeals for change, some of them happy to sustain styles just as in years past. As Sharon Hays and other cultural sociologists have pointed out, just because elements of cultural systems tend to remain largely intact over time does not mean that little or no agency or creative action has taken place among the individuals and groups that use them.[22] All of this is to say that while we see the clear influence of campus-level cul-

tural repertoires on college students' conservative ideas and practices, we must keep our eyes trained as well on the ways that individuals and groups play with those meanings, and to note how
styles end up changing at least to some extent.[23]

THE CONTINUOUS NEGOTIATION OF CULTURE

Last, we think an argument about the effects of local institutional
culture—in isolation from other sources of meaning—risks under-
appreciating the dynamism that exists when people draw from in-
terconnecting repertoires. In our case, this means attending to not
just the two neighboring repertoires at the campus level (campuswide settings and those that are more specific to conservative students and their organizations), but also with the larger world of
conservative politics. We have argued as much using our data, but
the point bears theoretical restatement: to understand the kind of
creative practice we see conservative college students engaged in,
we must employ a rich understanding of the interplay that occurs
when people make use of *multiple cultural repertoires*, both local
and distal. As Roger Friedland and Robert Alford persuasively
pointed out more than twenty years ago, and many scholars from a
variety of subfields have underscored since then, society is an interinstitutional system made up of different social sectors, or fields,
where each field features a unique set of assumptions—sometimes
explicit, sometimes tacit—for what is suitable thought and action.[24]
If we think of fields as analogous to the many different organizational and cultural forms that students are exposed to during college, we realize that conservative undergraduates are embedded in a
variety of fields, from the two campus-level systems just discussed
to the numerous discourses and practices found at the broader level,
which include the mainstream media, the Internet, regional and national politics, and the world of student conferences, seminars, and
fellowships sponsored by conservative organizations. The cultural
material found in these different arenas is not all the same, and sort-

ing through it requires the active and creative sense-making of people in interaction with one another.

Following work being done by Tim Hallett and Marc Ventresca and a few others in a body of research called inhabited institutions, we see broader cultural repertoires and people in local settings as "doubly embedded," such that people's "interactions take place within, and are shaped by, broader institutional contexts," but the practical meaning of their actions emerges locally through social interaction.[25] Conservative style is a form of action that both filters from the top down and emerges from the bottom up, getting worked out in the middle. Keeping track of all these levels of meaning—from the most personal and privately held to the most widely shared and disseminated—allows us to comprehend how and why students use different dominant and submerged conservative styles on different campuses. This provides a rich understanding of how individuals and groups "locate themselves in social relations and interpret their context."[26] To sum up, conservative culture on campus is the ongoing and negotiated result of students' constant interactions with local and national political repertoires.

SOCIAL AND CULTURAL CAPITAL IN TWO RELATIONAL FIELDS, HIGHER EDUCATION AND POLITICS

Having now theoretically laid out how college students live in a web of coexisting cultural repertoires in society at large and on their particular campuses, we take up a final question: What are the factors at play in the larger field of higher education that give rise to the particular dominant conservative styles of civilized discourse at Eastern Elite, provocation in the Western Public university system, and the submerged styles that we see on these different campuses? In this section we work out more formally the significance of what we have stated in the previous chapters about universities' reputations for being particular kinds of places, which are derived from those institutions' positions in the larger field of higher education.

As we showed empirically in chapters 4 through 7, students' shared understandings about their specific university shape their assumptions about the kinds of people they are supposed to be while in college, the ways they should express themselves while there, and the lives they should expect to lead once they graduate. In theoretical terms, different universities foster unique symbolic boundaries marking off who is included as "someone like us"—a phenomenon the sociologist John Meyer refers to as chartering identities.[27] These boundaries result from students' own sometimes conscious, sometimes unconscious alignment of preferences and sensibilities to likely outcomes in their life trajectories.

How does this work generally, and for conservative styles in particular? As Pierre Bourdieu and others have written, academia is a relational field in which institutions of higher education occupy dominant and subordinate positions, depending on the specific resources in their possession compared to other universities and colleges.[28] These resources take many forms but include most prominently (though in no particular order) the historical legacy and traditions of the university; the research profiles and national reputations of faculty members; the size of the university's endowment; the visible connections that the institution sustains in the worlds of policymaking, business, and elite culture; and the admissions criteria, future promise, and actual social outcomes of its undergraduate and graduate student populations. Inhabitants of colleges and universities (students, faculty, administrators, staff) keep close tabs on their campus's position in this relational field, as do those outside those boundaries.[29] So, for example, elite private universities exist atop the educational hierarchy in the United States, while state-funded universities, small liberal arts colleges, religious colleges and universities, and a variety of other institutional forms exist at various levels below.[30]

As bearers of distinctive kinds of symbolic capital, universities are expected to cultivate not only students' human capital (that is, their talents and skills) but also (if less transparently) society's status cultures through the distinctive development of students' social networks and cultural dispositions as, for example, Paul DiMaggio and

John Mohr have shown for university-influenced marriage markets.[31] Students and graduates who possess valued cultural and social capital can more seamlessly participate in exclusive social networks with others who share similar tastes. The cultural capital
imbued in the political style of civilized discourse, for example, is
better suited to some networks, while provocation fits more comfortably with others. Not to put too fine a point on it, but cultural
capital in the service of civilized discourse is much likelier to be developed at an institution like Eastern Elite University than at one
like Western Flagship, for the reasons Bourdieu and others lay out.

Most of the literature on higher education's role in producing
class cultures has focused on elite universities and their role in reproducing privilege and distinction—that is, showing how elite institutions serve to ratify social and cultural capital among those already habituated to social advantage.[32] But higher education studies
of capital acquisition and reproduction have generally overlooked a
couple of other facets of capital production. First, there are fewer
studies than one might expect of *nonprivileged students* who,
through the intervention of elite education, come to have elite tastes
and dispositions. Second, there are few studies of *less elite postsecondary settings*, such as large state schools, that address the issue of
regional elite formation. Third, most of the studies that look at students' cultural capital acquisition in higher education have not shed
light on the forms of *political capital* that are created in universities.
In fact, several recent qualitative studies of college-age students
argue that students more or less turn their backs on political commitments—or most any other deep commitments except, perhaps,
for a vague notion of community service—during their years having
fun in school.[33]

What our study adds to current scholarship on cultural capital
production is attention to these three gaps, specifically by asking
how two university systems—uniquely offering a variety of local
contexts where student interactions take place, differently located in
the college and university hierarchical field, and cultivating in their
heterogeneous students different forms of social, cultural, and political capital—serve as the settings where students develop distinctive

styles of conservatism. Eastern Elite provides models for conservative students to adopt civilized discourse: 18-year-olds arrive on campus, see what kinds of people they would like to become, and then work on themselves to become it.[34] Using the university's legacy as a guide, Eastern Elite students become versed in a more refined style of conservatism. The Western Public system, meanwhile, presents enticing opportunities to students—at least those who have the fortitude to pull it off—to enter a more rough-and-tumble world of conservative politics, to imagine themselves as local pundits or politicians in their future careers, and to think of liberals as adversaries, not future colleagues—in short, to engage in a provocative style.

Which of these styles is more valuable in today's conservative world? As we write this just after the "anybody-but-Romney" 2012 Republican Party primaries, Tea Party politics have put the style of provocative action practiced by groups like the Western Flagship College Republicans in much higher demand—at least for the conservative base—than the more refined styles of their peers at Eastern Elite. Jon Huntsman, the candidate who most clearly embodied the civilized discourse style—serving as Obama's ambassador to China, advocating bipartisan teamwork to solve the nation's problems—hardly made a dent in the presidential race.[35] The Party's eventual nominee Mitt Romney—fundamentally a "campaigning" candidate in disposition—has tried throughout the primary season to perform the provocative style, fumbling nearly every step of the way, and making his ascent to the nomination all the more fraught.[36] Throughout it all, the provocative style has carried the day, with vituperative super-PAC campaign ads adding fuel to the fire, leading candidate after candidate to decide they have "no choice" but to go negative.[37]

In many ways, these stylistic differences have risen to the forefront of campaign strategy: political style, rather than ideological position or even one's own record, has become perhaps the most important way that candidates, pundits, activists, and others position themselves in political discourse. Courting Tea Party voters, for example, appears to be more about embracing the provocative style than advocating specific policy stances.[38] Because these stylistic divisions are so relevant, it's important to look carefully at where they come from, what allows them to flourish or fail in different settings, who embraces them and who shies away—and *why*. Political style is not simply a given; styles emerge and are shaped by people, even as they shape the world around us. To understand where we may be headed, we must situate these political styles in the context of their development. We hope this book on universities' influence has been a solid step toward greater understanding.

Notes

Preface

1. William F. Buckley in his *God and Man at Yale* (1951) was the first conservative critic to have gotten a lot of traction for this critique. For examples of more recent articulations, see Black (2004), Horowitz (2006), Bennett (1984), Bloom (1988), and D'Souza (1992).

2. In January 2012, a group of conservative students at San Diego State University published a list of professors whom they considered to be real teachers versus those they criticized for being indoctrinating preachers. See Reno (2012).

3. Recent careful studies by Neil Gross and Solon Simmons (2012) have demonstrated that professors are far likelier to be Democrats than Republicans, but these authors do not make the leap to saying that campuses are therefore hostile political environments.

4. See two Students for Academic Freedom web pages for these quotations: for the first, http://www.studentsforacademicfreedom.org/documents/1925/abor.html; for the second, http://www.studentsforacademicfreedom.org/news/2037/letter-secondyearachievementreport060605.htm (accessed January 11, 2012).

5. The main organizer of the Conservative Political Action Committee is the American Conservative Union; the main organizer of the National Conservative Student Conference is the Young America's Foundation.

6. "Take back your campus" is a battle cry of the Leadership Institute, which has several initiatives on behalf of students. See http://www.campusreform.org/ (accessed November 10, 2010). The Clare Boothe Luce Policy Institute sent out an email to members titled "MEDIA ALERT: Luce Student Activists on Glenn Beck, 5/13 at 5pm" on May 12, 2011.

7. Information for the Institute for Humane Studies Charles G. Koch Summer Fellows program can be found at http://www.theihs.org/koch-summer -fellow-program (accessed April 7, 2011).

8. See McAdam (1988) and Rojas (2007). For the few exceptions of scholars studying conservative students and the historical antecedents of today's conservative student politics, see Klatch (1999) and Andrew (1997).

9. For two examples, see Colapinto (2003) and Tower (2006).

10. We mention many websites in this book, but one that is especially prominent is the Young America's Foundation website, www.yaf.org.

11. For work on faculty's politics, see Gross and Simmons (2007). Elaine Ecklund (2007) addresses faculty religious beliefs in "Religion and Spirituality among University Scientists." For work on conservative students, see Woessner and Woessner (2006, 2007); Fosse, Freese, and Gross (2011); and Fosse and Gross (2012). Others, including Tom Medvetz, have written trenchantly on conservative think tanks. See Medvetz (2012).

Chapter 1: Introduction

1. The names of campuses, campus organizations, and individual students and alumni/ae are pseudonyms. Some identifying details have been altered to protect their anonymity. For a full discussion of our methods and data and why we are masking the identities of these two universities, see the discussion later in this chapter.

2. For the 2003 Berkeley event, see Fox News (2003). For the 2011 event, see CNN.com (2011).

3. For more on submerged styles, see Eliasoph and Lichterman (2003).

4. Sam Tanenhaus writes about the increasingly confrontational factions in the GOP in *The Death of Conservatism* (2009).

5. There are many other examples from more recent years, but both of these examples had occurred by the time of our data collection.

6. For examples of conservative writing on the "liberal campus," see Horowitz (2007); Kors and Silverglate (1998); and Maranto, Redding, and Hess (2009).

7. The Pelosi-Moore-Clinton-Chomsky poster was distributed by the Young America's Foundation to email subscribers in 2008. Other organizations sponsoring this conservative style include the Leadership Institute, David Horowitz's Students for Academic Freedom, and the Heritage Foundation. We discuss the Young America's Foundation and the Leadership Institute, as well as one other national conservative organization, the Intercollegiate Studies Institute, in chapter 3.

8. There are many fine scholarly works on conservative politics and its vari-

eties. For two recent examples, see Farber (2010) and Gross, Medvetz, and Russell (2011).

9. On the high rates of racial and ethnic homogeneity of Republican voters, see the September 2010 Gallup poll report, "Republicans Remain Disproportionately White and Religious" (Newport 2010).

10. Brooks (1996, vv). For the Pew report, see Pew Research Center (2011).

11. See Tanenhaus (2009, 43). For information on William F. Buckley's agitator style, see his *God and Man at Yale* (1951).

12. See Clark (1992) and Stevens (2007). This process also occurs at earlier stages of schooling; see, e.g., Shamus Khan's (2011) ethnography of the institutional character of the elite St. Paul's boarding school in *Privilege: The Making of an Adolescent Elite at St. Paul's School*, and Rubén Gaztambide-Fernandez's (2009) ethnographic study of the "Weston School."

13. For other sources on campus culture and its effects on discourse and action, see Colby (2003, 2007).

14. A variety of studies have demonstrated the impact of a college's cultural context on students. For examples, see Pascarella and Terenzini (2005); Astin (1993); Feldman and Newcomb (1994); Holland and Eisenhart (1990); Knox, Lindsay, and Kolb (1993); Arum and Roksa (2011); and Trow (1979).

15. Both Steven Brint (2009) and Mitchell Stevens (2008) have written insistently on this point, especially how culture and education should be studied more thoroughly. See also how Stevens, Elizabeth Armstrong, and Richard Arum (2008) think of higher education institutions serving as "incubators" for particular types of cultural competencies and social paths in "Sieve, Incubator, Temple, Hub."

16. This is the idea of cultural repertoires developed by Ann Swidler (1986) and expanded by Nina Eliasoph (1998) and Eliasoph and Paul Lichterman (2003). As we develop our ideas about these repertoires below, it is important to note that when we refer to the shared meanings of these symbols, practices, and so forth, we do not mean to imply that all bits of culture are equally, coherently, and consistently used by all members of a group. We do emphasize, though, that there are prevailing ideas and practices on campuses that are familiar to students on that campus, and that these ideas and practices exert considerable power.

17. Although much about the provocative style would suggest that our Western Public respondents would be involved with the Tea Party, the majority of our interviews done on the Western Public campuses *predated* the rise of this movement. We did most of our data collection in the summer and fall of 2008; the Tea Party movement really gained steam in February 2009. For a sociological analysis of the Tea Party's effects on the Republican Party, see Skocpol and Williamson (2012).

18. Both Rebecca Klatch (1999) and John Andrew (1997) have written about Young Americans for Freedom. For a few key entries in this growing library on

conservatism, see Gross, Medvetz, and Russell (2011); Micklethwait and Wooldridge (2004); Himmelstein (1990); and Glenn and Teles (2009).

19. For studies of conservative students, see Woessner and Woessner (2006, 2007). For work on students'—including conservative students'—plans for graduate school, see Fosse, Freese, and Gross (2012).

20. For one study of conservative student mobilization into pro-life activity, see Ziad Munson (2010).

21. Richard Arum and Josipa Roksa make a similar point about academic effort, writing that "both institutional and individual characteristics shape students' life in college. Although individual-level characteristics are a powerful determinant of many social choices, differing campus cultures influence which options are available or are more widely embraced" (2011, 84).

22. For more information on the individualistic account of human action, see Bellah et al. (1986). For an example of how scholars rather simplistically attribute causality to "culture," see Fordham and Ogbu (1986).

23. In addition, our choice of generic-sounding names for these universities should not be interpreted to mean that we think of our case-study campuses as perfectly representative of other institutions of the same type.

24. We conducted our interviews before the Tea Party movement really caught fire, which means that we can only speculate in this book how our interviewees might connect to that ideology and its various actors—grassroots activists, government leaders, and very wealthy donors.

25. Four of the seven alumni/ae were within four years of graduating.

26. Twelve of the 14 were within four years of graduating.

27. Binder and undergraduate students in a small seminar class on college-age conservatism conducted the interviews at UC San Diego.

28. The Young Americans for Freedom chapter at Michigan State University has a reputation for sponsoring extremist actions and was labeled a "hate group" by the Southern Poverty Law Center (SPLC) in 2007. As the SPLC writes, the chapter not only organized a Catch an Illegal Alien Day but also "sponsored a 'Koran desecration contest,' jokingly threatened to distribute smallpox infected blankets to Native American students, posted 'Gays spread AIDS' fliers, called Latino students and faculty members 'savages,' and invited Nick Griffin, the chairman of the neo-fascist British National Party, to speak on the MSU campus." http://www.splcenter.org/blog/?s=%22Young+Americans+for+Freedom%22 & submit (accessed May 12, 2011).

29. For example, the Social Science Research Council has a whole initiative related to questions of college students' religious expression. See http://religion .ssrc.org/reguide.

30. Other conservative college students who may have an especially strong influence on national politics are those who attend Christian liberal arts colleges such as Liberty University and Patrick Henry College.

31. Interestingly, most of this difference came from Eastern Elite students' fathers' occupations and educational levels. There was not a substantial difference between the education levels and occupations of Eastern Elite and Western Public students' mothers.

32. Methodologists who write about case-study analysis argue that the potential for learning from an extreme case is a "different and sometimes superior criterion to representativeness" in selecting cases. See, e.g., Stake (2000, 243).

33. Clark (1992).

34. For more on the all-American education ideal, see the work in progress by Kate Wood (2012).

35. This quotation has been slightly altered from a report on http://college prowler.com.

36. According to the College Board, a senior scoring 1200 on the combined critical reading and mathematics SAT tests in 2006 is in the 79th percentile, which means that the average Western Flagship student scored better than 79 percent of all other college-bound seniors taking the test that year. See "SAT Percentile Ranks: 2006 College-Bound Seniors—Critical Reading + Mathematics," http://www.collegeboard.com/prod_downloads/highered/ra/sat/SATPercentile RanksCompositeCR_M.pdf (accessed December 13, 2011).

37. Western Flagship has higher SAT admissions criteria than other campuses in the Western Public system, which means that applicants self-select, based on their perceived ability to get in. These rates of admission would suggest that students with combined SAT scores lower than 1200 mostly do not apply to the Western Flagship campus.

38. For an overview of such studies, see Stevens, Armstrong, and Arum (2008).

39. Fosse and Gross (2012); Bérubé (2006).

40. Wendy Roth and Jal Mehta write about how to analyze contested events, in their case, school shootings. Their article includes a very nice meditation on positivist and interpretivist approaches to studying such events. See Roth and Mehta (2002, 132).

Chapter 2: Who Are Conservative Students?

1. For information on the Young Americans for Freedom, see Klatch (1999).

2. The term "multiversity" was coined by Clark Kerr, former president of the University of California, to refer to the enormous organizational complexity that came to characterize universities in the twentieth century. For a very nice primer, see the 2007 essay by James W. Wagner, then president of Emory University, "Multiversity or University? Pursuing Competing Goods Simultaneously."

HERI surveys universities and colleges that are private and public; elite and nonelite; eastern, western, southern, and northern; urban and rural; historically black, Roman Catholic, secular, evangelical; and large and small. That said, all the colleges in the sample are four-year, baccalaureate-granting institutions. See the 2007 HERI report, *The American Freshman: Forty Year Trends*.

3. Data on freshmen are collected by administering the survey instrument during registration, freshman orientation, or the first few weeks of classes (HERI 2007, appendix A, p. 208).

4. The fall 2001 survey of freshmen "included 411,970 entering freshmen at 704 of the nation's higher education institutions. Data culled from 281,064 of those students at 421 baccalaureate institutions [were] statistically adjusted to be representative of the 1.2 million freshmen entering four-year colleges and universities as first-time, full-time students" (HERI 2001).

5. Given that freshmen in the 2001 sample were likely surveyed during August and September 2001, the events of September 11, 2001, may well have influenced some of the responses students gave. We cannot know the exact dates these surveys were given (and for most colleges and universities, orientation and registration would have been in mid- to late August and thus pre-9/11), and so we can only speculate that this may have affected the data. We choose to flag this here because 9/11 was cited by several students in our interviews as an important ideological turning point.

6. Unfortunately, HERI does not ask a political party identification question, so we do not know whether "conservative" here necessarily always means "Republican." It is also likely that many of the students who describe themselves as "middle of the road" are registered voters with some kind of formal party affiliation.

7. Of the 421 baccalaureate institutions surveyed by HERI in 2001, 42 were designated by the survey team as "private very highly selective universities and colleges" (in other words, those institutions most like Eastern Elite University) and 14 were designated "public highly selective universities" (in other words, those institutions most like Western Flagship University). The selectivity of a school is based on the mean score of entering freshmen on the Verbal plus Mathematical portions of the SAT or the converted SAT Math and Verbal equivalents from the American College Test (ACT) composite. See HERI (2001).

We made several decisions about which institutions to include in our two campus types. The "private very highly selective" category is composed of all private, Research I universities and liberal arts colleges that were surveyed by HERI in the year we selected and were categorized by HERI as "very highly selective" on the basis of median SAT/ACT scores. No institutions satisfying both criteria of "private" and "very highly selective" were excluded, regardless of whether they were in the East or not. There were 13 very highly selective universities and 29 very highly selective liberal arts colleges from across the country (for a total of 42) that were included in the dataset for the year we analyzed, with approximately 30,000 respondents. The "public highly selective" category is composed of public, Research I universities, regardless of geographic region, such as those institutions in the Big 10 and Pac 10. There were 14 of these institutions in the dataset for the year we analyzed, with information on 50,000 respondents.

While making the decision to include institutions in these two categories regardless of geographic location presented something of a degradation of specificity for comparison to our two campuses, it also significantly increased our sample size of similar institutions on two more important dimensions, selectivity and the public/private divide.

Although confidentiality does not permit us to say whether the actual Eastern Elite or Western Flagship campuses are included in the HERI 2001 dataset, the characteristics of each of our schools are well captured by these two categorizations.

8. It could be argued that the conservative critique of liberal campuses has more to do with the proportion of left-leaning faculty on campus than left-leaning undergraduates. Neil Gross's research (forthcoming) shows that more faculty in four-year higher educational institutions identify with the Left than with the Right.

9. As noted earlier, this ideological orientation variable is not the same as party affiliation, so we do not know how these categories match up with students' voter registrations or party identifications.

10. For an analysis of the general population's tendency to self-identify as "moderate" (despite media and political claims of a "culture war" that is afoot), see DiMaggio, Evans, and Bryson (1996); DiMaggio (2003); and Evans (2003).

11. The figure shows data from 1970 to 2006. While there is ambiguity in what any of the political orientation terms mean precisely to recent high school graduates, "middle of the road" is perhaps the most difficult to pin down. Middle of the road may indicate that respondents are genuinely moderate on most issues, or that they have not thought very much about the issues (and hence choose a middle category as a path-of-least-resistance type of response), or that they are noncommittal about stating their politics. Whatever the case, we know that it is in relation to the poles of conservative and liberal, and that most students at any given point in the last 40 years have been more comfortable reporting a stance away from the extremes.

12. See pp. 76–77 for these exact percentages in HERI (2007).

13. See, e.g., Helen Lefkowitz Horowitz (1987).

14. In 2006, liberals hit 28.4 percent. In 2008 they peaked at 31 percent, and then their relative proportion went down to 29 percent in 2009. Conservatives, meantime, also gained ground against middle-of-the-roaders, hitting an all-time high of 23.9 percent in 2006. See HERI (2010).

15. When we report on all students from 2001, we use the adjusted numbers provided by HERI for a nationally representative sample.

16. Our tables do not report chi-square testing for the independence of the tabulated variables. Standard errors are very low because of the large sample collected by HERI. Most of the tables in this chapter present breakdowns across several variables at once; chi-square tests for all of the separate bivariate relationships within the tables are statistically significant at the .001 level and have been omitted for clarity.

17. Though we were able to find some evidence of at least one libertarian student at Eastern Elite (via op-eds in the mainstream student newspaper), we were unable to successfully interview any Eastern Elite libertarians. For a more thorough discussion of libertarianism at Western Public, including the lack of success of libertarian student groups on the Western Public campuses (despite the evidently larger numbers of libertarians), see chapter 5.

18. On the high rates of racial and ethnic homogeneity of Republican voters, see a September 2010 Gallup poll report titled "Republicans Remain Disproportionately White and Religious" (Newport 2010). While we acknowledge that "conservatism" and "Republican Party" do not refer to perfectly overlapping populations (and again, the HERI survey lacks a party identification question), the national GOP serves as a useful comparison of the general population of conservative voters to the conservative students we study in this book.

19. The example about how diversity is defined is illustrated in Kozol (2005). For extensive and thoughtful discussions of white identity, see Alba (1990), Frankenberg (1993), and Perry (2002).

20. This is also important to examine in light of concerns about ways that whiteness is deployed as an identity within the Tea Party movement, particularly around issues such as immigration. A 2010 *New York Times*/CBS News poll of Tea Party supporters found that 89 percent identified as white (Zernike and Thee-Brennan 2010, A1).

21. Table 2.5 shows that at private elite institutions, 42.8 percent of all liberals are men while 57.2 percent are women; on public flagship campuses 44.4 percent of liberals are men and 55.6 percent are women. Middle-of-the-road men and women are more equally distributed at private elite institutions (48.4 percent men, 51.6 percent women), but the distribution is intriguingly lopsided on public flagship campuses (45.1 percent men, 54.9 percent women)—suggesting that women at public flagships may be more reluctant to claim one or the other ends of the spectrum than their male classmates are, or that that they are genuinely more moderate on the issues (again, this is the problem with the meaning of "middle of the road").

22. Pew Forum on Religion and Public Life (2008).

23. This finding matches those of other studies of religious affiliation among young people. See Mayrl and Oeur (2009); Cherry, DeBerg, and Porterfield (2001); and Smith and Denton (2005).

24. On something of a side note, it is perhaps not surprising—given the oft-

repeated critique of the Ivy League as "godless"—to observe that the more elite the campus type is, the fewer students describing themselves as "born-again" there are in the student population (self-identified "born-again" students constitute 20.4 percent of conservative freshmen at private elite institutions, but 23.2 percent on public flagship campuses and 29.2 percent in the general sample). Nevertheless, this still means that one-fifth of all conservative students at universities and colleges like Princeton, Vanderbilt, and Vassar consider themselves born-again. See Goldman (1991) and Campolo and Willimon (2002).

25. While it may be tempting to guess that the larger number of Catholic conservatives at private elite institutions than at flagship institutions is explained by the inclusion of elite Catholic universities and colleges like Georgetown University in the "private very highly selective institutions," only two of the 42 very highly selective universities or colleges included in the 2001 sample were Catholic, so this explanation is not compelling. Further, plenty of non-Catholic students attend Catholic universities; attendance at an elite Catholic university is not predicated on students' religious affiliations. We reiterate here that our use of the HERI dataset obligates us not to use real names of institutions, but some examples of Catholic universities are Boston College, Georgetown University, and Notre Dame University.

26. That is not to say that all Catholic conservatives use this political style. However, we do see this combination of Catholicism and civility utilized elsewhere, notably by the Intercollegiate Studies Institute, one of the national conservative organizations profiled in chapter 3.

27. Christian Smith and Melinda Lundquist Denton (2005) devote considerable time to debunking the idea that there has been a surge in the number of American youth who identify as "spiritual but not religious," picking and choosing among elements of different religious traditions in order to develop a personalized relationship to faith that falls outside the realm of organized religion. While they argue that this is a much less widespread phenomenon than the mainstream media have made it appear, our findings suggest that it may be that this is not so much a national trend but a particularly institutional one.

28. Note that we began our "snowball" samples by finding interviewees through their political activities. Though we did find many right-leaning students who were involved in faith-based groups, and some who were not active in political organizations, this may be one reason why we did not find more evangelical conservatives on the Western Public campuses.

29. Unfortunately, the lack of political identification questions on the HERI survey makes us unable to move beyond speculation about this at the national level as well.

30. Smith and Denton (2005).

31. The following authors and works are famously identified with the cultural investigation of social class and taste: Max Weber, *Economy and Society*

(1978); Pierre Bourdieu, "Cultural Reproduction and Social Reproduction" (1977); Paul DiMaggio and John Mohr, "Cultural Capital, Educational Attainment, and Marital Selection" (1985); Michèle Lamont, *Money, Morals, and Manners* (1992) and *The Dignity of Working Men* (2000); Annette Lareau, *Unequal Childhoods: Class, Race, and Family Life* (2003); and Thorstein Veblen, *The Theory of the Leisure Class* (1912). A good summary of the complexities surrounding how social class shapes policy attitudes and political preferences is provided in Leslie McCall and Jeff Manza's "Class Differences in Social and Political Attitudes in the United States" (2011).

32. Though HERI offers a third social class variable, freshmen's reports of their parents' household income, we chose not to include an analysis of this here. As other authors have noted, high school and college students' self-reports of their parents' incomes tend not to be terribly accurate (most inflate their families' incomes); also, while we have data from our interviewees about parents' and guardians' occupations and educational attainment, we do not have comparable data on income. On the reliability of students' reporting family incomes, see Massey et al. (2003, 27).

33. HERI data are organized into eight categories of educational attainment; we have condensed these categories to the three we show in table 2.7. See Perrin et al. (2011).

34. For examples of sociological work in this area, see Massey et al. (2003) and Jerome Karabel's critical work *The Chosen: The Hidden History of Admission and Exclusion at Harvard, Yale, and Princeton* (2005).

35. Though we have reason to doubt self-reported income levels and do not report on the data here, it is interesting to note that these educational attainments (and occupational levels, as we will see in the following section) are not perfectly correlated with income levels. We find in the HERI data that conservative freshmen's families are overrepresented in the two wealthiest income strata, yet are underrepresented in the highest levels of education and occupational prestige. In other words, the families of conservative freshmen at private elite universities like Eastern Elite earn more income with less education and less prestigious jobs than the parents of the general freshman cohort at those schools.

36. The HERI survey records parental occupations for each student in the sample. Our research team assigned a prestige score to each answer by matching these to occupations in the most comprehensive prestige listing available, that of Ganzeboom, De Graaf, and Treiman (1992). For each HERI response occupation, the equivalent occupation in the report was identified with the highest possible level of precision and its score was recorded. A detailed list of occupational categories and scores assigned is available from the authors.

37. One issue with this system of scoring, however, is that no occupational prestige scores are applied to the categories of homemaker, unemployed, other, or undecided. As we will see with our interviews below, this appears to be particu-

larly significant in assessing the status of households in which the mothers are homemakers. In the national data, 16.9 percent of conservatives list their mother's occupation as "homemaker," while just 8.9 percent of liberals and 10.7 percent of moderates do. For further explanation of issues with undercounting women's employment, see Beller (2009).

38. Recall also that in the HERI data, we saw that conservative freshmen are not that different from others, but the parents of conservative freshman at private elite schools have lower graduate school attainments than do other freshmen parents (especially mothers). In contrast, at public flagship institutions the parents of conservative freshmen have higher graduate school attendance than other parents. Because we do not have data on students outside our sample at our schools, we cannot speculate as to how the attainments we see here compare with the national data.

39. See note 36 above for more on the limitations of this scoring system.

40. The U.S. Census Bureau divides the country by state into nine divisions, which make up four regions. For example, the Northeast Region encompasses two divisions, New England (Vermont, New Hampshire, Maine, Massachusetts, Rhode Island, and Connecticut) and Middle Atlantic (New York, New Jersey, Pennsylvania). See U.S. Census Bureau, "Census Bureau Regions and Divisions with State FIPS Codes," http://www.census.gov/geo/www/reg_div.text.

41. It is important to note, however, that these data are based on interviewees' self-reports of where they consider themselves to be "from," which was clarified as the place or places where they spent most of their time growing up. The only places we did not count were places interviewees described as having been born in but then quickly moving away from (a not uncommon situation for interviewees on both campuses with parents in the military). Thus, some Western Public students, though they grew up in other states, had families that relocated to the state where the Western Public university system is located enough years prior to their college enrollment to qualify for in-state status. Others, however, were out-of-state students paying higher fees and tuition.

42. One wonders whether left-leaning students share a sense of themselves as an aggrieved minority. We can think of a few possible arguments why liberal collegians might not view themselves as such. First, in light of the broad stereotypes of young people in general, and college students in particular, as leaning to the left, such students might assume that their middle-of-the-road peers agree with them (or would if pressed). For more on American beliefs about the "typical college student," see Wood's forthcoming dissertation (2012). Another possibility is that right-leaning students are more likely than those on the left to draw on national-level templates for viewing themselves as aggrieved. As we discuss in chapter 3, numerous national conservative organizations provide students with language and imagery for understanding themselves as embattled on campuses. A further possibility, which in some ways combines these first two and which we

discuss in more detail in chapter 4, is that conservative students view their minority status as an asset, and as such it is to their advantage to perceive themselves as outnumbered (while if their liberal counterparts see themselves as more akin to "typical" college students, they lack such reason to adopt this kind of combative identity). In some ways, this argument articulates with Christian Smith's (1998) work on the "subcultural identity" of evangelical Christians.

Chapter 3: Sponsored Conservatism: The Landscape of National Conservative Organizations

1. The Institute for Humane Studies offers fellowships to students who engage in "liberty-advancing research" in the areas of economics, philosophy, law, political science, history, and sociology, among others. See http://www.theihs.org/humane-studies-fellowships.

2. This information is provided on a web page headlined "Extreme Makeover: Job-seeker Edition," on the Leadership Institute's website at http://www.leadershipinstitute.org/news/?NR=6124.

3. Erica Tanner is a pseudonym for a young woman who had attended college in the Midwest, and who at the time of our interview was working part-time for CPAC. Unless otherwise noted, the names used in this chapter for organization leaders are real names.

4. Young America's Foundation promotes "aggressive" conservatism, as seen in its "battleplan." See Coyle and Robinson (2005). The boot camp reference for the Leadership Institute can be found at http://www.leadershipinstitute.org/training/.

5. When social scientists speak of ideal types, they mean that the categories constructed are formed from characteristics and elements of the given *phenomena*, but are not meant to correspond to all of the *characteristics* of any one particular case.

6. On what we know about conservative organizations set up for college students, see Andrew (1997) and Klatch (1999). Steven Teles's wonderful book on new conservative legal organizations, *The Rise of the Conservative Legal Movement* (2008), includes an important chapter on the Federalist Society, but undergraduates generally are not included in this organization.

An additional word should be said here about the Young Americans for Freedom, founded by conservative students in 1960 on the estate of William F. Buckley, Jr. This organization, with its principles of limited government and an unfettered market economy as set forth in the famous Sharon Statement, was once the central hub of conservative student activism. But throughout the decades the or-

ganization suffered internal cleavages, with libertarians at odds with moral tradi-
tionalists and the Vietnam War a deeply divisive issue. But the organization has
had staying power. Currently the Young America's Foundation has subsumed the
Young Americans for Freedom organization, and the new YAF advocates that
students consider starting Young Americans for Freedom chapters on their campuses. For information on the current relationship between the two YAFs, see
"Young Americans for Freedom Old Home Page" at http://www.yaf.org/yafree
dom.aspx.

7. Cloud (2006).

8. The information in the first part of this paragraph can be found on various
pages of the Young America's Foundation website (http://www.yaf.org). An organization called University Information Services, founded at Vanderbilt University,
was renamed the Young America's Foundation in 1971.

9. Again, the Young America's Foundation is not to be confused with the earlier conservative organization using the acronym YAF, Young Americans for Freedom, founded on the Sharon, Connecticut, estate of William F. Buckley, Jr., in
1960.

10. The Young America's Foundation has captured the attention of some
mainstream and liberal writers and publications. See Cloud (2006) and Tower
(2006).

11. Young America's Foundation, "Our Mission," http://www.yaf.org/Mission
.aspx.

12. Media Matters Action Network provides a public record of the organization's finances. For an overview of the YAF's revenues, grants, and total expenses
from 1997 to 2008, see http://mediamattersaction.org/transparency/organization/
Young_America_s_Foundation/financials. For a list of funders dating back to
1985, see http://mediamattersaction.org/transparency/organization/Young_Amer
ica_s_Foundation/funders. (The YAF itself also makes its tax forms available online; for example, its 2009 form 990 can be found at http://www.yaf.org/uploaded
Files/Webpages/About_Us/2009%20YAF%20990%20-%20Public%20
Copy%20with%20Sch%20B.pdf?n=7696).

13. See http://mediamattersaction.org/transparency/organization/Young_Amer
ica_s_Foundation/connections. The Intercollegiate Studies Institute quotation
can be found at http://home.isi.org/about.

14. Most of this information on board members can be found on the Media
Matters website, http://mediamattersaction.org. For information about the Phillips Foundation fellowship programs, see http://www.thephillipsfoundation
.org/#about.cfm.

15. All quoted text is from an online pdf file of the 2009 edition. March's activities are described on pp. 86–93 of the document. See also Coyle (2009).

16. Images of the cover of the wall calendar and the bumper sticker can be

found at http://www.yaf.org/marketplace.aspx. A poster with Joseph Stalin, Angela Davis, and Karl Marx is featured at http://www.yaf.org/uploadedFiles/Web pages/Students/YAF%20Battleplan_October.pdf.

17. See Coyle and Robinson (2005, 1).

18. See Coyle (2009, 7–8).

19. See ibid., 4-5.

20. For the quotation on the purpose of bringing "motivational" speakers to campus, see http://www.yaf.org/conservativespeakers.aspx.

21. For the quotation on the purpose of conferences, see http://www.yaf.org/Conservative-Conferences.aspx.

22. Reagan went on to say, "Young America's Foundation remains a source of refuge for such students. . . . I know the conference will send you back to your campuses better informed, motivated, and trained." See http://www.yaf.org/RonaldReaganYAF.aspx.

23. The full list of speakers is at http://www.yaf.org/conservativespeakers.aspx.

24. This, at least, was the price range Rick Santorum commanded before his star shone brightly as a presidential candidate. In all likelihood his fees have risen dramatically.

25. Roger Custer is the real name (not a pseudonym) of the former conference director. As of early 2012, Custer is the executive director of an organization called America's Future Foundation.

26. Always provocative, Coulter repeatedly referred to then presidential candidate Barack Obama as "B. Hussssssein Obama," and generally derogated "Mussssssssslims" who practice "Isssslam." The audience laughed, clapped, and hooted appreciatively whenever she used this purposively sibilant terminology, as they also did when she called Muslims "head-chopping savages" (field notes, Ann Coulter event at UC Irvine, May 22, 2008).

27. Our information about the Conservative Political Action Committee, or CPAC, was given to us by a young intern, whom we call Erica Tanner, during a phone interview in 2007.

28. From the YAF webpage promoting the 2011 National Conservative Student Conference. See http://www.yaf.org/eventdetails.aspx?id=6453.

29. See http://www.leadershipinstitute.org/aboutus/mission.cfm.

30. For information on the LI's net assets, see http://www.leadershipinstitute.org/aboutus/Files/2010Form990.pdf.

31. For the 74,000 number, see http://www.leadershipinstitute.org/news/?NR=1522; for the 94,000 number, see http://www.leadershipinstitute.org/training/; for the 97,000 number, see http://www.leadershipinstitute.org/aboutus/Morton.cfm.

32. For most of this information, see the LI's profile of Blackwell at http://www.leadershipinstitute.org/aboutus/Morton.cfm.

33. Again, the LI's 2010 990 tax form can be found at http://www.leader shipinstitute.org/aboutus/Files/2010Form990.pdf. For information on contrib-utors, see http://mediamattersaction.org/transparency/organization/Leadership _Institute/funders. Information on the Lynde and Harry Bradley Foundation can be found at http://mediamattersaction.org/transparency/organization/The_Lynde _and_Harry_Bradley_Foundation/grants.

34. This is from the LI's mission statement, found at http://www.leader-shipinstitute.org/aboutus/mission.cfm.

35. It is certainly "multifaceted" in its approach to web design. The complex-ity of navigation is either an irony, since one of the training sessions offered to young conservatives is how to create an effective, easy-to-navigate web presence, or it is intentional: One of our interviewees at Western State, Conor Denning, suggested that the LI doesn't "like a whole lot of in-depth detail about what they do." Whatever the case, the website is not easy to find one's way around in.

36. See http://www.leadershipinstitute.org/training/.

37. Again, see http://www.leadershipinstitute.org/training/.

38. Still more information on training can be found at http://www.leader shipinstitute.org/aboutus/kirby.cfm.

39. Again, see the LI's 2010 990 tax form at http://www.leadershipinstitute .org/aboutus/Files/2010Form990.pdf.

40. For more on the 9/12 Project, see http://the912-project.com/.

41. Information about this event can be found at http://www.leadershipinsti-tute.org/news/?NR=1509.

42. Information on the number of campuses included in the CampusReform .org database can be found at http://www.campusreform.org/about/faq.

43. See http://www.campusreform.org/about/help.

44. See http://www.campusreform.org/.

45. For resources, see http://www.campusreform.org/resources/publicity -resources; for manuals, see http://www.campusreform.org/resources/manuals-and -writings.

46. See http://www.campusreform.org/about/faq.

47. Again, for 2010 tax information, see http://www.leadershipinstitute.org/ aboutus/Files/2010Form990.pdf.

48. See http://www.campusreform.org/about/about-clp.

49. See http://www.leadershipinstitute.org/aboutus/Files/2010Form990.pdf.

50. Conor's paper had condemned a liberal columnist at another campus publication for using explicit language in a story on American foreign policy.

51. In 2009, O'Keefe posed with a student from UCLA, Hannah Giles, who was dressed as a prostitute. Together, O'Keefe and Giles recorded two members of the liberal community organizing group ACORN taking advice from them on how to hide their "criminal activities." As a result of the recording, which was distributed widely by the conservative provocateur Andrew Breitbart, ACORN

eventually lost its congressional funding, and it shut down shortly thereafter. In 2011, O'Keefe caught on tape the top fundraiser for National Public Radio (NPR) telling two people dressed as Muslims and posing as potential donors to the radio network that Tea Party supporters were "seriously racist, racist people." NPR's executive director quickly stepped down in the aftermath of the scandal. In 2010, O'Keefe and three others were charged with attempting to tamper with the phones in Louisiana senator Mary Landrieu's office. This and other information on O'Keefe can be found in a profile published in the *New York Times* online edition (2011) and in an article by Zev Chafets that appeared in the *New York Times Sunday Magazine*, "Stinger: James O'Keefe's Greatest Hits" (2011).

52. The details are a bit unclear as to what precisely O'Keefe's job was at the LI. See the main blog post by Blackwell, and responses to threads in the comment section, in Blackwell (2009).

53. See Vogel (2010).

54. These are the words of the LI's Steven Sutton, who heads the LI's campus journalism outreach program, as quoted in Vogel (2010).

55. See Blackwell (2009).

56. Ibid., article II.

57. For a conservative statement about how NPR is being funded by taxpayers for the good of liberal causes, see a 2011 *Washington Times* editorial titled "NPR's Taxpayer-funded Lobbyists: Liberal Public Radio Battles Congress with Your Money."

58. Email received on July 25, 2011, titled "ISI e-update, July 2011." The rest of the newsletter was also included in this email.

59. Each year, the ISI has a slot on the NCSC schedule, according to our survey of a handful of events. The observations we report on from the 2007 NCSC were given to us by an undergraduate student who self-identifies as a "moderate conservative" but who wished not to be identified.

60. Because the student we knew who attended the NCSC did not have a recording device, we cannot claim that these quotes are absolutely verbatim. But they are as close to verbatim as the student was able to capture.

61. For information on Buckley's and Frank Meyer's role in "fusionism," see Himmelstein (1990).

62. The ISI explicitly positions itself as elite, saying that it serves the "best and the brightest college students." See "ISI in Depth," at http://home.isi.org/about.

63. See http://mediamattersaction.org/transparency/organization/Intercol legiate_Studies_Institute/financials.

64. Information on the number of events sponsored can be found at http://home.isi.org/about/faq. Basic information on the debates between Hitchens and D'Souza and between Churchill and D'Souza (the names and dates of the events) can be found by searching for their names on the ISI site, but the text of their statements is available only to ISI members.

65. See http://home.isi.org/about.

66. The CN refers to the publications it funds as independent, not conservative. See http://www.collegiatenetwork.org/about.

67. Among the information offered in the college guide: "the quality of curricula, the rigor and vigor of major academic departments, the intellectual freedom that prevails—or not—on each campus, the schools that have safe campuses and wholesome living arrangements—and those that don't, the professors to seek out, and the courses that ought to be avoided entirely." See http://www.collegeguide.org/about_cg.aspx.

68. This list can be found at http://home.isi.org/about.

69. See http://www.isi.org/lecture.aspx.

70. Ibid.

71. Ibid.

72. See http://www.isi.org/lectures/content/cicero_bro.pdf. ISI formerly kept a topical database of its lectures online (http://www.isi.org/western_civ/lectures.html, accessed July 21, 2011), but as of 2012 this appears to no longer be the case.

73. See http://www.isi.org/programs/conferences/conferences.html.

74. The webpage listing information on this seminar is no longer online. (http://www.isi.org/programs/seminars/fpu11/index.html, accessed July 22, 2011).

75. The webpage giving information on the 2009 conference is no longer available online (http://www.isi.org/programs/conferences/indy09/index.html, accessed July 22, 2011).

76. John Podhoretz is the son of the neoconservative writers Norman Podhoretz and Midge Decter, and in 2009 was made editor of *Commentary*, where his father was a longtime editor-in-chief.

77. See their homepage at http://www.collegiatenetwork.org/.

78. See http://www.collegiatenetwork.org/internships.

79. Again, see http://www.collegiatenetwork.org/internships.

80. Formerly at http://www.collegiatenetwork.org/news/303:apply-for-the-eric-breindel-collegiate-journalism-award (accessed July 22, 2011). When we tried to revisit this page in December 2011, it had been removed. More information on Breindel's role in conservative news outlets can be found in a 1999 *New York* magazine article by Craig Horowitz (1999).

81. The ISI's Facebook page provides limited information on the 50,000 students and faculty in its network. See https://www.facebook.com/pages/Intercollegiate-Studies-Institute/108520352505838 (accessed January 18, 2012). Long became president of the ISI in 2011, after T. Kenneth Cribb, Jr., "built ISI to unprecedented financial and program levels since taking the helm in 1989." Long's quote on the ambivalence and hostility of campuses can be found in Kern (2011).

82. A copy of this memo can be found online. See Powell (1971).

83. See http://home.isi.org/about.

Chapter 4: How Conservatives Think about Campus: The Effects of College Reputations, Social Scenes, and Academics on Student Experience

1. The authors of both of these books are affiliated with the organizations we described in chapter 3. Alan Kors, co-author, with Harvey Silverglate, of *The Shadow University* (1998), lectures at ISI functions; David Horowitz, the author of *Indoctrination U* (2007), participates in the YAF speakers program.

2. According to the online *Merriam-Webster's Dictionary*, a policy is "politically correct" when it seeks to eliminate "language and practices which could offend political sensibilities (as in matters of sex or race)." This can be a positive assessment, but most usage is negative, indicating an overweening protectiveness of certain classes of people. See http://www.merriam-webster.com/dictionary/politically%20correct (accessed January 20, 2012).

3. Jonah Goldberg, for example, goes partway in the indoctrination thesis and says that while it is true that "conservative college students routinely find themselves in the crosshairs of the professors as well as their peers," it is not helpful to be "seduced by the narrative of victimization" (2010, xi).

4. In recent years, a handful of scholars have analyzed the conservative critique of the university, looking at both the language used in the discourse and whether the critics' assessment of the academy bears up under empirical scrutiny. See Michael Bérubé, *What's Liberal about the Liberal Arts? Classroom Politics and "Bias" in Higher Education* (2006), Melanie Bush, "The Movement for an 'Academic Bill of Rights,'" (2005), and Neil Gross and Solon Simmons, "The Social and Political Views of American Professors" (2007).

5. Clark and Trow (1966).

6. As is true in other chapters as well, this chapter's description of campus features is based on our amalgam institutions. See chapter 1 for a description.

7. We will see in chapter 5 that the parents of some of our conservative interviewees were wary of sending their offspring to Western Flagship because of its liberal reputation.

8. In many ways, Western Flagship is much like the university Mary Grigsby describes in *College Life through the Eyes of Students* (2009).

9. For information on admissions selectivity and the term "highly selective," see HERI (2001).

10. Many scholars have noted that elite universities have cohesive communities, among them most recently Camille Zubrinsky Charles and co-authors, *Taming the River: Negotiating the Academic, Financial, and Social Currents in Selective Colleges and Universities* (2009).

11. For analyses of how elite institutions came to have such student diversity, see, e.g., William G. Bowen and Derek Curtis Bok, *The Shape of the River: Long-Term Consequences of Considering Race in College and University Admissions*

(1998), and Douglas S. Massey et al., *The Source of the River: The Social Origins of Freshmen at America's Selective Colleges and Universities* (2003).

12. As we saw in chapter 3, however, our sample of conservative students and alumni/ae does not reflect the institution's racial and ethnic diversity.

13. In this respect, Eastern Elite University is a good deal like the college studied in Mitchell L. Steven's *Creating a Class: College Admissions and the Education of Elites* (2007). See also Mitchell Stevens and Josipa Roksa (2011), who have written of the "diversity imperative" embraced by elite colleges and universities.

14. According to data from UCLA's 2001 Higher Education Research Institute (HERI) survey of freshmen and as described in chapter 2, 18.5 percent of college freshmen at schools that are most similar to Eastern Elite (four-year, very selective private institutions) identify as conservative, while nearly 50 percent identify as liberal and about 33 percent identify as middle of the road. We recall also that data on individual schools are unavailable owing to confidentiality restrictions.

15. Burton R. Clark in *The Distinctive College* (1992) reserves the label "organizational saga" for those liberal arts colleges with very particular missions; we expand the meaning somewhat here to mean institutional character, without the added meaning of defining college purpose.

16. On the latter point, see Espeland and Sauder (2007).

17. George D. Kuh and his colleagues have written a great deal about institutions with an overarching sense of purpose, which leads to student academic success. See, e.g., Kuh (2010).

18. A telling example of conservative critics who nonetheless send their children to purportedly liberal schools is John Leo, once a columnist for *US News & World Report* and now the editor of mindingthecampus.com for the Manhattan Institute, a conservative think tank. Although he told us in an interview that he had misgivings about sending his daughter to Wesleyan University ("which is awful . . . it is a primitive place") because it is so liberal, he had done so because she really wanted to go there. He promised not to write about Wesleyan during the time she attended the school (John Leo, Manhattan Institute).

19. In her dissertation research, Alexandria Walton Radford finds that valedictorians in the state of California are more likely to stay in-state than to go to elite universities out of state. We may be seeing a similar pattern in the state where Western Flagship is located. See Radford (2009).

20. For some of the most-cited works in the area of the effects of peer climate, see Coleman et al. (1966) and Astin (1993).

21. Once again, this is undoubtedly truer of the religious students who decided to apply to and attend Eastern Elite University than of, say, religious students a lot like them who decided in advance that they did not want to attend a "godless" university.

22. For more extensive discussions on the content of outside-the-classroom

learning and the value college students place on it, see Moffat (1989) and Nathan (2005).

23. Thomas Ehrlich and Anne Colby in "Political Bias in Undergraduate Education" (2004) make a similar point, writing that while colleges and universities should be the types of setting where people of varying strong political opinions get to know one another, generally they are not.

24. For studies of peer culture, see (among many others) Adler and Adler (1998); Armstrong and Hamilton (2010, forthcoming); and Coleman (1961).

25. Lamont (1999, 2000).

26. See Reuben (1996, 260–61).

27. In total, 98 percent of Eastern Elite University undergraduates live in on-campus housing.

28. For example, a post on collegeconfidential.com (the specific URL is removed to mask the identity of the school) estimates that fewer than 10 percent of the Eastern Elite student body even socialize at these clubs, let alone belong to them.

29. Calculated from the HERI (2001) freshman survey. For confidentiality reasons, schools' names are omitted.

30. Douthat (2005).

31. This is not to say that Eastern Elite students had no gripes about their left-leaning campus. Some conservative students did express distress at some of the events that the university sponsored or endorsed, such as a talk by a sex educator at which sex toys were given as door prizes. But respondents across the board emphasized that the university did not bar conservative groups from hosting events or receiving equal funding.

32. Arum and Roksa (2011). See also Labaree (1997).

33. Others have referred to this type of orientation among students—collegiate academics as a sort of necessary pill to swallow in order to obtain the "college experience" or simply to receive the necessary diploma—variously as credentialism, utilitarianism, or a prioritization of "outside-the-classroom" learning. See Moffat (1989), Nathan (2005), and Grigsby (2009).

34. Though we have limited data on the other Western Public university campuses besides Western Flagship, a few interviewees at Western Satellite discussed the smaller class sizes and generally more intimate feel of Western Satellite versus Western Flagship.

35. As Charles et al. point out, these kinds of decisions made in the first and second years of college about courses and majors can have significant downstream effects on students' lives. For example, "if a student takes no math or science courses in college, it will be difficult later on to become not just a scientist or mathematician but also a physician, dentist, engineer, architect, statistician, actuary, or veterinarian" (2009, 23). Armstrong and Hamilton (forthcoming) make similar points about the effects on the benefits of college education for students in "mismatched" majors.

36. On depersonalized faculty-student relationships, see Arum and Roksa (2011) and Clark and Trow (1966).

37. This is true not only of our conservative interviewees but also of Western Flagship students more broadly, as deduced from information found on student-oriented websites like collegeprowler.com.

38. For these two quotations, see, respectively, Boyer and Carnegie Foundation for the Advancement of Teaching (1987) and Grigsby (2009).

39. As a former president of the Western Flagship chapter of College Republicans, Chuck may have known of Christina Hoff Sommers and her critique of liberal feminism through the Young America's Foundation; she is a member of the YAF's speakers' program.

40. See Gross and Simmons (2012) and Gross (forthcoming)

41. For more on comparative findings of students' assessments of faculty, see Arum and Roksa (2011, esp. 62–67).

42. These "noncanonical" departments include occupational and professional fields, such as undergraduate majors in engineering, allied health sciences, and business. Steven Brint (2002) has termed these fields, in contrast to the traditional liberal arts, the "practical arts."

43. As we pointed out earlier in this chapter and in chapter 2, UCLA HERI data on similar institutions show that these perceptions are accurate. Though conservatives may overestimate the numbers of liberal versus middle-of-the-road students, right-leaning students are indeed in the minority on these types of campuses. This rough sense of the numbers that right-leaning students have may be one reason that conservative identity is so salient for these students. In one example of this phenomenon, Peter Bearman and Hannah Brückner (2001), looking at chastity oaths, have theorized that young people are most likely to keep their pledges—in other words, to have the chaste identity be a salient one—when there are some fellow pledgers (offering support and, in this example, accountability), but not so many that there is a majority (similar to the situation described in chapter 2 by interviewees who came from conservative communities). It is possible that identities are activated once a certain critical mass has been reached, but shift when a group becomes the majority (and thus the unmarked, normal category).

44. Again, we do not claim that this is true for all conservative students. For example, those with predominantly negative feelings may have dropped out of the institutions and therefore would not have been present for us to interview.

45. A few conservative critics have pointed out that conservative students reap some benefit from being in the political minority, much as we found here. See Jonah Goldberg's *Proud to Be Right: Voices of the Next Conservative Generation* (2010).

46. John Leo is the real name of the former *U.S. News & World Report* journalist who is now housed as a Senior Fellow at the Manhattan Institute.

47. Armstrong and Hamilton (forthcoming).

48. Granfield (1991); Granfield and Koenig (1992).

49. Nannerl O. Keohane, the former president of both Wellesley College and Duke University, similarly notes in *Higher Ground* that elite universities seek to socialize students, not merely to train or inform but "to shape their qualities of mind, feeling and character" (2006).

Chapter 5: Provoking Liberals and Campaigning for Republicans: Two Conservative Styles at the Western Public Universities

1. Fligstein and McAdam (2011).

2. We could not locate a description of a Bake Sale in California that occurred before the one at Western Flagship, but we did find this account of an event staged at the University of Washington in 2003, published on David Horowitz's frontpagemag.com. It is hard not to notice the similarities between this student's and Chuck's telling of events:

> With a little flour, sugar and a dash of street comedy, we set out to show the campus that Affirmative Action, which judges people based solely on their skin color, is inherently racist. . . .
>
> Early in the afternoon, we were warned by a few students that we had just ten minutes to shut down our booth "or else." We declined to heed their ultimatum. Approximately 150 students were gathered around our booth discussing the issue by about 12:30 in the afternoon, when our booth was finally *attacked* by leftists. These "sensitive" left-wing students tore down our signs, threw our baked goods and literature off the table and attempted to tear down our tent. One College Republican tried to salvage a few boxes of cookies from the table, but the "peaceful" activists got to the goods first and struck the Republican in the head with a flying cookie.
>
> Fortunately, a College Republican had called the police a few minutes prior to the attacks, when a few conversations had become heated, afraid the Left would incite violence (and the Left did not disappoint). Rather than step in and arrest our attackers, the police stood by while the University said we, the peaceful ones, had to be shut down because *we* had created an unsafe environment.

See also Jason E. Chambers's article on the same site, "Smashing Affirmative Action: Bake Sales" (2003).

3. This event got a good deal of media attention in the years after 9/11 and has been presented at other universities such as the University of Michigan, the University of California–Berkeley, and Columbia University. Among some of our

interviewees we heard the story circulated that Columbia University, an elite private institution, had canceled the event because the administration had deemed it too controversial. In fact, this was not the case; the event went on, but the administration tightly restricted the audience just before the event, in part to bar protesters from getting in. This, however, led to further conflict over the meaning of the event and the university's actions: Many in the conservative media and blogosphere accused the university of, in effect, shutting down the event. See, e.g., John Leo of the Manhattan Institute's blog post on mindingthecampus.com, "No Free Speech, Please—This Is Columbia." (Leo 2007).

4. We should note here that such a style has been long used by liberal students and other activists across the country, such as the Yippies. We briefly consider liberal students' use of the provocative style in chapter 8 and in footnote 42 in chapter 2.

5. At Western Flagship, as well as at Eastern Elite, campus conservatives who are particularly committed to the pro-life cause are generally members of the College Republicans but also devote time separately to pro-life groups.

6. Such clubs may have become more robust after the election of President Obama, when the Tea Party phenomenon took off.

7. There is minimal staff oversight of the students elected to the Funds Board.

8. For an account of the "You lie" comment, see CNN.com (2009). For information on Palin's targets, see Berman (2011). For one of thousands of articles on Republicans during the debt ceiling debate, see Davis (2011).

9. See, e.g., Lind (1995, 2009).

10. For a seminar offered on teaching the "activist mentality" to conservative students, see YAF.org, "Emerging Activist Seminar" (2011).

11. At least in this sense, one could argue that they have some awareness of the "middle-of-the-road" constituency on their campuses, though they do not describe those they believe to be politically apathetic partiers in these terms.

12. Although both these incidents are hearsay, the one at Western Flagship involving Ward Connerly was described by another of our interviewees in a guest op-ed piece in a major metropolitan newspaper in the state where Western Flagship is located. We also have heard several reports from other sources that David Horowitz is often heckled at university events. In fact, it would not be without merit to argue that some conservative students invite David Horowitz to campus *because* he will be heckled, thus winning media and political attention.

13. The phrase "they cling to guns and religion" received an enormous amount of negative attention in 2008, after then candidate Barack Obama used it in reference to small-town voters who, he said, were suffering economically and lashing out at politicians they considered elitist. See Seelye and Zeleny (2008). On this same subject, Robert Horwitz (2011) has an excellent chapter in a book manuscript revisiting Richard Hofstadter's work on the conservative "paranoid style," which also sheds light on Western Public students' concerns about liberal arrogance.

14. Conservative students around the country also complain that university administrators require expensive security details at conservative events, thereby driving up the cost—sometimes prohibitively—for such events. Students argue this has a chilling effect on their ability to host such events (field notes, National Conservative Students Conference, 2007; Young America's Foundation, "Young America's Foundation Campus Conservative Battle Plan: Your Month to Month Plan for Activism," http://www.yaf.org/uploadedFiles/Webpages/Students/2009%20YAF%20Battleplan%20Final.pdf.

15. Chuck allowed us to see this handwritten note from the governor.

16. Even skilled provocateurs at the Western Public campuses generally claimed their events always had an educational aspect to them, and that this was their intended outcome—something of a "you'll attract more flies with vinegar" argument. For example, at the Global Warming Beach Party held at Western Satellite, participants were given brochures explaining the Western Satellite College Republicans' opposition to the Kyoto Treaty, along with party treats:

> We had Bob Marley playing . . . and we had the stage set up and we were grilling. . . . We gave away hot dogs and stuff that day . . . [and] we had the signs and just literature on like Kyoto. . . . We did have some really informative pieces of literature that some of our guys put together about Kyoto, about some of the myths behind global warning and some of the facts from our perspective. . . . [The event] is meant to recruit people. It's meant to draw attention and get them there. And once you get them there, then you can kind of, "Well this is what we're about. Here's what we want to do." (Karl Hayes, Western Satellite)

17. For a discussion of socially skilled actors, see Fligstein (2001).

18. Several conservative critics provide fuel for students' grading concerns, including most prominently David Horowitz (e.g., Horowitz 2007). Some academics take the time to consider such critiques and argue strongly against Horowitz-style accusations. See, e.g., Bérubé (2006).

19. It is politically *moderate* students who profess the greatest amount of academic dissatisfaction. See Woessner and Woessner (2007).

20. This was true essentially only of Eastern Elite University women—see chapter 7.

Chapter 6: Civilized Discourse, Highbrow Provocation, and a Fuller Embrace of Campaigning: Three Conservative Styles at Eastern Elite University

1. The membership of college clubs ebbs and flows from year to year, depending on the national context and leadership on campus. Membership in East-

ern Elite College Republicans hit a high of "three to four hundred" just after George W. Bush was elected president in 2000, when conservatives were pleased to come out the woodwork (Henry Quick, Eastern Elite). At the time we conducted most of our interviews, in the fall of 2008, we were told that the Eastern Elite College Republicans had about 200 members. Here as elsewhere, the names of all student organizations, as well as of the interviewees themselves, are pseudonyms.

2. ROTC, or the Reserve Officers' Training Corps, was barred from several elite university and college campuses after the military instituted the Don't Ask, Don't Tell policy regarding military personnel's homosexuality. The issue of shaming university administrations into bringing ROTC back to campus has been a mainstay of many conservative campus organizations.

3. For an example of George Washington University's Young America's Foundation chapter's Global Warming Beach Party, reported by campusreform .org, see Theodosopolous (2010). For the University of Michigan Young Americans for Freedom's version of "Catch an Illegal Immigrant Day," see Domsic (2006).

4. Though as we have noted, Western Public conservatives do often make claims about their events' informative content.

5. As a reminder, these organizational and cultural factors at Western Flagship consist of students' dispersal into more atomized off-campus housing situations, depersonalized relationships with faculty, and few informal or formal university-sponsored bipartisan events, as well as attending a school whose institutional ethos is centrally "party" and "recreation." Recall also the example of the Western Flagship Objectivists' unsuccessful attempts at having a dialogue-based club and their shift into a more provocative style.

6. Here we focus on those organizations with specifically *political* content in which our interviewees were most directly involved. However, other right-leaning organizations exist at Eastern Elite University about which we have less information (usually, just one interviewee was actively involved with each group). Still, it is worth noting that Eastern Elite also boasts a Federalist Society, a libertarian group, a politically oriented debate club, and several evangelical campus ministries. Also, we ignore for the moment the Eastern Elite *Searchlight* and the pro-abstinence group. The conservative newspaper, one of the most vibrant right-leaning student groups on campus, will be the focus of its own section later in this chapter; the abstinence group is treated in chapter 7.

7. As noted in chapter 5, fiscal—even libertarian-identified—conservatives were the more visible faces of active conservatism at Western during the time we conducted interviews, although most of these fiscal conservatives professed religious beliefs. But for the most part they were uninterested in the hard-core Christian right issues. We had heard about past Western Flagship College Republicans leaders who were anti–gay rights and vocally anti-abortion, but in the main, the

organizations we studied (the ones that were multi-issue Republican clubs) did not want to be known for hugely divisive issues. Immigration, affirmative action, and small government were of greater interest to them. The relative absence of evangelicals in the ranks of College Republicans on the Western Flagship campus, as we have stated elsewhere, may be due to evangelicals' decisions not to have come to a campus as "radical" as Western Flagship in the first place, or due to our not having recruited interviewees on any of the campuses specifically via religious organizations.

8. Student newspapers are a hot issue on the Western Public campuses. On one campus, the university's administration outsources the mainstream school newspaper to an independent company, so that the university can keep its hands clean of any contentious content that goes on in its pages. On the Western State campus (as we saw in chapter 5), conservative students stirred up considerable outrage over a liberal editorial in the mainstream campus paper, garnering attention not only from Fox News but also from the Leadership Institute. Thus, the type of discourse in the Western Public campuses' papers appears to be more confrontational than that in Eastern Elite's mainstream newspaper.

9. See Granfield and Koenig (1992). Other authors have demonstrated how elite cultural identification of this sort gets manufactured at exclusive boarding schools as well. See Howard and Gaztambide-Fernandez (2010) and Khan (2011). The "best and the brightest" label can be found in several places on the Intercollegiate Studies Institute website, of which the following page is one example: http://home.isi.org/about.

10. The *Searchlight* members, for their part, turned to the populist provocative—and well-resourced—Young America's Foundation to make up their deficit and host the speaker: an interesting pragmatic use of an arm's-length ally.

11. Note here that Darren is invested in thinking that "most" of his peers are liberals, but as chapter 2 demonstrates, just under 50 percent of incoming freshmen at higher education institutions most like Eastern Elite self-identify as liberal. There is certainly identity work put toward thinking of conservatives as a significant minority on both of these campuses.

12. The *Dartmouth Review* is one of the most widely recognized examples of this style, and made huge waves in the 1980s. For more on this conservative student newspaper, see http://s14929.gridserver.com/about/.

13. D'Souza (2007).

14. Ibid., 91–92.

15. Ibid., 92.

16. Ibid., 92.

17. Fiona Graham has written about the debate club at Oxford University, the Oxford Union, that evokes something of the same sense of the stuffy upper class. It is clear from Graham's description, however, that the Oxford Union's

members come from more solidly elite backgrounds than do the students involved in Eastern Elite's *Searchlight*. See Graham (2005).

18. Harvey Mansfield is something of a mentor to many conservative undergraduates at Harvard, a role played somewhat similarly by Robert (Robbie) George at Princeton University and Donald Kagan at Yale. Students at Eastern Elite University have such a faculty member to look up to, though we refrain from offering that person's name in order to keep Eastern Elite's identity masked. See Mansfield (2006).

19. The coed example is made up but is extrapolated from an article written about another aspect of gender that created a true firestorm on campus. Once again, we refrain from using direct quotes from the newspaper in this section because they are searchable online and the identity of the paper and the university could be revealed.

20. That is to say, within our study. These styles most likely occur as well on other campuses that share characteristics with Eastern Elite, and based on media accounts, provocation certainly seems to exist on many university campuses besides those of the Western Public system.

21. For analysis of media depictions of the "typical college experience," see Wood (2012).

22. As Michèle Lamont has vividly written about the pleasures that faculty take in their scholarly work, so too do students at Eastern Elite resonate with the intellectuality inherent in academic pursuits. See her *How Professors Think* (2009).

23. At the same time, we do not want to be interpreted as saying that Eastern Elite students (on the whole) are saints, and that they engage in no "college life" activities such as drinking, having sex, or doing drugs. What we want to emphasize here is that academics and other campus pursuits create heightened expectations for these students for acting appropriately, and that academic concerns, and the careers that are the rewards of doing one's academic work, appear to be paramount for most students.

24. See, e.g., Ronald Story's *The Forging of an Aristocracy: Harvard and the Boston Upper Class, 1800–1870* (1980).

25. See chapter 4 for a discussion of how Eastern Elite undergraduates choose classes and majors.

26. It is remarkable how similar Molly's analysis of her education is to Shamus Khan's sardonic depiction of what constitutes learning at St. Paul's Boarding School, where he says emphasis is placed on teaching students to *sound like* they have learned something, not to have actually, concretely learned something. See Khan (2011).

27. We have changed the details of this exchange slightly so as not to identify the university.

28. We cannot provide a citation for this figure of Eastern Elite graduates going into finance since it could identify the university.

29. This quote echoes Lauren Rivera's findings about the incredible power of specific extracurricular affiliations at "super-elite" universities for gaining jobs in prestigious firms. Rivera shows that elite employers sort résumés on the basis of elite education, and then within those institutions, to select students with similar extracurricular experiences as their own, reproducing inequality at the highest levels of the labor force. See Rivera (2011).

30. We should note here that Eastern Elite has a few highly regarded conservative faculty on campus who make it part of their mission to provide support and succor to right-leaning undergraduates. Undergraduates love these faculty members. By way of contrast, Western Public students were largely unaware of such mentors on their campuses, although the first author did conduct an interview with one political scientist at Western Flagship who has advised a handful of conservative students.

31. Max Blumenthal (2009) writes about movement conservatism, while Sam Tanenhaus (2009) believes this spells the end of intellectual conservatism as we know it.

32. For example, Calvin himself came from a much more humble and less high-status background than most of his peers at Eastern Elite.

Chapter 7: Conservative Femininity

1. For the evocative language of "building up" and "pulling down," we are indebted to Walter W. Powell and Jeannette A. Colvyas (2008).

2. Only one woman interviewee, an Eastern Elite alumna, did not address gender-related topics at any point in her interview. All other women, both at Eastern Elite and on the Western Public campuses, explicitly brought in gender-related concerns. Intriguingly, the Eastern Elite woman who did not discuss gender had a highly gender-stereotyped self-presentation.

3. West and Zimmerman (1987).

4. For what is arguably the opening bell for the sociology of masculinity, see Tim Carrigan, Bob Connell, and John Lee, "Towards a New Sociology of Masculinity" (1985). See also R. W. Connell, *Masculinities* (2005). Connell's introduction to the second edition offers a useful overview of the progress of the sociology of masculinities, both historically and in terms of more current debates.

5. The landmark piece here is West and Zimmerman's (1987) *Doing Gender*. See also the works in the 2002 collection *Doing Gender, Doing Difference: Inequality, Power, and Institutional Change*, edited by Sarah Fenstermaker and Candace West.

6. It does, however, fit well with the cultural dictates of hegemonic masculinity in the United States, which have changed surprisingly little over the years. For an older but still frequently cited formulation, see Robert S. Brannon, "The Male Sex Role: Our Culture's Blueprint of Manhood, and What It's Done for Us Lately" (1976). For a newer formulation (one that explicitly draws on Brannon's work) specific to this age group, see also Michael S. Kimmel, *Guyland: The Perilous World Where Boys Become Men* (2008).

7. Though it is beyond our scope to engage this question here, this does present an opportunity for future research on conservatism and masculinity. It seems possible that conservative political ideology presents an easier "fit" with the dictates of hegemonic masculinity than a liberal one would, given conservatism's emphasis on "traditional" values and personal responsibility. Hence, we could speculate that gender would not only be less of an issue for conservative men than for conservative women, it would also be less of an issue for conservative men than for men with other political beliefs.

8. See also Ronnee Schreiber, *Righting Feminism: Conservative Women and American Politics* (2008), and "But Does She Speak for Me? Feminist and Conservative Women's Organizations React to Palin" (2009).

9. For a concise (if somewhat dated) discussion of emphasized femininity, see R. W. Connell's *Gender and Power: Society, the Person, and Sexual Politics* (1987, esp. 186–88). For a contemporary collegiate version of emphasized femininity, see the description of "the blonde" in Hamilton (2007).

10. For one example of a conservative intellectual who argues for a bright line separating men and women's essential natures, see Harvey Mansfield, especially his *Manliness* (2006).

11. Though of course the majority of these women came to prominence subsequent to our data collection.

12. See Schreiber (2009).

13. Easton flyer described in Colapinto (2003).

14. Field notes, National Conservative Student Convention, 2007. Though Easton decried feminists who "sneer at full-time moms," and her posters imply motherhood as women's primary goal, she went on to frame herself as a woman who balanced career and family: "I got my BA in 1973, I went from an intern to being promoted to assistant director of my program due to my hard work, then I applied to law school *and* got married. And guess what—I'm married and a working woman with a family and I am still conservative. Oh! And I'm *happy*! Shocker, huh? Women like me are ignored by feminism."

15. See, e.g., Cary (2010) and Daum (2010).

16. Colapinto (2003).

17. This type of strategy for reconciling the conflicting demands of work and family is not unique to conservative women. We can find throughout the sociological literature examples of women attempting to bridge these divides in differ-

ent and creative ways, including crafting more flexible options within elite workplaces (Blair-Loy 2003), undertaking home-schooling as a version of "amplified womanhood" (Stevens 2001), and embracing more traditional forms of religion (Davidman 1991).

18. We learned of this exchange from a student who attended that year's conference. This student is a moderate conservative herself and is quite aligned with the call for recapturing femininity. For example, she was very taken with Michelle Malkin as a speaker at the conference, in no small part because Malkin personifies conservative femininity for her. According to her notes, "Malkin is a small petite woman who gives of[f] a powerful combination of strength and femin[in]ity. As a young woman, this is the type of aura I look up to."

19. No women on either campus expressed solely negative views of Palin. The responses of women interviewees ranged from mixed to positive, the only exceptions being the few women who did not mention Palin at all.

20. For a similar case, see the description of how pro-life women seek to protect their special status as mothers in Luker (1984).

21. On American campus norms for women, see Bogle (2008).

22. Though not as prominent at Western Public, this point of view *was* seen among women interviewees who were from other campuses or who were interviewed after graduation in their roles as representatives of national conservative organizations. For example, Erica Tanner described starting a group for conservative women on her Midwestern campus as a counterpoint to the school's Women's Center, which she saw as an opportunistically homogenizing organization: "[Our group members] were saying, hey, we don't think it's appropriate that [the Women's Center] claims some sort of representation. How is that even going to work? I mean, you can't represent *three* people with one group, much less 4,000 or 5,000, however many women were on campus at the time" (Erica Tanner, CPAC). Of note here is that this was one area where our Eastern Elite interviewees appeared more similar to students at other schools; in most other areas, Eastern Elite University was an outlier and the *Western Public* interviewees were closer to the national norm.

23. Of the seven women interviewed at Eastern Elite, five discussed the campus social climate as problematic, with only one of them describing herself as in any way subscribing to these more permissive social mores. The other two interviewees did not bring this up as an issue or express an opinion on it either way (including the one outlier noted earlier who did not discuss gender-related issues at all). As we see below, only two Eastern Elite men discussed this.

24. The two exceptions were young men who were involved with the Eastern Elite pro-abstinence group, both of whom identified as Catholic. Interestingly, though, both talked about their commitment to abstinence advocacy in abstract terms—discussions of physiology and faith—rather than tying these to the personal experiences of themselves or others as did the women. We only have one

mention from either of them about their campus peers: "Those were my main, kind of experienced-based reasons like what I saw around Eastern Elite that I was like, 'This needs to change.' Just a sense of this is what sexuality and marriage could be, is this vision, and this is what I'm seeing; like no serious relationships forming, no commitment, no trust. Just one-night stands that leave people crying and not getting their call back that they were expecting and all these different things that are just driving people crazy" (Kris Nagle, Eastern Elite). This contrasts strongly with the Eastern Elite women, who consistently contextualized this as an intensely personal issue. We can also argue, however, that as women the Eastern Elite women were more likely to draw on the wider ideas about conservative womanhood and gendered campus expectations and thus to have experienced conflict with the campus environment.

This finding stands in contrast to some work that examines sexual expectations and pressures placed on men on college campuses (e.g., Kimmel 2008). However, we argue that unlike the women in our sample (and unlike the evangelical Christian men cited in note 25 below), these men do not appear to have a broader discourse of conservative male sexuality to draw from, and as such are more likely to use other ways to describe the issue, such as biology and religion. Differing experiences of gender lead to divergent interpretations of issues within the local environment of the university campus.

25. Again, many of these types of issues are viewed as too divisive for these groups to engage them. For example, though a good number of its members (both men and women) identify themselves as pro-life, abortion is not an issue that the Eastern Elite College Republicans are eager to take on, for fear of alienating those who are not as animated by this issue.

26. In many ways, their ability to draw on this conservatism to forge a different path as undergraduates is similar to findings by Wilkins (2008) that evangelical Christian students' religious identity can serve as a strategy allowing them to drop out of campus sexual culture. Perry and Armstrong (2007) likewise ascribe some of the success of campus organizations for evangelical youth to their ability to provide a comprehensive and satisfying alternative to mainstream social life, complete with different expectations for courtship and managing sexuality.

27. Women at Eastern Elite recalled similar experiences, describing being looked down on by their peers for taking stances on "women's issues" that appeared to be contradicted by their sex. For example, Eastern Elite alumna Melissa Preston, who was heavily involved with pro-life causes during her time at the school, recalled, "it is really important to have that community that can [support you] . . . because people can be very vicious." She continued, "I think even being a woman and being pro-life makes people think twice" (Melissa Preston, Eastern Elite).

28. Eastern Elite women described their religious beliefs as: Protestant (3), Catholic (2), Evangelical (2). One of the Protestant women was initially raised

Catholic but became Episcopalian later in childhood. Of the seven, five described themselves as being very involved with and committed to their faiths; two of the women (both Protestant) expressed lower levels of religious involvement. In contrast, Western Public women described their religious beliefs as: Protestant (1), Catholic (1), Evangelical (1), Jewish (1), Spiritual (2), and None (1) (we are missing data on one interviewee's religious beliefs). The two Western Public interviewees who characterized themselves as "spiritual" described being raised in religious households (one Protestant, one evangelical) but not currently subscribing to any particular faith. The one interviewee coded as not religious had been gravitating toward becoming born-again as a teenager but had left that path and opted not to practice any form of religion, organized or otherwise. Of the seven Western Public women for whom we have data on religious beliefs, only one described a high level of religious activity.

Why might religion play such a minor role for our Western Public interviewees? Given Western Flagship's reputation for a party-oriented undergraduate lifestyle, it would be unsurprising if students for whom this is most strongly a concern would have opted to attend Christian colleges or other more conservative institutions. However, given the number of evangelical Christians in the state and the economic rationale for sending in-state students to state schools, it is more likely that on large campuses such as those in the Western Public system, religious students are able to more comfortably create spiritual homes for themselves through campus ministries such as InterVarsity Christian Fellowship or Campus Crusade for Christ.

29. There are also, quite simply, fewer students who participate in these faiths. According to national data from UCLA HERI, in 2001 23.5 percent of all students at schools like Eastern Elite identified themselves as Catholic, compared to 27.4 percent of students at schools similar to Western Flagship and 30.1 percent at other schools. There is a further drop among evangelical Christians. In these data, 11.4 percent of students at schools similar to Eastern Elite identified themselves as "born-again," versus 17.5 percent of students at schools like Western Flagship and 26.6 percent at other schools. We do not report data on our specific schools for reasons of confidentiality.

30. For descriptions of avoidance of religious commitments in college life, see Clydesdale (2007); see also Freitas (2008).

31. For descriptions of the norms of "typical" American colleges and universities, see, e.g., Bogle (2008), Kimmel (2008), Moffatt (1989), and Nathan (2005).

32. For expectations of "typical" college women, see Hamilton (2007) and Bogle (2008); see also Hamilton and Armstrong (2009).

33. This is not to say that there were no conservative men at Eastern Elite University who engaged in such provocation or were actively involved with causes such as the pro-life movement. It is notable, however, that as a group, Eastern Elite women were more consistently outspoken in style than the total group of Eastern Elite men.

34. Of the seven Eastern Elite women interviewed, two described themselves as conservative and one as Republican. Three offered their own descriptors, combining social conservatism with moderate stances on issues such as the environment: "moderate conservative," "social conservative or crunchy conservative," and "progressive conservative." The seventh interviewee described herself as "none of the above," unable to put any single label on her political views.

Of the eight Western Public women interviewed, five described themselves as wholly or partially libertarian, with three libertarians, one "conservative with libertarian sympathies," and one Republican with "libertarian leanings." The other three described themselves as conservative, though one of these hedged considerably and would more likely be best classified as "none of the above," as one Eastern Elite interviewee labeled herself.

35. For further description of the "typical" collegiate experience, see Kate Wood's unpublished manuscript, "Constructing the College Experience: Culture, Community, and Diversity in Undergraduate Life" (2012).

36. This again fits with the overall libertarian ethos prevalent on the Western Public campuses, and the contradictory nature of libertarian politics. Western Public interviewees like Samantha often described themselves as not personally supporting various issues but supporting others' rights to their own opinions on them. The overall emphasis for both men and women practicing any version of libertarianism at Western Public was on government nonintervention.

37. See Blair-Loy (2003) and Hamilton and Armstrong (2009).

38. For more on the Independent Women's Forum and its work on campus life, see http://www.iwf.org/campus. For the Clare Boothe Luce Policy Institute's Sense & Sexuality, see http://www.cblpi.org/senseandsexuality/.

39. For more on these organizations, see the Network of Enlightened Women website at http://enlightenedwomen.org/ and the Love & Fidelity Network website at http://loveandfidelity.org/.

Chapter 8: The Theory behind the Findings: How Studying College Conservatives Extends Our Understanding of Higher Education, Politics, and Culture

1. See Skowronek (2009, 348).

2. But for a highly critical view of the American academy's attenuated attention to conservatism, see Mark Lilla, "Taking the Right Seriously: Conservatism Is a Tradition, Not a Pathology" (2009).

3. For cogent arguments for why conservatism cannot be considered a fixed set of ideas or actors see Brian J. Glenn and Steven Michael Teles, *Conservatism and American Political Development* (2009), and Neil Gross, Tom Medvetz, and Rupert Russell, "The Contemporary American Conservative Movement" (2011). For examples of analyses of conservatism through the lens of movement leaders,

see, e.g., Rick Perlstein, *Before the Storm: Barry Goldwater and the Unmaking of the American Consensus* (2001), and Farber, *The Rise and Fall of Modern American Conservatism* (2010).

4. For information on fusionism, see, e.g., Himmelstein, *To the Right* (1990), and John Micklethwait and Adrian Wooldridge, *The Right Nation: Conservative Power in America* (2004).

5. On conservative think tanks, see Medvetz, *Think Tanks in America* (2012). For an example of organizational acumen in creating a conservative legal movement, including the establishment of the Federalist Society, see Teles, *The Rise of the Conservative Legal Movement* (2008).

6. See Lisa McGirr, *Suburban Warriors: The Origins of the New American Right* (2001). Isaac Martin and colleagues have written about tax revolts. See, e.g., Martin (2008).

7. On creationists, see Amy Binder, *Contentious Curricula: Afrocentrism and Creationism in American Public Schools* (2002). On conservative African Americans, see Corey Fields, "Multicultural Conservatives" (2009). On women on the right, see Schreiber, *Righting Feminism* (2008), and Rebecca E. Klatch, *Women of the New Right* (1987). The earliest scholarly book to come out about the Tea Party and its institutional backers is Skocpol and Williamson, *The Tea Party and the Remaking of Republican Conservatism* (2012).

8. The exact styles of liberals and conservatives will very likely not be identical on each campus, however, since (1) liberals are not plugged in to the same national-level repertoires as conservative students are and (2) liberals may well have a different sense of their place on campus (which of course is in part due to national discourses). We would, however, anticipate seeing systematic variation in liberal style by campus owing to the influence of campus-level variables—that is, we would expect liberals at Western Public to enact different styles from those at Eastern Elite.

9. See Pascarella and Terenzini (2005).

10. Ibid.

11. See Highton (2009, 1567).

12. See Kaufman and Feldman (2004, 404).

13. Clark and Trow write of the social forces and conditions that shape student life on campus in "The Organizational Context" (1966, esp. 18).

14. On group style, see Eliasoph and Lichterman (2003). For a study of political culture, see Lichterman and Cefai (2006).

15. See Eliasoph and Lichterman (2003, 737).

16. On avoiding politics, see Eliasoph (1998). Several of our interviewees complained about the majority of their classmates being apathetic and using the "avoiding politics" style. At the other end of the spectrum, both Aldon Morris and Doug McAdam have written about such a mobilization frame for political activity in the civil rights era. See esp. Morris (1984) and McAdam (1982). For absurdist theater, see, e.g., Gitlin (1980).

17. Max Weber's *The Protestant Ethic and the Spirit of Capitalism* ([1904-5], 1985) is sociology's touchpoint text for the concept of cultural determinism.

18. Tilly (1995). See also Gross (2010, 3).

19. On the concept of "rules" of the field, see Fligstein and McAdam (2011).

20. John Evans has an excellent discussion of inconsistent ideology in his book, *Contested Reproduction: Genetic Technologies, Religion, and Public Debate* (2010).

21. Ann Swidler writes of unsettled times, during which people use culture profligately. See her "Culture in Action: Symbols and Strategies" (1986) and *Talk of Love: How Culture Matters* (2001). Ziad Munson writes specifically about college as a transition point in people's lives, a period during which lives change rapidly, making them more biographically available for political mobilization. See Munson (2010, 769).

22. For more on culture and agency even during times of maintaining a relative status quo, see Sharon Hays, "Structure and Agency and the Sticky Problem of Culture" (1994), and William H. Sewell, Jr., "A Theory of Structure: Duality, Agency, and Transformation" (1992).

23. The same style is often used for different issues, a phenomenon we look at closely in chapter 5, where, for example, we see the Western Flagship College Republicans use the provocative style to confront liberals about affirmative action one year but about national security issues the next.

24. On society as an interinstitutional field, see Friedland and Alford (1991); Duffy, Binder, and Skrentny (2010); Fligstein and McAdam (2011); Medvetz (2012); and Thornton and Ocasio (2008). When we say that "each field features a unique set of assumptions . . . for what is suitable thought and action," we do not mean that all assumptions are held by all members of the field. We mean that they are available to those in the field.

25. Hallett (2010); Hallett and Ventresca (2006). See also Fine (1984) and Binder (2007).

26. Powell and Colvyas (2008, 2).

27. For more on symbolic boundaries generally see Lamont (1992). For more on symbolic boundaries within higher education, see Stuber (2009). For one of the most powerful statements on how education's institutional effects "charter" certain identities, see Meyer (1977).

28. For more on this, see Bourdieu and Johnson (1993) and Naidoo (2004).

29. A good illustration of how much people care about universities' position in the relational field of higher education can be found in the skirmishes following the release of the National Research Council's university rankings in October 2010. For an example, see Jason Thomas Parker, "Let's Make Rankings That Matter" (2010). For a theoretical treatment of rankings, see Espeland and Sauder (2007).

30. For a brief overview of the expansion of, and stratification within, Amer-

ican higher education, see Ann L. Mullen, *Degrees of Inequality: Culture, Class, and Gender in American Higher Education* (2010, esp. 4–9).

31. On human capital, see Arum and Roksa (2011). On universities' contributions to status cultures, see DiMaggio and Mohr (1985).

32. We do not address the much larger literature on class mobility here but rather the more restricted subject of class *cultures*. For excellent reading on how elite higher education produces class cultures, see Bowen and Bok (1998), Karabel (2005), Massey (2003), and Stevens (2007).

33. See Clydesdale (2007) and Nathan (2005). William Damon also writes about young people's "directionless drift" while in college, away from academics, politics, or other senses of purpose in *The Path to Purpose: Helping Our Children Find Their Calling in Life* (2008).

34. As Paul DiMaggio nicely pointed out to us, this is not to say that all Eastern Elite conservatives are miniature versions of F. Scott Fitzgerald's Jay Gatsby who must reinvent themselves in the manner of the elite. In fact, we see this pattern of self-socialization into adulthood even among students who are born to that style, insofar as they model their behavior on older versions of themselves.

35. In Huntsman's exit speech following the 2012 New Hampshire primary, he characterized the problem facing American conservatism using language that could have come from the lips of any of the Eastern Elite College Republicans leaders we spoke with: "At its core, the Republican Party is a party of ideas, but the current toxic forum for political discourse does not help our cause, and it's just one of the many reasons the American people have lost trust in their elected leaders." Quoted in Henneberger (2012).

36. See, e.g., Frum (2012).

37. For just one example of this type of exchange, see this *New York* magazine online piece on Mitt Romney's super-PAC's Florida ads, then a Reuters article describing Newt Gingrich's response as those ads followed him to the next primary in Nevada—"in a defiant news conference after the Nevada vote, Gingrich said he had no choice but to go negative to keep pace with Romney's 'level of ruthlessness and the level of dishonesty.'" For the latter quote, see Krasny (2012). On Romney's super-PAC ads, see Benson and Giles (2012).

38. As David Meyer (2012) has pointed out, it is difficult to pin down exactly where the Tea Party stands on numerous key issues, such as immigration. This would leave those most interested in capturing the hearts and minds of Tea Partiers stuck in the nebulous territory of "values" and "ideals" rather than discussions of specific policy recommendations and ideas. One of the few areas where the Tea Party appears most clear—taxation—brought forth some of the more specific talking points from 2012 Republican candidates (for example, Herman Cain's 9-9-9 tax plan).

References

The 9/12 Project. http://the912project.com/ (accessed February 28, 2012).

Adler, Patricia A., and Peter Adler. 1998. *Peer Power: Preadolescent Culture and Identity*. New Brunswick, NJ: Rutgers University Press.

Alba, Richard D. 1990. *Ethnic Identity: The Transformation of White America*. New Haven, CT: Yale University Press.

Andrew, John A. 1997. *The Other Side of the Sixties: Young Americans for Freedom and the Rise of Conservative Politics*. New Brunswick, NJ: Rutgers University Press.

Armstrong, Elizabeth A., and Laura Hamilton. 2010. "How and Why Some Women Benefit More from College Than Others: An Organizational Approach to College Experiences and Outcomes." Unpublished manuscript, University of Michigan, Ann Arbor.

———. Forthcoming. *Partying and Privilege: Women's Pathways through an American University*. Cambridge, MA: Harvard University Press.

Arum, Richard, and Josipa Roksa. 2011. *Academically Adrift: Limited Learning on College Campuses*. Chicago: University of Chicago Press.

Astin, Alexander W. 1993. *What Matters in College? Four Critical Years Revisited*. San Francisco, CA: Jossey-Bass.

Bearman, Peter, and Hannah Bruckner. 2001. "Promising the Future: Virginity Pledges and First Intercourse." *American Journal of Sociology* 106:859–12.

Bellah, Robert, et al. 1986. *Habits of the Heart: Individualism and Commitment in American Life*. New York: Harper & Row.

Beller, Emily. 2009. "Bringing Intergenerational Social Mobility Research into the Twenty-first Century: Why Mothers Matter." *American Sociological Review* 74:507–28.

Bennett, William J. 1984. *To Reclaim a Legacy: A Report on the Humanities in Higher Education*. Washington, DC: National Endowment for the Humanities.

Benson, Eric, and Matt Giles. 2012. "Three of Romney's Most Devastating Florida Ads, and Why They Worked." http://nymag.com/daily/intel/2012/02/romneys-negative-florida-ad.html (accessed February 15, 2012).

Berman, John. 2011. "Sarah Palin's 'Crosshairs' Ad Dominates Gabrielle Giffords Debate." http://abcnews.go.com/Politics/sarah-palins-crosshairs-ad-focus-gabrielle-giffords-debate/story?id=12576437 (accessed April 12, 2011).

Bérubé, Michael. 2006. *What's Liberal about the Liberal Arts? Classroom Politics and "Bias" in Higher Education*. New York: W. W. Norton.

Binder, Amy. 2002. *Contentious Curricula: Afrocentrism and Creationism in American Public Schools*. Princeton, NJ: Princeton University Press.

———. 2007. "For Love and Money: Organizations' Creative Responses to Multiple Environmental Logics." *Theory and Society* 36:547–71.

Black, Jim Nelson. 2004. *Freefall of the American University: How Our Colleges Are Corrupting the Minds and Morals of the Next Generation*. Nashville, TN: WND Books.

Blackwell, Morton. 2009. "The Leadership Institute Connection to James O'Keefe." http://www.campusreform.org/blog/the-leadership-institute-connection-to-james-okeefe (accessed February 27, 2012).

Blair-Loy, Mary. 2003. *Competing Devotions: Career and Family among Women Executives*. Cambridge, MA: Harvard University Press.

Bloom, Allan David. 1988. *The Closing of the American Mind*. New York: Simon and Schuster.

Blumenthal, Max. 2009. *Republican Gomorrah: Inside the Movement That Shattered the Party*. New York: Nation Books.

Bogle, Kathleen A. 2008. *Hooking Up: Sex, Dating, and Relationships on Campus*. New York: New York University Press.

Bourdieu, Pierre. 1977. "Cultural Reproduction and Social Reproduction." In *Power and Ideology in Education*, ed. J. K. and A. H. Halsey, 487–511. New York: Oxford University Press.

Bourdieu, Pierre, and Randal Johnson. 1993. *The Field of Cultural Production: Essays on Art and Literature*. New York: Columbia University Press.

Bowen, William G., and Derek Curtis Bok. 1998. *The Shape of the River: Long-Term Consequences of Considering Race in College and University Admissions*. Princeton, NJ: Princeton University Press.

Boyer, Ernest L., and Carnegie Foundation for the Advancement of Teaching. 1987. *College: The Undergraduate Experience in America*. New York: Harper and Row.

Brannon, Robert S. 1976. "The Male Sex Role: Our Culture's Blueprint of Manhood, and What It's Done for Us Lately." In *The Forty-nine Percent Majority:*

The Male Sex Role, ed. Deborah S. David and Robert Brannon, 1–45. Reading, MA: Addison-Wesley.

Brint, Steven. 2002. "The Rise of the Practical Arts." In *The Future of the City of Intellect: The Changing American University*, ed. S. Brint, 231–59. Stanford, CA: Stanford University Press.

———. 2009. "The 'Collective Mind' at Work: A Decade in the Life of U.S. Sociology of Education." Plenary lecture, Portuguese Sociology of Education Society, Lisbon, January 23, 2009.

Brooks, David. 1996. *Backward and Upward: The New Conservative Writing.* New York: Vintage Books.

Buckley, William F. 1951. *God and Man at Yale.* Chicago: Regnery.

Bush, Melanie. 2005. "The Movement for an 'Academic Bill of Rights': A New Assault on Academic Freedom." *North American Dialogue: Newsletter for the Society for the Anthropology of North America* 8:16–19.

Campolo, Tony, and William Willimon. 2002. *The Survival Guide for Christians on Campus: How to Be Students and Disciples at the Same Time.* West Monroe, LA: Howard Publishing.

Campus Reform Website. http://www.campusreform.org/ (accessed February 27, 2012).

———. "About CLP." http://www.campusreform.org/about/about-clp (accessed February 27, 2012).

———. "Frequently Asked Questions." http://www.campusreform.org/about/faq (accessed February 27, 2012).

———. "Help." http://www.campusreform.org/about/help (accessed February 27, 2012).

———. "Manuals and Writings." http://www.campusreform.org/resources/manuals-and-writings (accessed February 27, 2012).

———. "Publicity Resources." http://www.campusreform.org/resources/publicity-resources (accessed February 27, 2012).

Carrigan, Tim, Bob Connell, and John Lee. 1985. "Towards a New Sociology of Masculinity." *Theory and Society* 14:551–604.

Cary, Mary Kate. 2010. "The New Conservative Feminist Movement." http://politics.usnews.com/opinion/articles/2010/06/23/the-new-conservative-feminist-movement.html (accessed August 9, 2010).

Chafets, Zev. 2011. "Stinger: James O'Keefe's Greatest Hits." http://www.nytimes.com/2011/07/31/magazine/stinger-james-okeefes-greatest-hits.html (accessed February 27, 2012).

Chambers, Jason E. 2003. "Smashing Affirmative Action: Bake Sales." http://archive.frontpagemag.com/readArticle.aspx?ARTID=15903 (accessed June 20, 2011).

Charles, Camille Zubrinsky, Mary Fischer, Margarita Mooney, and Douglas Massey. 2009. *Taming the River: Negotiating the Academic, Financial, and*

Social Currents in Selective Colleges and Universities. Princeton, NJ: Princeton University Press.

Cherry, Conrad, Betty A. DeBerg, and Amanda Porterfield. 2001. *Religion on Campus*. Chapel Hill: University of North Carolina Press.

Clare Boothe Luce Policy Institute. "Sense & Sexuality." http://www.cblpi.org/senseandsexuality/ (accessed July 28, 2011).

Clark, Burton R. 1992. *The Distinctive College*. New Brunswick, NJ: Transaction Publishers.

Clark, Burton R., and Martin Trow. 1966. "The Organizational Context." In *College Peer Groups*, ed. T. Newcomb and E. Wilson, 17–70. Chicago: Aldine.

Cloud, John. 2006. "Campaign '04: The Right's New Wing." http://www.time.com/time/magazine/article/0,9171,994964,00.html (accessed February 27, 2012).

Clydesdale, Tim. 2007. *The First Year Out: Understanding American Teens after High School*. Chicago: University of Chicago Press.

CNN.com. 2009. "Rep. Wilson Shouts, 'You Lie' to Obama during Speech." September 9. http://articles.cnn.com/2009-09-09/politics/joe.wilson_1_rep-wilson-illegal-immigrants-outburst (accessed January 24, 2012).

———. 2011. "Campus Erupts over Campus Republicans Bake Sale Plans." September 25. http://www.cnn.com/2011/09/25/us/california-racial-bake-sale/index.html (accessed December 5, 2011).

Colapinto, John. 2003. "The Young Hipublicans." http://www.nytimes.com/2003/05/25/magazine/25REPUBLICANS.html (accessed February 27, 2012).

Colby, Anne. 2003. *Educating Citizens: Preparing America's Undergraduates for Lives of Moral and Civic Responsibility*. San Francisco, CA: Jossey-Bass.

———. 2007. *Educating for Democracy: Preparing Undergraduates for Responsible Political Engagement*. San Francisco and Stanford, CA: Jossey-Bass and Carnegie Foundation for the Advancement of Teaching.

Coleman, James, et al. 1966. *Equality of Educational Opportunity*. Washington, DC: U.S. Department of Health, Education and Welfare, Office of Education.

Coleman, James Samuel. 1961. *The Adolescent Society: The Social Life of the Teenager and Its Impact on Education*. New York: Free Press.

College Guide. "About CollegeGuide.org." http://www.collegeguide.org/about_cg.aspx (accessed February 27, 2012).

Collegiate Network. http://www.collegiatenetwork.org/ (accessed February 27, 2012).

———. "About the Collegiate Network." http://www.collegiatenetwork.org/about/ (accessed February 27, 2012).

———. "Professional Journalist Development." http://www.collegiatenetwork.org/internships/ (accessed February 27, 2012).

————. "Apply for the Eric Breindel Collegiate Journalism Award." http://www
.collegiatenetwork.org/news/303:apply-for-the-eric-breindel-collegiate
-journalism-award (accessed July 22, 2011).

Connell, R.W. 1987. *Gender and Power: Society, the Person, and Sexual Politics*.
Stanford, CA: Stanford University Press.

————. 2005. *Masculinities*, 2nd ed. Berkeley: University of California Press.

Coyle, Patrick X. 2009. "Campus Conservative Battleplan: Your Month-by-
Month Plan to Activism on Campus." http://www.yaf.org/uploadedFiles/
Webpages/Students/2009%20YAF%20Battleplan%20Final.pdf (accessed
July 7, 2011).

Coyle, Patrick X., and Ron Robinson. 2005. *The Conservative Guide to Campus
Activism*, 2nd ed. Herndon, VA: Young America's Foundation.

Damon, William. 2008. *The Path to Purpose: Helping Our Children Find Their
Calling in Life*. New York: Free Press.

Dartmouth Review. "About." http://s14929.gridserver.com/about/ (accessed January 27, 2012).

Daum, Meghan. 2010. "Sarah Palin, Feminist." http://www.latimes.com/news/
opinion/commentary/la-oe-0520-daum-fword-20100520,0,4933552.column
(accessed August 9, 2010).

Davidman, Lynn. 1991. *Tradition in a Rootless World: Women Turn to Orthodox Judaism*. Berkeley: University of California Press.

Davis, Julie Hirschfield. 2011. "Debt Challenge Makes for Two Lonely Republicans." http://www.businessweek.com/magazine/content/11_25/
b4233031734925.htm (accessed January 24, 2012).

DiMaggio, Paul. 2003. "The Myth of Culture War: The Disparity between Private Opinion and Public Politics." In *The Fractious Nation? Unity and Division in Contemporary American Life*, ed. J. Rieder, 79–97. Berkeley: University of California Press.

DiMaggio, Paul, John Evans, and Bethany Bryson. 1996. "Have Americans' Social Attitudes Become More Polarized?" *American Journal of Sociology*
102:690–755.

DiMaggio, Paul, and John Mohr. 1985. "Cultural Capital, Educational Attainment, and Marital Selection." *American Journal of Sociology* 90:1231–61.

Domsic, Melissa. 2006. "'Catch an Immigrant' Game Fires Up Debate on Campuses." http://articles.cnn.com/2006-10-23/politics/CNNU.msu.immi-
grant_1_illegal-immigration-student-group-freedom (accessed January 26,
2012).

Douthat, Ross. 2005. *Privilege: Harvard and the Education of the Ruling Class*.
New York: Hyperion.

D'Souza, Dinesh. 1992. *Illiberal Education: The Politics of Race and Sex on
Campus*. New York: Vintage Books.

————. 2007. "Recollections of a Campus Renegade." In *Why I Turned Right:*

Leading Baby Boom Conservatives Chronicle their Political Journeys, ed. M. Eberstadt, 85–108. New York: Threshold Editions.

Duffy, Meghan, Amy Binder, and John Skrentny. 2010. "Elite Status and Social Change: Using Field Analysis to Explain Policy Formation and Implementation." *Social Problems* 57:49–73.

Ecklund, Elaine Howard. 2007. "Religion and Spirituality among University Scientists." Social Science Research Council Essay Forum on the Religious Engagements of American Undergraduates. http://religion.ssrc.org/reforum/Ecklund.pdf (accessed February 27, 2012).

Ehrlich, Thomas, and Anne Colby. 2004. "Political Bias in Undergraduate Education." *Liberal Education* 90:36–39.

Eliasoph, Nina. 1998. *Avoiding Politics: How Americans Produce Apathy in Everyday Life*. New York: Cambridge University Press.

Eliasoph, Nina, and Paul Lichterman. 2003. "Culture in Interaction." *American Journal of Sociology* 108:735–94.

Espeland, Wendy, and Michael Sauder. 2007. "Rankings and Reactivity: How Public Measures Recreate Social Worlds." *American Journal of Sociology* 113:1–40.

Evans, John H. 2003. "Have Americans' Attitudes Become More Polarized? An Update." *Social Science Quarterly* 84:71–90.

———. 2010. *Contested Reproduction: Genetic Technologies, Religion, and Public Debate*. Chicago: University of Chicago Press.

Farber, David R. 2010. *The Rise and Fall of Modern American Conservatism: A Short History*. Princeton, NJ: Princeton University Press.

Feldman, Kenneth A., and Theodore Newcomb. 1994. *The Impact of College on Students*. New Brunswick, NJ: Transaction Publishers.

Fenstermaker, Sarah, and Candace West, eds. 2002. *Doing Gender, Doing Difference: Inequality, Power, and Institutional Change*. New York: Routledge.

Fields, Corey. 2009. "Multicultural Conservatives." In *Culture Wars: An Encyclopedia of Issues, Voices, and Viewpoints*, ed. R. Chapman, 373. Armonk, NY: M. E. Sharpe.

Fine, Gary Alan. 1984. "Negotiated Orders and Organizational Cultures." *Annual Review of Sociology* 10:239–62.

Fligstein, Neil, and Doug McAdam. 2011. "Toward a General Theory of Strategic Action Fields." *Sociological Theory* 29:1–26.

Fligstein, Neil. 2001. "Social Skill and the Theory of Fields." *Sociological Theory* 19:105–25.

Fordham, Signithia and John U. Ogbu. 1986. "Black Students' School Success: Coping with the Burden of 'Acting White.'" *Urban Review* 18:176–206.

Fosse, Ethan, Jeremy Freese, and Neil Gross. 2012. "Political Liberalism and Graduate School Attendance: A Longitudinal Analysis." Working paper, University of British Columbia, Vancouver.

Fosse, Ethan, and Neil Gross. 2012. "Why Are Professors Liberal?" *Theory and Society* 41:127–68.

Fox News. 2003. "Berkeley Group Holds Anti-Affirmative Action Bake Sale." http://www.foxnews.com/story/0,2933,79811,00.html (accessed June 1, 2011).

Frankenberg, Ruth. 1993. *White Women, Race Matters: The Social Construction of Whiteness*. Minneapolis: University of Minnesota Press.

Freitas, Donna. 2008. *Sex and the Soul: Juggling Sexuality, Spirituality, Romance, and Religion on America's College Campuses*. New York: Oxford University Press.

Friedland, Roger, and Robert Alford. 1991. "Bringing Society Back In: Symbols, Practices, and Institutional Contradictions." In *The New Institutionalism in Organizational Analysis*, ed. W. P. Powell and P. DiMaggio, 232–63. Chicago: University of Chicago Press.

Frum, David. 2012. "Mitt Romney's 'Severely' Bad Moves." http://www.cnn.com/2012/02/13/opinion/frum-romney-moves/index.html (accessed February 15, 2012).

Ganzeboom, Harry B. G., Paul M. De Graaf, and Donald J. Treiman. 1992. "A Standard International Socio-economic Index of Occupational Status." *Social Science Research* 21:1–56.

Gaztambide-Fernandez, Rubén A. 2009. *The Best of the Best: Becoming Elite at an American Boarding School*. Cambridge, MA: Harvard University Press.

Gitlin, Todd. 1980. *The Whole World Is Watching: Mass Media in the Making & Unmaking of the New Left*. Berkeley: University of California Press.

Glenn, Brian J., and Steven Michael Teles. 2009. *Conservatism and American Political Development*. New York: Oxford University Press.

Goldberg, Jonah. 2010. *Proud to Be Right: Voices of the Next Conservative Generation*. New York: Harper Paperbacks.

Goldman, Ari. 1991. *The Search for God at Harvard*. New York: Ballantine Books.

Graham, Fiona. 2005. *Playing at Politics: An Ethnography of the Oxford Union*. Edinburgh: Dunedin Academic Press.

Granfield, Robert. 1991. "Making It by Faking It: Working-Class Students in an Elite Academic Environment." *Journal of Contemporary Ethnography* 20:331–51.

Granfield, Robert, and Thomas Koenig. 1992. "Learning Collective Eminence: Harvard Law School and the Social Production of Elite Lawyers." *Sociological Quarterly* 33:503–20.

Grigsby, Mary. 2009. *College Life through the Eyes of Students*. Albany, NY: SUNY Press.

Gross, Neil, and Solon Simmons. 2007. "The Social and Political Views of American Professors." Working paper, Harvard University, Cambridge, MA.

Gross, Neil, Tom Medvetz, and Rupert Russell. 2011. "The Contemporary American Conservative Movement." *Annual Review of Sociology* 37:325–54.

Gross, Neil. 2010. "Charles Tilly and American Pragmatism." *American Sociologist* 41:337–57.

Gross, Neil. Forthcoming. *Why Are Professors Liberal and Why Do Conservatives Care?* Cambridge, MA: Harvard University Press.

Hallett, Tim. 2010. "The Myth Incarnate: Recoupling Processes, Turmoil, and Inhabited Institutions in an Urban Elementary School." *American Sociological Review* 75:52–74.

Hallett, Tim, and Marc Ventresca. 2006. "Inhabited Institutions: Social Interactions and Organizational Forms in Gouldner's *Patterns of Industrial Bureaucracy*." *Theory and Society* 35:213–36.

Hamilton, Laura. 2007. "Trading on Heterosexuality: College Women's Gender Strategies and Homophobia." *Gender & Society* 21:145–72.

Hamilton, Laura, and Elizabeth A. Armstrong. 2009. "Gendered Sexuality in Young Adulthood: Double Binds and Flawed Options." *Gender & Society* 23:589–616.

Hays, Sharon. 1994. "Structure and Agency and the Sticky Problem of Culture." *Sociological Theory* 12:57–72.

Henneberger, Melinda. 2012. "Jon Huntsman Lectures GOP on Civility Even He Wouldn't Have Been Able to Deliver." http://www.washingtonpost.com/blogs/she-the-people/post/jon-huntsman-lectures-gop-on-civility-even-he-wouldnt-have-been-able-to-deliver/2012/01/16/gIQAN4OX3P_blog.html (accessed February 15, 2012).

HERI (Higher Education Research Institute). 2001. *College Freshmen More Politically Liberal than in the Past, UCLA Survey Reveals: The American Freshman National Norms for 2001.* Los Angeles: UCLA Higher Education Research Institute.

———. 2007. *The American Freshman: Forty Year Trends.* Los Angeles: UCLA Higher Education Research Institute.

———. 2010. *The American Freshman: National Norms Fall 2009 Research Brief.* Los Angeles: UCLA Higher Education Research Institute.

Highton, Benjamin. 2009. "Revisiting the Relationship between Educational Attainment and Political Sophistication." *Journal of Politics* 71:1564–76.

Himmelstein, Jerome L. 1990. *To the Right: The Transformation of American Conservatism.* Berkeley: University of California Press.

Holland, Dorothy C., and Margaret A. Eisenhart. 1990. *Educated in Romance: Women, Achievement, and College Culture.* Chicago: University of Chicago Press.

Horowitz, Craig. 1999. "The Connection Man." http://nymag.com/nymetro/news/media/features/916/ (accessed February 27, 2012).

Horowitz, David. 2006. *The Professors: The 101 Most Dangerous Academics in America*. Washington, DC: Regnery.

———. 2007. *Indoctrination U.: The Left's War against Academic Freedom*. New York: Encounter Books.

Horowitz, Helen Lefkowitz. 1987. *Campus Life: Undergraduate Cultures from the End of the Eighteenth Century to the Present*. New York: A. A. Knopf.

Horwitz, Robert. 2011. "Richard Hofstadter's 'Paranoid Style' Revisited: The Tea Party, Past as Prologue." Working Paper, Department of Communication, University of California, San Diego, La Jolla, CA.

Howard, Adam, and Rubén A. Gaztambide-Fernandez. 2010. *Educating Elites: Class Privilege and Educational Advantage*. Lanham, MD: Rowman & Littlefield.

Independent Women's Forum. http://www.iwf.org/ (accessed July 28, 2011).

Institute for Humane Studies. "Humane Studies Fellowships." http://www.theihs .org/humane-studies-fellowships (accessed February 27, 2012).

Intercollegiate Studies Institute. "Cicero's Podium." http://www.isi.org/lectures/ content/cicero_bro.pdf (accessed February 27, 2012).

———. "Conferences." http://home.isi.org/programs/conferences (accessed February 27, 2012).

———. "Frequently Asked Questions." http://home.isi.org/about/faq (accessed February 27, 2012).

———. "ISI in Depth." http://home.isi.org/about (accessed February 27, 2012).

———. "Lectures and Debates." http://www.isi.org/lecture.aspx (accessed July 27, 2011).

Intercollegiate Studies Institute Facebook Page. https://www.facebook.com/ pages/Intercollegiate-Studies-Institute/108520352505838 (accessed February 27, 2012).

Karabel, Jerome. 2005. *The Chosen: The Hidden History of Admission and Exclusion at Harvard, Yale, and Princeton*. Boston: Houghton Mifflin.

Kaufman, Peter, and Kenneth Feldman. 2004. "Forming Identities in College: A Sociological Approach." *Research in Higher Education* 45:463–96.

Keohane, Nannerl O. 2006. *Higher Ground: Ethics and Leadership in the Modern University*. Durham, NC: Duke University Press.

Kern, David. 2011. "An Interview with the New President of ISI." http://circe institute.com/2011/06/an-interview-with-the-new-president-of-isi/ (accessed February 27, 2012).

Khan, Shamus. 2011. *Privilege: The Making of an Adolescent Elite at St. Paul's School*. Princeton, NJ: Princeton University Press.

Kimmel, Michael S. 2008. *Guyland: The Perilous World Where Boys Become Men*. New York: Harper.

Klatch, Rebecca E. 1987. *Women of the New Right*. Philadelphia, PA: Temple University Press.

————. 1999. *A Generation Divided: The New Left, the New Right, and the 1960s.* Berkeley: University of California Press.

Knox, William E., Paul Lindsay, and Mary Kolb. 1993. *Does College Make a Difference? Long-Term Changes in Activities and Attitudes.* Westport, CT: Greenwood Press.

Kors, Alan Charles, and Harvey Silverglate. 1998. *The Shadow University: The Betrayal of Liberty on America's Campuses.* New York: Free Press.

Kozol, Jonathan. 2005. *The Shame of the Nation: The Restoration of Apartheid Schooling in America.* New York: Crown.

Krasny, Ros. 2012. "Anger, Disarray and Double Defeat Take Toll on Gingrich." http://www.reuters.com/article/2012/02/06/us-usa-campaign-gingrich-idUS-TRE8140LH20120206 (accessed February 15, 2012).

Kuh, George D. 2010. *Student Success in College: Creating Conditions That Matter.* San Francisco, CA: Jossey-Bass.

Labaree, David F. 1997. *How to Succeed in School without Really Learning: The Credentials Race in American Education.* New Haven, CT: Yale University Press.

Lamont, Michèle. 1992. *Money, Morals, and Manners: The Culture of the French and American Upper-Middle Class.* Chicago: University of Chicago Press.

————. 1999. *The Cultural Territories of Race: Black and White Boundaries.* Chicago: University of Chicago Press.

————. 2000. *The Dignity of Working Men: Morality and the Boundaries of Race, Class, and Immigration.* New York: Russell Sage Foundation; Cambridge, MA: Harvard University Press.

————. 2009. *How Professors Think: Inside the Curious World of Academic Judgment.* Cambridge, MA: Harvard University Press.

Lareau, Annette. 2003. *Unequal Childhoods: Class, Race, and Family Life.* Berkeley: University of California Press.

Leadership Institute. "CampusReform.org to Challenge Dominance of College Leftists." http://www.leadershipinstitute.org/news/?NR=1522 (accessed February 27, 2012).

————. "F.M. Kirby Training Center." http://www.leadershipinstitute.org/aboutus/kirby.cfm (accessed February 27, 2012).

————. "Mission." http://www.leadershipinstitute.org/aboutus/mission.cfm (accessed February 27, 2012).

————. "Morton Blackwell." http://www.leadershipinstitute.org/aboutus/Morton.cfm (accessed February 27, 2012).

————. "The Leadership Institute Trains over 400 Students in Conjunction with the 9/12 Project March on Washington." http://www.leadershipinstitute.org/news/?NR=1509 (accessed February 27, 2012).

————. "Training." http://www.leadershipinstitute.org/training/ (accessed February 27, 2012).

————. 2010 Form 990. http://www.leadershipinstitute.org/aboutus/Files/2010 Form990.pdf (accessed February 27, 2012).

Leo, John. 2007. "No Free Speech, Please—This Is Columbia." http://www.mind ingthecampus.com/forum/2007/09/no_free_speech_please_this_is.html (accessed August 29, 2011).

Lichterman, Paul, and Daniel Cefai. 2006. "The Idea of Political Culture." In *The Oxford Handbook of Contextual Political Analysis*, ed. R. E. Goodin and C. Tilly, 392–414. New York: Oxford University Press.

Lilla, Mark. 2009. "Taking the Right Seriously: Conservatism Is a Tradition, Not a Pathology." http://chronicle.com/article/Taking-the-Right-Seriously/48333/ (accessed January 30, 2012).

Lind, Michael. 1995. "Why Intellectual Conservatism Died." *Dissent* 42:42–47.

————. 2009. "Intellectual Conservatism, RIP." http://www.salon. com/2009/09/22/neoconservatism/ (accessed January 24, 2012).

Love & Fidelity Network Website. http://loveandfidelity.org/ (accessed February 27, 2012).

Luker, Kristin. 1984. *Abortion and the Politics of Motherhood*. Berkeley: University of California Press.

Mansfield, Harvey Claflin. 2006. *Manliness*. New Haven, CT: Yale University Press.

Maranto, Robert, Richard E. Redding, and Richard M. Hess. 2009. "The PC Academy Debate: Questions Not Asked." In *The Politically Correct University: Problems, Scope and Reform*, ed. R. Maranto, R. E. Redding, and R. E. Hess, 3–14. Washington, DC: American Enterprise Institute.

Martin, Isaac William. 2008. *The Permanent Tax Revolt: How the Property Tax Transformed American Politics*. Stanford, CA: Stanford University Press.

Massey, Douglas S., Camille Z. Charles, Garvey F. Lundy, and Mary J. Fischer. 2003. *The Source of the River: The Social Origins of Freshmen at America's Selective Colleges and Universities*. Princeton, NJ: Princeton University Press.

Mayrl, Damon, and Freeden Oeur. 2009. "Religion and Higher Education: Current Knowledge and Directions for Future Research." *Journal for the Scientific Study of Religion* 48:260–75.

McAdam, Doug. 1982. *Political Process and the Development of Black Insurgency, 1930–1970*. Chicago: University of Chicago Press.

————. 1988. *Freedom Summer*. New York: Oxford University Press.

McCall, Leslie, and Jeff Manza. 2011. "Class Differences in Social and Political Attitudes in the United States." In *The Oxford Handbook of American Public Opinion and the Media*, ed. L. Jacobs and R. Shapiro, 552–70. New York: Oxford University Press.

McGirr, Lisa. 2001. *Suburban Warriors: The Origins of the New American Right*. Princeton, NJ: Princeton University Press.

Media Matters Action Network. "Intercollegiate Studies Institute." http://media

mattersaction.org/transparency/organization/Intercollegiate_Studies_Insti-tute/financials (accessed February 27, 2012).

———. "The Leadership Institute." http://mediamattersaction.org/transparency/organization/Leadership_Institute/funders (accessed February 27, 2012).

———. "The Lynde and Harry Bradley Foundation." http://mediamattersaction.org/transparency/organization/The_Lynde_and_Harry_Bradley_Foundation/grants (accessed February 27, 2012).

———. "Young America's Foundation." http://mediamattersaction.org/transparency/organization/Young_America_s_Foundation/connections (accessed February 27, 2012).

———. "Young America's Foundation." http://mediamattersaction.org/transparency/organization/Young_America_s_Foundation/financials (accessed February 27, 2012).

———. "Young America's Foundation." http://mediamattersaction.org/transparency/organization/Young_America_s_Foundation/funders (accessed February 27, 2012).

Medvetz, Tom. 2012. *The Rise of Think Tanks in America: Merchants of Policy and Power.* Chicago: University of Chicago Press.

Meyer, David. 2012. "Populists and Plutocrats: The Tea Party and Protest Politics in Contemporary America." Presented at the Workshop for the Study of Conservative Movements and Conservatism, University of California, San Diego, La Jolla, February 9.

Meyer, John. 1977. "The Effects of Education as an Institution." *American Journal of Sociology* 83:55–77.

Micklethwait, John, and Adrian Wooldridge. 2004. *The Right Nation: Conservative Power in America.* New York: Penguin Press.

Moffatt, Michael. 1989. *Coming of Age in New Jersey: College and American Culture.* New Brunswick, NJ: Rutgers University Press.

Morris, Aldon D. 1984. *The Origins of the Civil Rights Movement: Black Communities Organizing for Change.* New York: Free Press.

Mullen, Ann L. 2010. *Degrees of Inequality: Culture, Class, and Gender in American Higher Education.* Baltimore, MD: Johns Hopkins University Press.

Munson, Ziad. 2010. "Mobilizing on Campus: Conservative Movements and Today's College Students." *Sociological Forum* 25:769–86.

Naidoo, Rajani. 2004. "Fields and Institutional Strategy: Bourdieu on the Relationship between Higher Education, Inequality and Society." *British Journal of Sociology of Education* 25:457–71.

Nathan, Rebekah. 2005. *My Freshman Year: What a Professor Learned by Becoming a College Student.* New York: Penguin.

Network of Enlightened Women Website. http://enlightenedwomen.org/ (accessed February 27, 2012).

New York Times. "Times Topics: James O'Keefe." http://topics.nytimes.com/top/
reference/timestopics/people/o/james_okeefe/index.html (accessed February
27, 2012).

Newport, Frank. 2010. "Republicans Remain Disproportionately White and
Religious." http://www.gallup.com/poll/142826/republicans-remain-dispro
portionately-white-religious.aspx (accessed February 27, 2012).

Parker, Jason Thomas. 2010. "Let's Make Rankings That Matter." http://
chronicle.com/article/Lets-Make-Rankings-That/124802 (accessed January
30, 2012).

Pascarella, Ernest T., and Patrick Terenzini. 2005. *How College Affects Students:
A Third Decade of Research.* San Francisco, CA: Jossey-Bass.

Perlstein, Rick. 2001. *Before the Storm: Barry Goldwater and the Unmaking of
the American Consensus.* New York: Hill and Wang.

Perrin, Andrew, Steven Tepper, Neal Caren, and Sally Morris. 2011. "Cultures of
the Tea Party." *Contexts* 10 (2): 74–75.

Perry, Evelyn M., and Elizabeth A. Armstrong. 2007. "Evangelicals on Campus."
Social Science Research Council Essay Forum on the Religious Engagements of
American Undergraduates. http://religion.ssrc.org/reforum/Perry_Armstrong
.pdf (accessed February 27, 2012).

Perry, Pamela. 2002. *Shades of White: White Kids and Racial Identities in High
School.* Durham, NC: Duke University Press.

Pew Forum on Religion and Public Life. 2008. "How the Faithful Voted." http://
pewforum.org/Politics-and-Elections/How-the-Faithful-Voted.aspx (accessed
February 27, 2012).

Pew Research Center. 2011. "Beyond Red vs. Blue: Political Typology." http://
people-press.org/2011/05/04/beyond-red-vs-blue-the-political-typology/ (accessed May 20, 2011).

Phillips Foundation. "About Us." http://www.thephillipsfoundation.org/#about
.cfm (accessed February 27, 2012).

Powell, Lewis F. 1971. "Confidential Memorandum: Attack of American Free
Enterprise System." http://reclaimdemocracy.org/corporate_accountability/
powell_memo_lewis.html (accessed February 27, 2012).

Powell, Walter W., and Jeannette A. Colvyas. 2008. "Microfoundations of Institutional Theory." In *The Sage Handbook of Organizational Institutionalism*,
ed. Royston Greenwood, Christine Oliver, Kerstin Sahlin, and Roy Suddaby,
276–98. Thousand Oaks, CA: Sage.

Radford, Alexandria Walton. 2009. "Where Do They Go? How Gender, Race,
and Social Class Shape High School Valedictorians' Paths to their Undergraduate Institutions." PhD diss., Princeton University, Princeton, NJ.

Reno, Jamie. 2012. "San Diego State Student Republicans Claim Bias in Class."
San Diego Union Tribune, January 9.

Reuben, Julie A. 1996. *The Making of the Modern University: Intellectual Trans-*

formation and the Marginalization of Morality. Chicago: University of Chicago Press.

Rivera, Lauren A. 2011. "Ivies, Extracurriculars, and Exclusion: Elite Employers' Use of Educational Credentials." *Research in Social Stratification and Mobility* 29:71–90.

Rojas, Fabio. 2007. *From Black Power to Black Studies: How a Radical Social Movement Became an Academic Discipline.* Baltimore, MD: Johns Hopkins University Press.

Roth, Wendy, and Jal Mehta. 2002. "The Rashomon Effect." *Sociological Methods & Research* 31:131–73.

Schreiber, Ronnee. 2008. *Righting Feminism: Conservative Women and American Politics.* New York: Oxford University Press.

———. 2009. "But Does She Speak for Me? Feminist and Conservative Women's Organizations React to Palin." Working paper, San Diego State University, San Diego, CA.

Seelye, Katharine Q., and Jeff Zeleny. 2008. "On the Defensive, Obama Calls His Words Ill-Chosen." http://www.nytimes.com/2008/04/13/us/politics/13campaign.html (accessed January 24, 2012).

Sewell, William H., Jr. 1992. "A Theory of Structure: Duality, Agency, and Transformation." *American Journal of Sociology* 98:1–29.

Skocpol, Theda, and Vanessa Williamson. 2012. *The Tea Party and the Remaking of Republican Conservatism.* New York: Oxford University Press.

Skowronek, Stephen. 2009. "Afterword: An Attenuated Reconstruction: The Conservative Turn in American Political Development." In *Conservatism and American Political Development*, ed. B. J. Glenn and S. M. Teles, 348–62. New York: Oxford University Press.

Smith, Christian. 1998. *American Evangelicalism: Embattled and Thriving.* Chicago: University of Chicago Press.

Smith, Christian, and Melinda Lundquist Denton. 2005. *Soul Searching: The Religious and Spiritual Lives of American Teenagers.* New York: Oxford University Press.

Stake, Robert E. 2000. "Case Studies." In *Handbook of Qualitative Research*, 2nd ed., ed. N. K. Denzin and Y. S. Lincoln, 236–47. Thousand Oaks, CA: Sage.

Stevens, Mitchell L. 2001. *Kingdom of Children: Culture and Controversy in the Homeschooling Movement.* Princeton, NJ: Princeton University Press.

———. 2007. *Creating a Class: College Admissions and the Education of Elites.* Cambridge, MA: Harvard University Press.

———. 2008. "Culture and Education." *Annals of the American Academy of Political and Social Science* 619:97–113.

Stevens, Mitchell, Elizabeth Armstrong, and Richard Arum. 2008. "Sieve, Incubator, Temple, Hub: Empirical and Theoretical Advances in the Sociology of Higher Education." *Annual Review of Sociology* 34:127–51.

Stevens, Mitchell, and Josipa Roksa. 2011. "The Diversity Imperative in Elite Admissions." In *Diversity in American Higher Education: Toward a More Comprehensive Approach*, ed. L. Stulberg and S. Weinberg, 63–73. New York: Routledge.

Story, Ronald. 1980. *The Forging of an Aristocracy: Harvard and the Boston Upper Class, 1800–1870*. Middletown, CT: Wesleyan University Press.

Stuber, Jenny M. 2009. "Class, Culture, and Participation in the Collegiate Extra-Curriculum." *Sociological Forum* 24:877–900.

Swidler, Ann. 1986. "Culture in Action: Symbols and Strategies." *American Sociological Review* 51:273–86.

———. 2001. *Talk of Love: How Culture Matters*. Chicago: University of Chicago Press.

Tanenhaus, Sam. 2009. *The Death of Conservatism*. New York: Random House.

Teles, Steven Michael. 2008. *The Rise of the Conservative Legal Movement: The Battle for Control of the Law*. Princeton, NJ: Princeton University Press.

Theodosopolous, Sam K. 2010. "GWU Students Protest Outside Thomas Friedman's Talk." http://gwu.campusreform.org/group/84/blog/gwu-students-protest-outside-thomas-friedmans-talk (accessed January 26, 2012).

Thornton, Patricia, and William Ocasio. 2008. "Institutional Logics." In *The Sage Handbook of Organizational Institutionalism*, ed. R. Greenwood, C. Oliver, R. Suddaby, and K. Sahlin, 99–129. Los Angeles, CA: Sage.

Tilly, Charles. 1995. *Popular Contention in Great Britain, 1758–1834*. Cambridge, MA: Harvard University Press.

Tower, Wells. 2006. "The Kids Are Far Right: Hippie Hunting, Bunny Bashing, and the New Conservatism." *Harper's Magazine*, November, 41–53.

Trow, Martin. 1979. "Aspects of Diversity in American Higher Education." In *On the Making of Americans*, ed. H. Gans et al., 271–90. Philadelphia: University of Pennsylvania Press.

U.S. Census Bureau. "Census Bureau Regions and Divisions with State FIPS Codes." http://www.census.gov/geo/www/reg_div.txt (accessed February 28, 2012).

Veblen, Thorstein. 1912. *The Theory of the Leisure Class*. New York: Macmillan.

Vogel, Kenneth P. 2010. "James O'Keefe and Accomplices Trained in Conservative Journalism." http://www.politico.com/news/stories/0110/32138.html (accessed February 27, 2012).

Wagner, James W. 2007. "Multiversity or University? Pursuing Competing Goods Simultaneously." http://www.emory.edu/ACAD_EXCHANGE/2007/febmar/wagneressay.html (accessed February 28, 2012).

Washington Times. 2011. "NPR's Taxpayer-funded Lobbyists: Liberal Public Radio Battles Congress with Your Money." http://www.washingtontimes.

com/news/2011/may/6/nprs-taxpayer-funded-lobbyists/ (accessed February 28, 2012).

Weber, Max. [1904–5] 1985. *The Protestant Ethic and the Spirit of Capitalism.* Translated by Talcott Parsons; introduction by Anthony Giddens. London and Boston: Unwin.

———. 1978. *Economy and Society: An Outline of Interpretive Sociology.* Edited by G. Roth and C. Wittich. Berkeley: University of California Press.

West, Candace, and Don H. Zimmerman. 1987. "Doing Gender." *Gender & Society* 1:125–51.

Whitfield, Dan. 2011. "Extreme Makeover: Job-seeker Edition: 10 Steps to Look Better when Finding Your Dream Job." http://www.leadershipinstitute.org/news/?NR=6124 (accessed February 27, 2012).

Wilkins, Amy C. 2008. *Wannabes, Goths, and Christians: The Boundaries of Sex, Style, and Status.* Chicago: University of Chicago Press.

Woessner, April Kelly, and Matthew Woessner. 2006. "My Professor Is a Partisan Hack: How Perceptions of a Professor's Political Views Affect Student Course Evaluations." *PS: Political Science and Politics* 39:495–501.

Woessner, Matthew, and April Kelly Woessner. 2007. "Left Pipeline: Why Conservatives Don't Get Doctorates." In *The Politically Correct University: Problems, Scope, and Reforms,* ed. R. Maranto, R. Redding, and F. Hess, 38–59. Washington, DC: American Enterprise Institute.

Wood, Kate. 2012. "Constructing the College Experience: Culture, Community, and Diversity in Undergraduate Life." Unpublished manuscript, Department of Sociology, University of California, San Diego.

Young America's Foundation Website. http://www.yaf.org/ (accessed February 28, 2012).

———. "2009 YAF 990—Public Copy with Schedule B." http://www.yaf.org/uploadedFiles/Webpages/About_Us/2009%20YAF%20990%20-%20Public%20Copy%20with%20Sch%20B.pdf?n=7696 (accessed February 28, 2012).

———. "2011 National Conservative Student Conference." http://www.yaf.org/eventdetails.aspx?id=6453 (accessed February 28, 2012).

———. "Conservative Conferences and Seminars." http://www.yaf.org/Conservative-Conferences.aspx (accessed February 28, 2012).

———. "Conservative Marketplace." http://www.yaf.org/marketplace.aspx (accessed February 28, 2012).

———. "Conservative Speakers." http://www.yaf.org/conservativespeakers.aspx (accessed February 28, 2012).

———. "Emerging Activist Seminar." http://www.yaf.org/eventdetails.aspx?id=6465 (accessed January 24, 2012).

———. "Our Mission." http://www.yaf.org/Mission.aspx (accessed February 28, 2012).

———. "Ronald Reagan & Young America's Foundation." http://www.yaf.org/
RonaldReaganYAF.aspx (accessed February 28, 2012).

———. "YAF Battleplan—October." http://www.yaf.org/uploadedFiles/Web-
pages/Students/YAF%20Battleplan_October.pdf (accessed February 28,
2012).

———. "Young Americans for Freedom Old Home Page." http://www.yaf.org/
yafreedom.aspx (accessed February 28, 2012).

Zernike, Kate, and Megan Thee-Brennan. 2010. "Poll Finds Tea Party Backers
Wealthier and More Educated." http://www.nytimes.com/2010/04/15/us/
politics/15poll.html (accessed August 7, 2011).

Index

Note: Page numbers followed by "t" represent references to tables.

PRINCETON STUDIES IN CULTURAL SOCIOLOGY

Paul J. DiMaggio, Michèle Lamont, Robert J. Wuthnow, Viviana A. Zelizer, Series Editors